ADOBE® INDESIGN® CS
DESIGN PROFESSIONAL

ADOBE® INDESIGN® CS
DESIGN PROFESSIONAL

Chris Botello

THOMSON

COURSE TECHNOLOGY

Adobe® InDesign® CS—Design Professional

Chris Botello

Executive Editor:
Nicole Jones Pinard

Product Manager:
Jane Hosie-Bounar

Associate Product Manager:
Emilie Perreault

Editorial Assistant:
Shana Rosenthal

Production Editor:
Catherine DiMassa

Developmental Editor:
Ann Fisher

Composition House:
GEX Publishing Services

QA Manuscript Reviewers:
John Freitas, Ashlee Welz,
Jeffrey Schwartz

Text Designer:
Ann Small

Illustrator:
Philip Brooker

Cover Design:
Philip Brooker

Design Professional Series Vision

The Design Professional Series is your guide to today's hottest multimedia applications. These comprehensive books teach the skills behind the application, showing you how to apply smart design principles to multimedia products such as dynamic graphics, animation, Web sites, software authoring tools, and video.

A team of design professionals including multimedia instructors, students, authors, and editors worked together to create this series. We recognized the unique learning environment of the multimedia classroom and created a series that:

- Gives you comprehensive step-by-step instructions
- Offers in-depth explanation of the "why" behind a skill
- Includes creative projects for additional practice
- Explains concepts clearly using full-color visuals

It was our goal to create a book that speaks directly to the multimedia and design community—one of the most rapidly growing computer fields today.

We would like to thank Philip Brooker for developing the inspirational artwork found on each chapter opener and book cover. We would also like to give special thanks to Ann Small of A Small Design Studio for developing a sophisticated and instructive book design.

—The Design Professional Series

Author's Vision

I am thrilled to have written this book on Adobe InDesign CS. For me, InDesign is something of a destination in what has been a long and fascinating journey through the world of computer graphics.

The first software package I ever used was Adobe Illustrator '88. Not everybody remembers that Adobe first presented Illustrator as *both* a drawing package *and* a layout package. Unfortunately for Adobe, users didn't see it quite that way, and despite the prominence of Illustrator and Photoshop, Adobe has been without a leading layout package ever since.

Enter Adobe InDesign CS. InDesign CS has so many great features enough to fill up this whole book, in fact. The most important feature though, the key to InDesign CS, is that it interfaces so well with Photoshop and Illustrator. Finally! Produce your entire project—illustration, imagery and layout—without ever leaving the world of Adobe. That's InDesign CS—the third member of the Adobe trinity. It's been a long time coming, but here it is. And it's been worth the wait.

As always, my most special thanks go to Ann Fisher. Before she was my crackerjack editor, she was my friend, and before she was my friend, she was my colleague. For this project, I did the writing, but Ann is the one who put it all together.

The godmother of this book is Product Manager Jane Hosie-Bounar. Jane shepherded this book through to completion with her trademark combination of patience, intelligence, and clarity of vision.

I also want to acknowledge the QA manuscript reviewers for their input: John Freitas, Ashlee Welz, and Jeff Schwartz. Thanks also to our manuscript and table of contents reviewers: Susan Oakes and Max Dutton of Briarcliffe College, Christine Shock of Front Range Community College, Mary Malinconico of Gloucester County College, Patrick Miller of Mississippi State University, and Jeremy Vest of Virginia College. Tamika Williams of Louisiana Tech University School of Art and Marcia Williams of Bellevue Community College also reviewed the table of contents.

Last but not least, this book is dedicated to my two dogs Blake and Rex. Their movie star good looks made them the perfect models for the many photos you'll see throughout the book. Most times, at least one of them was sleeping on my lap as I was writing.

Introduction to Adobe InDesign CS

Welcome to *Adobe InDesign CS—Design Professional*. This book offers creative projects, concise instructions, and complete coverage of basic to advanced InDesign skills, helping you to create polished, professional-looking layouts. Use this book both in the classroom and as your own reference guide.

This text is organized into twelve chapters. In these chapters, you will explore the many options InDesign provides for creating comprehensive layouts, including formatting text and body copy, designing display headlines, setting up a document, working with process and non-process colors, placing graphics from Adobe Illustrator and Adobe Photoshop, working with tabs and tables, and preparing an InDesign layout for output. By the end of the book, you'll be able to create professional-looking layouts that incorporate illustrations and bitmap graphics as well as sophisticated presentations of text and typography.

What You'll Do

A What You'll Do figure begins every lesson. This figure gives you an at-a-glance look at what you'll do in the chapter, either by showing you a page or pages from the current project or a tool you'll be using.

Comprehensive Conceptual Lessons

Before jumping into instructions, in-depth conceptual information tells you "why" skills are applied. This book provides the "how" and "why" through the use of professional examples. Also included in the text are tips and sidebars to help you work more efficiently and creatively, or to teach you a bit about the history or design philosophy behind the skill you are using.

Step-by-Step Instructions

This book combines in-depth conceptual information with concise steps to help you learn InDesign CS. Each set of steps guides you through a lesson where you will create, modify, or enhance an InDesign CS file. Step references to large colorful images and quick step summaries round out the lessons.

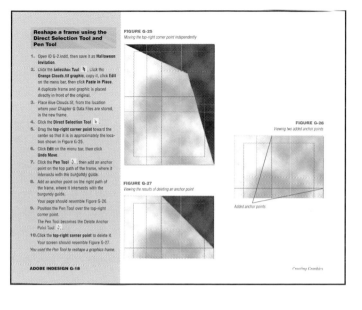

Projects

This book contains a variety of end-of-chapter materials for additional practice and reinforcement. The Skills Review contains hands-on practice exercises that mirror the progressive nature of the lesson material. The chapter concludes with four projects: two Project Builders, one Design Project, and one Group Project. The Project Builders and the Design Project require you to apply the skills you've learned in the chapter. Group Projects encourage group activity as students use the resources of a team to address and solve challenges based on the content explored in the chapter.

What Instructor Resources Are Available with This Book?

The Instructor Resources CD-ROM is Course Technology's way of putting the resources and information needed to teach and learn effectively into your hands. All the resources are available for both Macintosh and Windows operating systems, and many of the resources can be downloaded from www.course.com.

Instructor's Manual

Available as an electronic file, the Instructor's Manual is quality-assurance tested and includes chapter overviews and detailed lecture topics for each chapter, with teaching tips. The Instructor's Manual is available on the Instructor Resources CD-ROM, or you can download it from www.course.com.

Syllabus

Prepare and customize your course easily using this sample course outline (available on the Instructor Resources CD-ROM).

PowerPoint Presentations

Each chapter has a corresponding PowerPoint presentation that you can use in lectures, distribute to your students, or customize to suit your course.

Figure Files

Figure Files contain all the figures from the book in bitmap format. Use the figure files to create transparency masters or use them in a PowerPoint presentation.

Data Files for Students

To complete most of the chapters in this book, your students will need Data Files. The Data Files are available on the CD at the back of this text book. Instruct students to use the Data Files List at the end of this book. This list gives instructions on organizing files.

30-Day Tryout Software

On the CD at the back of this book, you will also find a 30-day tryout version of Adobe® InDesign® CS software for both Macintosh and Windows operating systems. Students can use this software to gain additional practice away from the classroom. *Note*: The tryout software will expire after 30 days. Check the Read Me file on the CD-ROM for more information.

Solutions to Exercises

Solution Files are Data Files completed with comprehensive sample answers. Use these files to evaluate your students' work. Or distribute them electronically so students can verify their work. Sample solutions to all lessons and end-of-chapter material are provided.

Test Bank and Test Engine

ExamView is a powerful testing software package that allows instructors to create and administer printed, computer (LAN-based), and Internet exams. ExamView includes hundreds of questions that correspond to the topics covered in this text, enabling students to generate detailed study guides that include page references for further review. The computer-based and Internet testing components allow students to take exams at their computers, and also save the instructor time by grading each exam automatically.

CHAPTER D   WORKING WITH FRAMES

CHAPTER F   PLACING AND LINKING GRAPHICS

CHAPTER G CREATING GRAPHICS

CHAPTER H — WORKING WITH TRANSPARENCY

CHAPTER I — WORKING WITH TABS AND TABLES

CHAPTER J · MAKING BOOKS, TABLES OF CONTENTS, AND INDEXES

CONTENTS

CHAPTER K EXPLORING ADVANCED TECHNIQUES

CHAPTER L   PREPARING, PACKAGING, AND EXPORTING DOCUMENTS

Units and Increments

The page layout measurements for the documents in this book are given in inches, not points or picas. In order to follow these exercises, it is important that the horizontal and vertical ruler units are set to inches. To verify this, click Edit (Win) or InDesign (Mac) on the menu bar, point to Preferences, then click Units & Increments.

All text sizes and rule weights are expressed in points.

You may or may not prefer to work with rulers showing. You can make rulers visible by clicking View on the menu bar, then clicking Show Rulers. You can make rulers invisible by clicking View on the menu bar, then clicking Hide Rulers. Having rulers visible or invisible will not affect your ability to follow the exercises in this book in any way, unless a step specifically refers to a measurement on the ruler.

Fonts

Because InDesign is a page layout program, text is involved in almost every exercise in the book, even those that focus on placed graphics. The fonts used in the exercises in this book were chosen from a set of very common typefaces that you are likely to have available on your computer. In most cases, the fonts used are either Impact or Garamond. If any of the fonts in use are not available on your computer, please make a substitution with another typeface that has a similar look. Also, please note that because Garamond is such a common typeface, it is possible that the Garamond font on your computer will be that of a different manufacturer than the Garamond used in the exercises. If that is the case, simply replace the "missing" Garamond in the exercises with the Garamond font on your computer. The following tip, which explains how to substitute fonts, appears in Chapter A.

QUICKTIP

You may see the Missing Fonts dialog box, which lets you know that one or more fonts used in the document you are opening are not available on your computer. You can either use the substitute font chosen by InDesign by clicking OK, or click Find Font and choose another font of your choice in the Find Font dialog box.

When you open an InDesign Data File, if any fonts used in the file are not available on your computer, the usages of that font will be highlighted in pink. Once you substitute the missing font with an available font, the pink highlight disappears.

Working with Guides

Chapter C focuses on creating and setting up a new document, which includes a thorough exploration of creating and positioning guides and changing the color of guides. Throughout the remainder of the book, the steps in the lessons will direct the user to make guides visible or invisible when necessary. However, when guides are inconsequential to the lesson, the steps do not instruct the user to make guides visible or not. Therefore, the user's document may differ from the figures in the book in terms of guides. For example, the user's document may have guides visible, whereas the figures in the book may not show guides.

Palettes

Chapter A explains palettes in depth. Students are shown how to group, ungroup, dock, and undock palettes. Like guides, the way that students choose to display palettes may differ from the figures in the book.

Hiding and Showing Frame Edges / Normal View Mode and Preview Mode

Objects on the page appear with frame edges. When an object is selected, the frame edges are more prominent, but even when the object is not selected, the frame edges are visible. Sometimes the frame edges can be distracting, especially at the end of a lesson when you want to view the final result of your work. You can choose to hide frame edges, so that an object's frame is visible only when the object is selected. An alternative to hiding frame edges is to switch from Normal View Mode to Preview Mode using the appropriate buttons on the Toolbox. In Preview Mode, all guides and frame edges are hidden.

The lessons in the book offer specific instruction for hiding and showing frame edges and for switching between Normal View Mode and Preview Mode. Once the user learns these commands, one can expect that he or she will work with the settings that are most comfortable. Because this is a personal choice,

the instructor and the user can expect that the user's work may differ from the figures in the book. For example, the user may be working in Preview Mode, whereas the figures in the book may be in Normal View Mode.

File Formats for Placed Graphics

Because InDesign is an Adobe product, it interfaces naturally with Adobe Photoshop and Adobe Illustrator. Therefore, Photoshop and Illustrator files can be placed in InDesign as "native" Photoshop and Illustrator files—it is not necessary to save them as TIFF or EPS files. For this reason, in the exercises that include placed images, the placed images are sometimes native Photoshop files, sometimes native Illustrator files, sometimes Photoshop TIFF files, and sometimes they are EPS files from Photoshop or Illustrator. The point is to stress that InDesign works with a variety of file formats, including native Photoshop and Illustrator files.

Working with Process Colors and Spot Colors

Chapter E focuses on creating colors in the Swatches palette. Some of these colors will be process colors, some will be spot colors. The narrative in this chapter provides substantial information on the offset printing process and the role of CMYK inks vs. non-process inks. Nevertheless, comprehensive coverage of the myriad concepts involved in offset printing is beyond the scope of this book. The author presumes that the user already has some familiarity with the basic concepts of 4-color process printing and that the instructor will be available to bridge any gaps that might confuse the user.

Updating Placed Graphics

Users will be working with Data Files that contain placed graphics throughout the book. These support files are stored in the same folder as the InDesign Data File they are placed in. Normally, there are no issues for opening files with placed graphics; nevertheless, for a number of reasons, a warning dialog box may appear stating that the placed graphics have been modified and the link needs to be updated. In most cases, the placed graphics themselves have not been modified—only their location has been modified. Because the placed graphics are now on a new computer, InDesign may decide that the link needs to be updated. When this occurs, click the button that says Fix Links Automatically.

After clicking the Fix Links Automatically button, an additional warning dialog box may appear stating that "Edits have been made to this object. You will lose these edits by updating. Update anyway?" This dialog box is referring to a handful of text documents used throughout the book. Make sure students click No in this dialog box so that the text file is not updated. Otherwise, the formatting applied to the text will be lost.

In Chapter F, which focuses on managing links to placed graphics, links from the InDesign document to the placed graphics have been modified or are missing intentionally to teach the user how to react to those situations. It is recommended that the instructor read the Chapter F Instructor's Manual thoroughly and the narrative in Chapter F to become familiar with the issues involved with updating modified and missing links. This knowledge will help the instructor address any linking issues that may occur in exercises in earlier chapters that include placed graphics.

Quick Keys

Quick keys are keyboard shortcuts that can be used in place of clicking a command in a pull-down menu. [Ctrl][X] (Win) or ⌘[X] (Mac), for example, are basic quick keys for the cut command. Mastering basic quick keys is essential for a smooth workflow, and it is suggested that the instructor encourage students to do so.

CHAPTER A

EXPLORING THE INDESIGN WORKSPACE

1. Explore the InDesign workspace.

2. Change document views.

3. Navigate through a document.

4. Use InDesign Help.

CHAPTER A

EXPLORING THE INDESIGN WORKSPACE

Introduction

Welcome to Adobe InDesign! It's an exciting time to begin working with InDesign. Adobe Systems has created a layout program that interfaces seamlessly with Adobe Photoshop and Illustrator.

If you love those two applications, you'll love InDesign too. In terms of its concept and its intuitive design, InDesign is pure Adobe. You'll feel right at home. In fact, at times, you may even have to remind yourself that you're working in InDesign, not Photoshop or Illustrator.

The key word to keep in mind is layout. That's InDesign's primary function. InDesign is a comprehensive software program that allows you to create output-ready layouts for anything from a simple coupon to an 8-page newsletter to a 120-page full-color magazine. Everything you need is here. Along with everything you expect, you're also in for some pleasant surprises. With InDesign, you can build tables quickly and easily. You'll also find that the table of contents and index features are fun and easy to learn. And try to remember that you're not using Illustrator when you're positioning that text on a curved path!

Best of all, you'll never have to leave the world of Adobe. The interface of InDesign with Photoshop and Illustrator allows them to work together as something of a trinity. From that combination, InDesign emerges as one of the most powerful layout production utilities ever devised.

Tools You'll Use

Toolbox

Pages palette

Navigator palette

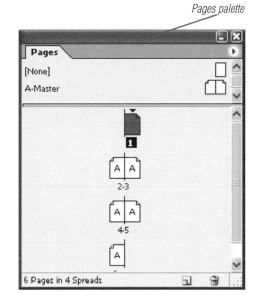

EXPLORE THE INDESIGN WORKSPACE

What You'll Do

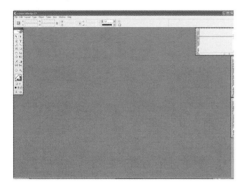

 In this lesson, you will start Adobe InDesign and explore the workspace.

Looking at the InDesign Workspace

The arrangement of windows and palettes that you see on your monitor after starting InDesign is called the **workspace**. InDesign's workspace features four areas: the document window, the Toolbox, the pasteboard, and the palette name tabs along the right edge of the document window, as shown in Figure A-1. You will find that you use the Toolbox the most when working in InDesign. You can customize the workspace to suit your working preferences; for example, you can change the location of the Toolbox, the document window, and other palettes in relation to each other.

Of these workspace elements, the role of the pasteboard is perhaps the least

FIGURE A-1
InDesign workspace

Toolbox

Palette name tabs

Pasteboard

Document window

obvious. The **pasteboard** is the area surrounding the document. The pasteboard provides space for extending objects past the edge of the page (known as creating a bleed), and it also provides space for storing objects that you may or may not use in the document. Objects that are positioned wholly on the pasteboard do not print, as shown in Figure A-2.

Exploring the Toolbox

As its name implies, the Toolbox houses all the tools that you will work with in InDesign. The first thing that you should note about the Toolbox is that not all tools are visible; many are hidden. Look closely and you will see that six tools have small black triangles beside them. These triangles indicate that other tools are hidden behind them. To access hidden tools, press and hold your mouse on the visible tool in the Toolbox; this will reveal a menu of hidden tools. The small black square to the left of a tool name in the menu indicates the tool that is currently visible in the Toolbox, as shown in Figure A-3. The Toolbox includes 29 tools, as shown in Figure A-4.

> **QUICK**TIP
>
> You can view the Toolbox as a single row or a single column instead of a double column. To do so, click Edit on the menu bar (Win) or InDesign on the menu bar (Mac), point to Preferences, click General, click the Floating Tools Palette list arrow in the General Options section, then click Single Column or Single Row.

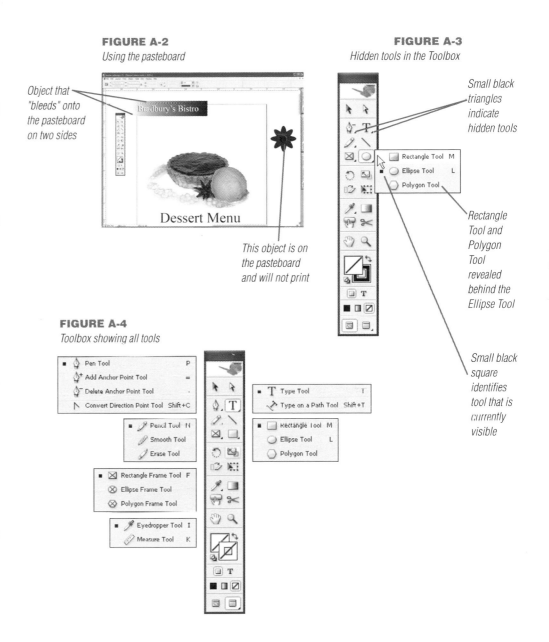

FIGURE A-2
Using the pasteboard

Object that "bleeds" onto the pasteboard on two sides

This object is on the pasteboard and will not print

FIGURE A-3
Hidden tools in the Toolbox

Small black triangles indicate hidden tools

Rectangle Tool and Polygon Tool revealed behind the Ellipse Tool

Small black square identifies tool that is currently visible

FIGURE A-4
Toolbox showing all tools

Horizontal lines divide the Toolbox into nine sections that are grouped by function. The top section contains the selection tools. The section beneath that contains item creation tools—drawing tools, shape tools, and type tools. Next is a section that contains transform tools, such as the Rotate Tool and the Scale Tool. Below that you'll find the Eyedropper Tool, the Gradient Tool, the Button Tool, and the Scissors Tool. You can think of the next section as the navigation section, which houses the Hand Tool—used for scrolling through the document—and the Zoom Tool—used for magnifying your view of the document.

The bottommost sections of the Toolbox contain functions for applying colors and gradients to objects and for choosing Normal View Mode or Preview Mode. Preview Mode allows you to view your document without the guides being visible.

To choose a tool, you simply click it; you can also press a single key to access a tool. For example, pressing [p] selects the Pen Tool. To learn the shortcut key for each tool, point to a tool until a tooltip appears with the tool's name and its shortcut key in parentheses. Figure A-5 shows the tooltip for the Type Tool.

Working with Palettes

InDesign features 34 palettes, all of which are listed and can be accessed from the Window menu. Some palettes are placed within categories on the Window menu. For example, all of the text and table-related palettes, such as the Character palette, the Tabs palette, and the Table palette, are listed in the Type & Tables category on the Window menu. Palettes offer controls for you to modify and manipulate your work; for example, the Character palette offers controls for changing the font, font size, and leading, as shown in Figure A-6.

By default, palettes appear in groups along the right side of the document window—this is necessary to conserve space on your monitor. The default groupings of palettes are designed so that palettes with similar functions are grouped together.

FIGURE A-5
Viewing a tool name and its shortcut key

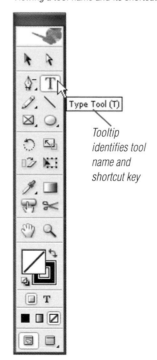

Tooltip identifies tool name and shortcut key

FIGURE A-6
Character palette

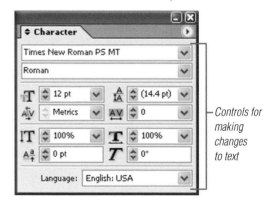

Controls for making changes to text

Figure A-7 shows the three palettes grouped together. The Paragraph palette is the active palette—it is in front of the others in the group and available for use. To activate a palette in a group, simply click its name tab. Some palette groups are collapsed along the right side of the workspace. Clicking the active palette name tab will expand the group of palettes. Once expanded, you can activate other palettes in the group by clicking the appropriate palette name tab; clicking it again will collapse the group of palettes. When you choose a palette from the Window menu, the palette will be displayed in its expanded view.

To ungroup palettes, simply click and drag a palette's name tab away from the other palettes. When you release your mouse, the palette is no longer part of a group. To add a palette to a group, simply drag and drop the palette into the group.

QUICKTIP

You can restore the default arrangement of palettes by clicking Window on the menu bar, pointing to Workspace, then clicking [Default].

Don't confuse grouping palettes with docking palettes; docking palettes is a different function. When you dock palettes, you connect

the bottom edge of one palette to the top edge of another palette, so that both move together. Drag a palette's name tab to the bottom edge of another palette. When the bottom edge of the other palette is highlighted, release your mouse and the two palettes will be docked. Figure A-8 shows docked palettes. To undock a palette, simply drag it away from its group.

QUICKTIP

You can temporarily hide all open palettes and the Toolbox simply by pressing [Tab]. Press [Tab] again to show the palettes and the Toolbox.

FIGURE A-7
Three grouped palettes

Character palette and Transform palette name tabs

The order of your palette name tabs may differ

Paragraph palette

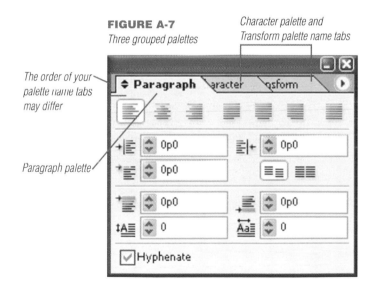

FIGURE A-8
Docked palettes

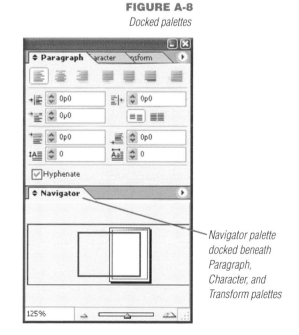

Navigator palette docked beneath Paragraph, Character, and Transform palettes

Explore the Toolbox

1. Click **Start** 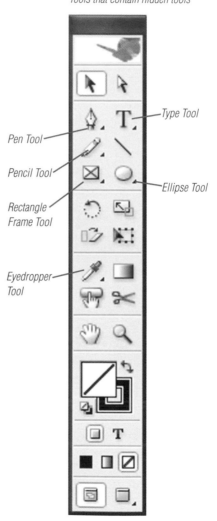 on the taskbar, point to **All Programs**, then click **Adobe InDesign CS** (Win) or double-click **the hard drive icon**, double-click the **Adobe InDesign CS folder**, then double-click **InDesign** (Mac).

2. Click **File** on the menu bar, click **Open**, navigate to the drive and folder where your Chapter A Data Files are stored, click **ID A-1.indd**, then click **Open**.

   TIP If you see the Missing Fonts dialog box, you can use the font chosen by InDesign by clicking OK, or click Find Font and choose another font in the Find Font dialog box.

3. Click **File** on the menu bar, click **Save**, navigate to the drive and folder where you store your Chapter A Solution Files, name the file **Dessert Menu**, then click **Save**.

4. Point to the **Type Tool** T , then press and hold the mouse over the Type Tool to see the Type on a Path Tool.

5. Using the same method, view the hidden tools behind the five other tools with small black triangles, as shown in Figure A-9.

   Your visible tools may differ from the figure.

6. Point to the **Selection Tool** until its tooltip appears.

7. Press the following keys: **[v]**, **[a]**, and **[p]**.

   The associated tools are selected.

8. Press **[Tab]** to temporarily hide all open palettes, then press **[Tab]** again.

   The palettes reappear.

You explored the Toolbox, revealed hidden tools, used shortcut keys to access tools quickly, hid the palettes, then displayed them again.

FIGURE A-9
Tools that contain hidden tools

Type Tool

Pen Tool

Pencil Tool

Ellipse Tool

Rectangle Frame Tool

Eyedropper Tool

Exploring the InDesign Workspace

FIGURE A-10

Removing the Paragraph palette from the group

Drag a palette by its name tab

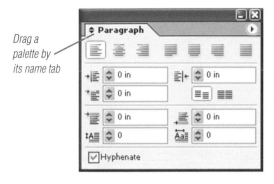

The order of your palette name tabs may differ

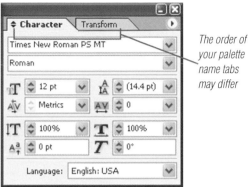

FIGURE A-12

Docking the Transform palette

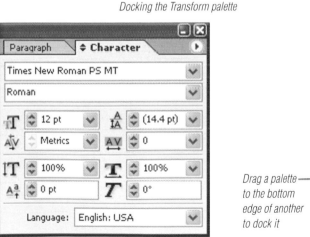

Drag a palette to the bottom edge of another to dock it

FIGURE A-11

Grouping the Character palette with the Paragraph palette

1. Click **Window** on the menu bar, point to **Type & Tables**, then click **Paragraph**.

2. Drag the **Paragraph palette name tab** to the left, away from the group, as shown in Figure A-10.

3. Drag the **Transform palette name tab** below the Paragraph and Character palettes.

4. Close the Transform palette.

5. Drag the **Character palette name tab** next to the Paragraph palette name tab, then release the mouse.

   The Character palette is grouped with the Paragraph palette, as shown in Figure A-11. Note that the order—from left to right—of palettes within the group on your computer may differ from the figure.

6. Click **Window** on the menu bar, then click **Transform**.

7. Drag the **Transform palette name tab** to the bottom edge of the Character and Paragraph palettes group, then release the mouse when the bottom edge of the top palette group is highlighted.

   The Transform palette is docked, as shown in Figure A-12.

8. Click the **Transform palette name tab**, then drag it away from the other two palettes.

   The Transform palette is undocked.

You explored methods for grouping and ungrouping palettes, and you docked and undocked a palette.

CHANGE DOCUMENT VIEWS

What You'll Do

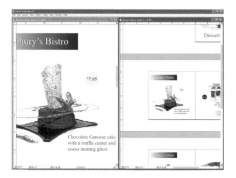

In this lesson, you will explore various methods for changing the magnification of your document.

Using the Zoom Tool

Imagine creating a layout on a traditional pasteboard—not on your computer. For precise work, you would bring your nose closer to the pasteboard so that you could better see what you were doing. At other times, you would hold the pasteboard away from you, say at arms' length, so that you could get a larger perspective of the artwork. When you're working in InDesign, the Zoom Tool performs these functions for you.

When you position the Zoom Tool over the document window, a plus sign appears in the Zoom pointer; when you click the Zoom Tool, the document is enlarged. To reduce the view of the document, press and hold [Alt] (Win) or [option] (Mac). The plus sign changes to a minus sign; when you click the tool, the document size is reduced.

Using the Zoom Tool, you can reduce or enlarge the view of the document from 5% to 4000%. Note that the current percentage appears in two places: in the title bar

next to the filename and in the Zoom text box in the lower-left corner of the document window, as shown in Figure A-13.

Accessing the Zoom Tool

As you work, you can expect to zoom in and out of the document more times than you can count. The most basic way of accessing the Zoom Tool is simply to click its icon in the Toolbox. Another method for accessing the Zoom Tool is to use keyboard shortcuts. When you are using any tool, for example the Selection Tool, don't switch to the Zoom Tool. Instead, press and hold [Ctrl][Spacebar] (Win) or ⌘ [Spacebar] (Mac). This keyboard combination changes the Selection Tool into the Zoom Tool (in the enlarge mode). Click the document to enlarge the view; when you release the keys, the Zoom Tool changes back to the Selection Tool.

To access the Zoom Tool in reduction mode, press and hold [Ctrl][Alt][Spacebar] (Win) or ⌘ [option][Spacebar] (Mac).

In addition to the Zoom Tool, InDesign
offers other ways to zoom in and out of your
document. You can choose a preset percentage from the Zoom menu in the lower-left
corner of the document window, or you can
double-click the current percentage in the
Zoom text box, then type a new percentage.

You can also use the Zoom In and Zoom
Out commands in the View menu.

Using the Hand Tool

When you zoom in on a document—when
you make it appear larger—eventually the
document will be too large to fit in the window. Therefore, you will need to scroll to
see other areas of it. You can use the scroll
bars along the bottom and the right sides of
the document window. You can also use the
Hand Tool to scroll through the document,
as shown in Figure A-14.

The best way to understand the concept of
the Hand Tool is to think of it as your own
hand. Imagine that you could put your hand
up to the document on your monitor, then
move the document left, right, up, or down,
like a paper on a table or against a wall. This
is analogous to how the Hand Tool works.

FIGURE A-13
A reduced view of the document

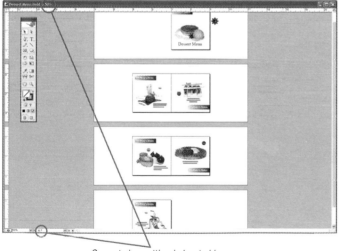

*Current view setting is located in
the title bar and Zoom text box*

FIGURE A-14
Scrolling through a document

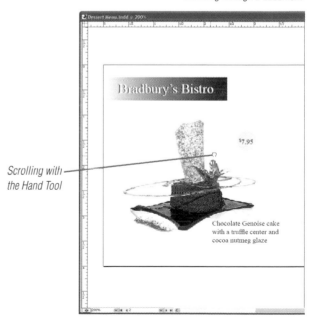

*Scrolling with
the Hand Tool*

The Hand Tool is often a better choice for scrolling than the scroll bars. Why? You can access the Hand Tool using a keyboard shortcut. Regardless of whatever tool you are using, simply press [Spacebar] to access the Hand Tool. Release [Spacebar] to return to whatever tool you were using, without having to choose it again.

Creating Multiple Views of a Document

You can create more than one view of a single document using multiple windows. A dual view is the most common—view the document at 100% in one window, then create another window to enlarge or reduce the document. In this method of working, you maintain a view of your document at actual size (100%) at all times.

Figure A-15 shows two tiled documents with different magnification settings.

Use the New Window command on the Window menu to create a new window. The document in the new window will have the number 2 in the title bar. Use the Tile command on the Window menu to view both windows simultaneously. Figure A-15 shows two views of the same document.

FIGURE A-15

Two views of the same document

Documents are tiled to view both simultaneously

FIGURE A-16

Scrolling with the Hand Tool

The Hand Tool
becomes a fist
when clicked and
dragged

Zoom Text Box   Zoom menu list arrow

1. Press **[z]** to access the Zoom Tool 🔍.

2. Position the Zoom Tool over the document window, click your mouse twice to enlarge the document, press **[Alt]** (Win) or **[option]** (Mac), then click twice to reduce the document.

3. Click the **Zoom menu list arrow** in the lower-left corner of the document window, then click **800%**.

   Note that 800% is listed in the title bar at the top of the document window.

4. Double-click **800%** in the Zoom text box, type **600**, then press **[Enter]** (Win) or **[return]** (Mac).

5. Click the **Hand Tool** ✋ in the Toolbox, then click and drag the document window so that the image in the window appears as shown in Figure A-16.

6. Double-click the **Zoom Tool** 🔍 in the Toolbox.

   The magnification changes to 100% (actual size).

7. Click the **Selection Tool** ▶, point to the center of the document window, then press and hold **[Ctrl][Spacebar]** (Win) or ⌘ **[Spacebar]** (Mac).

   The Selection Tool changes to the Zoom Tool.

8. Click the mouse three times, then release [Ctrl][Spacebar] (Win) or ⌘[Spacebar] (Mac).

   (continued)

9. Press **[Spacebar]** to access the Hand Tool, then scroll around the image.

10. Press and hold **[Ctrl][Alt][Spacebar]** (Win) or ⌘**[option][Spacebar]** (Mac), then click the mouse six times.

   Your document window should resemble Figure A-17.

You explored various methods for accessing and using the Zoom Tool for enlarging and reducing the document. You also used the Hand Tool to scroll around an enlarged document.

Create a new window

1. Click **View** on the menu bar, then click **Fit Page in Window**.

   TIP   Make it a point to memorize the keyboard shortcuts for Fit Page in Window— [Ctrl][0] (Win) or ⌘[0] (Mac)—and Fit Spread in Window—[Ctrl][Alt][0] (Win) or ⌘[option][0] (Mac).

2. Press **[Tab]** to hide the palettes.

3. Click **Window** on the menu bar, point to **Arrange**, then click **New Window**.

4. Click **Window** on the menu bar, point to **Arrange**, then click **Tile**.

   The two windows are positioned side-by-side, as shown in Figure A-18.

   (continued)

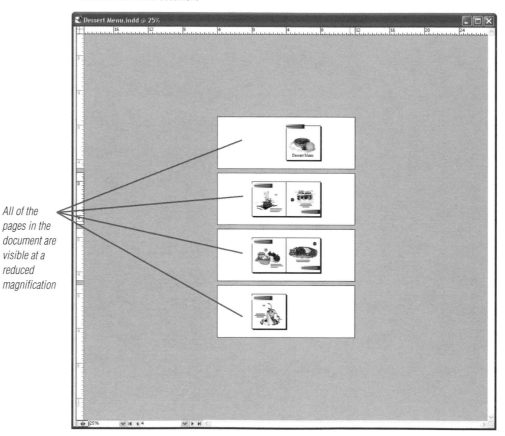

All of the pages in the document are visible at a reduced magnification

5. Click the title bar of the new window to make it the active window.

6. Press and hold **[Ctrl][Spacebar]** (Win) or ⌘ **[Spacebar]** (Mac), position the Zoom Tool over the center of the new window, then click your mouse two times.

7. Close the new window.

8. Click the **Maximize button** (Win) or the **Resize button** (Mac) on the title bar to return the window to its full width.

9. Press **[Tab]** to make the palettes visible again.

You created a new window and used the Zoom Tool to enlarge the view of the new document.

FIGURE A-18

Two views of the same document

NAVIGATE THROUGH A DOCUMENT

What You'll Do

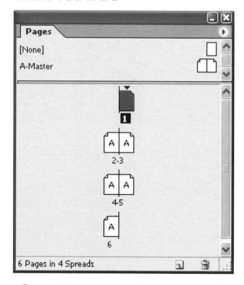

 In this lesson, you will use various methods for viewing individual pages and navigating through a multiple page document.

Navigating to Pages in a Document

When you are creating a layout for a magazine, a book or a brochure, by definition you will create a document that has multiple pages. **Spreads** are two pages that face each other; a left page and a right page in a multi-page document. You have a variety of methods at your disposal for navigating to pages or spreads in your document. You can use the scroll bars on the bottom and right sides of the document window or choose a page from the Page menu in the lower-left corner of the document window. You can also use the First Spread, Previous Spread, Next Spread, and Last Spread buttons at the bottom of the document window, as shown in Figure A-19. These navigation buttons have corresponding menu commands on the Layout menu.

FIGURE A-19
Page buttons and the Page menu

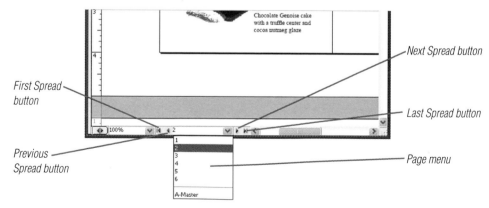

The Pages palette, shown in Figure A-20, is a comprehensive solution for moving from page to page in your document. The Pages palette shows icons for all of the pages in the document. Double-clicking a single page icon brings that page into view. The current page icon appears as blue in the palette and is identified as the targeted page in the palette.

Double-clicking the numbers under page icons representing a spread, as shown in Figure A-21, centers the spread in the document window. In this case, both icons representing the spread will appear as blue in the Pages palette.

FIGURE A-20
Pages palette

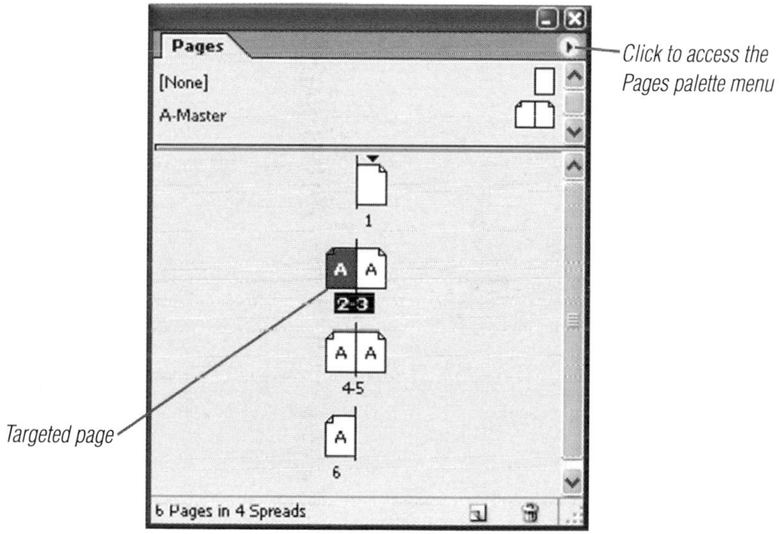

FIGURE A-21
A two-page spread selected in the Pages palette

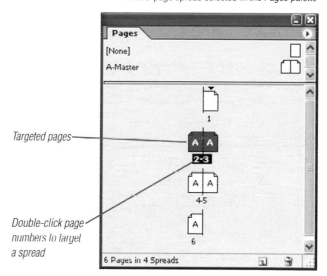

Click to access the Pages palette menu

Targeted page

Targeted pages

Double-click page numbers to target a spread

Using the Navigator Palette

The Navigator palette, shown in Figure A-22, is an excellent resource for moving through a document. Though you certainly can use the Navigator palette to move from page to page, many designers use the Pages palette for that function and use the Navigator palette to move around a single page. This is why it's a great idea to group the Navigator palette with the Pages palette.

The red box in the Navigator palette is called the View box and identifies the area of the page currently being viewed in the document window. Moving the View box is akin to scrolling—moving it to a different area of the page moves the view to that area of the page.

QUICKTIP

You can change the color of the View box by clicking the Navigator palette list arrow, clicking Palette Options, then choosing a new color from the Color list.

Additionally, you can use the Zoom Slider and the Zoom In and Zoom Out buttons in the Navigator palette to change the view of the document. You can also enter a percentage in the Zoom text box at the lower-left corner of the palette.

As stated above, you can move from page to page by dragging the View box up or down. You can also use the View box to move from spread to spread. To do so, first choose View All Spreads from the Navigator palette menu, then drag the View box to move from spread to spread, as shown in Figure A-23.

FIGURE A-22
Navigator palette

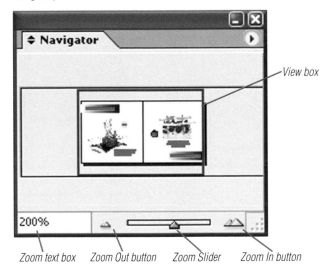

View box

Zoom text box   Zoom Out button   Zoom Slider   Zoom In button

FIGURE A-23
Viewing all spreads in a document

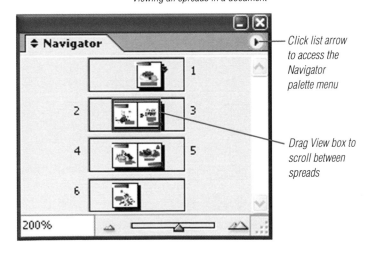

Click list arrow to access the Navigator palette menu

Drag View box to scroll between spreads

FIGURE A-24

Page menu and the Previous Spread and Next Spread buttons

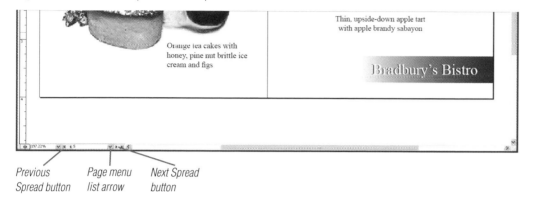

Previous Spread button   *Page menu list arrow*   *Next Spread button*

FIGURE A-25

Targeting page 6 in the Pages palette

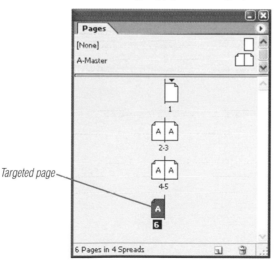

Targeted page

Navigate to pages in a document

1. Click the **Page menu list arrow** at the bottom of the document window, then click **3**.

    The document view changes to page 3.

2. Click **View** on the menu bar, then click **Fit Spread in Window**.

3. Click the **Next Spread button** ▶.

    Your screen should resemble Figure A-24.

4. Click the **Previous Spread button** ◀ twice.

5. Click **Window** on the menu bar, then click **Pages** to display the Pages palette, if necessary.

    > TIP Checked items in the Window menu indicate palettes that are already displayed and those that are the active palettes within their groups.

6. Double-click the **page 6 icon** in the Pages palette.

    The document view changes to page 6, page 6 is targeted in the Pages palette, and the icon changes to blue, as shown in Figure A-25.

7. Double-click the **page 3 icon** in the Pages palette.

    The right half of the spread—page 3—is centered in the document window.

    (continued)

8. Double-click the numbers **2-3** beneath the page 2 and page 3 icons in the Pages palette.

   TIP Double-clicking numbers below the icons in the Pages palette centers the full spread in the document window.

9. Click **Layout** on the menu bar, then click **First Page**.

You explored various methods for moving from one page to another. You chose a page from the Pages menu, you clicked the Next Spread and Previous Spread buttons, you clicked page icons in the Pages palette, and you used the Layout menu.

Use the Navigator palette

1. Click **Window** on the menu bar, then click **Navigator**.

   TIP Clicking a palette's name in the Window menu makes that palette the active palette.

2. Drag the **Zoom Slider** to the right until the Zoom text box is approximately at 500%, as shown in Figure A-26.

3. Double-click the percentage in the Zoom text box to select it, type **500**, then press **[Enter]** (Win) or **[return]** (Mac).

4. Click the **Zoom In button** ◿ once.

   The magnification increases to 600%.

   (continued)

FIGURE A-26
Dragging the Zoom Slider in the Navigator palette

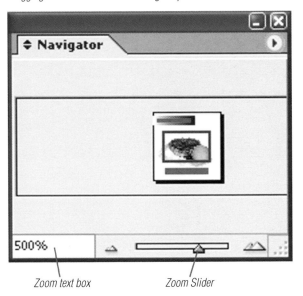

Zoom text box   Zoom Slider

FIGURE A-27

Navigator palette showing all spreads

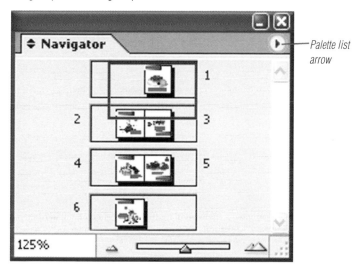

Palette list arrow

5. Drag the **View box** in the Navigator palette to scroll around the page.

6. Click the **Zoom Out button** five times.

   The magnification is reduced to 125%.

7. Click the **Navigator palette list arrow**, then click **View All Spreads**.

   The palette now shows all spreads, as shown in Figure A-27.

8. Close Dessert Menu.indd.

You used the Navigator palette to enlarge and reduce the view of the document and to scroll around the document.

USE INDESIGN HELP

What You'll Do

In this lesson, you will access help using Adobe's online Help page.

Accessing InDesign Help

Help! At some point we all need it. When you do, you can use it to search for answers to your questions using the InDesign Help command in the Help menu.

InDesign Help is an online resource. Clicking the InDesign Help command will launch your browser and take you to the Adobe InDesign CS Help Web site. This site contains all the information in the user guide, plus keyboard shortcuts and additional information, as shown in Figure A-28.

QUICKTIP

The Help menu also contains commands for registering your software, finding out if there are any updates to the software, and viewing the InDesign page of the Adobe Systems Web site. The Online Support command brings you to the support page for InDesign where you can read about top issues and access tutorials, forums, and announcements.

You can find information quickly by conducting a search using keywords. To do so, you click the Search link, type your keyword(s) into the Find pages containing text box, then click Search. Searching for information this way is more powerful than using a software manual.

The Web site offers you the power to do much broader searches and to view a number of different topics at a glance that relate to your search. For example, if you search for information about guides, you are given a very thorough list of topics relating to guides, as shown in Figure A-29. Compare that to using the traditional index in a book and you will probably agree that this is a much more comprehensive and effective solution for accessing information.

FIGURE A-28
InDesign Help Web site

Search link

Preset
search links

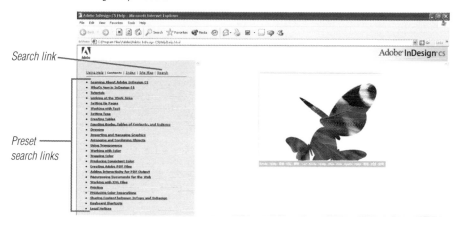

FIGURE A-29
"Guides" search results

Find pages
containing
text box

Pages containing
guides

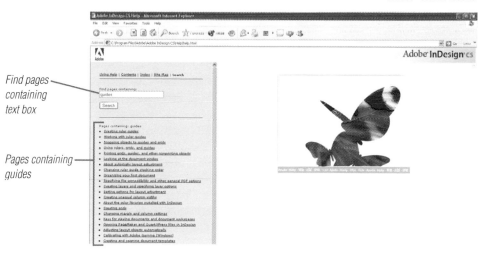

Explore the InDesign workspace.

1. Open ID A-2.indd. (*Hint*: You may see the Missing Fonts dialog box which lets you know that one or more fonts used in the document you are opening are not available on your computer. You can either use the substitute font chosen by InDesign by clicking OK, or click Find Font and choose another font of your choice in the Find Font dialog box.)

2. Press and hold the Type Tool until you see the hidden tools beneath it.

3. Using the same method, view the hidden tools behind the five other tools with small black triangles.

4. Click Window on the menu bar, point to Workspace, then click [Default].

5. Click Window on the menu bar, then click Pages (if necessary).

6. Drag the Pages palette away from its group to the center of the document window.

7. Drag the Layers palette away from its group, then dock it beneath the Pages palette.

8. Drag the Layers palette away from the Pages palette, so that it is no longer docked.

9. Drag the Layers palette name tab next to the Pages palette name tab so that the two palettes are grouped.

Change document views.

1. Click the Zoom Tool, then click inside the document window twice to enlarge the document, press and hold [Alt] (Win) or [option] (Mac), then click twice to reduce the document.

2. Click the Zoom menu list arrow, then click **600**%.

3. Double-click 600% in the Zoom text box, type **800**, then press [Enter] (Win) or [return] (Mac).

4. Double-click the Zoom Tool in the Toolbox.

5. Click the Selection Tool, position it over the center of the document window, then press and hold [Ctrl][Spacebar] (Win) or ⌘ [Spacebar] (Mac).

6. Click the mouse once, then release [Ctrl][Spacebar] (Win) or ⌘ [Spacebar] (Mac).

7. Press [Spacebar] to access the Hand Tool, then scroll around the document.

8. Press and hold [Ctrl][Alt][Spacebar] (Win) or ⌘ [option][Spacebar] (Mac), then click the mouse three times.

Navigate through a document.

1. Click the Page menu list arrow, then click 3.

2. Click View on the menu bar, then click Fit Spread in Window.

3. Click the Previous Spread button.

4. Click the Next Spread button two times.

5. In the Pages palette, double-click the page 5 icon.

6. Double-click the numbers 2-3 beneath the page 2 and page 3 icons in the Pages palette.

7. Click Layout on the menu bar, then click First Page.

8. Click Window on the menu bar, then click Navigator.

9. Drag the Zoom Slider to the right until the Zoom text box is approximately at 300%.
10. Double-click the percentage in the Zoom text box to select it, type **400**, then press [Enter] (Win) or [return] (Mac).
11. Click the Zoom In button once.
12. Drag the View box in the Navigator palette to scroll around the page.
13. Click the Zoom Out button five times.
14. Close ID A-2.indd.

FIGURE A-30
Skills Review

You work at a local design studio. Your boss has informed you that the studio will be switching to Adobe InDesign for its layout software. She tells you that she wants you to spend the day investigating the software and creating simple layouts. You decide first to group and dock palettes in a way that you think will be best for working with type and simple layouts.

1. Start Adobe InDesign.
2. Without creating a new document, group the Paragraph, Character, and Tabs palettes together, then click the Character palette name tab so that it is the active palette. (*Hint*: The Character, Paragraph, and Tabs palettes can be found on the Window menu under Type & Tables.)
3. Dock the Pages palette to the bottom of the Character palette group.
4. Group the Navigator and Layers palettes with the Pages palette, then click the Navigator palette name tab so that it is the active palette.
5. Dock the Swatches palette below the Navigator palette group.
6. Group the Color, Stroke, and Gradient palettes with the Swatches palette, then click the Stroke palette name tab so that it is the active palette.
7. Dock the Align palette below the Stroke palette group.

8. Group the Transform and the Transparency palettes with the Align palette, then click the Align palette name tab so that it is the active palette.
9. Dock the Paragraph Styles palette below the Align palette group. (*Hint*: The paragraph Styles palette is in the Type & Tables submenu on the Windows menu.)
10. Group the Character Styles and Text Wrap palettes with the Paragraph Styles palette.
11. Compare your palettes with Figure A-31.

FIGURE A-31
Completed Project Builder 1

Exploring the InDesign Workspace

You are the creative director at a design studio. The studio has recently switched to Adobe InDesign as its layout software. You will be conducting a series of in-house classes to teach the junior designers how to use InDesign. Before your first class, you decide to practice some basic skills for viewing a document.

1. Open ID A-3.indd.
2. Click the Selection Tool, then press [Ctrl][Spacebar] (Win) or [⌘][Spacebar] (Mac) to access the Zoom Tool.
3. Position the Zoom Tool over the dog's left eye, click and drag the Zoom Tool pointer around the dog's eye (you'll see a dotted rectangle emerge as you drag), then release your mouse.
4. Press [Spacebar], then scroll with the Hand Tool to the dog's right eye.
5. Press [Ctrl][Alt][Spacebar] (Win) or [⌘][option][Spacebar] (Mac), then click the Zoom Tool three times on the dog's right eye.
6. Drag the View box in the Navigator palette so that both of the dog's eyes and his snout are visible in the window and your screen resembles Figure A-32.
7. Close ID A-3.indd.

FIGURE A-32
Completed Project Builder 2

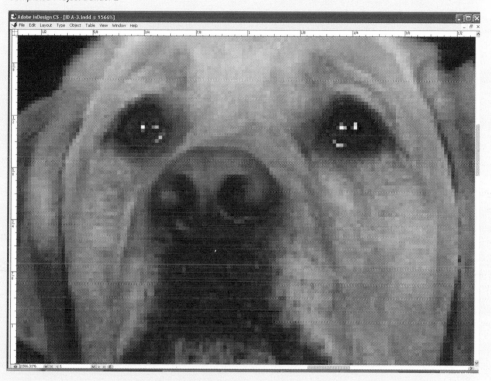

DESIGN PROJECT

You will be teaching a small, in-house class on InDesign, and you will need to design handouts for students to take away from your lecture. To get ideas, you decide to visit a site created by a local design firm and look at solutions devised by other users of Adobe InDesign.

1. Connect to the Internet, go to *www.course.com*, navigate to the page for this book, click the Online Companion link, then click the link for this chapter.
2. Click through the Web site, as shown in Figure A-33, looking at a variety of pages.
3. Regard each layout from a design perspective: note the use of typography, imagery, color, and layout.
4. Write a brief summary stating why you like or dislike the design of this Web site, then save it as **Web Notes**.

FIGURE A-33
Design Project

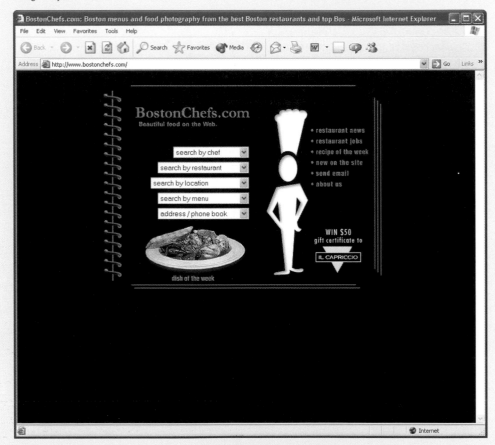

In this project, your group will examine the layout that they worked with in the lessons of this chapter. The group is encouraged to critique the layout from a design perspective, to comment on the elements that they think are effective, and to suggest ways that the presentation may be improved.

1. Open ID A-4.indd.
2. Use the Pages palette to move from page to page, so that the group has seen each of the six pages at least one time. You may also refer to Figure A-34 during the discussion.
3. What does the group think of the photographs? Are they effective? Does the fact that they are "silhouetted" against a white background make them more effective, or does the group think it would be better if they were photographed in context, such as on a plate or on a table in a restaurant setting?
4. How does the clean white background add to the look and feel of the piece, given that this is a layout about food?
5. Move through all the pages again. The layout changes from page to page. Though the restaurant's name doesn't move and the desserts are all positioned at the center of the page, the location of the menu descriptions changes, as does the location of the prices. Also, the circle behind the prices changes color. What does the group think about these changes from page to page?

Would the layout be improved if all items were consistent from page to page?
6. Should the prices be in a bold typeface?
7. None of the pages features a title of the food item; the food is described only in the menu description. Does the group think it would be better if a title appeared on every page? If so, would the group be willing to discard the restaurant's name in the upper-left corner in favor of a title?
8. Submit your answers to these three questions in a document called **Design Critique**.
9. Close ID A-4.indd.

FIGURE A-34
Completed Group Project

CHAPTER

B

WORKING WITH TEXT

1. Format text.

2. Format paragraphs.

3. Create and apply styles.

4. Edit text.

WORKING WITH TEXT

Earth, air, fire, and water—it is said that these are the four essential elements of our world. A different quartet establishes itself as the four main elements of any layout: text, color, illustration, and imagery. Take a moment to read them again, and make a mental note of them. We will use these four elements—text, color, illustration, and imagery—throughout this book to reduce the myriad features of InDesign into four simple categories.

In this chapter, we will focus on working with text. Like Proteus, the mythological figure who could change his outer form at will, text in a layout can appear in a variety of ways. It is *protean*—it is versatile. It can be display text—a bold, dramatic headline at the center of a page, for example, or a miniscule footnote tucked away unobtrusively. It can be flowed as body copy—paragraphs of text; or it can appear as simple page numbers at the lower corner of a page.

You will be pleased to find that InDesign is a first-rate application for generating and editing text. Everything that you want to do—you can do. With InDesign, your ability to generate functional, readable text and beautiful typographic artwork is limited only by your imagination.

Tools You'll Use

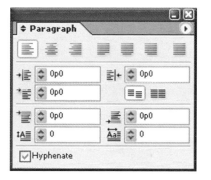

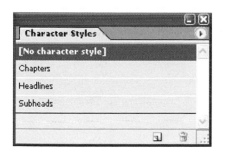

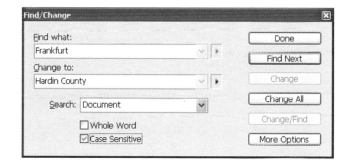

FORMAT TEXT

What You'll Do

Introducing the Min-Pin

by Christopher Smith

 In this lesson, you will use the Character palette and various keyboard commands to modify text attributes.

Using the Character Palette

The Character palette, shown in Figure B-1, is the command center for modifying text. The Character palette works hand in hand with the Paragraph palette, which is why they are often grouped together. Where the Paragraph palette, as its name implies, focuses on manipulating paragraphs or blocks of text, the Character palette focuses on more specific modifications, such as font, font style, and font size.

In addition to these basic modifications, the Character palette offers other controls for manipulating text. You use the palette to modify leading; to track and kern text; to apply a horizontal scale or a vertical scale to text; to perform a baseline shift; or to skew text.

Understanding Leading

Leading is the term used to describe the vertical space between lines of text. This space is measured from the baseline of one line of text to the baseline of the next line of text. As shown in Figure B-2, the **baseline** is the invisible line on which a line of text sits. As with font size, leading is measured in points.

DESIGNTIP   The origins of leading

"Where in the world does the term leading come from?" you might ask. The answer is interesting. In the early days of the printing press, text was set using little pieces of lead, one piece of lead for each character, like tiles in a Scrabble game. (Imagine creating an entire newspaper story one letter at a time!) When one full line of text was created, typographers inserted a strip of lead beneath those letters to create vertical space before setting the next line of text. Hence, the term "leading."

Font Family text box

Font Size text box

Kerning list arrow

Vertical Scale text box

Baseline Shift text box

Skew text box

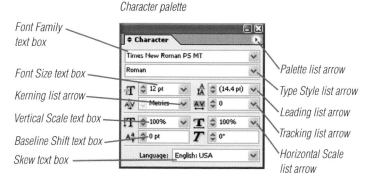

Palette list arrow

Type Style list arrow

Leading list arrow

Tracking list arrow

Horizontal Scale list arrow

12 pt text with 14 pt leading

As soon as the Min-Pin climbs onto the bed, he usually slips under the covers like a mole, all the way to the very foot of the bed.

Baseline

As soon as the Min-Pin climbs onto the

bed, he usually slips under the covers

12 pt text with 24 pt leading

like a mole, all the way to the very foot

of the bed.

As soon as the Min-Pin climbs onto the bed, he usually slips under the covers like a mole, all the way to the very foot of the bed.

12 pt text with 8 pt leading

Leading

Making text selections

to select:	do the following:
One word	Double-click word
One line	Triple-click any word in the line
One paragraph	Click any word in the paragraph four times
Entire story	Click any word in the story five times
Entire story	[Ctrl][A] (Win) or ⌘ [A] (Mac)
One character to the right of insertion point	[Shift]→
One character to the left of insertion point	[Shift]←
One line up from insertion point	[Shift]↑
One line down from insertion point	[Shift]↓
One word to the right of insertion point	[Shift][Ctrl]→ (Win) or [Shift] ⌘ → (Mac)
One word to the left of insertion point	[Shift][Ctrl]← (Win) or [Shift] ⌘ ← (Mac)
One paragraph above insertion point	[Shift][Ctrl]↑ (Win) or [Shift] ⌘ ↑ (Mac)
One paragraph below insertion point	[Shift][Ctrl]↓ (Win) or [Shift] ⌘ ↓ (Mac)

Scaling Text Horizontally and Vertically

When you format text, your most basic choice is which font you want to use and at what size you want to use it. Once you've chosen a font and a font size, you can further manipulate the appearance of the text with a horizontal or vertical scale.

In the Character palette, horizontal and vertical scales are expressed as percentages. By default, text is generated at a 100% horizontal and 100% vertical scale, meaning that the text is not scaled at all. Decreasing the horizontal scale only, for example, maintains the height of the characters but decreases the width—on the horizontal axis. Conversely, increasing only the horizontal scale again maintains the height but increases the width of the characters on the horizontal axis. Figure B-3 shows four examples of horizontal and vertical scales.

Kerning and Tracking Text

Though your computer is a magnificent instrument for generating text in myriad fonts and font sizes, you will often want to manipulate the appearance of text after you have created it—especially if you have the meticulous eye of a designer. **Kerning** is a long-standing process of increasing or decreasing space between a pair of characters. **Tracking** is more global. Like kerning, tracking affects the spaces between letters, but it is applied globally to an entire word or paragraph.

Kerning and tracking are standard features in most word processing applications, but they are more about typography than word processing—that is, they are used for setting text in a way that is pleasing to the eye. Spacing problems with text are usually more prominent with large size headlines than with smaller body copy—this is why many designers will spend great amounts of time tracking and kerning a headline. Figures B-4 and B-5 show examples of kerning and tracking applied to a headline. Note, though, that kerning and tracking are also used often on body copy as a simple solution for fitting text within an allotted space.

FIGURE B-3
Scaling text horizontally and vertically

original text

50% horizontal scale

150% horizontal scale

50% vertical scale

150% vertical scale

FIGURE B-4
Kerning text

Without kerning, some letters are spaced further apart

Wonderful

Without kerning, some letters are very close

Wonderful

After kerning, all letters are evenly spaced

FIGURE B-5
Tracking text

Wonderful

Kerned text with no tracking

Wonderful

Tracked text with greater space between characters

InDesign measures both kerning and tracking in increments of 1/1000 em, a unit of measure that is determined by the current type size. In a 6-point font, 1 em equals 6 points; in a 12-point font, 1 em equals 12 points. It's good to know this, but you don't need to have this information in mind when kerning and tracking text. Just remember that the increments are small enough to provide you with the specificity that you desire for creating eye-pleasing text.

Creating Superscript Characters

You are already familiar with superscript characters, even if you don't know them by that term. When you see a footnote in a book or document, the superscripted character is the footnote itself, the small number positioned to the upper-right of a word. Figure B-6 shows a superscripted character.

The only tricky thing about applying a superscript is remembering how to do it. The Superscript command, as shown in Figure B-7, is listed in the Character palette menu. Wait—there's one more tricky thing you need to remember about superscripts. If, for example, you select a 12-point character and then apply the Superscript command, by definition the character will be smaller in size. However, its point size will still be identified in the Character palette as 12 points.

Underlining Text

InDesign offers many different options, commands, and dialog boxes for creating rules—horizontal, vertical, or diagonal lines—and for underlining text. That said, when you want simply to underline selected text, the most basic method is to use the Underline command in the Character palette's menu. With this command, the weight of the underline is determined by the point size of the selected text. The greater the point size, the greater the weight of the line.

FIGURE B-6
Identifying a superscripted character

FIGURE B-7
Locating the Superscript command

Palette list arrow

Superscripted character

Superscript command

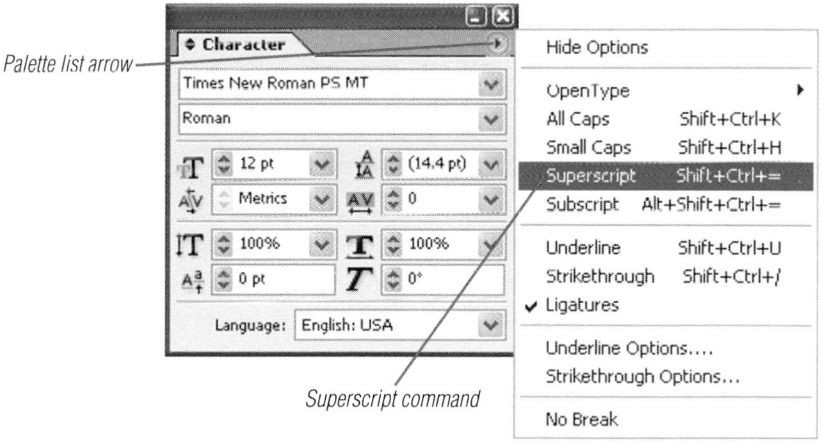

Modify text attributes

1. Open ID B-1.indd, then save it as **Min-Pin Intro**.

2. Click **Edit** (Win) or **InDesign** (Mac) on the menu bar, point to **Preferences**, then click **Units & Increments**.

3. In the Keyboard Increments section, change the Size/Leading value to 1 pt (if necessary), as shown in Figure B-8.

4. Click **OK**, click the **Type Tool** **T.**, then double-click the word **Introducing** at the top of the page.

5. Triple-click **Introducing** to select the entire line.

6. In the Character palette, click the **Font Family list arrow**, click **Impact**, click the **Font Size list arrow**, then click **48 pt**, as shown in Figure B-9.

7. Press and hold **[Shift][Ctrl]** (Win) or **[Shift]** ⌘ (Mac), then press **[<]** ten times.

   The point size is reduced by one point size every time you press **[<]**.

8. Press and hold **[Shift][Ctrl]** (Win) or **[Shift]** ⌘ (Mac), then press **[>]** two times.

   The point size is increased by two points.

9. Triple-click **by** on the second line, change the font to Garamond, click the **Type Style list arrow**, click **Italic**, click the **Font Size list arrow**, then click **18 pt**.

10. Click the **Selection Tool** ▶, then note that the text frame is highlighted, as shown in Figure B-10.

11. Click **Object** on the menu bar, click **Text Frame Options**, click the **Align list arrow**, click **Center**, then click **OK**.

You used keyboard commands and the Character palette to modify text.

INDESIGN B-8

FIGURE B-8
Units & Increments section of the Preferences dialog box

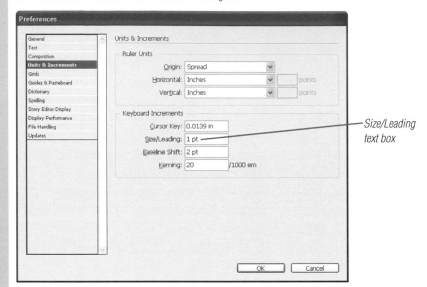

Size/Leading text box

FIGURE B-9
Character palette

Font Family list arrow

Font Size list arrow

FIGURE B-10
Text frame indicates a selected text box

Text frame

Text frame handles

Increasing the tracking value of selected text

Introducing the Min-Pin

by Christopher Smith

Decreasing the kerning value between two letters

Introducing the Min-Pin

by Christopher Smith

Decreased kerning

Track and kern text

1. Click the **Zoom Tool** 🔍, click and drag the **Zoom Tool pointer** around the light green frame that encompasses the entire headline, then release your mouse.

    When you drag the Zoom Tool pointer, a dotted-lined selection rectangle appears. When you release the mouse, the contents within the rectangle are magnified.

2. Click the **Type Tool** T, then triple-click the word **Introducing**.

3. Click the **Tracking list arrow** in the Character palette, then click **200**.

    The horizontal width of each word increases, as a consistent amount of space is applied between each letter, as shown in Figure B-11.

4. Change the tracking value to 25.

5. Click between the letters h and e in the word the, click the **Kerning list arrow**, then click **-50**.

    The space between the two letters decreases.

6. Click the **Kerning up arrow** twice to change the kerning value to -30.

7. Click the **Selection Tool** ▶.

    Your headline should resemble Figure B-12.

You used the Character palette to modify tracking and kerning values applied to text.

Create superscript characters

1. Click **View** on the menu bar, click **Fit Page in Window**, click the **Zoom Tool** 🔍 , then drag a selection box that encompasses all of the body copy on the page.

2. Click the **Type Tool** **T.** , then select the number 1 after the words Doberman Pinscher at the end of the fourth paragraph.

3. Click the **Character palette list arrow**, then click **Superscript**.

   The character's size is reduced and it is positioned higher than the characters that precede it, as shown in an enlarged view in Figure B-13.

4. Select the number 2 after the word cows in the last paragraph, then apply the Superscript command.

   TIP When the Superscript command is applied to text, its designated font size remains the same.

5. Select the number 1 beside the footnote at the bottom of the page, apply the Superscript command, select the number 2 below, apply the Superscript command again, then deselect the text.

   Your footnotes should resemble Figure B-14.

You applied the Superscript command to format selected text as footnotes.

Pinscher[1]. — *Superscript character*

Superscript characters ⟨ [1] Montag, Scott: In Love with the Min-Pin, All Breeds Publishing, 1997
[2] Miltenberger, William: Working Toy Breeds, CJP Press, 2002

¹ Montag, Scott: In Love with the Min-Pin, All Breeds
² Miltenberger, William: Working Toy Breeds, CJP Pre

¹ Montag, Scott: In Love with the Min-Pin, All Breeds Publishing, 1997

²/Miltenberger, William: Working Toy Breeds, CJP Press, 2002

8 pt text

Underline text

1. Click **View** on the menu bar, click **Fit Page in Window**, click the **Zoom Tool** 🔍, then drag a selection box that encompasses both footnotes at the bottom of the page.

2. Click the **Type Tool** **T.**, then select In Love with the Min-Pin in the first footnote.

3. Click the **Character palette list arrow**, then click **Underline**.

   Only the selected text is underlined, as shown in Figure B-15.

   > TIP The weight of the line is automatically determined, based on the point size of the selected text.

4. Select **Working Toy Breeds** in the second footnote, then apply the Underline command.

5. Select the entire first footnote except the number 1, double-click the **Font Size text box**, type **8**, then press **[Enter]** (Win) or **[return]** (Mac).

6. Select the entire second footnote except the number 2, change its font size to 8 pt, then click to deselect the text.

   Your footnotes should resemble Figure B-16.

You selected text, then applied the Underline command from the Character palette menu.

FORMAT PARAGRAPHS

What You'll Do

Introducing the Min-Pin
by Christopher Smith

The Miniature Pinscher is a smooth coated dog in the Toy Group. He is frequently - and incorrectly - referred to as a Miniature Doberman. The characteristics that distinguish the Miniature Pinscher are his size (ten to twelve and a half inches), his racy elegance, and the gait which he exhibits in a self-possessed, animated and cocky manner.

The Miniature Pinscher is part of the larger German Pinscher family, which belonged to a prehistoric group that dates back to 3000 B.C. One of the clear-cut traits present in the ancient Pinschers was that of the two opposing size tendencies: one toward the medium to larger size and the other toward the smaller "dwarf" of miniature size. This ancient miniature-sized Pinscher was the forerunner of today's Miniature pinscher.

"Is the Miniature Pinscher bred down from the Doberman Pinscher?"

The answer is a definite "No." Since ancient times, the Min Pin was developing with its natural tendency to smallness in stature. In fact, as a recognized breed, the Miniature Pinscher predates the development of the well-known Doberman Pinscher.

The Min Pin is an excellent choice as a family pet. The breed tends to attach itself very quickly to children and really delights in joining a youngster in bed. As soon as the Min-Pin climbs onto the bed, he usually slips under the covers like a mole, all the way to the foot of the bed.

The Min Pin is intelligent and easily trained. He has a tendency to be clean in all respects, the shedding of the short coat constitutes minimal, if any, problems to the apartment dweller. On the other hand, the Miniature Pinscher certainly is not out of his element on the farm and has been trained to tree squirrels, chase rabbits, and even help herd cows'. It is not unusual for the Miniature Pinscher on a farm to catch a rabbit that is equal to or larger than the size of the dog.

[1] Manring, Scott: In Love with the Min Pin, All Breeds Publishing, 1997

[2] Miltenberger, William: Working Toy Breeds, CJP Press, 2002

 In this lesson, you will use the Paragraph palette and various keyboard commands to modify paragraph attributes.

Using the Paragraph Palette

The **Paragraph palette**, shown in Figure B-17, is the command center for modifying paragraphs, blocks of text also known as body copy. The Paragraph palette works hand in hand with the Character palette, which is why they are often grouped together.

The Paragraph palette is divided into three main sections. The top section controls alignment. Of the seven icons offering

FIGURE B-17
Paragraph palette

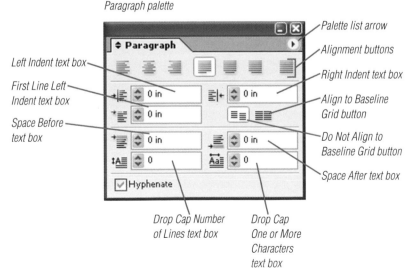

Working with Text

options for aligning text, the first four—Align left, Align center, Align right, and Justify with last line aligned left—are the most common. The remaining three are subtle modifications of justified text and are used less often.

The next section offers controls for indents. Use an indent when you want the first line of each paragraph to start further to the right than the other lines of text, as shown in Figure B-18. This figure also shows what is commonly referred to as a **pull quote**. You have probably seen pull quotes in most magazines. They are a typographical design solution in which text is used at a larger point size and positioned prominently on the page. Note the left and right indents applied to the pull quote in Figure B-18. They were created using the Left Indent and Right Indent buttons in the Paragraph palette.

The third section of the Paragraph palette controls vertical spacing between paragraphs and applying drop caps. For large blocks of text, it is often most pleasing to the eye to create either a subtle or distinct space after every paragraph. In InDesign, you create these by entering values in the

FIGURE B-18

First line indent and left and right indents

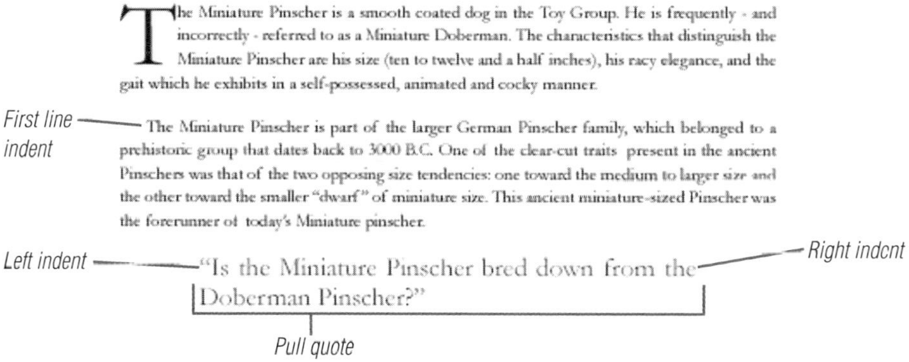

The Miniature Pinscher is a smooth coated dog in the Toy Group. He is frequently - and incorrectly - referred to as a Miniature Doberman. The characteristics that distinguish the Miniature Pinscher are his size (ten to twelve and a half inches), his racy elegance, and the gait which he exhibits in a self-possessed, animated and cocky manner.

First line indent — The Miniature Pinscher is part of the larger German Pinscher family, which belonged to a prehistoric group that dates back to 3000 B.C. One of the clear-cut traits present in the ancient Pinschers was that of the two opposing size tendencies: one toward the medium to larger size and the other toward the smaller "dwarf" of miniature size. This ancient miniature-sized Pinscher was the forerunner of today's Miniature pinscher.

Left indent — "Is the Miniature Pinscher bred down from the — Right indent Doberman Pinscher?"

Pull quote

Space After or the Space Before text boxes in the Paragraph palette. Of the two, the Space After text box is more commonly used. The Space Before text box, when it is used, is often used in conjunction with the Space After text box to offset special page elements, such as a pull quote.

A **drop cap** is a design element in which the first letter or letters of a paragraph are increased in size to create a visual effect. In the figure, the drop cap is measured as being three text lines in height. If you click your cursor to the right of the drop cap then increase the kerning value in the

Character palette, the space between the drop cap and all three lines of text will be increased. Figure B-19 shows a document with a drop cap and a .25 inch space after every paragraph.

FIGURE B-19

A drop cap and paragraphs with vertical space applied after every paragraph

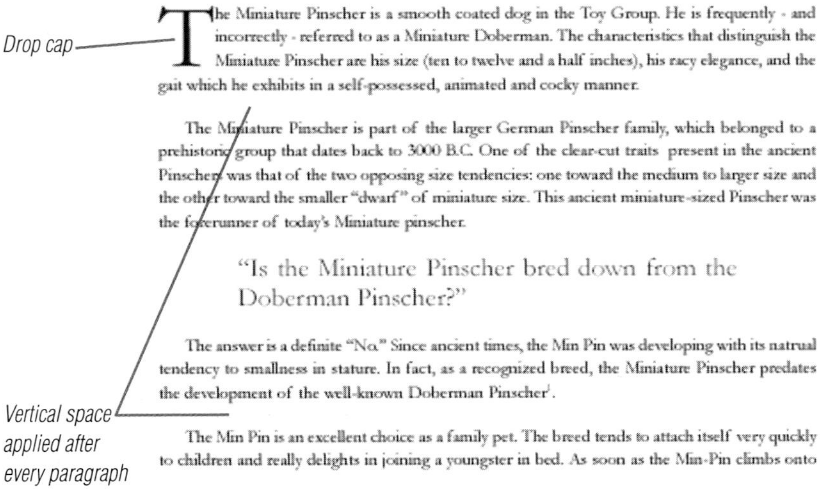

Drop cap

The Miniature Pinscher is a smooth coated dog in the Toy Group. He is frequently - and incorrectly - referred to as a Miniature Doberman. The characteristics that distinguish the Miniature Pinscher are his size (ten to twelve and a half inches), his racy elegance, and the gait which he exhibits in a self-possessed, animated and cocky manner.

The Miniature Pinscher is part of the larger German Pinscher family, which belonged to a prehistoric group that dates back to 3000 B.C. One of the clear-cut traits present in the ancient Pinscher was that of the two opposing size tendencies: one toward the medium to larger size and the other toward the smaller "dwarf" of miniature size. This ancient miniature-sized Pinscher was the forerunner of today's Miniature pinscher.

"Is the Miniature Pinscher bred down from the Doberman Pinscher?"

The answer is a definite "No." Since ancient times, the Min Pin was developing with its natrual tendency to smallness in stature. In fact, as a recognized breed, the Miniature Pinscher predates the development of the well-known Doberman Pinscher.

Vertical space applied after every paragraph

The Min Pin is an excellent choice as a family pet. The breed tends to attach itself very quickly to children and really delights in joining a youngster in bed. As soon as the Min-Pin climbs onto

Understanding Returns and Soft Returns

In terms of formatting text, the definition of a paragraph is that of a word, a line of text, or a block of text that is followed by a paragraph return. A **paragraph return**, also called a **hard return**, is inserted into the text formatting by pressing [Enter] (Win) or [return] (Mac). For example, if I type my first name and then enter a paragraph return, that one word—my first name—is a paragraph. You are more familiar with paragraphs as blocks of text, which is fine. But the definition doesn't change. When working with body copy, paragraphs appear as blocks of text, each separated by a single paragraph return.

Here's an example of incorrect formatting. When typing body copy, often many designers will want a space after each paragraph because it is visually pleasing and helps to keep paragraphs visually distinct. The mis-take many designers make is that they press [Enter] (Win) or [return] (Mac) twice to create that space after the paragraph. Wrong! What they've done is created two paragraphs. The correct way to insert space between paragraphs is to enter a value in the Space After text box in the Paragraph palette.

Here's a similar problem: When creating a first line paragraph indent, many users will press [Spacebar] 5 or 10 times and then start typing. This too is incorrect format-ting. Paragraph indents are created using the First Line Left Indent setting in the Paragraph palette, not by inserting multi-ple spaces.

Why is this a problem? For one thing, it's an example of not using the features of the soft-ware properly. Also, space characters are not always consistent. If you press [Spacebar] 5 times to indent every paragraph in a docu-ment, you might be surprised to find that your indents will not necessarily be consis-tent from paragraph to paragraph.

Untold numbers of formatting problems occur from these incorrect typesetting behaviors, especially from misusing paragraph returns. "But," you may ask, "what if I need to move a word down to the next line?"

As you edit text, you may encounter a "bad line break" at the end of a line, such as an oddly hyphenated word or a phrase that is split from one line to the next. In many cases, you will want to move a word or phrase to the next line. You can do this by entering a **soft return**. A soft return moves words down to the next baseline but does not create a new paragraph. You enter a soft return by press-ing and holding [Shift] and then pressing [Enter] (Win) or [return] (Mac).

Use the Paragraph palette and Character palette to modify leading and alignment

1. Click **View** on the menu bar, click **Fit Page in Window**, then click the first instance of **The** in the first paragraph four times.

   TIP Clicking a word four times selects the entire paragraph.

2. Click the same word five times.

   TIP Clicking a word five times selects all the text in the text frame.

3. Click the **Leading list arrow** in the Character palette, then click **30 pt**.

   The vertical space between each line of text is increased, as shown in Figure B-20.

   TIP Because leading can be applied to a single selected word as well as to an entire paragraph, the Leading setting is in the Character palette.

4. Double-click the **Leading text box**, type **16**, then press **[Enter]** (Win) or **[return]** (Mac).

5. Click the **Paragraph palette name tab** to display the Paragraph palette, then click the **Justify with last line aligned left button** ▤ .

6. Click **Introducing** at the top of the document three times, then click the **Align center button** ▤ in the Paragraph palette.

7. Click **Edit** on the menu bar, then click **Deselect All**.

   Your document should resemble Figure B-21.

You modified the leading and alignment of a block of selected text.

Introducing the Min-Pin
by Christopher Smith

The Miniature Pinscher is a smooth coated dog in the Toy Group. He is frequently - and incorrectly - referred to as a Miniature Doberman. The characteristics that distinguish the Miniature Pinscher are his size (ten to twelve and a half inches), his racy elegance, and the gait which he exhibits in a self-possessed, animated and cocky manner.

The Miniature Pinscher is part of the larger German Pinscher family, which belonged to a prehistoric group that dates back to 3000 B.C. One of the clear-cut traits present in the ancient Pinschers was that of the two opposing size tendencies: one toward the medium to larger size and the other toward the smaller "dwarf" of miniature size. This ancient miniature-sized Pinscher was the forerunner of today's Miniature pinscher.

New fanciers of the breed often ask: "Is the Miniature Pinscher bred down from the Doberman Pinscher?"

The answer is a definite "No." Since ancient times, the Min Pin was developing with its natural tendency to smallness in stature. In fact, as a recognized breed, the Miniature Pinscher predates the development of the well-known Doberman Pinscher.

The Min Pin is an excellent choice as a family pet. The breed tends to attach itself very quickly to children and really delights in joining a youngster in bed. As soon as the Min-Pin climbs onto the bed, he usually slips under the covers like a mole, all the way to the foot of

Increased leading adds more vertical space between lines of text

Introducing the Min-Pin
by Christopher Smith

The Miniature Pinscher is a smooth coated dog in the Toy Group. He is frequently - and incorrectly - referred to as a Miniature Doberman. The characteristics that distinguish the Miniature Pinscher are his size (ten to twelve and a half inches), his racy elegance, and the gait which he exhibits in a self-possessed, animated and cocky manner.

The Miniature Pinscher is part of the larger German Pinscher family, which belonged to a prehistoric group that dates back to 3000 B.C. One of the clear-cut traits present in the ancient Pinschers was that of the two opposing size tendencies: one toward the medium to larger size and the other toward the smaller "dwarf" of miniature size. This ancient miniature-sized Pinscher was the forerunner of today's Miniature pinscher.

"Is the Miniature Pinscher bred down from the Doberman Pinscher?"

The answer is a definite "No." Since ancient times, the Min Pin was developing with its natural tendency to smallness in stature. In fact, as a recognized breed, the Miniature Pinscher predates the development of the well-known Doberman Pinscher[1].

The Min Pin is an excellent choice as a family pet. The breed tends to attach itself very quickly to children and really delights in joining a youngster in bed. As soon as the Min-Pin climbs onto the bed, he usually slips under the covers like a mole, all the way to the foot of the bed. The Min Pin is intelligent and easily trained. He has a tendency to be clean in all respects, the shedding of the short coat constitutes minimal, if any, problems to the apartment dweller. On the other hand, the Miniature Pinscher certainly is not out of his element on the farm and has been trained to tree squirrels, chase rabbits, and even help herd cows[2]. It is not unusual for the Miniature Pinscher on a farm to catch a rabbit that is equal to or larger than the size of the dog.

[1] Morang, Scott. In Love with the Min-Pin, All Breeds Publishing, 1997

[2] Miltonburger, William. Working Toy Breeds, CIP Press, 2002

Text justified with last line aligned left

Introducing the Min-Pin
by Christopher Smith

The Miniature Pinscher is a smooth coated dog in the Toy Group. He is frequently - and incorrectly - referred to as a Miniature Doberman. The characteristics that distinguish the Miniature Pinscher are his size (ten to twelve and a half inches), his racy elegance, and the gait which he exhibits in a self-possessed, animated and cocky manner.

The Miniature Pinscher is part of the larger German Pinscher family, which belonged to a prehistoric group that dates back to 3000 B.C. One of the clear-cut traits present in the ancient Pinschers was that of the two opposing size tendencies: one toward the medium to larger size and the other toward the smaller "dwarf" of miniature size. This ancient miniature-sized Pinscher was the forerunner of today's Miniature pinscher.

"Is the Miniature Pinscher bred down from the Doberman Pinscher?"

The answer is a definite "No." Since ancient times, the Min Pin was developing with its natural tendency to smallness in stature. In fact, as a recognized breed, the Miniature Pinscher predates the development of the well-known Doberman Pinscher[1].

The Min Pin is an excellent choice as a family pet. The breed tends to attach itself very quickly to children and really delights in joining a youngster in bed. As soon as the Min-Pin climbs onto the bed, he usually slips under the covers like a mole, all the way to the foot of the bed.

The Min Pin is intelligent and easily trained. He has a tendency to be clean in all respects, the shedding of the short coat constitutes minimal, if any, problems to the apartment dweller. On the other hand, the Miniature Pinscher certainly is not out of his element on the farm and has been trained to tree squirrels, chase rabbits, and even help herd cows[2]. It is not unusual for the Miniature Pinscher on a farm to catch a rabbit that is equal to or larger than the size of the dog.

[1] Mornag, Scott: In Love with the Min-Pin, All Breeds Publishing, 1997

[2] Mihrmberger, William: Working Toy Breeds, CIP Press, 2002

Space before value increased

Apply vertical spacing between paragraphs

1. Click the **Type Tool** T., click anywhere in the body copy, click **Edit** on the menu bar, then click **Select All**.

   TIP The keyboard shortcut for Select All is [Ctrl][A] (Win) or ⌘[A] (Mac).

2. Click the **Space After up arrow** in the Paragraph palette three times, so that the value reads .1875 in, then deselect all.

   .1875 inches of vertical space is applied after every paragraph, as shown in Figure B-22.

3. Select the two footnotes at the bottom of the document, double-click the **Space After text box**, type **0**, then press [Enter] (Win) or [return] (Mac).

4. Select only the first of the two footnotes, double-click the **Space Before text box** in the Paragraph palette, type **.25**, then press [Enter] (Win) or [return] (Mac).

   .25 inches of vertical space is positioned above the first footnote.

5. Click **Edit** on the menu bar, then click **Deselect All**.

   Your document should resemble Figure B-23.

You used the Space After and Space Before text boxes in the Paragraph palette to apply vertical spacing between paragraphs.

Apply paragraph indents

1. Click **Type** on the menu bar, then click **Show Hidden Characters**.

   As shown in Figure B-24, hidden characters appear in blue, showing blue dots for spaces, created by pressing [Spacebar], and paragraph marks for paragraph returns.

2. Select all the body copy on the page except the two footnotes, then click the **First Line Left Indent up arrow** in the Paragraph palette four times to change the value to .25 in, as shown in Figure B-25.

   The first line of each paragraph is indented .25 in.

3. Select by Christopher Smith, then change the left indent to .5 in.

4. Click anywhere in the third paragraph, change the First Line Left Indent value to 0 in, change the Left Indent value to .75 in, then change the Right Indent value to .75 in.

5. Click any word in the third paragraph four times to select the paragraph, click the **Character palette name tab**, change the font size to 18 pt, change the leading to 20 pt, then deselect the paragraph.

   Your document should resemble Figure B-26.

You showed hidden characters so that you could better identify each paragraph. You indented the first lines of every paragraph, and then you added substantial left and right indents to a paragraph and increased its point size to create a "pull quote."

FIGURE B-24
Showing hidden characters

The·characteristics·that
Space symbol

lf·inches),·his·racy·elegan

ocky·manner.¶
Paragraph return symbol

FIGURE B-26
Using indents to format text as a pull quote

Introducing·the·Min-Pin¶
by Christopher Smith#

The Miniature Pinscher is a smooth coated dog in the Toy Group. He is frequently - and incorrectly - referred-to as a Miniature Doberman. The characteristics that distinguish the Miniature Pinscher are his size (ten to twelve and a half inches), his racy elegance, and the gait which he exhibits in a self-possessed, animated and cocky manner¶

The Miniature Pinscher is part of the larger German Pinscher family, which belonged to a prehistoric group that dates back to 3000 B.C. One of the clear-cut traits present in the ancient Pinschers was that of the two opposing size tendencies: one toward the medium to larger size and the other toward the smaller "dwarf" of miniature size. This ancient miniature-sized Pinscher was the forerunner of today's Miniature pinscher¶

"Is the Miniature Pinscher bred down from the Doberman Pinscher?" ¶

The answer is a definite "No." Since ancient times, the Min Pin was developing with its natrual tendency to smallness in stature. In fact, as a recognized breed, the Miniature Pinscher predates the development of the well-known Doberman Pinscher[1] ¶

The Min Pin is an excellent choice as a family pet. The breed tends to attach itself very quickly to children and really delights in joining a youngster in bed. As soon as the Min-Pin climbs onto the bed, he usually slips under the covers like a mole, all the way to the foot of the bed. ¶

The Min Pin is intelligent and easily trained. He has a tendency to be clean in all respects, the shedding of the short coat constitutes minimal, if any, problems to the apartment dweller. On the other hand, the Miniature Pinscher certainly is not out of his element on the farm and has been trained to tree squirrels, chase rabbits, and even help herd cows[2]. It is not unusual for the Miniature Pinscher on a farm to catch a rabbit that is equal to or larger than the size of the dog¶

[1] Marring, Scott. In Love with the Min-Pin, All Breeds Publishing, 1997¶
[2] Mishenberger, William. Working Toy Breeds, CTF Press, 2002¶

Pull quote formatted with increased left and right indents

FIGURE B-25
Applying a first line left indent

First line left indent value

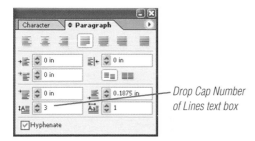

Drop Cap Number
of Lines text box

Apply drop caps and soft returns

1. Click the **Paragraph palette name tab**, click anywhere in the first paragraph, then change the First Line Left Indent value to 0.

2. Click the **Drop Cap Number of Lines up arrow** three times, so that the text box displays a 3, as shown in Figure B-27.

   A drop cap at the height of three text lines is added to the first paragraph.

3. Select all the body copy text, including the two footnotes, then change the font to Garamond.

4. Click the **Zoom Tool** 🔍 , then drag a selection box around the entire last paragraph.

5. Click the **Type Tool** T , click before the capital letter O of the word On in the third sentence of the last paragraph, press and hold **[Shift]**, then press **[Enter]** (Win) or **[return]** (Mac) to create a soft return.

6. Click **Type** on the menu bar, click **Hide Hidden Characters**, click **View** on the menu bar, then click **Hide Guides**.

   Your document should resemble Figure B-28.

7. Click **File** on the menu bar, click **Save**, then close Min-Pin Intro.

You created a drop cap and a soft return, which moved text to the next line without creating a new paragraph.

FIGURE B-28
Viewing the finished document

Introducing the Min-Pin

by Christopher Smith

The Miniature Pinscher is a smooth coated dog in the Toy Group. He is frequently - and incorrectly - referred to as a Miniature Doberman. The characteristics that distinguish the Miniature Pinscher are his size (ten to twelve and a half inches), his racy elegance, and the gait which he exhibits in a self-possessed, animated and cocky manner.

The Miniature Pinscher is part of the larger German Pinscher family, which belonged to a prehistoric group that dates back to 3000 B.C. One of the clear-cut traits present in the ancient Pinschers was that of the two opposing size tendencies: one toward the medium to larger size and the other toward the smaller "dwarf" of miniature size. This ancient miniature sized Pinscher was the forerunner of today's Miniature pinscher.

"Is the Miniature Pinscher bred down from the Doberman Pinscher?"

The answer is a definite "No." Since ancient times, the Min Pin was developing with its natrual tendency to smallness in stature. In fact, as a recognized breed, the Miniature Pinscher predates the development of the well-known Doberman Pinscher[1].

The Min Pin is an excellent choice as a family pet. The breed tends to attach itself very quickly to children and really delights in joining a youngster in bed. As soon as the Min-Pin climbs onto the bed, he usually slips under the covers like a mole, all the way to the foot of the bed.

The Min Pin is intelligent and easily trained. He has a tendency to be clean in all respects, the shedding of the short coat constitutes minimal, if any, problems to the apartment dweller. On the other hand, the Miniature Pinscher certainly is not out of his element on the farm and has been trained to tree squirrels, chase rabbits, and even help herd cows[2]. It is not unusual for the Miniature Pinscher on a farm to catch a rabbit that is equal to or larger than the size of the dog.

No new
paragraph

[1] Moning, Scott: *In Love with the Min-Pin*, All Breeds Publishing, 1997

[2] Miltenberger, William: *Working Toy Breeds*, CJP Press, 2002

CREATE AND APPLY STYLES

Jake's Diner

Early Bird Breakfast Menu

Eggs and Bacon

Two eggs any style, two strips of lean bacon, one biscuit with our homestyle gravy, and home fries.

$5.95

Egg Sandwich

One egg over easy, served with American or Jack cheese on a soft French croissant.

$5.25

Belgian Waffle

A golden brown buttery waffle served with fresh-picked strawberries, raspberries and blueberries. Whipped fresh cream on request.

$4.95

Silver Dollar Pancakes

1 stack of eight golden pancakes served with fresh creamery butter and warm maple syrup.

$4.95

French Toast

Four triangles of thick peasant bread dipped in a cinnamon-egg batter. Served with French Fries.

$6.95

Biscuits and Gravy

Light fluffy southern biscuits served with a hearty sausage gravy.

$3.95

Eggs Hollandaise

Three eggs lightly poached served on a bed of romaine lettuce and topped with a rich Hollandaise sauce.

$6.95

Steak and Eggs

A 6 oz. strip of peppered breakfast steak cooked to your liking, served with two eggs, any style.

$7.95

 In this lesson, you will use the Character Styles and Paragraph Styles palettes to create and apply styles to text.

Working with Character and Paragraph Styles

Imagine that you are writing a book—let's say a user's manual for how to care for houseplants. This book will contain seven chapters. In each chapter, different sections will be preceded by a headline that is the same font as the chapter title, but a smaller font size. Within those sections would be subheads—same font, smaller size. This would be a perfect scenario for using styles.

A **style** is a group of formatting attributes, such as font, font size, color, and tracking, that is applied to text—whenever and wherever you want it to appear—throughout a document or multiple documents. Using styles saves you time, and it keeps your work consistent. Styles are given descriptive names for the type of text they are applied to. Figure B-29 shows three styles in the Character Styles palette. You use the Character Styles palette to create styles for individual words or characters, such as a footnote, and you use the Paragraph Styles palette to apply a style to a paragraph. Paragraph styles include formatting options such as indents and drop caps. The Paragraph Styles palette is shown in Figure B-30.

In the above scenario of the houseplant book, if you weren't using styles, you would be required to format those chapter headlines one at time, for all seven chapter heads. You'd need to remember the font size, the font style, and any tracking, kerning, scaling, or other formatting. Then you'd need to do the same for every section headline, then every sub-headline. For any body copy, you'd risk inconsistent spacing, indents, and other formatting options. Using styles, you define those formats one time and one time only. A much better solution, don't you think?

QUICKTIP

Glyphs are alternate versions of the characters available in the current font being used. Click Type on the menu bar, then click Glyphs to display the Glyph palette. Click the document window with the Type Tool, then double-click the glyph in the Glyph palette that you wish to insert.

FIGURE B-29
Character Styles palette

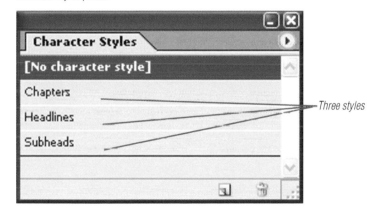

Three styles

FIGURE B-30
Paragraph Styles palette

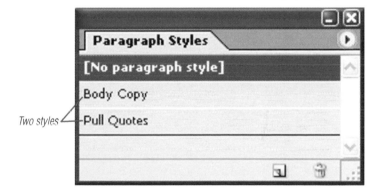

Two styles

Create character styles

1. Open ID B-2.indd, then save it as **Jake's Diner**.

2. Click **Window** on the menu bar, point to **Type & Tables**, then click **Character Styles**.

   TIP Pull the Character Styles palette away from the right side of the document window, if necessary.

3. Click the **Character Styles palette list arrow**, then click **New Character Style**.

4. Type **Dishes** in the Style Name text box of the New Character Style dialog box as shown in Figure B-31, then click **Basic Character Formats** in the left column.

5. Click the **Font Family list arrow**, click **Impact**, click the **Size list arrow**, click **14 pt**, click the **Leading text box**, type **16 pt**, then click **Advanced Character Formats** in the left column.

6. Type **85** in the Horizontal Scale text box, then click **OK**.

   The style "Dishes" now appears in the Character Styles palette.

7. Click the **Character Styles palette list arrow**, click **New Character Style**, type **Descriptions** in the Style Name text box, then click **Basic Character Formats** in the left column.

8. Click the **Font Family list arrow**, click **Garamond**, click the **Font Style list arrow**, click **Italic**, change the font size to 10 pt, change the leading to 12 pt, then click **OK**.

   The style "Descriptions" now appears in the Character Styles palette.

continued

FIGURE B-31
New Character Style dialog box

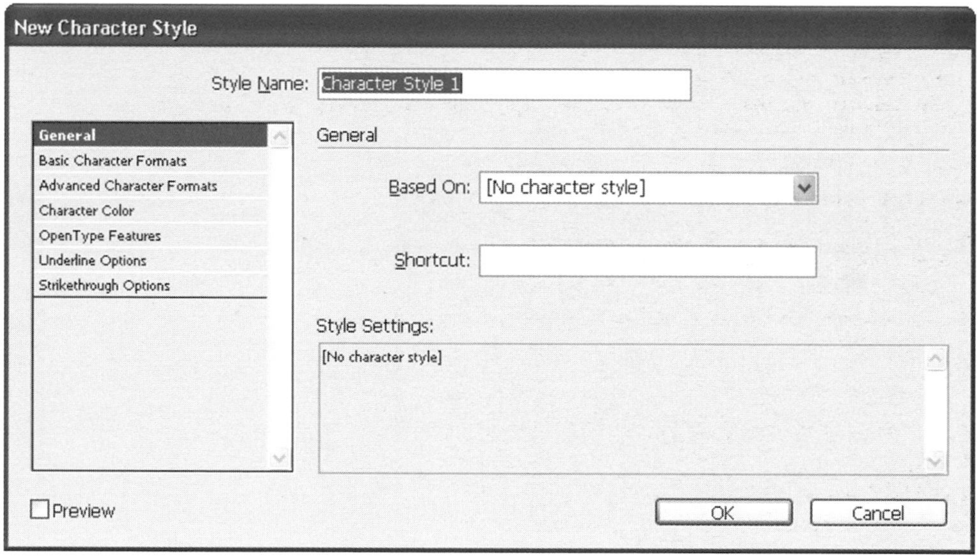

FIGURE B-32
Character Styles palette

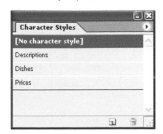

FIGURE B-33
Applying three different character styles

Dishes style ——— **Eggs and Bacon**

Descriptions style ╱ *Two eggs any style, two strips of lean bacon, one*
biscuit with our homestyle gravy, and home fries.

$5.95

Prices style

FIGURE B-34
Viewing the document with all character styles applied

Jake's Diner
Early Bird Breakfast Menu

Eggs and Bacon
*Two eggs any style, two strips of lean bacon, one
biscuit with our homestyle gravy, and home fries.*
$5.95

Egg Sandwich
*One egg over easy, served with American or Jack
cheese on a soft French croissant.*
$5.25

Belgian Waffle
*A golden brown buttery waffle served with fresh-
picked strawberries, raspberries and blueberries.
Whipped fresh cream on request.*
$4.95

Silver Dollar Pancakes
*A stack of eight golden pancakes served with fresh
creamery butter and warm maple syrup.*
$4.95

French Toast
*Four triangles of thick peasant bread dipped in a
cinnamon-egg batter. Served with French Fries.*
$6.95

Biscuits and Gravy
*Light fluffy southern biscuits served with a hearty
sausage gravy.*
$3.95

Eggs Hollandaise
*Three eggs lightly poached served on a bed of
romaine lettuce and topped with a rich Hollandaise
sauce.*
$6.95

Steak and Eggs
*A 16 oz. strip of peppered breakfast steak cooked
to your liking, served with two eggs, any style.*
$7.95

9. Click the **Character Styles palette list arrow**, click **New Character Style**, type **Prices** in the Style Name text box, then click **Basic Character Formats** in the left column.

10. Change the font to ITC Garamond, change the font style to Bold, change the font size to 12 pt, change the leading to 14 pt, then click **OK**.

   Your Character Styles palette should resemble Figure B-32.

You created three new character styles.

Apply character styles

1. Click the **Type Tool** T, triple-click the word **Eggs** in the first title to select the entire title "Eggs and Bacon," then click **Dishes** in the Character Styles palette.

   The Dishes character style is applied to the title.

2. Select the entire next paragraph (beginning with the word Two), then click **Descriptions** in the Character Styles palette.

3. Select the first price ($5.95), click **Prices** in the Character Styles palette, click **Edit** on the menu bar, then click **Deselect All**.

   Your first menu item should resemble Figure B-33.

4. Apply the Dishes style to the remaining seven dish titles.

5. Apply the Descriptions style to the remaining seven descriptions.

6. Apply the Prices style to the remaining seven prices, then deselect so that your document resembles Figure B-34.

You applied character styles to format specific areas of a document.

Create paragraph styles

1. Click **Window** on the menu bar, point to **Type & Tables**, then click **Paragraph Styles**.

   TIP Pull the Paragraph Styles palette away from the right side of the document window, if necessary.

2. Click the **Paragraph Styles list arrow**, then click **New Paragraph Style**.

3. Type **Prices** in the Style Name text box, then click **Indents and Spacing** in the left column.

   TIP Note that the New Paragraph Style dialog box contains Basic Character Formats and Advanced Character Formats windows— the same that you find when working in the New Character Style dialog box.

4. Click the **Alignment list arrow**, then click **Center**.

5. Type **.25** in the Space After text box, then click **Paragraph Rules** in the left column.

   TIP The term **rules** is layout jargon for lines. Rules can be positioned on a page as a design element, or text can be underlined with rules.

6. Click the **Paragraph Rules list arrow**, click **Rule Below**, then click the **Rule On check box** to add a check mark.

7. Type **.125** in the Offset text box, type **.25** in the Left Indent text box, type **.25** in the Right Indent text box, press **[Tab]** so that your dialog box resembles Figure B-35, then click **OK**.

   The paragraph style "Prices" now appears in the Paragraph Styles palette, as shown in Figure B-36.

You created a paragraph style, which included a center alignment, a space after value, and a paragraph rule.

Paragraph Rules window in the New Paragraph Style dialog box

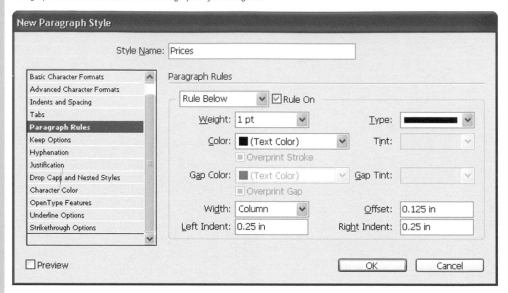

FIGURE B-36
Paragraph Styles palette

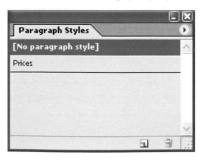

Working with Text

FIGURE B-37

Applying a paragraph style to two prices

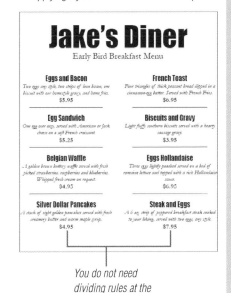

Eggs and Bacon

Two eggs any style, two strips of lean bacon, one biscuit with our homestyle gravy, and home fries.

$5.95

Egg Sandwich

One egg over easy, served with American or Jack cheese on a soft French croissant.

$5.25

Prices paragraph style applied

FIGURE B-38

Applying styles to all but the bottom two prices

You do not need dividing rules at the bottom of the menu

FIGURE B-39

Viewing the final document

Hollandaise sauce moves to a new line

Apply paragraph styles

1. Click the **Type Tool** T, then select all the text in the document except for the two headlines at the top of the page.

2. Activate the Paragraph palette (if necessary), then click the **Align center button** ≡.

   For this layout, all the menu items will be aligned center. It's not necessary to create a paragraph style for all items to align center, because you can simply use the Align center button in the Paragraph palette.

3. Select the first price (**$5.95**), click **Prices** in the Paragraph Styles palette, select the second price (**$5.25**), click **Prices** in the Paragraph Styles palette again, then deselect.

   Your first two menu items should resemble Figure B-37.

4. Apply the Prices paragraph style to the remaining prices in the document *except* the Silver Dollar Pancakes and Steak and Eggs prices, then deselect so that your document resembles Figure B-38.

   You do not need dividing rules at the bottom of the menu.

5. Click **View** on the menu bar, then click **Hide Guides**.

6. Click before the second instance of the word Hollandaise, press and hold **[Shift]**, then press **[Enter]** (Win) or **[return]** (Mac).

   Hollandaise sauce is moved to the next line, as shown in Figure B-39.

7. Save your work, then close Jake's Diner.

You applied a paragraph style to specific areas of the menu.

EDIT TEXT

What You'll Do

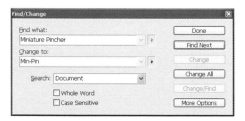

In this lesson, you will use the Find/Change and Check Spelling commands to edit the text of a document.

Using the Find/Change Command

One of the great things about creating documents using a computer is the ability to edit text quickly and efficiently. Imagine the days before the personal computer: When you were finished typing a document, you needed to read through it carefully looking for any errors. If you found any, you had only three options: cover it up, cross it out, or type the whole document again.

The Find/Change dialog box, shown in Figure B-40, is a very powerful tool for editing a document. With this command, you can search for any word in the document, then change that word to another word or delete it altogether with a click of your mouse. For example, imagine that you have typed an entire document about Abraham Lincoln's early years growing up in Frankfurt, Kentucky. Then the fact checker informs you that Lincoln actually grew up in Hardin County, Kentucky. You could use the Find/Change command to locate every instance of the word "Frankfurt" and change it to "Hardin County." One click would correct every instance of that error, throughout the entire document. Try that with a typewriter!

Checking Spelling

Since the earliest days of the personal computer, the ability to check and correct spelling errors automatically has been a much-promoted benefit of creating documents digitally. It has stood the test of time. The spell checker continues to be one of the most powerful features of word processing.

InDesign's Check Spelling dialog box, shown in Figure B-41, is a comprehensive utility for locating and correcting typos and other misspellings in a document. If you've done word processing before, you will find yourself on familiar turf. The spell checker identifies words that it doesn't find in its dictionary, offers you a list of suggested corrections, and asks you what you want to do. If it is indeed a misspelling, type the correct spelling or choose the correct word from the suggested corrections list, then click Change to correct that instance or click Change All to correct all instances of the misspelling throughout the document.

Sometimes the spell checker identifies a word that is not actually a misspelling. For example, say you were typing a letter about your dog whose name is Gargantua. The spell checker is not going to find that word/name in its dictionary, and it is going to ask you what you want to do with it. You have two options. You could click Ignore, which tells the spell checker to make no changes and move on to the next questionable word. However, because in the future you will probably type the dog's name in other documents, you don't want the spell checker always asking you if this word/name is a misspelling. In this case, you'd be better off clicking the Add button. Doing so adds the name Gargantua to the spell checker's dictionary, and in the future, the spell checker will no longer identify Gargantua as a misspelling.

When adding an item to the dictionary, you can choose whether you want the term to be available in InDesign's User Dictionary or a custom dictionary specific to an individual document. After clicking Add in the Check Spelling dialog box, click the Target list arrow in the Dictionary dialog box, then click User Dictionary or a specific document. If you choose a document, rather than User Dictionary, the term will only belong to the dictionary used when you spell check that particular document. If you choose User Dictionary, the term will not show up as a misspelling when you spell check any InDesign document.

QUICKTIP

You can remove words from a dictionary using the Dictionary command on the Edit menu.

FIGURE B-40

Find/Change dialog box

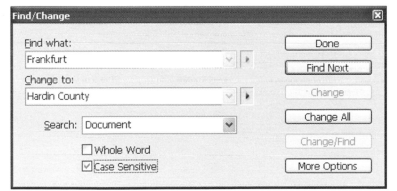

FIGURE B-41

Check Spelling dialog box

Use the Find/Change command

1. Open ID B-3.indd, then save it as **Final Edit**.

2. Click **Edit** on the menu bar, then click **Find/Change**.

3. Type **Miniature Pincher** in the Find what text box, then type **Min-Pin** in the Change to text box, as shown in Figure B-42.

4. Click **Find Next**.

   The first use of "Miniature Pincher" in the document is highlighted. As this is the first use of the term, you don't want to change it to a nickname.

   | TIP   Drag the dialog box out of the way if you cannot see your document.

5. Click **Find Next** again, then click **Change**.

   The second use of "Miniature Pincher" is changed to "Min-Pin."

6. Click **Find Next** again, then click **Change**.

7. Click **Find Next** three times.

   You don't want to change *all* instances of Miniature Pincher to Min-Pin.

8. Click **Change**, then click **Done**.

9. Click **Edit** on the menu bar, then click **Find/Change**.

10. Type **Pincher** in the Find what text box, type **Pinscher** in the Change to text box, then click **Change All**.

    A dialog box appears stating that the search is completed and 14 replacements were made.

11. Click **OK**, then click **Done**.

You used the Find/Change command to replace specific words in the document with other words.

FIGURE B-42
Find/Change dialog box

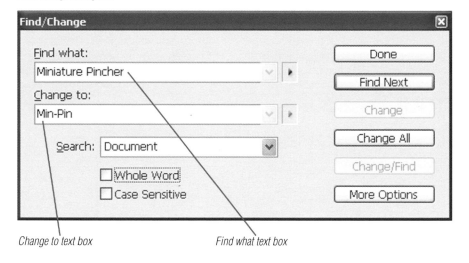

Change to text box   Find what text box

FIGURE B-43

Check Spelling dialog box

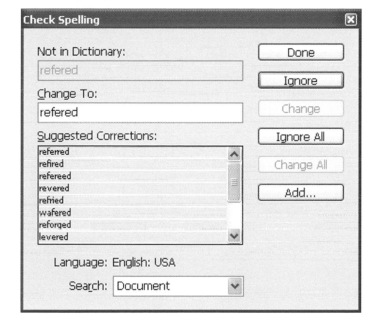

1. Click to the right of the drop cap **T** (between the T and the h) at the top of the page.

   Positioning your cursor at the top of a document forces the spell checker to begin checking for misspellings from the start of the document.

2. Click **Edit** on the menu bar, click **Check Spelling**, then click **Start**.

   As shown in Figure B-43, the first word the spell checker can't find in the dictionary—"refered"—is listed and suggested corrections are listed below.

3. Click **referred** in the Suggested Corrections list—then click **Change**.

   The spell checker lists the next word that it can't find in the dictionary—"Min-Pin."

4. Click **Add** to open the Dictionary dialog box, click the **Target list arrow**, click **Final Edit.indd**, click **Add**, click **Done**, then click **Ignore**.

5. Click **raoy** in the Suggested Corrections list, then click **Change**.

   The spell checker lists "Pinscher1" as not in the dictionary because of the number 1 footnote.

6. Click **Ignore**, then click **Ignore** for the remaining queries, click **OK**, then click **Done**.

7. Save your work, then close Final Edit.

   TIP Never rely on the spell checker as the sole means for proofreading a document.

You used the Check Spelling dialog box to proof a document for spelling errors.

Format text.

1. Open ID B-4.indd, then save it as **Independence**.
2. Click the Type Tool, then triple-click the word Declaration at the top of the page.
3. In the Character palette, type **80** in the Horizontal Scale text box, then press [Enter] (Win) or [return] (Mac).
4. Click the Font Family list arrow, click Impact, click the Font Size list arrow, then click 36 pt.
5. Press and hold [Shift] [Ctrl] (Win) or [Shift] ⌘ (Mac), then press [<] two times.
6. Triple-click the word July on the next line, change the type face to Garamond (if necessary), change the type style to Italic, then click the Font Size up arrow until you change the font size to 18 pt.
7. Click Object on the menu bar, click Text Frame Options, change the Align setting to Center, then click OK.
8. Triple-click the word July (if necessary).
9. Type **100** in the Tracking text box.
10. Click between the letters r and a in the word Declaration, click the Kerning list arrow, then click 10.
11. Click View on the menu bar, click Fit Page in Window, click the Zoom Tool, then drag a selection box that encompasses all of the body copy on the page.

12. Click the Type Tool, then select the number 1 at the end of the first paragraph.
13. Click the Character palette list arrow, then click Superscript.
14. Select the number 1 at the beginning of the last paragraph, then apply the Superscript command.

Format paragraphs.

1. Click View on the menu bar, click Fit Page in Window, then click the first word When in the body copy five times to select all the body copy.
2. Double-click the Leading text box in the Character palette, type **13**, then press [Enter] (Win) or [return] (Mac).
3. Click the Paragraph palette name tab to display the Paragraph palette, then click the Justify with last line aligned left button.
4. Triple-click the word Independence at the top of the document, then click the Align center button in the Paragraph palette.
5. Click Edit on the menu bar, then click Deselect All.
6. Click the Type Tool, click anywhere in the body copy, click Edit on the menu bar, then click Select All.

7. In the Paragraph palette, click the Space After up arrow three times, so that the value reads .1875 in, then apply the Deselect All command.
8. Select the last paragraph of the document, double-click the Space Before text box in the Paragraph palette, type **.5**, then press [Enter] (Win) or [return] (Mac).
9. Click Edit on the menu bar, then click Deselect All.
10. Click Type on the menu bar, then click Show Hidden Characters.
11. Select all the body copy on the page except for the last paragraph (the footnote), double-click the First Line Left Indent text box in the Paragraph palette, type **.25**, then press [Enter] (Win) or [return] (Mac).
12. Select July 4, 1776 beneath the headline, then click the Align right button in the Paragraph palette.
13. Double-click the Right Indent text box in the Paragraph palette, type **.6**, then press [Enter] (Win) or [return] (Mac).
14. Click anywhere in the first paragraph, then change the First Line Left Indent value to 0.
15. Click the Drop Cap Number of Lines up arrow three times, so that the text box displays a 3.

16. Click the Zoom Tool, then drag a selection box that encompasses the entire second to last paragraph in the body copy.

17. Click the Type Tool, position your cursor before the word these—the second to last word in the paragraph.

18. Press and hold [Shift] then press [Enter] (Win) or [return] (Mac).

19. Click Type on the menu bar, click Hide Hidden Characters, click View on the menu bar, then click Hide Guides.

20. Click View on the menu bar, then click Fit Page in Window.

21. Compare your document to Figure B-44, click File on the menu bar, click Save, then close Independence.

FIGURE B-44
Completed Skills Review, Part 1

The Declaration of Independence
July 4, 1776

When in the Course of human events, it becomes necessary for one people to dissolve the political bands which have connected them with another, and to assume among the powers of the earth, the separate and equal station to which the Laws of Nature and of Nature's God entitle them, a decent respect to the opinions of mankind requires that they should declare the causes which impel them to the separation.[1]

We hold these truths to be self-evident, that all men are created equal, that they are endowed by their Creator with certain unalienable Rights, that among these are Life, Liberty and the pursuit of Happiness. That to secure these rights, Governments are instituted among Men, deriving their just powers from the consent of the governed. That whenever any Form of Government becomes destructive of these ends, it is the Right of the People to alter or to abolish it, and to institute new Government, laying its foundation on such principles and organizing its powers in such form, as to them shall seem most likely to effect their Safety and Happiness.

Prudence, indeed, will dictate that Governments long established should not be changed for light and transient causes; and accordingly all experience hath shown, that mankind are more disposed to suffer, while evils are sufferable, than to right themselves by abolishing the forms to which they are accustomed. But when a long train of abuses and usurpations, pursuing invariably the same Object evinces a design to reduce them under absolute Despotism, it is their right, it is their duty, to throw off such Government, and to provide new Guards for their future security.

Such has been the patient sufferance of these Colonies; and such is now the necessity which constrains them to alter their former Systems of Government. The history of the present King of Great Britain [George III] is a history of repeated injuries and usurpations, all having in direct object the establishment of an absolute Tyranny over these States.

We, therefore, the Representatives of the united States of America, in General Congress,Assembled, appealing to the Supreme Judge of the world for the rectitude of our intentions, do, in the Name, and by the Authority of the good People of these Colonies, solemnly publish and declare, That these United Colonies are, and of Right ought to be Free and Independent States; that they are Absolved from all Allegiance to the British Crown, and that all political connection between them and the State of Great Britain, is and ought to be totally dissolved; and that as Free and Independent States, they have full Power to levy War, conclude Peace, contract Alliances, establish Commerce, and to do all other Acts and Things which Independent States may of right do. And for the support of this Declaration, with a firm reliance on the protection of divine Providence, we mutually pledge to each other our Lives, our Fortunes and our sacred Honor.

[1] This document is an excerpt of the full text of the Declaration of Independence. For space considerations, the lengthy section listing the tyranny and transgressions of King George III has been removed.

Create and apply styles.

1. Open ID B-5.indd, then save it as **Toy Breeds**.
2. Click the Character Styles palette list arrow, then click New Character Style.
3. Type **Breeds** in the Style Name text box, then click Basic Character Formats in the left column.
4. Change the font to Tahoma, change the size to 14 pt, change the leading to 16 pt, click Advanced Character Formats in the left column, then click OK.
5. Click the Character Styles palette list arrow, click New Character Style, type **Blurbs** in the Style Name text box, then click Basic Character Formats in the left column.
6. Change the font to Garamond, change the style to Italic, change the size to 10 pt, change the leading to 12 pt, then click OK.
7. Select all of the text except for the top two lines, then click Blurbs in the Character Styles palette.
8. Double-click the Affenpinscher headline, then click Breeds in the Character Styles palette.
9. Apply the Breeds character style to the remaining seven breed headlines.
10. Click the Paragraph Styles palette list arrow, then click New Paragraph Style.
11. Type **Blurbs** in the Style Name text box, then click Indents and Spacing in the left column.
12. Click the Alignment list arrow, then click Center.
13. Type **.25** in the Space After text box, then click Paragraph Rules in the left column.

14. Click the Paragraph Rules list arrow, click Rule Below, then click the Rule On check box.
15. Type **.1625** in the Offset text box, type **1** in the Left Indent text box, type **1** in the Right Indent text box, then click OK.
16. Select all of the text except for the top two lines, then click the Align center button in the Paragraph palette.
17. Select the Affenpinscher blurb copy, then click Blurbs in the Paragraph Styles palette.
18. Apply the Blurbs paragraph style to all the remaining descriptions except for the Pomeranian and the Pug.

FIGURE B-45
Completed Skills Review, Part 2

TOY BREEDS
A Guide to Small Dog Breeds

Affenpinscher
One of the oldest of the toy breeds, the Affenpinscher originated in Europe. The Affenpinscher is noted for its great loyalty and affection.

Chihuahua
A graceful, alert and swift dog, the Chihuahua is a clannish breed which tends to recognize and prefer its own breed for association.

Maltese
Known as the "ancient dog of Malta," the Maltese has been known as the aristocrat of the canine world for more than 28 centuries.

Manchester Terrier
Dubbed "the gentleman's terrier," this dog was bred in Manchester, England to kill vermin and to hunt small game.

Pekingese
Sacred in China, the Pekingese is a dignified dog who is happy in a rural or urban setting.

Poodle
The national dog of France, Poodles are known for their retrieving capabilities in cold water.

Pomeranian
A descendant of the sled dogs of Iceland and Lapland, the "Pom" is hearty and strong despite his fragile appearance.

Pug
One of the oldest breeds, the Pug is an even-tempered breed who is playful, outgoing and dignified.

19. Click View on the menu bar, then click Hide Guides.
20. Click before the word bred in the Manchester Terrier description, press and hold [Shift], then press [Enter] (Win) or [return] (Mac).
21. Click before the phrase even-tempered in the "Pug" description, press and hold [Shift], press [Enter] (Win) or [return] (Mac), click before the word and in the "Pug" description, press and hold [Shift], then press [Enter] (Win) or [return] (Mac).
22. Save your work, compare your screen to Figure B-45, then close Toy Breeds.

Working with Text

Edit text.

1. Open ID B-6.indd, then save it as **Declaration Edit**.
2. Click at the beginning of the first paragraph.
3. Click Edit on the menu bar, then click Find/Change.
4. Type **IV** in the Find what text box, then type **III** in the Change to text box. (*Hint*: Drag the dialog box out of the way if you cannot see your document.)
5. Click Find Next. (*Hint*: You want to change the IV in George IV to III, as in George III, however, the spell checker finds all instances of "IV" such as in the word "deriving.")
6. Click the Case Sensitive check box to add a check mark, then click Find Next again.
7. Click Change All, click OK in the dialog box that tells you that two replacements were made, then click Done in the Find/Change dialog box.
8. Click before the drop cap in the first paragraph, click Edit on the menu bar, then click Check Spelling.
9. Click Start.
10. Click Ignore to ignore the query on "separation.1."
11. Click Safety at the top of the Suggested Corrections list, then click Change.
12. Click Ignore to ignore the query on hath.

13. Click Ignore All to ignore all instances of III.
14. Click before Assembled in the Change to text box in the Check Spelling dialog box, press [Spacebar] once, then click Change.

FIGURE B-46
Completed Skills Review, Part 3

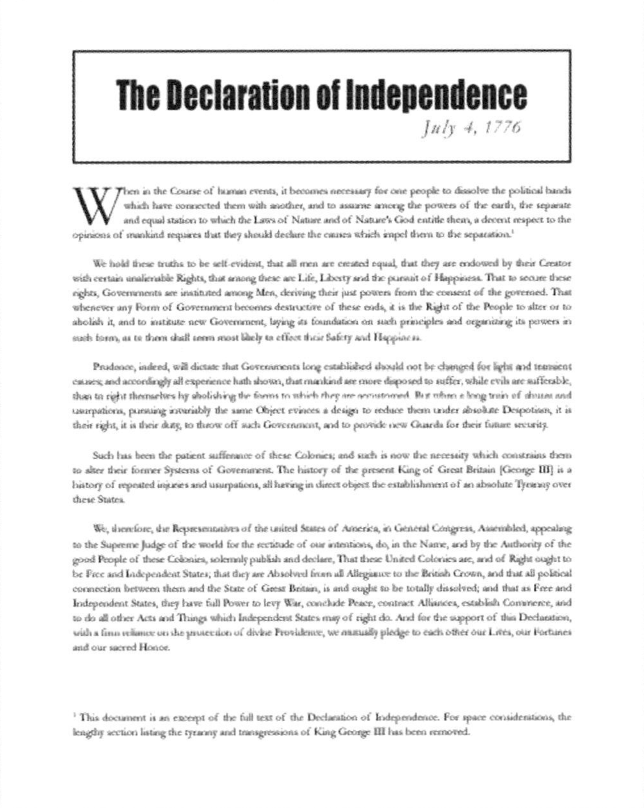

15. Click OK in the dialog box that tells you that the spell check is complete, then click Done.
16. Save your work, deselect, compare your screen to Figure B-46, then close Declaration Edit.

You are a freelance designer. Your client returns a document to you, telling you that she wants you to make a change to a drop cap. She says that, instead of the first letter only being formatted as a drop cap, she wants the entire first word to be more prominent on the page.

1. Open ID B-7.indd, then save it as **Drop Cap Modifications**.

2. Click the Zoom Tool, then drag a selection box around the first paragraph.

3. Click the Type Tool, click after the W drop cap, then change the Drop Cap One or More Characters text box in the Paragraph palette to 4.

4. Select the letters "hen," click the Character palette list arrow, click All Caps, click the Character palette list arrow again, then click Superscript.

5. Click between the N in when and the I in the word in, then type **100** in the Kerning text box.

6. Select "HEN," then type **–10** in the Baseline Shift text box in the Character palette.

7. Click between the W and H in the word When, then type **–50** in the Kerning text box.

8. Save your work, compare your screen to Figure B-47, then close Drop Cap Modifications.

FIGURE B-47
Completed Project Builder 1

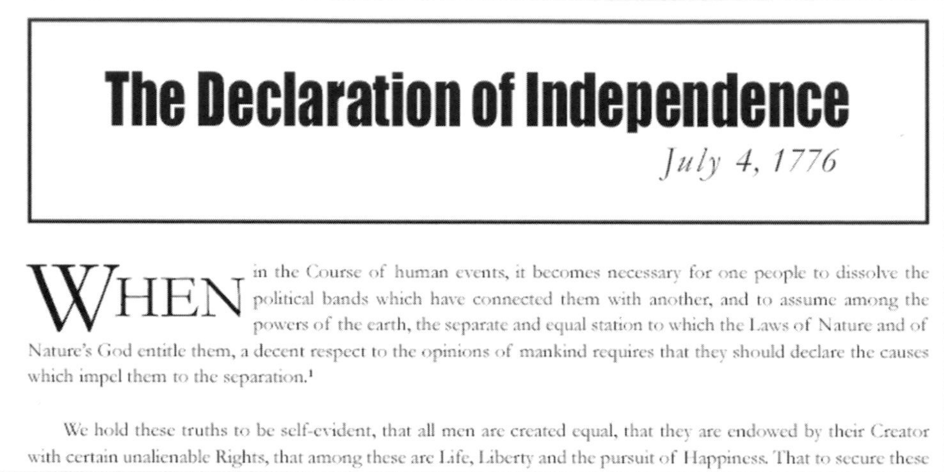

The Declaration of Independence
July 4, 1776

WHEN in the Course of human events, it becomes necessary for one people to dissolve the political bands which have connected them with another, and to assume among the powers of the earth, the separate and equal station to which the Laws of Nature and of Nature's God entitle them, a decent respect to the opinions of mankind requires that they should declare the causes which impel them to the separation.[1]

We hold these truths to be self-evident, that all men are created equal, that they are endowed by their Creator with certain unalienable Rights, that among these are Life, Liberty and the pursuit of Happiness. That to secure these

You have designed a document about miniature pinschers. Your client calls you with changes. He wants to show small pictures of miniature pinschers in the document, one beside each paragraph. He asks you to reformat the document to create space where the small pictures can be inserted.

1. Open ID B-8.indd, then save it as **Hanging Indents**.

2. Select the four paragraphs of body copy, then change the first line left indent to 0.

3. Change the left indent to 2 in, then change the right indent to .5 in.

4. Create a half-inch space after each paragraph.

5. Type **–1.5** in the First Line Left Indent text box, then deselect all.

6. Select the second paragraph, then type **–10** in the Tracking text box to move the word Pinscher up to the previous text line.

7. Save your work, deselect all, compare your screen to Figure B-48, then close Hanging Indents.

FIGURE B-48
Completed Project Builder 2

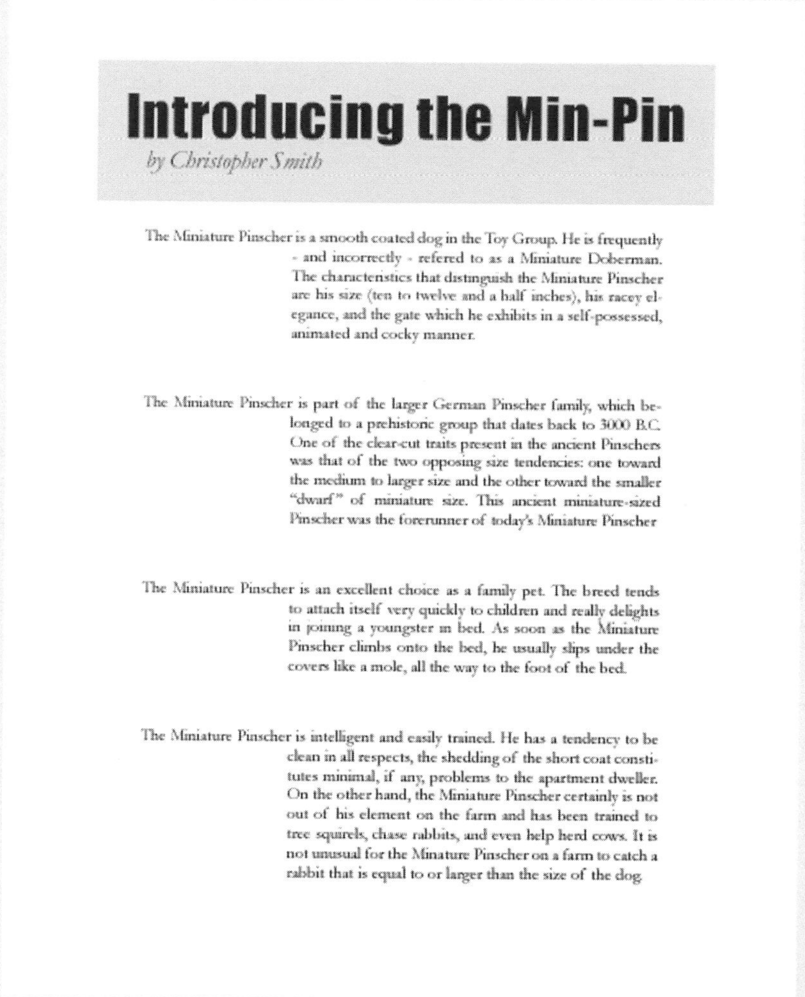

Introducing the Min-Pin
by Christopher Smith

The Miniature Pinscher is a smooth coated dog in the Toy Group. He is frequently - and incorrectly - refered to as a Miniature Doberman. The characteristics that distinguish the Miniature Pinscher are his size (ten to twelve and a half inches), his racey elegance, and the gate which he exhibits in a self-possessed, animated and cocky manner.

The Miniature Pinscher is part of the larger German Pinscher family, which belonged to a prehistoric group that dates back to 3000 B.C. One of the clear-cut traits present in the ancient Pinschers was that of the two opposing size tendencies: one toward the medium to larger size and the other toward the smaller "dwarf" of miniature size. This ancient miniature-sized Pinscher was the forerunner of today's Miniature Pinscher

The Miniature Pinscher is an excellent choice as a family pet. The breed tends to attach itself very quickly to children and really delights in joining a youngster in bed. As soon as the Miniature Pinscher climbs onto the bed, he usually slips under the covers like a mole, all the way to the foot of the bed.

The Miniature Pinscher is intelligent and easily trained. He has a tendency to be clean in all respects, the shedding of the short coat constitutes minimal, if any, problems to the apartment dweller. On the other hand, the Miniature Pinscher certainly is not out of his element on the farm and has been trained to tree squirrels, chase rabbits, and even help herd cows. It is not unusual for the Miniature Pinscher on a farm to catch a rabbit that is equal to or larger than the size of the dog.

You are designing a title treatment for a poster for the new music CD titled "Latin Lingo." After typing the title, you realize immediately that the phrase poses obvious kerning challenges. You note that the central letters—TIN LIN—appear close together, but the outer letters are much further apart. You decide to kern the outer letters to bring them closer together.

1. Open ID B-9.indd, then save it as **Latin Lingo**.

2. Using the Type Tool, click between the A and T, then apply a kerning value of –100.

3. Apply a kerning value of –75 between the N and the G.

4. Apply a kerning value of –30 between the G and the O.

5. Save your work, compare your screen to Figure B-49, then close Latin Lingo.

FIGURE B-49
Completed Design Project

Your group has been assigned the task of designing a headline for a billboard for the movie "Crushing Impact." The client has asked for a finished design in black letters on a white background. As the leader of the group, you decide first to engage the group in a discussion before you design the title.

Discussion.

1. Open ID B-10.indd, then save it as **Crushing Impact**.

2. Have the group regard the title for a full minute.

3. Have the group discuss what font family might be best for the title.

4. Does the title demand a big, bold font, or could it work in a fine, delicate font?

5. Should the two words be positioned side by side, or one on top of the other?

6. Does the title itself suggest that, visually, one word should be positioned on top of the other?

Exercise.

1. Position the word Impact on a second line, select all the text, change the font to Impact, then change the font size to 60 pt.

2. Select the word Impact, change the horizontal scale to 200, then change the vertical scale to 75.

3. Select the word Crushing, change the horizontal scale to 50, change the font size to 177, then change the leading to 203.

FIGURE B-50
Completed Group Project

4. Expand the height of the text box, select the word Impact, then change the leading to 39.

5. Save your work, compare your screen to Figure B-50, then close Crushing Impact.

CHAPTER C

SETTING UP A DOCUMENT

1. Create a new document.

2. Create master pages.

3. Apply master pages to document pages

4. Place text and thread text.

5. Modify master pages and document pages.

6. Create new sections and wrap text.

CHAPTER C
SETTING UP A DOCUMENT

Starting a new document is often a critical phase, for you will make decisions that determine the fundamental properties of the layout. When you start a new document, you specify the size of the document, the number of pages in the document, and the basic layout of the document. At this stage, you also position columns and guides to help you plan out and work with the layout. Though all of these elements can be modified, it is best if you have already determined these basic properties beforehand, so that you will not need to go back and "retro-fit" the document and its design.

Chapter C explores all of the basic principles and features that Adobe InDesign offers for setting up a new document. You will create a simple layout using master pages, and you will create placeholders for text, graphics, and page numbers. You will also learn how to import or place text into a document and how to "thread" text from page to page.

Keep in mind that this is not a chapter about *design* or designing a layout. Instead, Chapter C is an exploration of InDesign's basic tools for setting up and structuring a layout so that you can simplify your work, avoid time-consuming repetition of your efforts, and ensure a consistent layout from page to page.

Tools You'll Use

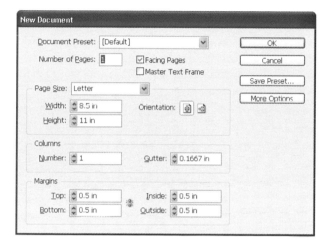

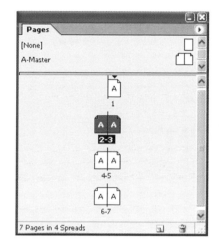

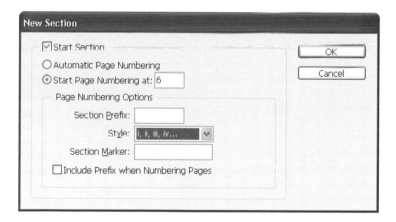

CREATE A NEW DOCUMENT

What You'll Do

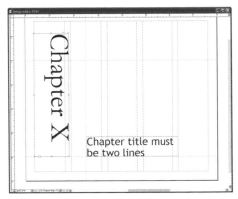

 In this lesson, you will create a new document, position guides on a master page, and create a placeholder for a headline.

Creating a New Document

When you are ready to create a new document in InDesign, you begin in the New Document dialog box, shown in Figure C-1. In the New Document dialog box, you specify the number of pages the document will contain. You also specify the **page size** or **trim size**—the width and height of the finished document. In addition, you specify whether or not the document will have **facing pages**. When you choose this option, the document is created with left and right pages that face each other in a spread, such as you would find in a magazine. If this option is not selected, each page stands alone, like a stack of pages.

The New Document dialog box also allows you to specify the width of margins on the outer edges of the page and the number of columns that will be positioned on the page. **Margins** and **columns** are very useful as layout guides, and they play an important role in flowing text. When working with

FIGURE C-1
New Document dialog box

Enter number of pages that you want in your document here

Page size options

New Document	
Document Preset: [Default]	OK
Number of Pages: 1 ☑ Facing Pages	Cancel
☐ Master Text Frame	Save Preset...
Page Size: Letter	More Options
Width: 8.5 in Orientation:	
Height: 11 in	
Columns	
Number: 1 Gutter: 0.1667 in	
Margins	
Top: 0.5 in Inside: 0.5 in	
Bottom: 0.5 in Outside: 0.5 in	

columns, the term **gutter** refers to the space between the columns. Figure C-2 shows margins and columns on a typical page.

All of the choices you make in the New Document dialog box can be changed after the document has been created.

Understanding Master Pages

Imagine that you are creating a layout for a book and that every chapter title page will have the same layout format. If that book had 20 chapters, you would need to create that chapter title page 20 times. And you'd need to be careful to make the layout consistent every time you created the page. Now imagine that you've finished your

layout, but your editor wants you to change the location of the title on the page. That would mean making the same change— 20 times!

Not so with master pages. **Master pages** are templates that you create for a page layout. Once created, you apply the master page to the document pages you want to have that layout. With master pages, you create a layout one time, then use it as many times as you like. Working with master pages saves you from time-consuming repetition of efforts, and it offers consistency between document pages that are meant to have the same layout.

So what happens when your editor asks for that change in location of the title? Simply make the change to the master page, and the change will be reflected on all the document pages based on that master.

When you create a new document, one default master page is created and listed in the Pages palette, shown in Figure C-3. The Pages palette is command central for all things relating to pages. You use the Pages palette to add, delete, and reorder document pages. You also use the Pages palette to add, delete, and apply master pages to document pages.

FIGURE C-2
Identifying margins and columns

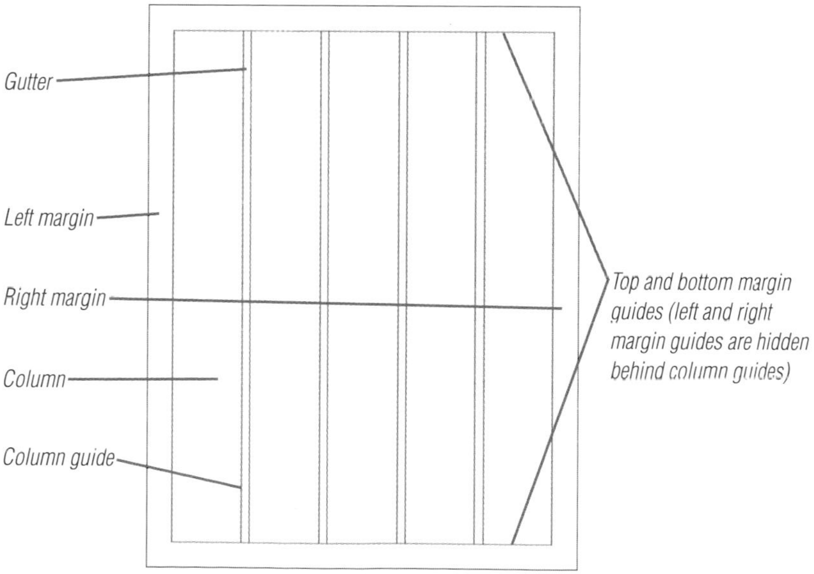

Gutter
Left margin
Right margin
Column
Column guide

Top and bottom margin guides (left and right margin guides are hidden behind column guides)

FIGURE C-3
Default master page

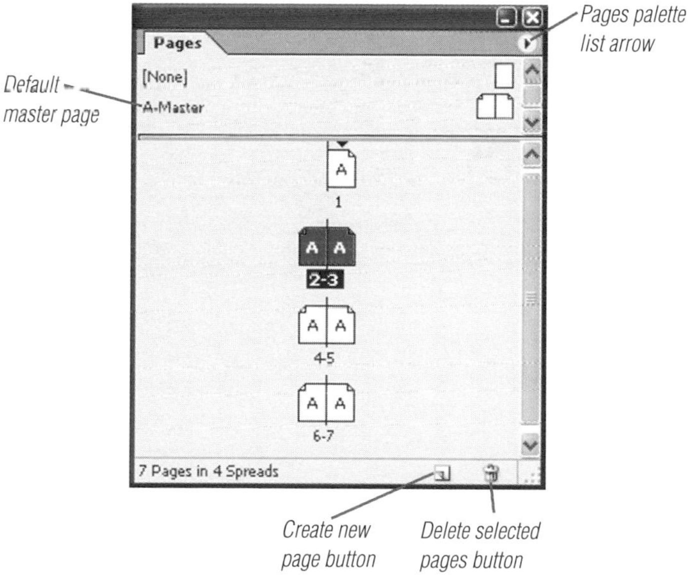

Pages palette list arrow
Default master page

7 Pages in 4 Spreads

Create new page button

Delete selected pages button

Creating Placeholder Frames on Master Pages

In InDesign, text is positioned in **text frames** and graphics are positioned in **graphics frames**. To create a text frame, you click the Type Tool and then drag it in the document window to create a text frame. You can then type text into the text frame. You use the Rectangle, Ellipse, or Polygon Frame Tools in the same way to create graphics frames.

When you create a frame for text or graphics on a master page, it is referred to as a **placeholder**. This term signifies that the frame on the master page is functioning as a place where objects on the document pages are to be positioned. For example, if you had a book broken down into chapters and you created a master page for the chapter title pages, you would create a text frame placeholder for the chapter title text. This text frame would appear on every document page that uses the chapter title master page. Working this way—with the text frame placeholder on the master page—you can feel certain that the location of the chapter title will be consistent on every chapter title page in the book.

Understanding Guides

Guides, as shown in Figure C-4, are horizontal or vertical lines that you position on a page. As their name suggests, guides are used to help guide you in aligning objects on the page. When the Snap to Guides command on the View menu is checked, objects adhere more readily to guides. When you position an object near a guide, the object jumps or "snaps" to the guide, making it very easy to align objects with guides.

Creating Guides

You have a number of options for creating guides. You can create them manually by "pulling" them out from the horizontal and vertical rulers on the page. You can also use the Create Guides command on the Layout menu. Once created, guides can be selected, moved, and deleted, if necessary. You can also change the color of guides, which sometimes makes it easier to see them, depending on the colors used in your document.

FIGURE C-4
Identifying guides

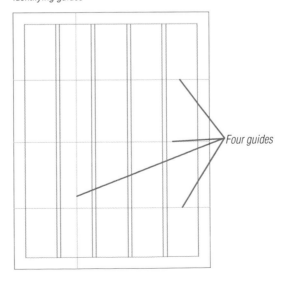

Four guides

Changing the Color of Guides, Margins, and Columns

By default, guides are cyan, columns are violet, and margins are magenta. Depending on
your preferences and on the color of objects
in the layout you are creating, you may want
to have guides, columns, and margins
appear with different colors.

In InDesign, you modify guide colors by
selecting them, then clicking the Ruler
Guides command on the Layout menu.
Choosing a new color in the Ruler Guides
dialog box affects only the selected guides.
When you create more guides, they will be
created in the default color.

You modify the color of margins and
columns in the Guides & Pasteboard section of the Preferences dialog box. Once
you've modified the color of margins and
columns, each new page you create in an
existing document will appear with those
colors. However, when you create a new
document, the margins and columns will
appear in their default colors.

Choosing Default Colors for Guides, Margins, and Columns

When you choose colors for guides, margins, and columns, you may want those
choices to affect every document you create. You do so by making the color changes
in the appropriate dialog boxes without any
documents open. The new colors will be
applied in all new documents created there-
after. Remember, if you change default colors when a document is open, the changes
are only applied to that document.

Using the Transform Palette

The Transform palette identifies a selected
object's width and height, and its horizontal
and vertical locations on the page. As shown
in Figure C-5, the width and height of the
selected object appears in the Width and
Height text boxes of the Transform palette.

When you position an object on a page, you
need some way to describe that object's
position on the page. InDesign defines the
position of an object using X and Y location
values in the Transform palette. To work
with X and Y locations, you first need to
understand that the **zero point** of the page
is, by default, at the top left corner of the
page. X and Y locations are made in reference to that zero point.

The **proxy** is a group of nine reference
points that correspond to the nine points
available on a selected item's bounding box.
Clicking a reference point on the proxy

FIGURE C-5
Transform palette

Proxy icon

Selected frame
is 1" × 1"

Width
text box

Height
text box

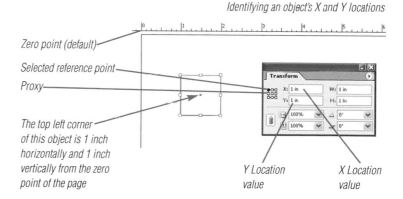

FIGURE C-6
Identifying an object's X and Y locations

Zero point (default)

Selected reference point

Proxy

The top left corner
of this object is 1 inch
horizontally and 1 inch
vertically from the zero
point of the page

Y Location
value

X Location
value

tells InDesign that you wish to see the horizontal and vertical locations of that point of the selected object.

When an object is selected, the X value is the horizontal location—how far it is across the page—and the Y value is the vertical location—how far it is down the page. The selected object in Figure C-6 has an X location of 1 inch and a Y location of 1 inch. This means that its top left point is 1 inch across the page and 1 inch down. Why the top left point? Because that is what has been clicked in the proxy, also shown in Figure C-6.

QUICKTIP

X and Y location values for circles are determined by the reference points of the bounding box that is placed around circles when they are selected.

Be sure to note that the text boxes in the Transform palette are interactive. For example, if you select an object and find that its X coordinate is 2, you can enter 3 in the X Location text box, press [Enter] (Win) or [return] (Mac), and the object will

be relocated to the new location on the page. You can also change the width or height of a selected object by changing the value in the Width or Height text boxes.

QUICKTIP

You can perform calculations in the text boxes in the Transform palette. For example, you could select an object whose width is three inches. By typing 3 - .625 in the W text box, you can reduce the object's width to 2.375 inches. What a powerful feature!

Using the Control Palette

The Control palette, docked at the top of the document window by default, is similar to the Transform palette. It offers the same settings and ability to modify a selected object. For example, you can change the width and height of a frame using the Control palette, just as you can with the Transform palette. Unlike the Transform palette, the Control palette offers additional options for frames including changing the frame's stroke weight and stroke style. The options in the Control palette

change based on the type of object selected. For example, if a block of text is selected, the Control palette changes to show all of the type-related options for modifying text, such as changing the font or font size. In Figure C-7, the Control palette shows options for a graphics frame. The Control palette can be docked at the top or bottom of the document window. Just click the Control palette list arrow and choose Dock at Top or Dock at Bottom. Choosing to use the Transform palette or the Control palette is really a matter of personal preference.

QUICKTIP

The Info palette displays information about the current document and selected objects, such as text and graphics frames. For example, if you click inside a text frame with the Type Tool, the Info palette displays the number of characters, words, lines, and paragraphs in the frame. If you click the same text frame with the Selection Tool, you can find out the size and location of the text frame. The Info palette is available only for viewing information. You cannot make changes to a selected object using this palette.

FIGURE C-7
Control palette

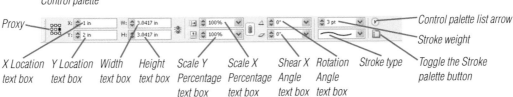

Proxy — X Location text box — Y Location text box — Width text box — Height text box — Scale Y Percentage text box — Scale X Percentage text box — Shear X Angle text box — Rotation Angle text box — Stroke type — Control palette list arrow — Stroke weight — Toggle the Stroke palette button

Using the Transform Palette to Transform Objects

Transform is a term used to describe the act of moving an object, scaling it, skewing it, or rotating it. You can do all of the above in the Transform or Control palettes. Figure C-8 shows a rectangular frame positioned between two guides. In Figure C-9, the same frame has been rotated 90 degrees—note the 90° value in the Rotation Angle text box in the Transform palette. Note also that the object was rotated at its center

point. This is because the center reference point has been selected in the proxy as the **point of origin** for the transformation. Think of the point of origin as the point from where the transformation happens. Whichever reference point is selected on the proxy determines the point of origin for the transformation of the selected object.

Figure C-10 shows the same frame rotated the same 90 degrees. However, this time, the point of origin for the rotation was set at the lower-left corner of the object.

Note how differently the rotation affected the object.

Don't trouble yourself trying to guess ahead of time how the choice of a point of origin in conjunction with a transformation will affect an object. Sometimes it will be easy to foresee how the object will be transformed; sometimes you'll need to use trial and error. The important thing for you to remember is that the point of origin determines the point where the transformation takes place.

FIGURE C-8

Rectangle with its center point identified

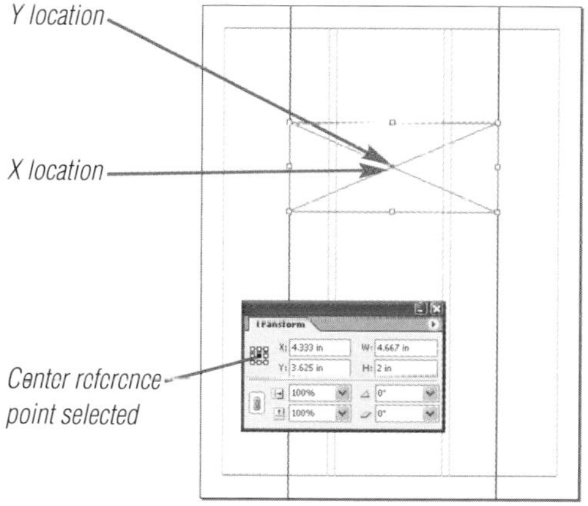

FIGURE C-9

Rectangle rotated 90 degrees at its center point

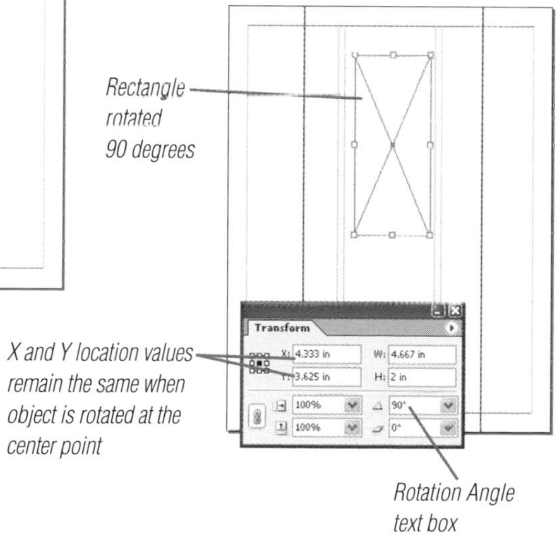

FIGURE C-10

Rectangle rotated 90 degrees at its lower-left corner point

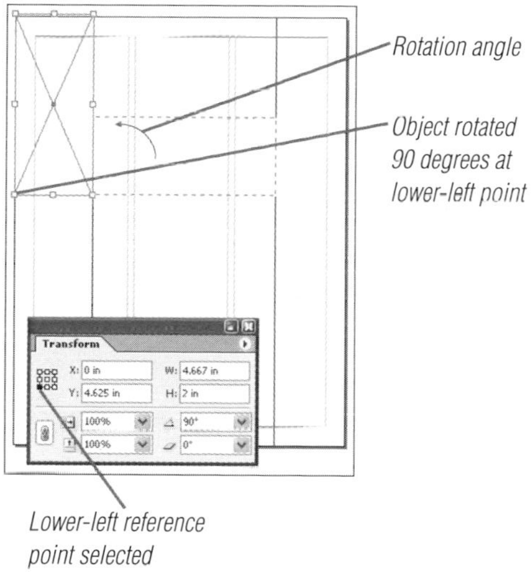

Y location

X location

Center reference point selected

Rectangle rotated 90 degrees

X and Y location values remain the same when object is rotated at the center point

Rotation Angle text box

Rotation angle

Object rotated 90 degrees at lower-left point

Lower-left reference point selected

Create a new document

1. Start InDesign, click **Edit** (Win) or **InDesign** (Mac) on the menu bar, point to **Preferences**, then click **Units & Increments**.

2. Click the **Horizontal list arrow**, click **Inches**, click the **Vertical list arrow**, click **Inches**, then click **OK**.

3. Click **File** on the menu bar, point to **New**, then click **Document**.

4. Type **12** in the Number of Pages text box, then verify that the Facing Pages check box is checked.

5. Type **8** in the Width text box, press **[Tab]**, then type **7** in the Height text box.

   TIP Press [Tab] to move your cursor forward from text box to text box in InDesign dialog boxes. Press [Shift][Tab] to move backward from text box to text box.

6. Type **5** in the Number text box in the Columns section, then type **.25** in the Gutter text box.

7. Type **.375** in the Top, Bottom, Inside, and Outside Margin text boxes so that your New Document dialog box resembles Figure C-11.

8. Click **OK**, then look at the first page of the document, which should resemble Figure C-12.

9. Save the document as **Setup**.

You set the Units & Increments preferences to specify that you will be working with inches for horizontal and vertical measurements. You then created a new document using the New Document dialog box. You specified the number of pages in the document, the page size for each page, and the number of columns on each page.

FIGURE C-11
Entering values in the New Document dialog box

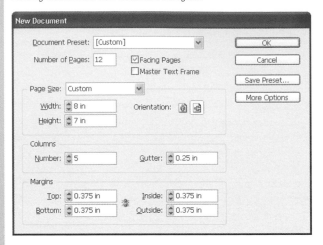

FIGURE C-12
Identifying basic elements on a page

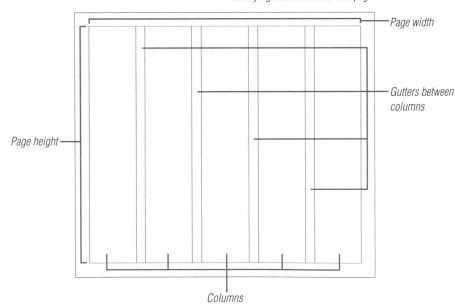

Page width

Gutters between columns

Page height

Columns

FIGURE C-13

Identifying icons in the Pages palette

Default A-Master master page

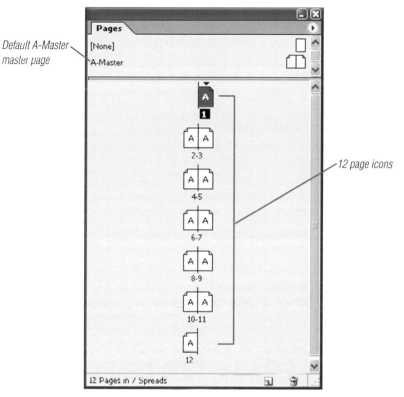

12 page icons

FIGURE C-14

Master Options dialog box

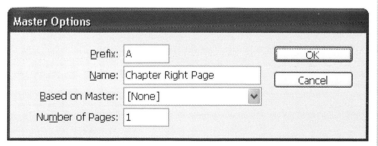

Rename and modify the default master page

1. Close all open palettes except for the Toolbox and the Pages palette.

2. Looking at the Pages palette, as shown in Figure C-13, note that the document contains the 12 pages that you specified in the New Document dialog box and that the default master page is named A-Master.

   TIP   You may need to resize the Pages palette to see all of the page icons.

3. Click **A-Master** once to select it, click the **Pages palette list arrow**, then click **Master Options for "A-Master"**.

4. Type **Chapter Right Page** in the Name text box of the Master Options dialog box, then type **1** in the Number of Pages text box so that the dialog box resembles Figure C-14.

   In this layout design, the chapter title page will always occur on a right-hand page. Therefore, this master needs to be only one page.

5. Click **OK**, then note the changes in the Pages palette.

   The default master page is now listed as a single page with its new title.

You renamed the A-Master master page and redefined it as a single page.

Add guides to a master page

1. Double-click **A-Chapter Right Page** in the Pages palette, then note that the page menu at the lower-left corner of the document window lists A-Chapter Right Page.

   A-Chapter Right Page is now the active page.

2. Click **Window** on the menu bar, then click **Transform**.

3. If rulers are not visible at the top and left of the document window, click **View** on the menu bar, then click **Show Rulers**.

4. Click the **Selection Tool** ▸, position your cursor over the horizontal ruler, then click and drag a guide down from the ruler about 1.5 inches down the page, as shown in Figure C-15.

   TIP As you drag the new guide onto the page, the value in the Y Location text box in the Transform palette continually changes to show the guide's current location.

5. Release your mouse to position the guide at approximately 1.5 inches down the page.

6. Type **1.9** in the Y Location text box in the Transform palette, then press **[Enter]** (Win) or **[return]** (Mac).

   The guide jumps to the specific vertical location you entered.

7. Drag a second guide down from the horizontal ruler, then release your mouse when the Y Location text box in the Transform palette reads approximately 5.9 in.

   (continued)

FIGURE C-15

Creating a horizontal guide

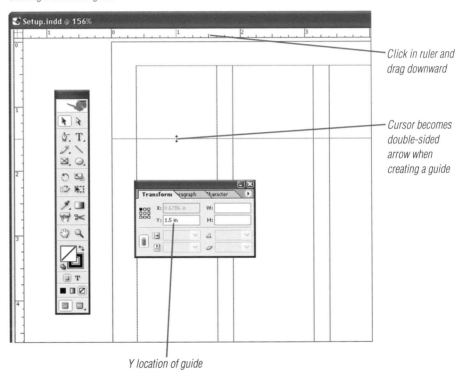

Click in ruler and drag downward

Cursor becomes double-sided arrow when creating a guide

Y location of guide

Setting up a Document

FIGURE C-16

Viewing the master page with three guides

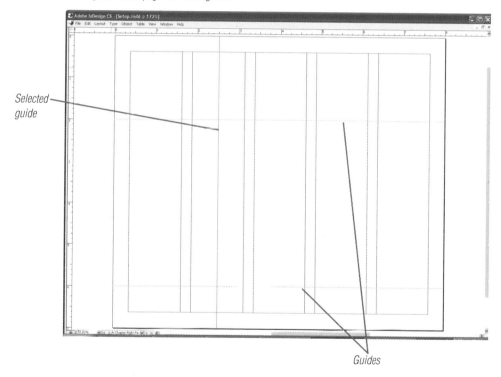

Selected guide

Guides

8. Drag a guide from the vertical ruler on the left side of the document window, then release your mouse when the X Location text box in the Transform palette reads approximately 2 in.

9. Click the **first horizontal guide** you positioned at 1.9 inches to select it, double-click the **Y Location text box** in the Transform palette, type **2**, then press **[Enter]** (Win) or **[return]** (Mac).

    The guide is moved and positioned exactly two inches from the top of the document.

    TIP   Selected guides appear darker blue in color.

10. Change the location of the horizontal guide positioned approximately at 5.9 inches to 6 inches, then change the location of the vertical guide to 2.5 inches.

    As shown in Figure C-16, the vertical guide is still selected.

You positioned guides on the master page by dragging them from the horizontal and vertical rulers. You used the Transform palette to position them at precise locations.

Create placeholder text frames

1. Click the **Type Tool** T, position the cursor approximately where the vertical guide intersects the top horizontal guide, then click and drag a **text frame** to the right margin.

   Your screen should resemble Figure C-17.

2. Type **Chapter X** in the text frame, then select the text.

3. Display the Character palette, set the font to Garamond, set the font size to 80 pt, then set the leading to 96 pt (if necessary).

4. Position the Type Tool cursor where the vertical guide intersects the bottom horizontal guide, click and drag toward the upper-right corner to create a text frame, then click the **Selection Tool** ▶.

   As shown in Figure C-18, the second text frame is selected.

5. Click the **Type Tool** T, click inside the second text frame, type **Chapter title must be two lines** in the text frame, then select the text.

6. Set the font to Trebuchet MS, set the font size to 32 pt, then set the leading to 33 pt.

7. Click the page to deselect the text so that your page resembles Figure C-19.

You created two text frames which will be used as placeholders for chapter numbers and chapter titles in the document.

FIGURE C-17
Drawing a text frame

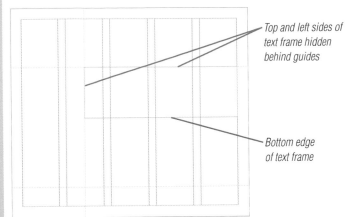

Top and left sides of text frame hidden behind guides

Bottom edge of text frame

FIGURE C-18
Viewing the second text frame

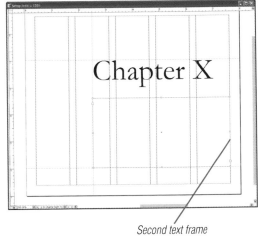

Second text frame

FIGURE C-19
Viewing the page with two placeholder text frames

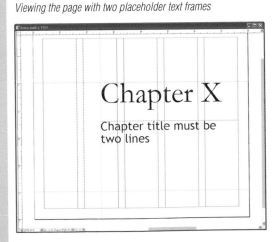

FIGURE C-20
Viewing the page with guides in back

Text frame borders
are in front of guides

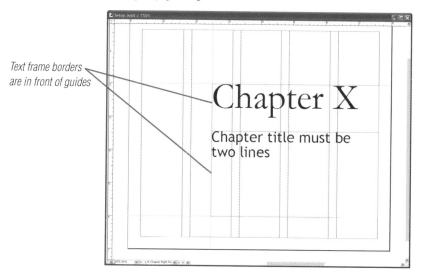

Chapter X

Chapter title must be
two lines

FIGURE C-21
Changing the colors of guides to better distinguish elements on the page

Guides in
grass green

Margins and
column guides
in peach

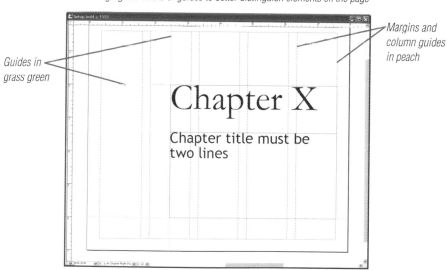

Chapter X

Chapter title must be
two lines

Change the color of guides, margins, and columns

1. Click **Edit** (Win) or **InDesign** (Mac) on the menu bar, point to **Preferences**, then click **Guides & Pasteboard**.

2. Click the **Guides in Back check box**, then click **OK**.

   As shown in Figure C-20, the text frame borders are in front of the guides.

3. Click **Edit** (Win) or **InDesign** (Mac) on the menu bar, point to **Preferences**, then click **Guides & Pasteboard**.

4. In the Color section, click the **Margins list arrow**, then click **Peach**.

5. Click the **Columns list arrow**, click **Peach**, then click **OK**.

6. Click the **Selection Tool** , click the **cyan vertical guide** to select it, press and hold **[Shift]**, click the **top horizontal guide**, then click the **lower horizontal guide**.

   All three cyan guides are selected and appear dark blue.

7. Click **Layout** on the menu bar, then click **Ruler Guides**.

8. Click the **Color list arrow**, click **Grass Green**, then click **OK**.

9. Click the **pasteboard** to deselect the guides, then compare your page to Figure C-21.

You changed the color of margins, columns, and guides to improve your ability to distinguish text frames from page guides.

Use the Transform palette to transform text frames

1. Click the **Selection Tool** ⬉ (if necessary), click anywhere in the lower text frame to select it, click **Object** on the menu bar, then click **Text Frame Options**.

2. In the Vertical Justification section, click the **Align list arrow**, click **Bottom**, then click **OK**.

3. Using Figure C-22 as a guide, drag the **top middle handle** of the text frame down to the top of the text.

4. With the text frame still selected, click the **middle-left reference point** on the proxy in the Transform palette, as shown in Figure C-23.

   | TIP The selected reference point specifies the point of origin for the transformation.

5. Double-click the **Width (W) text box** in the Transform palette, type **3.875**, then press **[Enter]** (Win) or **[return]** (Mac).

   The width of the selected text frame is reduced to 3.875 inches. Since the point of origin for the transformation was specified as the left edge, only the right side of the text frame moves when the new width is applied.

   (continued)

FIGURE C-22
Resizing the height of a text frame

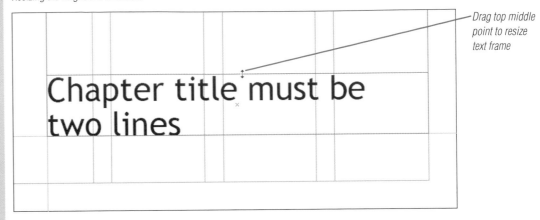

Drag top middle point to resize text frame

FIGURE C-23
Selecting a reference point on the proxy

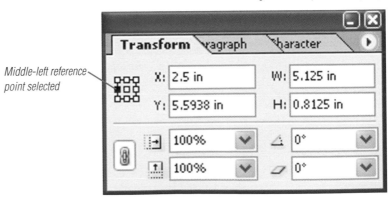

Middle-left reference point selected

Setting up a Document

FIGURE C-24
Repositioning the text frame

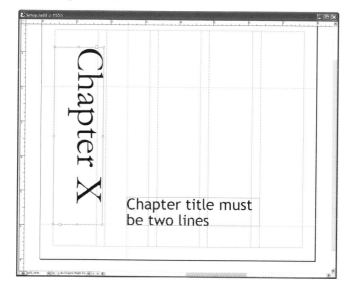

6. Click the **"Chapter X" text frame**, then click the **center reference point** on the proxy in the Transform palette.

7. Click the **Transform palette list arrow**, then click **Rotate 90° CW**.

   The text frame is rotated at its center point.

8. Drag the rotated **Chapter X** text frame to the same location shown in Figure C-24.

9. Display the **Paragraph palette**, then click the **Align right button** ▤ .

10. Click **Edit** on the menu bar, click **Deselect All**, click the **Preview Mode button** ▢, in the Toolbox, then press **[Tab]** to hide all palettes.

    Your page should resemble Figure C-25.

You used the Transform palette to change the width of one text frame and to rotate the other.

FIGURE C-25
Viewing the page in preview mode

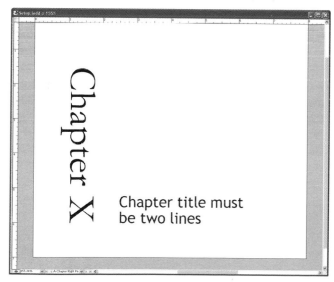

CREATE MASTER PAGES

What You'll Do

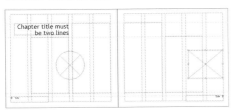

 In this lesson, you will create two new master pages, create placeholder text frames for body copy, create automatic page numbering, and create placeholder frames for graphics.

Creating a New Master Page

When you create a new document, a default master page, called A-Master, appears in the top section of the Pages palette. You can use this default master as your first master for the document, and you can also create as many new master pages as you need for the document. You create new master pages by clicking the New Master command in the Pages palette menu.

When you create a new master page, you have the option of giving the master page a title. This is often very useful for distinguishing one master page from another. For example, you might want to use the title "Body Copy" for master pages that will be used for body copy and then use the title "Chapter Start" for master pages that will be used as a layout for a chapter title page. Figure C-26 shows three titled master pages in the Pages palette.

When you create a new master page, you have the option of changing the values for the margins and for the number of columns on the new master page.

Creating Automatic Page Numbering

When you create a document with multiple pages, chances are you'll want to have page numbers on each page. You could create a text frame on every page, then manually type the page number on every page, but think of what a nightmare that could turn out to be! You would have to create a text frame of the same size and in the same location on every page. Imagine what would happen if you were to remove a page from or add a page to the middle of the document. You'd need to go back and renumber your pages!

Fortunately, InDesign offers a solution for this. You can create placeholders for page numbers on your master pages. Each newly created page will have an automatic page number on it, assuming the page is based on a master page with a page number placeholder. Simply create a text frame on the master page (if you are working with facing pages, create a text frame on both the left and right pages of the spread). Click inside the text frame, click Type, point to Insert Special Character, then click Auto Page Number. A letter (that of the master page) will appear in the text frame, as shown in Figure C-27.

That letter represents the page number. You can format it using any font, size, and

FIGURE C-26
Three master pages in the Pages palette

Master pages with titles

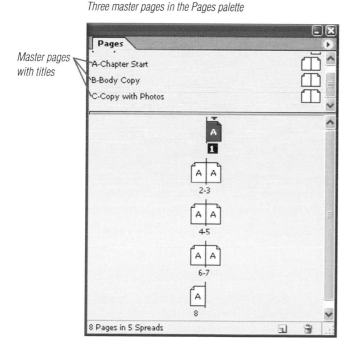

FIGURE C-27
A text frame on a master page containing an auto page number character

Auto page number character represents that of the master page

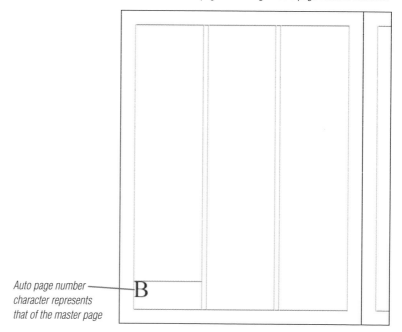

alignment that you desire. On the document pages based on that master, the letter in the text frame will appear as the number of the page. The page numbering is automatic. This means that the page number is automatically updated when pages are added to or removed from the document.

When you work with multiple master pages, you position the text frame with the auto page numbering character on all the master pages that you want to show page numbers in the document. Just be sure that the text frame is in the same location on all masters and that the text for the number is formatted in the same way. This will make the appearance of page numbers consistent from page to page, regardless of which master a given document page is based on.

Inserting White Space Between Text Characters

In Chapter B, you learned that you should not press [Spacebar] more than once to create extra spacing between characters. However, sometimes a single space does not provide enough space between words or characters. You may want to insert additional space to achieve a certain look. In this case, you insert white space.

The Type menu contains commands for inserting white space between words or characters. The two most-used white spaces are **em space** and **en space**. The width of an em space is equivalent to that of the lowercase letter m in the current typeface at that type size. The width of an en space is narrower—that of the lowercase letter n in that typeface at that type size. Use these commands—not multiple spaces—to insert white space. To insert an em space or an en space, click Type on the menu bar, point to Insert White Space, then click either Em Space or En Space. Figure C-28 shows an em space between an auto page number character and a word.

Inserting Em Dashes and En Dashes

Sometimes you'll want to put a dash between words or characters and you'll find that the dash created by pressing the dash

FIGURE C-28

Identifying an em space

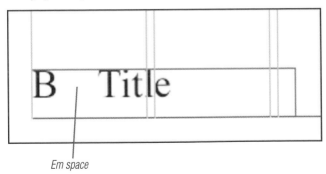

Em space

key is not wide enough. That's because there is no dash key on a keyboard. What you think of as a dash is actually a hyphen, and hyphens are shorter than dashes.

InDesign offers two types of dashes—the em dash and the en dash—that you can insert between words or characters. The width of an em dash is equivalent to that of the lowercase letter m in the current typeface at that type size. The width of an en dash is narrower—that of the lowercase letter n in that typeface at that type size. To insert an em dash or an en dash, click Type on the menu bar, point to Insert Special Character, then click either Em Dash or En Dash. Figure C-29 shows an example of an en dash.

Creating a New Master Page Based on Another Master Page

Imagine that you've created a master page for a page in a magazine layout. The master contains placeholder text frames for the headline, for the body copy, and for the page number. It also contains placeholder graphics frames for pictures that will appear on the page. Now imagine that you need to create another master page that will be identical to this master page, with the one exception, that this new master will not contain frames for graphics. You wouldn't want to duplicate all of the work you did to create the first master, would you?

You can create a new master page based on another master page. You do this to avoid repeating efforts and for consistency between masters. In the above example, you would create the new master based on the first master. The new master would appear identical to the first master. You would then modify only the elements that you want to change on the new master, keeping all of the elements that you don't want to change perfectly consistent with the previous master.

Basing a new master on another master is not the same thing as duplicating a master.

When one master is based on another, any changes you make to the first master will be updated on the master based on it. Think of how powerful this is. Let's say that your editor tells you to change the type size of the page numbers. If you make that change to the first master, the change will automatically be updated on the master(s) based on it. This offers you a substantial savings in time and effort and provides you with the certainty that the page numbers will be consistent from master to master.

When you base a new master on another master, you will find that you cannot select the objects on the new master that were created on the first master. Or, it should be said, that you cannot select those objects in the usual way. You must press and hold [Shift][Ctrl] (Win) or [Shift]⌘ (Mac) to select those objects on the new master. InDesign does this so that you don't accidentally move or delete objects from the previous master.

FIGURE C-29
Identifying an en dash

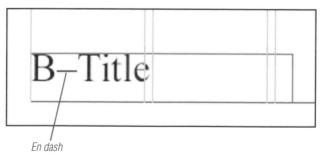

En dash

Create a new master page

1. Press **[Tab]** to show the palettes again, then click the **Normal View Mode button** 🔲 on the Toolbox.

2. Click the **Pages palette list arrow**, then click **New Master**.

3. Type **Body Copy with Pics** in the Name text box, then type **2** in the Number of Pages text box (if necessary) so that your New Master dialog box resembles Figure C-30.

   You need two pages for this master since it will be used for both left and right pages.

4. Click **OK**, note the new master page listing in the Pages palette, click **View** on the menu bar, then click **Fit Spread in Window** (if necessary).

5. Click **Layout** on the menu bar, then click **Margins and Columns**.

6. Double-click the **Inside text box** to select it, type **.5**, then click **OK**.

   The inner margins on both the left and right pages are increased—only on the B-Body Copy with Pics master page.

7. Press and hold **[Ctrl]** (Win) or ⌘ (Mac), then drag a **horizontal guide** onto the spread, positioning it one inch from the top of the page.

(continued)

FIGURE C-30
New Master dialog box

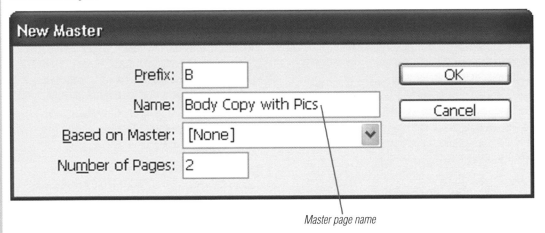

Master page name

FIGURE C-31

Viewing the new master page with guides

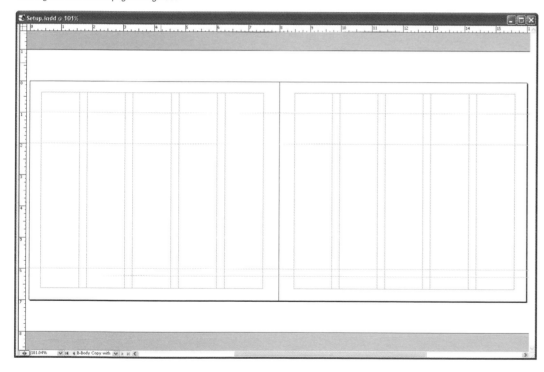

TIP Pressing and holding [Ctrl] (Win) or ⌘ (Mac) creates a spread ruler guide, which extends across both pages of the spread.

8. Using the same method, position three more horizontal guides, one at two inches from the top of the page, one at six inches from the top of the page, and one at 6.225 inches from the top of the page.

9. Click the page to deselect.

Because this is a new master page, the guides have reverted to the default cyan color for guides. Your screen should resemble Figure C-31.

10. Select all four guides, click **Layout** on the menu bar, click **Ruler Guides**, click the **Color list arrow**, click **Grass Green**, then click **OK**.

TIP To change the default guide color, open the Ruler Guides dialog box with no InDesign documents open, then select the color you want.

You created and named a new master page, then you modified its margin settings. You also created four spread guides and changed their colors.

Create text frames on a master page

1. Click the **Type Tool** T, then draw two text frames on the left page of the B-Body Copy with Pics master in the same locations shown in Figure C-32.

2. Click the **Selection Tool** , select the text frame on the right, click **Edit** on the menu bar, then click **Copy**.

3. Click **Edit** on the menu bar, then click **Paste in Place**.

   A copy is pasted exactly above the first text frame.

4. Press and hold **[Shift]**, then drag the copy of the text frame to the right page, positioning it so that it is positioned inside the first two columns on the right page.

   > TIP Pressing and holding [Shift] when dragging an object constrains that object to the axis on which you are moving it.

5. Deselect all, select the smaller text frame on the left page, press and hold **[Shift][Alt]** (Win) or **[Shift][option]** (Mac), then drag a copy to the right page.

   (continued)

FIGURE C-32
Positioning two text frames on the left page of the B-Body Copy with Pics master

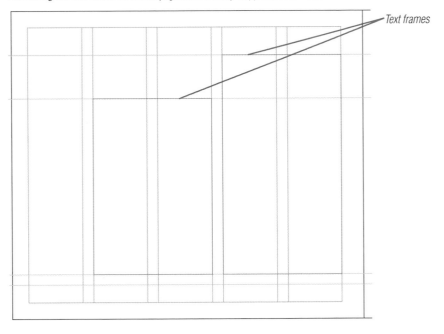

Text frames

FIGURE C-33

Positioning two text frames on the right page of the B-Body Copy with Pics master

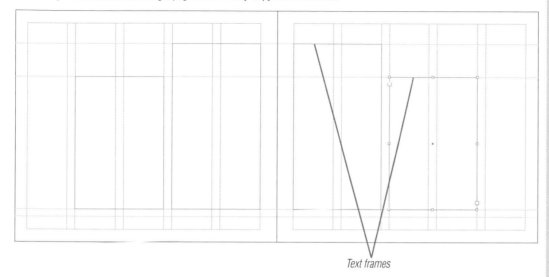

Text frames

FIGURE C-34

Positioning a text frame for a headline

Text frame
for headline

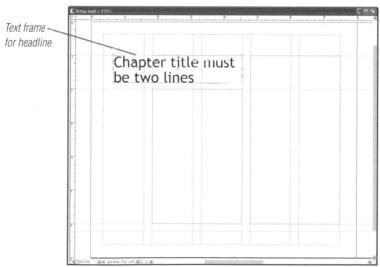

TIP Pressing and holding [Shift][Alt] (Win) or [Shift][option] (Mac) when dragging an object makes a copy of the object.

6. Position the frame so that it is aligned with the third and fourth columns on the right page, as shown in Figure C-33.

7. Double-click the **A-Master page title**, select the text frame that includes the text "Chapter title must be two lines," then copy it.

8. Double-click the **B-Master page title**, double-click the **left page Icon** of the B-Body Copy with Pics master page to center the left page in the window, click **Edit** on the menu bar, then click **Paste**.

9. Position the text frame in the location shown in Figure C-34.

10. Display the Paragraph palette (if necessary), then click the **Align right button** .

You created four text frames on the B master page, which will be used as placeholders for body copy.

Create automatic page numbering and insert white space between characters

1. Click the **Type Tool** T, then draw a text frame on the left page of the B-Body Copy with Pics master, as shown in Figure C-35.

2. Click **Type** on the menu bar, point to **Insert Special Character**, then click **Auto Page Number**.

   The letter B appears in the text frame. This letter will change on document pages to reflect the current document page. For example, on page 4, the B will appear as the number 4.

3. Click **Type** on the menu bar, point to **Insert White Space**, then click **Em Space**.

4. Type the word **Title** so that your text box resembles Figure C-36.

5. Click the **Selection Tool** , select the text frame, click **Edit** on the menu bar, click **Copy**, click **Edit** on the menu bar again, then click **Paste in Place**.

   (continued)

FIGURE C-35
Positioning the left page text frame

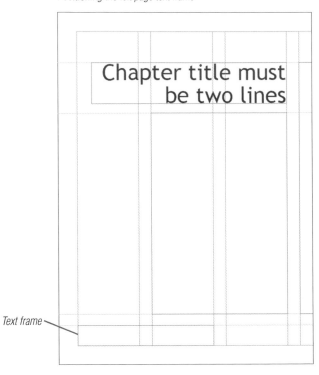

Chapter title must be two lines

Text frame

FIGURE C-36
Viewing the text frame with automatic page numbering

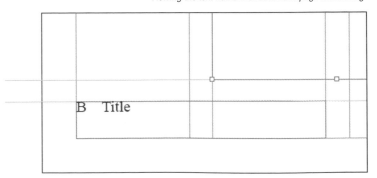

B   Title

Setting up a Document

FIGURE C-37

Positioning the right page text frame

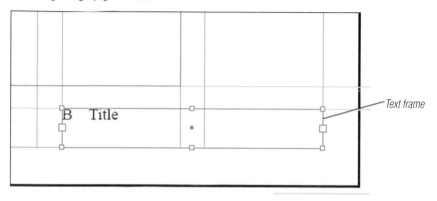

Text frame

6. Press and hold **[Shift]**, then drag the copy of the text frame so that it is positioned on the right page of the B-Body Copy with Pics master, as shown in Figure C-37.

7. Click the **Align right button** in the Paragraph palette, then delete the B and the white space after the B.

8. Click after the word Title, click **Type** on the menu bar, point to **Insert White Space**, then click **Em Space**.

9. Click **Type** on the menu bar, point to **Insert Special Character**, then click **Auto Page Number**.

   Your text box should resemble Figure C-38.

You created automatic page numbering on the left and right pages of the B-Body Copy with Pics master.

FIGURE C-38

Viewing the right text frame with automatic page numbering

Title   B

Create graphics frames on a master page

1. Double-click the **left page icon** of the B-Body Copy with Pics master in the Pages palette to center it in the document window.

2. Click the **Ellipse Frame Tool** ⊗ , press and hold **[Shift]**, then drag the cursor to create an ellipse frame of any size on the left page, as shown in Figure C-39.

   Pressing and holding [Shift] constrains the Ellipse Frame Tool to create only a perfect circle.

   TIP   The Ellipse Frame Tool may be hidden beneath the Rectangle Frame Tool or the Polygon Frame Tool.

3. Type **2** in the Width text box in the Transform palette, press **[Tab]**, type **2** in the Height text box, then press **[Enter]** (Win) or **[return]** (Mac).

   The size of the frame changes to a diameter of two inches.

4. Click the **center reference point** on the proxy in the Transform palette, double-click the **X Location text box**, type **4.65**, press **[Tab]**, type **4** in the Y Location text box, then press **[Enter]** (Win) or **[return]** (Mac).

5. Double-click the **right page icon** of the B-Body Copy with Pics master in the Pages palette to center the page in the window.

6. Click **Edit** (Win) or **InDesign** (Mac) on the menu bar, point to **Preferences**, click **Guides & Pasteboard**, click **Units & Increments**, click the **Origin list arrow**, click **Page**, then click **OK**.

   (continued)

FIGURE C-39
Creating an ellipse frame

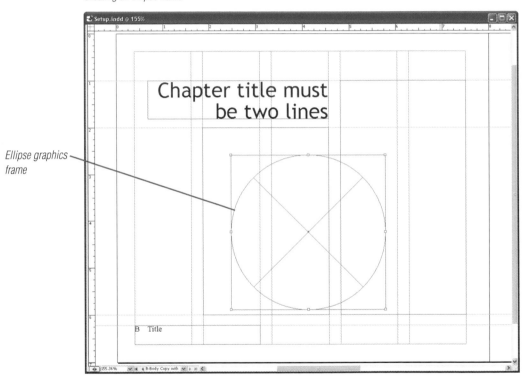

Ellipse graphics frame

FIGURE C-40

Viewing the spread

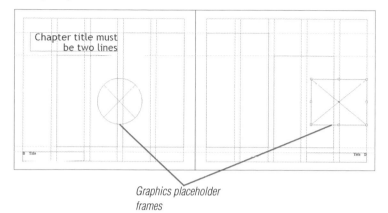

Graphics placeholder
frames

FIGURE C-41

Creating a rectangle frame

Graphics placeholder
frame

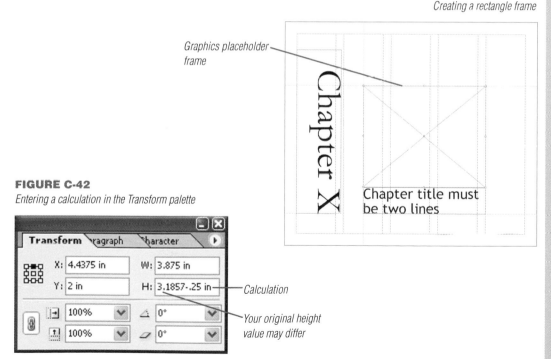

FIGURE C-42

Entering a calculation in the Transform palette

Transform	ragraph	haracter
X: 4.4375 in	W: 3.875 in	
Y: 2 in	H: 3.1857-.25 in	— Calculation
100%	0°	— Your original height
100%	0°	value may differ

The horizontal ruler now measures each page, not the entire spread.

7. Click the **Rectangle Frame Tool** ⊠ , draw a rectangle frame of any size anywhere on the right master page, then click the **top-left reference point** on the proxy in the Transform palette.

8. In the Transform palette, type **5.125** in the X Location text box, type **3** in the Y Location text box, type **2.5** in the Width text box, type **2** in the Height text box, then press **[Enter]** (Win) or **[return]** (Mac).

9. Click **View** on the menu bar, then click **Fit Spread in Window** so that your spread resembles Figure C-40.

10. Double-click **A-Chapter Right Page** in the Pages palette, then draw a rectangle frame in the position shown in Figure C-41.

    The bottom of the rectangular graphics frame abuts the top of the text frame beneath it.

11. Select the **top-middle reference point** on the proxy in the Transform palette, click to the immediate right of the value in the Height text box, then type **-.25**, as shown in Figure C-42.

    The current value in the Height text box in your Transform palette might differ slightly from the figure.

12. Press **[Enter]** (Win) or **[return]** (Mac).

    The height of the rectangle frame is reduced by .25 inches, and only the bottom edge of the box moves to accommodate the reduction.

You created three frames, which will be used as placeholders for graphics. You used the Transform palette to specify the sizes of the frames and their locations on the master pages.

Create a new master page based on another master page

1. Click the **Pages palette list arrow**, then click **New Master**.

2. Type **Copy No Pics** in the Name text box of the New Master dialog box.

   The C-Copy No Pics master page will be applied to pages in the document that do not have pictures, only text.

3. Click the **Based On Master list arrow**, click **B-Body Copy with Pics**, then click **OK**.

   > TIP Since the new master is based on the B-Body Copy with Pics master, it will include everything already positioned on the B-Body Copy with Pics master, such as the automatic page numbering.

   The C-Copy No Pics icons display a B in each of the page icons, as shown in Figure C-43. This indicates that the C-Copy No Pics master page is based on the B-Body Copy with Pics master page.

4. Click the **Selection Tool** ▶, press and hold **[Shift][Ctrl]** (Win) or **[Shift]** ⌘ (Mac), click the **ellipse frame**, click the **headline placeholder text frame**, click **Edit** on the menu bar, then click **Cut**.

   The two objects are deleted from the page. Because the ellipse frame was created on the B-Body Copy with Pics master, you cannot select it unless you press and hold [Shift][Ctrl] (Win) or [Shift] ⌘ (Mac) while selecting it.

   (continued)

FIGURE C-43

Viewing the new master in the Pages palette

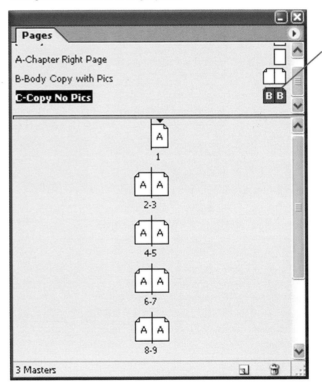

The B letters in the Copy No Pics master page icons indicate that it is based on the Body Copy with Pics master page

FIGURE C-44

Creating a new text frame

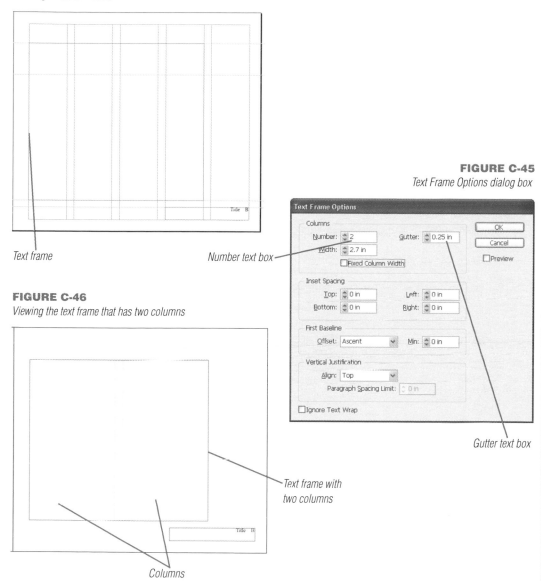

Text frame

Number text box

FIGURE C-46

Viewing the text frame that has two columns

Text frame with
two columns

Columns

FIGURE C-45

Text Frame Options dialog box

Gutter text box

5. Press and hold **[Shift][Ctrl]** (Win) or **[Shift]** ⌘ (Mac), click the **first text frame** on the right page, click the **second text frame**, then click the **rectangle frame**.

All three objects on the right page are selected.

6. Click **Edit** on the menu bar, then click **Cut**.

7. Click the **Type Tool** T., then draw a text frame on the right page in the position shown in Figure C-44.

Note that the single text frame covers the width of four columns.

8. Click the **Selection Tool** ▶, click **Object** on the menu bar, then click **Text Frame Options**.

9. Double-click the **Number text box**, type **2**, double-click the **Gutter text box**, then type **.25**, then press **[Tab]** so that your Text Frame Options dialog box resembles Figure C-45.

10. Click **OK**, click the page to deselect all, click **View** on the menu bar, click **Hide Guides**, then compare your right page to Figure C-46.

You created a new master page based on the B-Body Copy with Pics master page. You named the new master C-Copy No Pics and modified it by deleting items from it and creating a new two-column text frame.

APPLY MASTER PAGES TO DOCUMENT PAGES

What You'll Do

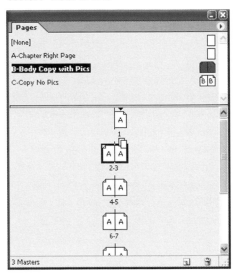

 In this lesson, you will apply master pages to document pages.

Applying Master Pages to Document Pages

Once you have created master pages, you then use the Pages palette to apply them to the document pages. One method for applying master pages is the "drag and drop" method. Using this method, you drag the master page icon or the master page name in the top section of the Pages palette down to the page icons in the lower section of the Pages palette. To apply the master to a single page, you drag the master onto the page icon, as shown in Figure C-47. To apply the master to a spread, you drag the master onto one of the four corners of the left and right page icons, as shown in Figure C-48.

When you apply a master page to a document page, the document page inherits all of the layout characteristics of the master.

QUICKTIP
You can apply the default None master page to a document page when you want the document page not to be based on any master.

A second method for applying master pages to document pages is to use the Apply Master to Pages command in the Pages palette menu. The Apply Master dialog box, shown in Figure C-49, allows you to specify which master you want to apply to which pages. This method is a good choice when you want to apply a master to a series of consecutive pages. When many pages are involved, it's faster than dragging and dropping.

FIGURE C-47

Applying the C-Copy No Pics master to page 2

FIGURE C-48

Applying the C-Copy No Pics master to pages 2 and 3

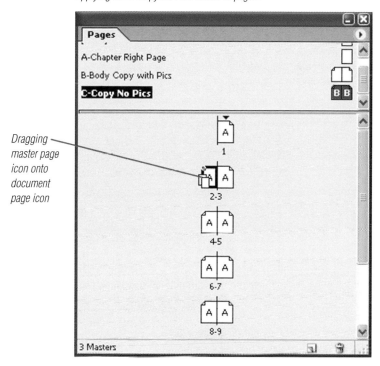

Dragging master page icon onto document page icon

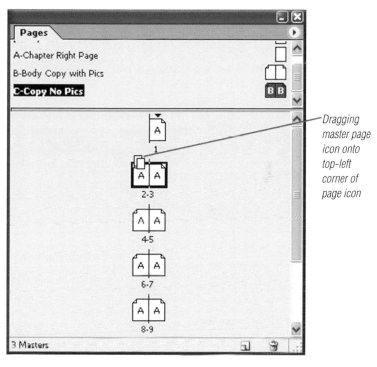

Dragging master page icon onto top-left corner of page icon

FIGURE C-49

Apply Master dialog box

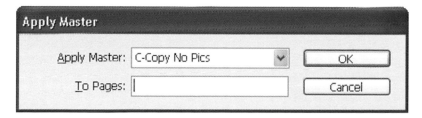

Apply master pages to document pages

1. Double-click **B-Body Copy with Pics** in the Pages palette, then drag the corresponding master page icon to the upper-right corner of the page 3 icon until a black frame appears around both pages 2 and 3, as shown in Figure C-50, then release your mouse.

   The master is applied to the spread.

2. Double-click **C-Copy No Pics** in the Pages palette, then drag the corresponding master icon on top of the page 4 icon, as shown in Figure C-51.

3. Apply the B-Body Copy with Pics master page to page 10, then apply the C-Copy No Pics master page to pages 11 and 12.

(continued)

FIGURE C-50
Applying the B-Body Copy with Pics master page to a spread

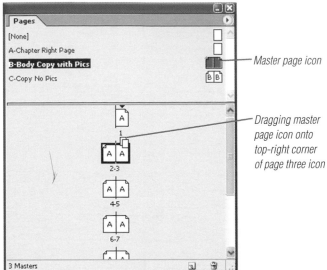

Master page icon

Dragging master page icon onto top-right corner of page three icon

FIGURE C-51
Applying the C-Copy No Pics master page to page 4

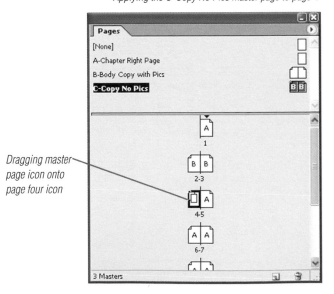

Dragging master page icon onto page four icon

Setting up a Document

FIGURE C-52

Viewing the masters applied to each page

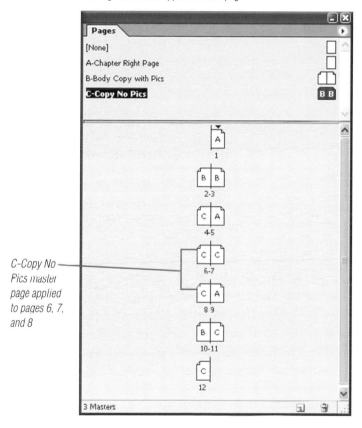

C-Copy No Pics master page applied to pages 6, 7, and 8

4. Click the **Pages palette list arrow**, then click **Apply Master to Pages**.

5. Click the **Apply Master list arrow**, click **C-Copy No Pics** (if necessary), press **[Tab]**, type **6-8** in the To Pages text box, then click **OK**.

As shown in Figure C-52, the C-Copy No Pics master page is applied to pages 6, 7, and 8.

You used the Pages palette to explore various ways for applying master pages to document pages and spreads.

PLACE TEXT AND THREAD TEXT

What You'll Do

 In this lesson, you will place text, thread text from frame to frame, then view text threads.

Placing Text

Once you have created a text frame—either on a master page or on a document page—you can type directly into the frame, or you can place text from another document into it. When creating headlines, you usually type them directly into the text frame. When creating body copy, however, you will often find yourself placing text from another document, usually a word processing document.

Placing text in InDesign is simple and straightforward. Click the Place command on the File menu, which opens the Place dialog box. Find the text document that you want to place, then click Open.

Your cursor changes to the loaded text icon. With a loaded text icon, you can drag to create a text frame or click inside an existing text frame. Float the loaded text icon over an existing text frame, and the icon appears in parentheses, as shown in Figure C-53. The parentheses indicate that you can click to place the text into the text frame. Do so, and the text flows into the text frame, as shown in Figure C-54.

FIGURE C-53

Loaded text icon positioned over a text frame

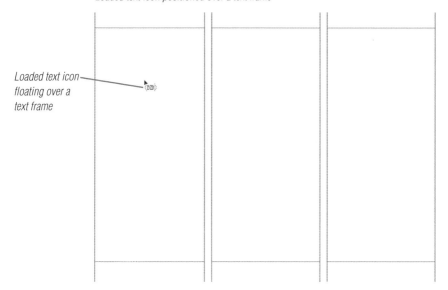

Loaded text icon
floating over a
text frame

FIGURE C-54

Text placed into a text frame

Text placed
in text frame

Lorem ipsum dolor sit amet, consect
adipiscing elit, sed diam nonummy nibh
euismod tincidunt ut laoreet dolore magna
aliquam erat volutpat. Ut wisi enim ad minim
veniam, quis nostrud exercitation ullam
corper suscipit lobortis nisl ut aliquip exea
commodo consequat.

Duis autem veleum iriure dolor in hendrerit
in vulputate velit esse molestie consequat.
Vel willum lunombro dolore eu feugiat nulla
facilisis.

At vero eros et accumsan et iusto odio
dignissim qui blandit praesent luptatum zzril
delenit augue duis dolore te feugait nulla
facilisi.

Li Europan lingues es membres del sam
familie. Lor separat existentie es un myth.
Por scientie, musica, sport etc, litot Europa
usa li sam vocabular.

Li lingues differe solmen in li grammatica,
li pronunciation e li plu commun vocabules.
Omnicos directe al desirabilite de un nov
lingua franca: On refusa continuar payar
custosi traductores.

It solmen va esser necessi far uniform
grammatica, pronunciation e plu sommun
paroles. Ma quande lingues coalesce, li
grammatica del resultant lingue es plu simpli
e regulari quam ti del coalescent lingues. Li

Threading Text

InDesign provides many options for **threading text**—linking text from one text frame to another. Text frames have an **in port** and an **out port**. When threading text, you use the text frame ports to establish connections between the text frames.

In Figure C-55, the center text frame is selected, and the in port and out port are identified. The in port represents where text would flow into the text frame, and the out port represents where text would flow out.

In the same figure, note that the out port on the first text frame is red and has a plus sign in its center. This indicates the presence of **overset text**—more text than can fit in the frame.

To thread text manually from the first to the second text frame, first click the Selection Tool, then click the frame with the overset text so that the frame is highlighted. Next, click the out port of the text frame. When you float your cursor over the next text frame, the cursor changes to the link icon, as shown in Figure C-56. Click the link icon and the text flows into the frame, as shown in Figure C-57. When the Show Text Threads command on the View menu is activated, a blue arrow appears between any two text frames that have been threaded, as shown in Figure C-58.

FIGURE C-55

Identifying in ports and out ports

FIGURE C-56

Link icon

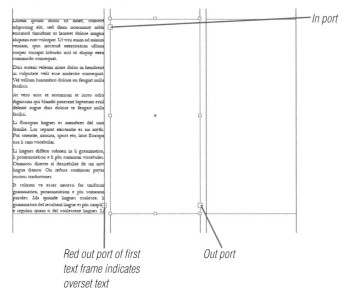

In port

Red out port of first text frame indicates overset text

Out port

Link icon floating over text frame

Setting up a Document

FIGURE C-57

Threading text between frames

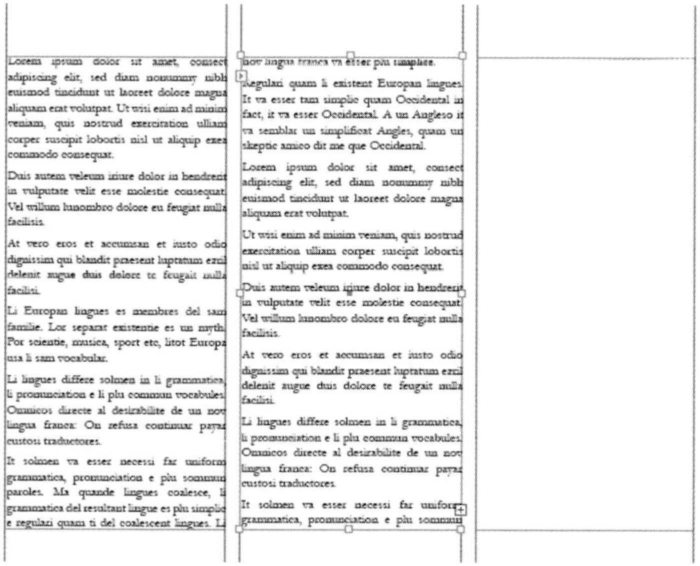

FIGURE C-58

Showing text threads

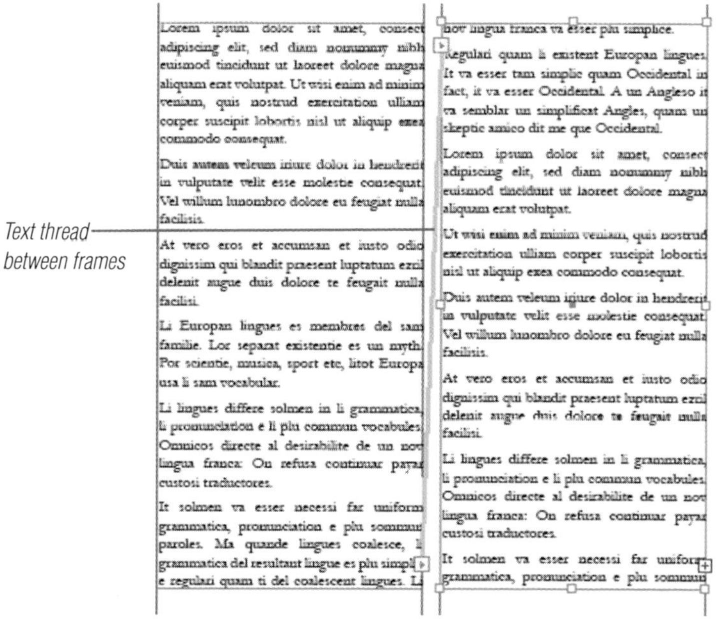

Text thread
between frames

Place text on document pages

1. Double-click the **page 2 icon** in the Pages palette.

   Because the left text frame on page 2 is a master page object, it cannot be selected as usual—however, you can place text into the frame without selecting the frame.

2. Click **File** on the menu bar, click **Place**, navigate to the drive and folder where your Chapter C Data Files are stored, then double-click **Chapter 1 text**.

3. Point to the **left text frame**.

   The loaded text icon appears in parentheses, signaling you that you can insert the loaded text into the text frame.

4. Click anywhere in the left text frame, then compare your work to Figure C-59.

   The red out port with the plus sign indicates that there is overset text—more text than can fit in the text frame.

You used the Place command to load text into a text frame on a document page.

FIGURE C-59

Placing text in a text frame

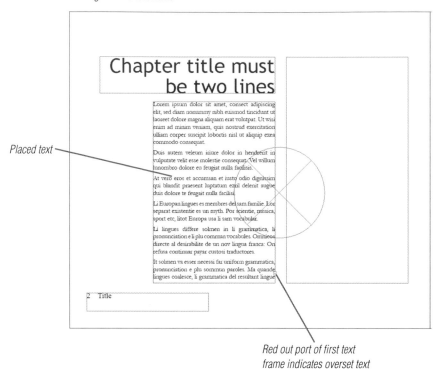

Placed text

Red out port of first text frame indicates overset text

Controlling how text is placed

When you place text in InDesign you have a number of options to choose from regarding how that text is placed. For example, you can choose to include or not include footnotes, endnotes, table of contents text and index text. You can also choose to remove any previous styles applied to text and any table formatting. Conversely you can opt to retain styles and table formatting applied to incoming text. After you click Place on the File menu and find the text document that you are going to place, click the Show Import Options check box, before you click Open. The Microsoft Word Import Options dialog box opens. Make your selections in this dialog box, then click OK. The text will be placed with or without the options that you chose.

FIGURE C-60

Threading text

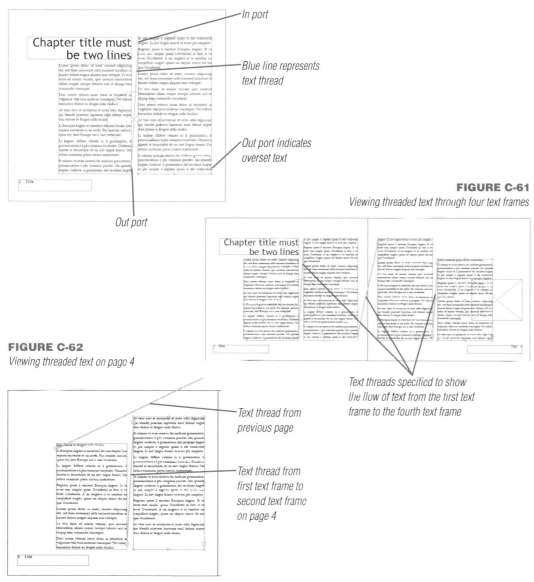

In port

Blue line represents
text thread

Out port indicates
overset text

Out port

FIGURE C-61

Viewing threaded text through four text frames

FIGURE C-62

Viewing threaded text on page 4

Text threads specified to show
the flow of text from the first text
frame to the fourth text frame

Text thread from
previous page

Text thread from
first text frame to
second text frame
on page 4

1. Click **View** on the menu bar, then click **Show Text Threads**.

   With the Show Text Threads command activated, blue arrows will appear between threaded text frames when they are selected.

2. Click the **Selection Tool** ▶, click the **left text frame** to select it, then click the **out port** of the left text frame.

3. Position your cursor on top of the right text frame so that you see the link icon.

4. Click anywhere in the right text frame.

   As shown in Figure C-60, a blue text thread appears and the text is threaded from the left to the right text frames.

   TIP A threaded text frame must be selected for the text threads to be visible.

5. Using the same process, thread text from the second text frame to the third text frame on the spread, then thread text from the third text frame to the fourth text frame, so that your two-page spread resembles Figure C-61.

6. Click the **out port** on the fourth text frame, then double-click the **page 4 icon** in the Pages palette.

7. Click anywhere in the first text frame on page 4.

8. Click the **out port** of the first text frame on page 4, then click anywhere in the second text frame.

   Your page 4 should resemble Figure C-62.

You threaded text manually on document pages.

MODIFY MASTER PAGES AND DOCUMENT PAGES

What You'll Do

Chapter X

Chapter title must
be two lines

 In this lesson, you will make modifications to both master pages and document pages and explore how each affects the other.

Modifying Master Page Items on Document Pages

Master pages are designed to allow you to lay out the basic elements for a page that will be used repeatedly throughout a document. In most cases, however, you will want to make modifications to the document page once it is created—you will even want to modify some objects on the document page that were created on the master page.

When you apply a master page to a document page, you may be surprised to find that you can't select the objects that were created on the master page.

Once a master page is applied to a document page, you can select the master page items on the document page by pressing and holding [Shift][Ctrl] (Win) or [Shift]⌘ (Mac). Once selected, you can modify those objects any way that you desire.

Making changes to a document page is often referred to as making a **local change**. Once you modify an object on a document page, that change will remain in effect, regardless of what you do on the master page.

Modifying Master Pages

When you modify an element of a master page, that modification, in theory, will be reflected on all the document pages that are based on that master page. This can be a very powerful option. Let's say that you have created a layout for a 36-page book, and you decide that you want to change the typeface of all the headlines. If they were created on master pages, you could simply reformat the headline in the text frame placeholders on the master pages, and those modifications would be updated on every document page in the book based on those master pages.

As a rule of thumb, remember that modifications you make to a master page will be reflected only if you haven't modified those elements on a document page; it won't overwrite your local changes. That's good, but it also means that the more changes you make locally, the fewer options you have for modifying master pages to make global changes throughout the document.

FIGURE C-63
Modifying master page items on a document page

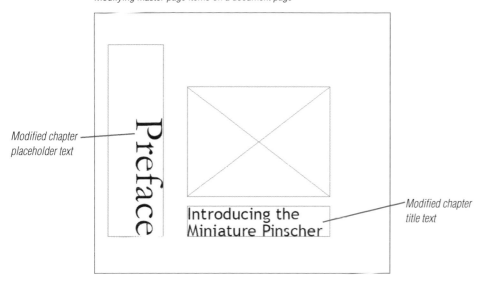

Modified chapter
placeholder text

Modified chapter
title text

FIGURE C-64
Viewing changes made to page 5

Modify master page items on a document page

1. Double-click the **page 1 icon** in the Pages palette, click the **Selection Tool** ➤, press and hold **[Shift][Ctrl]** (Win) or **[Shift]** ⌘ (Mac), then click the **Chapter X text frame**.

2. Click the **Type Tool** T, select all the text in the box, type **Preface**, then click the pasteboard to deselect.

3. Press and hold **[Shift][Ctrl]** (Win) or **[Shift]** ⌘ (Mac), click the **horizontal text frame**, click the text four times to select all of it, type **Introducing the Miniature Pinscher**, then click the pasteboard to deselect so that your page resembles Figure C-63.

4. Click the **Selection Tool** ➤, then click the **"Preface" text frame**.

   Since this is the second time you are selecting the placeholder text frame, it can now be selected the normal way.

5. Double-click the **page 5 icon** in the Pages palette, press and hold **[Shift][Ctrl]** (Win) or **[Shift]** ⌘ (Mac), click the **Chapter X text frame**, click the **Type Tool** T, then change the letter X to 1.

6. Change the title on page 5 to read **Feeding the Miniature Pinscher**.

   | TIP Use a soft return so that "Miniature Pinscher" is on one line.

   Your document window should resemble Figure C-64.

You modified document pages by editing the text within text frames that were created from placeholders on master pages.

Modify master pages

1. Click **View** on the menu bar, click **Show Guides**, then double-click **A-Chapter Right Page** in the Pages palette.

2. Click the **Selection Tool** ▶ (if necessary), then click the **Chapter X placeholder frame**.

3. Click the **center reference point** on the proxy in the Transform palette, double-click the **Rotation Angle text box**, type **90**, then press **[Enter]**(Win) or **[return]**(Mac).

4. Double-click the **X Location text box** in the Transform palette, type **1.75**, then press **[Enter]** (Win) or **[return]** (Mac).

5. Double-click the **page 1 icon** in the Pages palette, then note how the changes made to the A-Chapter Right Page master are reflected on the document page.

    As shown in Figure C-65, both the rotation and the relocation of the text frame on the A-Chapter Right Page master are reflected on the document page.

6. View pages 5 and 9 to see the same changes.

7. Double-click **A-Chapter Right Page** in the Pages palette, click the **Chapter X text frame**, click the **Align left button** ≣ in the Paragraph palette, click the **horizontal title text frame**, then click the **Align center button** ≣ so that your master page resembles Figure C-66.

(continued)

FIGURE C-65
Viewing changes to page 1

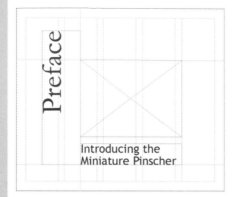

FIGURE C-66
Viewing text alignment changes to the A-Chapter Right Page master

FIGURE C-67

Viewing changes to page 9

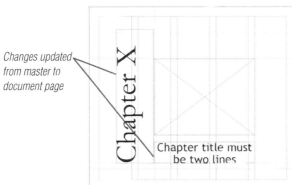

Changes updated
from master to
document page

Chapter X

Chapter title must
be two lines

8. View pages 1 and 5.

Because you have modified the chapter text and the title text on pages 1 and 5, formatting changes to the master have not affected the local formatting.

9. View page 9.

As shown in Figure C-67, because you did not modify any text formatting on page 9, the formatting changes you made to the master are reflected on page 9.

10. Double-click **B-Body Copy with Pics** in the Pages palette, then change the typeface for the automatic page numbering text place-holders on both the left and right page to Garamond.

> TIP   Footer is a term given to information at the bottom of every document page, such as the page number or the date.

11. Double-click **C-Copy No Pics** in the Pages palette.

The footers on both the left and right pages of the C-Copy No Pics master are Garamond because C-Copy No Pics is based on B-Body Copy with Pics.

You modified elements on a master page, then noted which modifications affected corresponding elements on document pages. Next, you modified text on the B-Body Copy with Pics master, and then noted that the C-Copy No Pics master was automatically updated with the modification.

CREATE NEW SECTIONS AND WRAP TEXT

What You'll Do

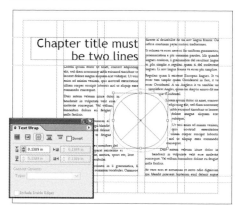

In this lesson, you will create two different numbering sections and create two text wraps around graphics frames.

Creating Sections in a Document

Sections are pages in a document where page numbering changes. For example, sometimes in the front pages of a book, in the introduction or the preface, the pages will be numbered with lowercase Roman numerals, then normal page numbering will begin with the first chapter.

You can create as many sections in a document as you wish. You determine the start page of a new section by clicking a page icon in the Pages palette, then choosing the Numbering & Section Options command in the Pages palette menu, which opens the New Section dialog box, as shown in Figure C-68. The example in this figure shows that, on the page targeted in the Pages palette, a new section will begin. The new section will begin with the page number 6 in lower-case Roman numerals—as defined in the Style section.

> **QUICKTIP**
>
> The first time you choose a type of page numbering for a document, the Numbering & Section Options dialog box opens instead of the New Section dialog box.

FIGURE C-68

New Section dialog box

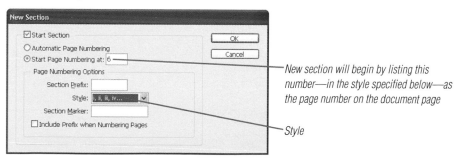

New section will begin by listing this number—in the style specified below—as the page number on the document page

Style

Wrapping Text Around a Frame

When you position a text frame or a graphics frame near another frame that contains text, you can apply a text wrap to the overlapping frame in order to force the underlying text to wrap around it. InDesign offers many options for wrapping text around a frame. One quick method is to click the Wrap around bounding box button in the Text Wrap palette, as shown in Figure C-69.

Figure C-70 shows a rectangular frame using the No text wrap option in the Text Wrap palette. Figure C-71 shows that same frame using the Wrap around bounding box option in the Text Wrap palette.

When you choose the Wrap around bounding box option, you can control the offset—the distance that text is repelled by the frame—by entering values in the Top, Bottom, Left, and Right Offset text boxes in the palette. Figure C-72 shows the frame with a .125-inch offset applied to all four sides of the frame.

FIGURE C-69

Text Wrap palette

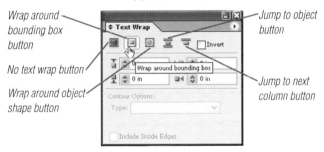

Wrap around bounding box button

No text wrap button

Wrap around object shape button

Jump to object button

Jump to next column button

FIGURE C-70

A frame using the no text wrap option

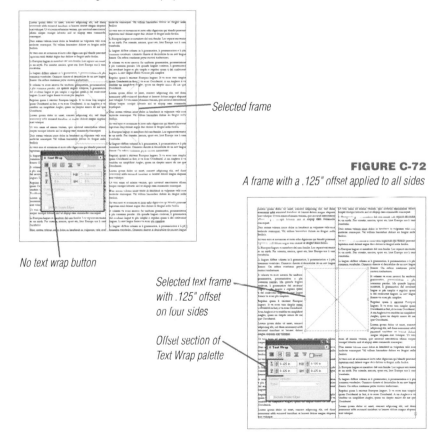

Selected frame

No text wrap button

FIGURE C-71

A frame using the wrap around bounding box option

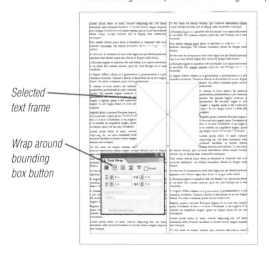

Selected text frame

Wrap around bounding box button

FIGURE C-72

A frame with a .125" offset applied to all sides

Selected text frame with .125" offset on four sides

Offset section of Text Wrap palette

Create sections in a document

1. Double-click the **page 1 icon** in the Pages palette, click the **Pages palette list arrow**, then click **Numbering & Section Options**.

2. Click the **Style list arrow**, then click the **lower-case Roman numeral style**, as shown in Figure C-73.

3. Click **OK**, then view the pages in the document, noting the new style of the page numbering on the pages and in the Pages palette.

4. Double-click the **page v icon** in the Pages palette (page 5), click the **Pages palette list arrow**, then click **Numbering & Section Options**.

5. Click the **Start Page Numbering at option button**, type **1** in the text box, then verify that the Style text box shows ordinary numerals as shown in Figure C-74.

   The fifth page in the document will be designated as Page 1.

6. Click **OK**, then view the pages in the document, noting the new style of page numbering beginning on page 6.

   Since page 5 is based on the A-Chapter Right Page master, it does not display a page number, even though it begins the new section.

7. Double-click the **page ii icon** in the Pages palette, click the **Selection Tool** , press and hold **[Shift][Ctrl]** (Win) or **[Shift]** (Mac), then select the footer text frame.

8. Click the **Type Tool** , double-click the word **Title**, type **Preface**, then click the pasteboard to deselect.

(continued)

FIGURE C-73
Choosing lower-case Roman numerals

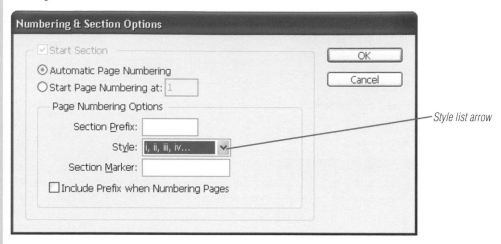

— *Style list arrow*

FIGURE C-74
Starting a new section

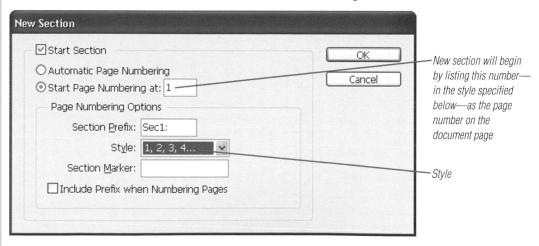

— *New section will begin by listing this number— in the style specified below—as the page number on the document page*

— *Style*

FIGURE C-75

Choosing the Wrap around object shape button

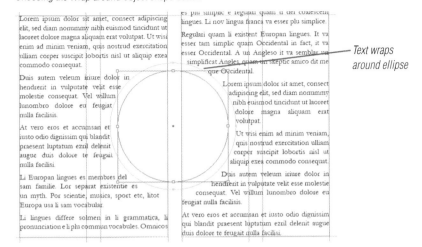

Text wraps
around ellipse

FIGURE C-76

Viewing the spread

Chapter title must
be two lines

ii Preface

Preface iii

Lesson 6 Create New Sections and Wrap Text

---

9. Replace the word Title with the word **Preface** on pages iii and iv, then deselect all.

You used the New Section dialog box to change the style of the page numbering in the Preface section of the book, and then again to start numerical page numbering with Chapter 1.

Wrap text around a frame

1. Double-click the **page ii icon** in the Pages palette, click the **Selection Tool** , press and hold [**Shift**][**Ctrl**] (Win) or [**Shift**] (Mac), then click the **ellipse frame**.

   TIP Clicking the center point of the ellipse frame is the easiest way to select it.

2. Click **Window** on the menu bar, point to **Type & Tables**, then click **Text Wrap**.

3. Click the **Wrap around object shape button** .

   The text wraps around the ellipse, as shown in Figure C-75.

4. Double-click the **page iii icon** in the Pages palette, select the empty rectangular frame, then click the **Wrap around bounding box button** in the Text Wrap palette.

5. Double-click the **Top Offset text box** in the Text Wrap palette, type **.125**, press [**Tab**], type **.125** in the Left Offset text box, then press [**Enter**] (Win) or [**return**] (Mac).

6. Click **View** on the menu bar, click **Fit Spread in Window**, then click anywhere to deselect any selected items.

7. Click the **Preview Mode button** . in the Toolbox, then press [**Tab**].

   Your spread should resemble Figure C-76.

8. Save your work, then close Setup.

You used the Text Wrap palette to flow text around two graphics frames.

INDESIGN C-49

Create a new document.

1. Start Adobe InDesign.
2. Without creating a new document, click Edit (Win) or InDesign (Mac) on the menu bar, point to Preferences, then click Guides & Pasteboard.
3. In the Guide Options section, click the Guides in Back check box to add a check mark, then click OK.
4. Click File on the menu bar, point to New, then click Document.
5. Type **8** in the Number of Pages text box, press [Tab], then verify that the Facing Pages check box is checked.
6. Press [Tab] three times, type **5** in the Width text box, press [Tab], then type **5** in the Height text box. (*Hint*: Mac users may not have to press [Tab].)
7. Using [Tab] to move from one text box to another, type **2** in the Number text box in the Columns section, then type **.2** in the Gutter text box.
8. Type **.25** in the Top, Bottom, Inside, and Outside Margins text boxes.
9. Click OK, then save the document as **Skills Review**.
10. Double-click A-Master in the Pages palette.
11. Click Window on the menu bar, then click Transform.
12. Click the Selection Tool, press and hold [Ctrl] (Win) or ⌘ (Mac), create a guide from the horizontal ruler on the left page, releasing your mouse when the Y Location

text box in the Transform palette reads approximately 2.5 in.
13. Press and hold [Ctrl] (Win) or ⌘ (Mac), create a guide from the vertical ruler on the left page, releasing your mouse when the X Location text box in the Transform palette reads approximately 2.5 in.
14. Click Edit (Win) or InDesign (Mac) on the menu bar, point to Prefer-ences, click Units & Increments, click the Origin list arrow, click Page, then click OK.
15. Press and hold [Ctrl] (Win) or ⌘ (Mac), create a guide from the vertical ruler on the right page, releasing your mouse when the X Location text box in the Transform palette reads approximately 2.5 in.
16. Click the horizontal guide, double-click the value in the Y Location text box of the Transform palette, type **2.5**, then press [Enter] (Win) or [return] (Mac).
17. Click the vertical guide on the left page, double-click the value in the X Location text box in the Transform palette, type **2.5**, then press [Enter] (Win) or [return] (Mac).
18. Click the vertical guide on the right page, double-click the value in the X Location text box in the Transform palette, type **2.5**, then press [Enter] (Win) or [return] (Mac).
19. Click the Rectangle Frame Tool, then draw a rectangle anywhere on the left page.
20. Click the upper-left reference point on the proxy in the Transform palette.
21. With the rectangle frame selected, type **0** in the X Location text box in the Transform

palette, type **0** in the Y Location text box, type **5** in the Width text box, type **5** in the Height text box, then press [Enter] (Win) or [return] (Mac).
22. Click Edit on the menu bar, click Copy, click Edit on the menu bar again, then click Paste in Place.
23. Drag the copied box anywhere on the right page, being sure that its upper-left corner is on the page.
24. Type **0** in the X Location text box in the Transform palette, type **0** in the Y Location text box, then press [Enter] (Win) or [return] (Mac).

Create master pages.

1. Click the Pages palette list arrow, then click New Master.
2. Type **Body Copy** in the Name text box, click the Based on Master list arrow, click A-Master, then click OK.
3. Click the Selection Tool, press and hold [Shift][Ctrl] (Win) or [Shift] ⌘ (Mac), select both rectangle frames, then delete them.
4. Double-click B-Body Copy in the Pages palette to center both pages of the master in your window.
5. Click Layout on the menu bar, then click Margins and Columns.
6. Type **2** in the Number text box in the Columns section (if necessary), then click OK.
7. Click the Type Tool, create a text frame of any size anywhere in the right column on the left page, then click the Selection Tool.

8. Verify that the upper-left reference point is selected on the proxy in the Transform palette, type **2.6** in the X Location text box, type **.25** in the Y Location text box, type **2.15** in the Width text box, type **4.5** in the Height text box, then press [Enter] (Win) or [return] (Mac).

9. Click Edit on the menu bar, click Copy, click Edit on the menu bar again, then click Paste in Place.

10. Press and hold [Shift], then drag the copy of the text frame onto the right page, releasing your mouse when it "snaps" into the left column on the right page.

11. Click the Type Tool, then draw a small text frame anywhere on the left page of the B-Body Copy master.

12. Verify that the upper-left reference point is selected on the proxy in the Transform palette, type **.25** in the X Location text box, type **4.5** in the Y Location text box, type **1.65** in the Width text box, type **.25** in the Height text box, then press [Enter] (Win) or [return] (Mac).

13. Click Type on the menu bar, point to Insert Special Character, then click Auto Page Number.

14. Click Type on the menu bar, point to Insert Special Character, then click En Dash.

15. Type the word **Title**.

16. Click the Selection Tool, select the footer text frame, click Edit on the menu bar, click

Copy, click Edit on the menu bar again, then click Paste in Place.

17. Press and hold [Shift], then drag the copy of the text frame so that it is positioned in the lower-right corner of the right page of the master page.

18. Click the Align right button in the Paragraph palette, then delete the B and the dash after the B.

19. Click after the word Title, click Type on the menu bar, point to Insert Special Character, then click En Dash.

20. Click Type on the menu bar, point to Insert Special Character, then click Auto Page Number.

Apply master pages to document pages.

1. Double-click the page 2 icon in the Pages palette.

2. Double-click B-Body Copy in the Pages palette, then drag the master page title to the top-left corner of the page 2 icon until you see a black rectangle around the page 2 and 3 icons, then release your mouse.

3. Drag the B-Body Copy title to the top-left corner of the page 4 icon until you see a black rectangle around the page 4 icon, then release your mouse.

4. Click the Pages palette list arrow, then click Apply Master to Pages.

5. Click the Apply Master list arrow, click B-Body Copy (if necessary), type **6-8** in the To Pages text box, then click OK.

6. Double-click the page 2 icon in the Pages palette.

Place text and thread text.

1. Click File on the menu bar, click Place, navigate to the drive and folder where your Chapter C Data Files are stored, then double-click Skills Review Text.

2. Click anywhere in the text frame on page two.

3. Click View on the menu bar, then click Show Text Threads.

4. Click the Selection Tool, click the text frame on page 2, then click the out port of the text frame on page 2.

5. Click the link icon anywhere in the text frame on page 3.

Modify master pages and document pages.

1. Double-click the page 6 icon in the Pages palette.

2. Click the bottom-middle reference point on the proxy in the Transform palette.

3. Click the Selection Tool, press and hold [Shift][Ctrl] (Win) or [Shift] $\mathcal{H}$ (Mac), then click the text frame.

4. Type **3** in the Height text box in the Transform palette, then press [Enter] (Win) or [return] (Mac).

5. Double-click A-Master in the Pages palette, then select the graphics placeholder frame on the left page.

6. Click the center reference point on the proxy in the Transform palette.

7. In the Transform palette, type **3** in the Width text box, type **3** in the Height text box, then press [Enter] (Win) or [return] (Mac).

8. Double-click the right page icon of the A-Master in the Pages palette, then select the graphics placeholder frame on the right page.

9. In the Transform palette, type **2** in the Width text box, type **4** in the Height text box, then press [Enter] (Win) or [return] (Mac).

10. View the two document pages in the Pages palette that are based on the A-Master to verify that the modifications were updated.

11. Double-click B-Body Copy in the Pages palette, click the Rectangle Frame Tool, then create a frame anywhere on the left page of the B-Body Copy master page.

12. Click the upper-left reference point on the proxy in the Transform palette, then type **2** in the X Location text box, type **2.6** in the Y Location text box, type **2.25** in the Width text box, type **1.5** in the Height text box, then press [Enter] (Win) or [return] (Mac).

Create new sections and wrap text.

1. Double-click the page 1 icon in the Pages palette, click the Pages palette list arrow, then click Numbering & Section Options.

2. Click the Style list arrow, click the lower-case style letters (a, b, c, d), click OK, then note the changes to the pages in the Pages palette and in the document.

3. Double-click the page e icon in the Pages palette, click the Pages palette list arrow, then click Numbering & Section Options.

4. Click the Start Page Numbering at option button, type **5** in the text box, then verify that the Style text box shows ordinary numerals (1, 2, 3, 4).

5. Click OK, then view the pages in the document noting the new style of the page numbering on the pages and in the Pages palette.

6. Double-click the page b icon in the Pages palette, click the Selection Tool, press and hold [Shift][Ctrl] (Win) or [Shift] ⌘ (Mac), then select the rectangular graphics frame.

7. Click Window on the menu bar, point to Type & Tables, then click Text Wrap.

8. Click the Wrap around bounding box button in the Text Wrap palette.

9. Type **.125** in the Right Offset text box in the Text Wrap palette.

10. Click View on the menu bar, click Fit Spread in Window, then click anywhere to deselect any selected items.

11. Compare your screen to Figure C-77, save your work, then close Skills Review.

FIGURE C-77

Completed Skills Review

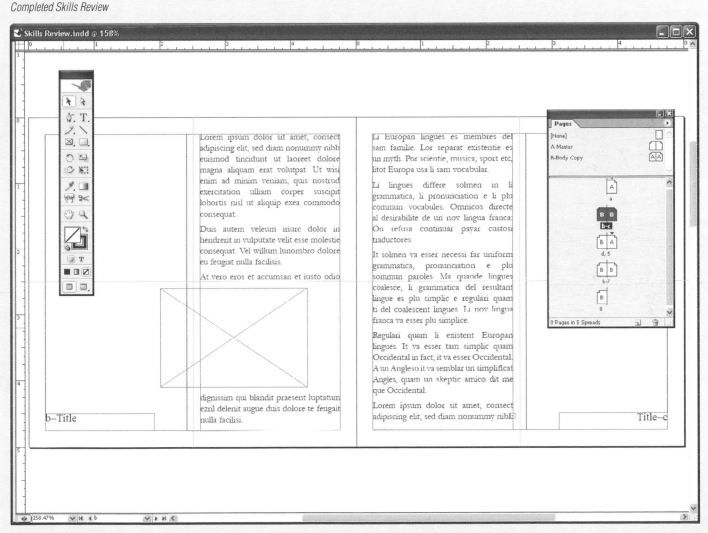

You are a graphic designer working out of your home office. You have one client— a local investment company who has contracted you to design their monthly 16-page newsletter. You've sketched out a design and created a new document at the correct size, and now you need to add automatic page numbering to the document.

1. Open ID C-1.indd, then save it as **Newsletter**.
2. Double-click A-Master in the Pages palette.
3. Click the Type Tool, then draw a text frame about one inch tall and one column wide.
4. Position the text frame at the bottom of the center column, being sure that the bottom edge of the text frame snaps to the bottom margin of the page.
5. Set the Preference settings so that the guides are sent to the back of the layout—so that all four sides of the text frame are visible.
6. Click the Type Tool, then click inside the text box.
7. Click Type on the menu bar, point to Insert Special Character, then click Em Dash.
8. Click Type on the menu bar, point to Insert Special Character, then click Auto Page Number.
9. Click Type on the menu bar, point to Insert Special Character, then click Em Dash.
10. Click the Align center button in the Paragraph palette.

11. Click the bottom center reference point on the proxy in the Transform palette, double-click the Height text box in the Transform palette, type **.25**, then press [Enter] (Win) or [return] (Mac).

FIGURE C-78
Completed Project Builder 1

12. Double-click the page 5 icon in the Pages palette, compare your page 5 to Figure C-78, save your work, then close Newsletter.

You work in the design department for a bank, and you are responsible for creating a new weekly bulletin, which covers various events within the bank's network of branches. You have just finished creating three master pages for the bulletin, and now you are ready to apply the masters to the document pages.

1. Open ID C-2.indd, then save it as **Bulletin Layout**.
2. Apply the B-Master to pages 2 and 3.
3. Click the Pages palette list arrow, then click Apply Master to Pages.
4. Apply the C-Master to pages 5 through 6, then click OK.
5. Place Bulletin text.doc in the text frame on page 1.
6. Select the text frame, click the out port on the text frame, double-click page 2 in the Pages palette, then click anywhere in the text frame on page 2.
7. Thread the remaining text through each page up to and including page 6 in the document.
8. Click the Preview Mode button, deselect any selected items, then compare your page 6 to Figure C-79.
9. Save your work, then close Bulletin Layout.

FIGURE C-79

Completed Project Builder 2

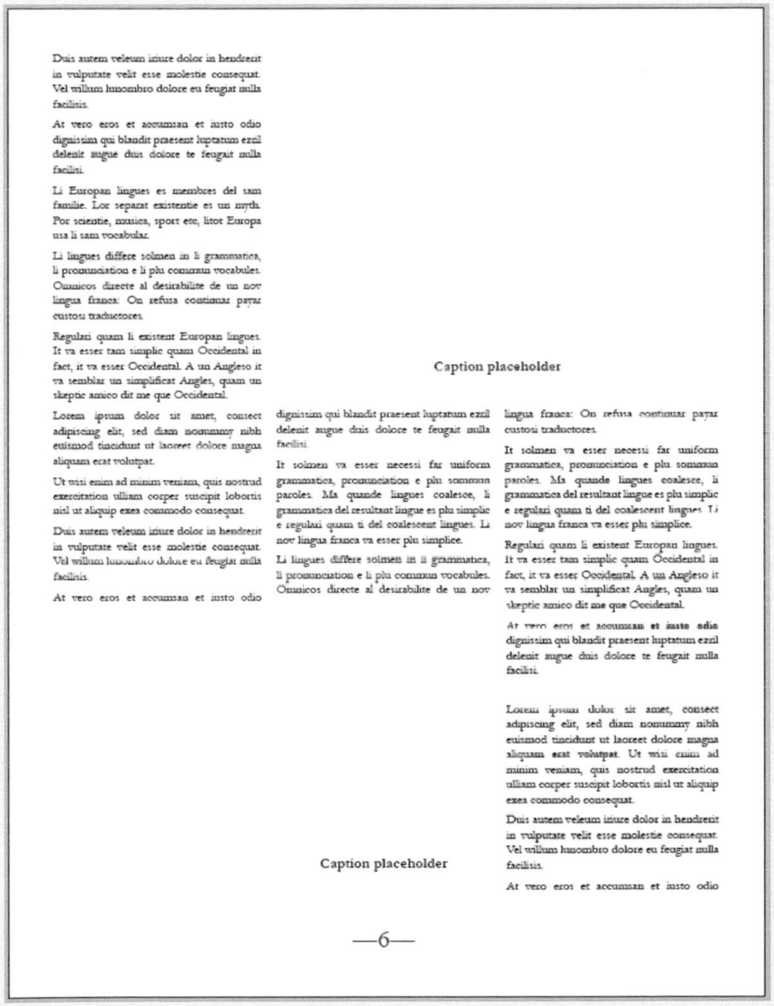

Your client has provided you with a page layout that she describes as her design for the background of her page. Knowing that she'll want to use this background design for multiple pages, you decide to "tweak" her document to be sure that the background elements are the same size and are aligned evenly.

1. Open ID C-3.indd, then save it as **Four Square**.
2. Click File on the menu bar, click Document Setup, note the width and height of the page, then close the Document Setup dialog box.
3. Hide the guides and the frame edges, then verify that only the Transform palette and the Toolbox are visible.
4. Click the Selection Tool, then click the upper-left reference point on the proxy in the Transform palette.
5. Click the upper-left square on the page, type **0** in the X Location text box, type **0** in the Y Location text box, type **7.75** in the Width text box, then press [Enter] (Win) or [return] (Mac).
6. Click your cursor after the number 7.75 in the Width text box, type **/2**, then press [Tab].
7. Type **3.875** in the Height text box, then press [Enter] (Win) or [return] (Mac).
8. Click the upper-right square, type **3.875** in the X Location text box, type **0** in the Y Location text box, type **3.875** in the Width and Height text boxes, then press [Enter] (Win) or [return] (Mac).

9. Click the lower-left square, type **0** in the X Location text box, type **3.875** in the Y Location text box, type **3.875** in the Width and Height text boxes, then press [Enter] (Win) or [return] (Mac).
10. Click the lower-right square, type **3.875** in the X Location text box, type **3.875** in the Y Location text box, type **3.875** in the Width and Height text boxes, then press [Enter] (Win) or [return] (Mac).
11. Compare your screen to Figure C-80, save your work, then close Four Square.

FIGURE C-80
Completed Design Project

Set up a Document

Your group is going to work on a fun puzzle, which will test your problem-solving skills when using X and Y locations. You will open an InDesign document with two pages. On the first page are four 1-inch squares at each corner of the page. On the second page, the four 1-inch squares appear again—this time forming a large black square that is positioned at the exact center of the 8-inch x 8-inch document page. The challenge is for the group to call out X and Y locations for all four of the squares on the first page so that they will be relocated to the same positions as the four squares on the second page.

Setup.

1. Have one computer set up to display the document so that the entire group can see it. If you can, use a large display projection against the wall.

2. Verify that only the Toolbox and the Transform palette are visible.

3. Have one member sit at the computer display to implement the groups' call-outs in the document, selecting the boxes and entering information in the Transform palette.

4. Explain to the group that, not only is this a challenge to use X and Y location values to reposition the boxes, it's also a challenge to find what the group will agree is the most straightforward method for doing so using the fewest steps.

5. Divide the group into groups of 4. Have each group choose a spokesperson. Tell the groups that they have exactly one minute to huddle among themselves to come up with a solution for the problem. (Group members should not be in front of computers during this time; they can use pencils and paper and base their calculations on the information given in the introduction.)

6. Have the first group spokesperson call out the changes to the student at the display until the first group spokesperson achieves the objective. Note that the rules of the challenge state that the spokesperson is allowed one try only for each square. This means that the spokesperson can call out a value for any of the X and Y text boxes in the Transform palette only one time for each square. The spokesperson is also free to specify a point of origin in the proxy in the Transform palette. If, at the end, the squares are not aligned, the spokesperson does not get a second chance.

7. Ask the second group spokesperson if he/she thinks she knows a better method. If she says yes, revert the document and let her try. If she says no, her group is out.

8. Proceed in this fashion until all four groups have had the opportunity to try the challenge. At the end, have the groups decide who found the best method.

9. Open ID C-4.indd, then save it as **Center Squares**.

10. Enter the correct X and Y location values in the Transform palette for all four squares.

11. Compare your work to Figure C-81, then close Center Squares.

FIGURE C-81
Completed Group Project

CHAPTER D

WORKING WITH FRAMES

1. Align and distribute objects on a page.

2. Stack and layer objects.

3. Work with graphics frames.

4. Work with text frames.

CHAPTER D
WORKING WITH FRAMES

When you position objects on a page, they are positioned in text or graphics frames. Chapter D focuses on frames and how you can best work with them.

The first lesson gives you the chance to pause and explore basic options for aligning and distributing frames on the page. In the second lesson, you'll learn how to manipulate the stacking order of frames, and you'll get a thorough tour of the Layers palette. After going through these lessons, you'll feel confident in your ability to position frames precisely on a page and to get them to overlap the way you want them to.

The third lesson is an immersion into the world of placing graphics in graphics frames. Put on your thinking caps—there's a lot going on here, all of it interesting. You'll learn the specifics of placing graphics—and the all-important difference between the graphics frame and the graphic itself. Finally, you'll finish by working with text frames and exploring the power of autoflowing text in a document. Watch InDesign create dozens of text frames with a click of a button. Now that's a lot of frames!

Tools You'll Use

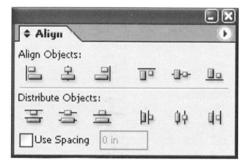

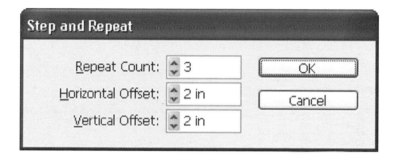

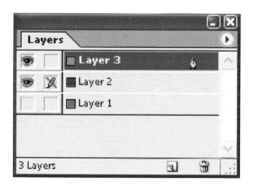

ALIGN AND DISTRIBUTE OBJECTS ON A PAGE

What You'll Do

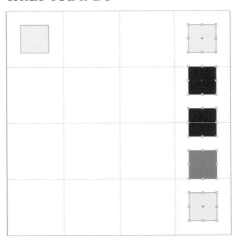

 In this lesson, you will explore various techniques for positioning objects in specific locations on the document page.

Applying Fills and Strokes

A **fill** is a color you apply that fills an object. A **stroke** is a color that you apply to the outline of an object. Figure D-1 shows an object with a blue fill and a yellow stroke.

InDesign offers you a number of options for filling and stroking objects. The simplest and most direct method for doing so is to select an object and then pick a color from the **Swatches palette**, shown in Figure D-2. The color that you choose in the Swatches palette will be applied to the selected object as a fill or as a stroke, depending on whether the fill or the stroke button is activated in the Toolbox.

To activate either the Fill or the Stroke button, simply click it once in the Toolbox. The Fill button is activated when it is in front of the Stroke button, as shown in Figure D-3. When the Fill button is activated, clicking a swatch in the Swatches palette applies that swatch color as a fill to the selected object(s). When the Stroke button is activated, as shown in Figure D-4, the swatch color is applied as a stroke.

Once a stroke is applied, you can modify the **stroke weight**—how heavy the outline appears—using the Stroke palette. Figure D-5 shows the Stroke palette and an object with a 10-pt red stroke. Note the Stroke palette list arrow, which you can click to display more stroke options in the palette.

QUICKTIP

You can merge the contents of two or more layers by selecting the layers in the Layers palette, clicking the Layers palette list arrow, then clicking Merge Layers. The first layer that you click upon selecting the layers to be merged becomes the resulting merged layer. **Flattening** a document refers to merging all of the layers in the Layers palette.

FIGURE D-1
An object with a fill and a stroke

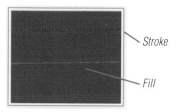

Stroke

Fill

FIGURE D-2
Swatches palette

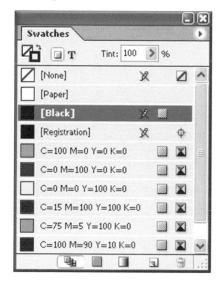

FIGURE D-3
Viewing the activated Fill button

Fill button is
in front of the
Stroke button

FIGURE D-4
Viewing the activated Stroke button

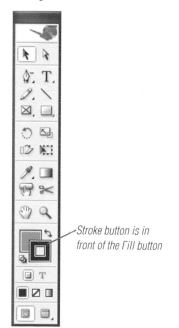

Stroke button is in
front of the Fill button

FIGURE D-5
A 10-pt stroke applied to an object

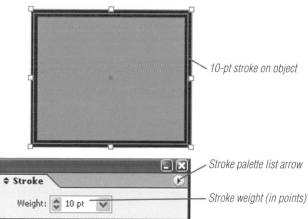

10-pt stroke on object

Stroke palette list arrow

Stroke weight (in points)

Lesson 1   Align and Distribute Objects on a Page

Using the Step and Repeat Command

Many times, when laying out a page, you will want to create multiple objects that are evenly spaced. Rather than draw each object one at a time, it's often best to use the **Step and Repeat** dialog box, as shown in Figure D-6.

Before you choose the Step and Repeat command, you need to decide which object you want to make copies of, and how many copies of the object you want to create. After selecting the object, choose Step and Repeat on the Edit menu. In the Step and Repeat dialog box, you choose the number of copies. You also specify the **offset** value

for each successive copy. The offset is easy to understand—it is the distance, horizontally and vertically, that the copy will be from the original. Figure D-7 shows an original 1-inch square frame and the three copies created using the Step and Repeat command. Note that the horizontal offset is two inches and the vertical offset is two inches. Thus, each copy is two inches to the right and two inches down from the previous copy.

Note that positive and negative offset values create copies in specific directions. On the horizontal axis, a positive value creates copies to the right of the original; a negative value creates copies to the left of the

original. On the vertical axis, a positive value creates copies below the original; a negative value creates copies above the original. Figure D-8 is a handy guide for remembering the result of positive and negative offset values.

Use the vertical ruler on the left side of the document page to remember positive and negative values on the vertical axis. You are used to thinking of positive as up and negative as down, but remember that in InDesign, the default (0, 0) coordinate is in the top-left corner of the page. On the ruler, positive numbers *increase* as you move down the ruler.

FIGURE D-6
Step and Repeat dialog box

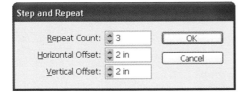

FIGURE D-7
Results of the Step and Repeat command

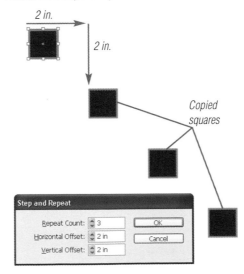

2 in.

2 in.

Copied squares

FIGURE D-8
Understanding positive and negative offset values

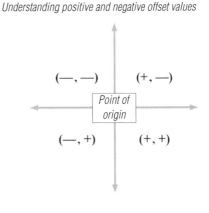

$(-, -)$ $(+, -)$

Point of origin

$(-, +)$ $(+, +)$

Aligning Objects

The Align palette offers quick and simple solutions for aligning and distributing multiple objects on a page. To **align** objects is to position them by their tops, bottoms, left sides, right sides or centers. To **distribute** objects is to space them equally on a page horizontally, vertically, or both. Using the top section of the Align palette, you can choose from six alignment buttons, shown in Figure D-9. Each option includes an icon that represents the resulting layout of the selected objects, after the button has been clicked. Figure D-10 shows three objects placed randomly on the page. Figure D-11 shows the same three objects after clicking the Align left edges button.

Compare Figure D-10 to Figure D-11. Only the bottom two objects moved; they moved left to align with the left edge of the top object. This is because the top object was originally the left-most object. Clicking the Align left edges button aligns all selected objects with the left-most object.

Figure D-12 shows the same three objects after clicking the Align top edges button. Clicking this button means that the top edges of each object are aligned.

The Align palette is a great feature of InDesign, one that you will use over and over again.

FIGURE D-9
Align Objects section of the Align palette

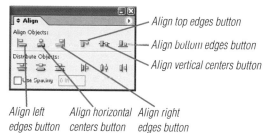

Align top edges button
Align bottom edges button
Align vertical centers button

Align left edges button
Align horizontal centers button
Align right edges button

FIGURE D-11
Viewing the results of the Align left edges button

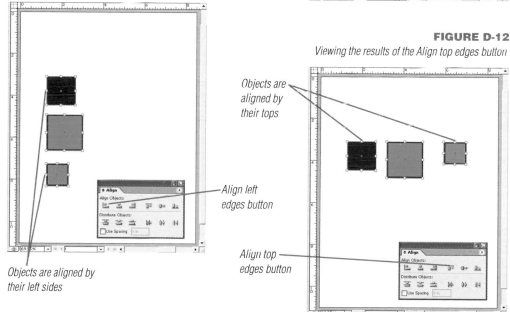

Align left edges button

Objects are aligned by their left sides

FIGURE D-10
Three objects not aligned

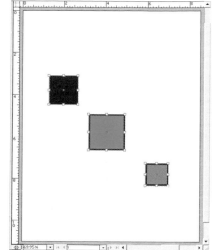

FIGURE D-12
Viewing the results of the Align top edges button

Objects are aligned by their tops

Align top edges button

Distributing Objects

You use the Distribute Objects section of the Align palette to distribute objects. As stated earlier, to distribute objects is to space them equally on a page horizontally, vertically, or both.

Figure D-13 shows three objects that are not distributed evenly on either the horizontal or vertical axis. Figure D-14 shows the same three objects after clicking the Distribute horizontal centers button. Clicking this button means that—on the horizontal axis—the distance between the center point of the first object and the center point of the second object is the same as the distance between the center point of the second object and the center point of the third object.

Figure D-15 shows the same three objects after clicking the Distribute vertical centers button. Clicking this button means that—on the vertical axis—the distance between the center points of the first two objects is the same as the distance between the center points of the second and third objects.

Why are the Align and Distribute buttons in the same palette? Because their power is how they work in conjunction with each other. Figure D-16 shows three text frames without any alignment or distribution applied. Figure D-17 shows the three frames after clicking the Align top edges button and the Distribute left edges button. Compare the two figures.

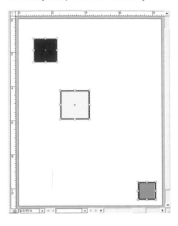

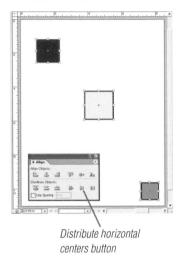

Distribute horizontal centers button

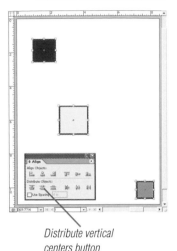

Distribute vertical centers button

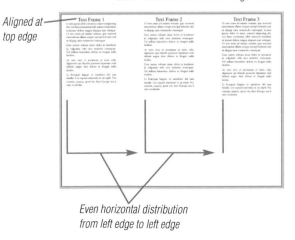

Aligned at top edge

Even horizontal distribution from left edge to left edge

FIGURE D-18
Positioning the rectangle frame

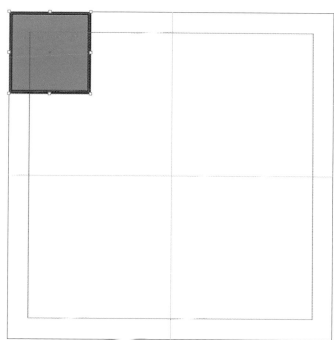

1. Open ID D-1.indd, then save it as **Orientation**.

2. Click the **Rectangle Tool** ⬜ , then click anywhere on the page.

   TIP   When a shape tool is selected in the Toolbox, clicking the document window opens the tool's dialog box, where you can enter values that determine the size of the resulting object.

3. Type **2** in the Width text box, type **2** in the Height text box, then click **OK**.

4. Click **Window** on the menu bar, then click **Swatches**.

5. Click the **Fill button** in the Toolbox (if necessary) to activate it.

6. Click **Green** in the Swatches palette.

   The rectangle frame fills with green.

7. Click the **Stroke button** in the Toolbox.

8. Click **Brick Red** in the Swatches palette.

9. Click **Window** on the menu bar, click **Stroke**, type **6** in the Weight text box, then press **[Enter]** (Win) or **[return]** (Mac).

10. Press **[V]** to access the Selection Tool, then drag the frame so that its top-left corner is aligned with the top-left corner of the page, as shown in Figure D-18.

11. Click **File** on the menu bar, then click **Save**.

You created a rectangle using the Rectangle dialog box. You then used the Swatches palette to choose a fill color and a stroke color for the rectangle frame. Finally, you used the Stroke palette to increase the weight of the stroke around the rectangle frame.

Use the Step and Repeat command

1. Click the **green rectangle**, click the **Stroke button** in the Toolbox, then click the **Apply None button** 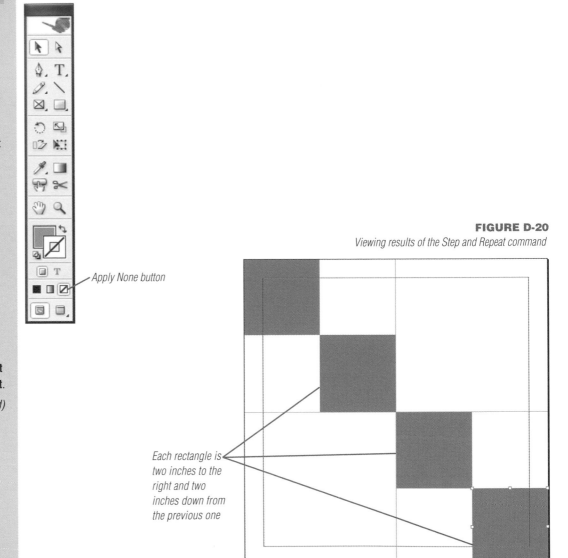, as shown in Figure D-19.

   The stroke is removed from the green rectangle. With the loss of the stroke, the rectangle is no longer aligned with the top-left corner.

2. Move the rectangle up and to the left so that it is once again aligned with the top-left corner of the page.

3. Click **Edit** on the menu bar, then click **Step and Repeat**.

4. Type **3** in the Repeat Count text box, type **2** in the Horizontal Offset text box, type **2** in the Vertical Offset text box, then click **OK**.

   Three new rectangles are created, each one two inches to the right and two inches down from the previous one, as shown in Figure D-20.

5. Click the **top-left rectangle**, press and hold **[Shift]**, click the **second rectangle**, click **Edit** on the menu bar, then click **Step and Repeat**.

   (continued)

FIGURE D-19
Removing the stroke from the rectangle

— *Apply None button*

FIGURE D-20
Viewing results of the Step and Repeat command

Each rectangle is two inches to the right and two inches down from the previous one

Working with Frames

FIGURE D-21

Viewing a checkerboard created using the Step and Repeat command

6. Type **1** in the Repeat Count text box, type **4** in the Horizontal Offset text box, type **0** in the Vertical Offset text box, then click **OK**.

7. Click the **bottom-right rectangle**, press and hold **[Shift]**, click the **rectangle** that is diagonally above the bottom-right rectangle, click **Edit** on the menu bar, then click **Step and Repeat**.

8. Type **1** in the Repeat Count text box, type **-4** in the Horizontal Offset text box, type **0** in the Vertical Offset text box, then click **OK**.

9. Press **[W]** to switch to Preview Mode, click anywhere to deselect the new rectangles, then compare your page to Figure D-21.

10. Click **File** on the menu bar, click **Revert**, then click **Yes** (Win) or **Revert** (Mac) in the dialog box that follows.

   TIP   The Revert command returns the document to its last saved status.

You used the Step and Repeat command to create a checkerboard pattern, duplicating a single rectangle seven times, then reverted the document.

Align objects

1. Press and hold **[Alt]** (Win) or **[option]** (Mac), then click and drag the **square** in the top-left corner down to the bottom-right corner, as shown in Figure D-22.

   TIP   Pressing and holding [Alt] (Win) or [option] (Mac) when dragging an object makes a copy of the object.

2. Press and hold **[Alt]** (Win) or **[option]** (Mac), then click and drag the **square** from the bottom-right corner up so that its center point is aligned with the intersection of the two guides, as shown in Figure D-23.

3. Click **Window** on the menu bar, then click **Align**.

4. Press **[Ctrl][A]** (Win) or **[⌘][A]** (Mac) to select all the objects on the page, then click the **Align left edges button** in the Align Objects section of the Align palette.

5. Click **Edit** on the menu bar, then click **Undo Horizontal Align Left**.

6. Click the **Align top edges button** in the Align palette.

7. Undo the previous step, then click the **Align horizontal centers button**.

8. Click the **Align vertical centers button**.

   All three frames are stacked upon one another, their center points aligned both horizontally and vertically.

9. Save your work, then close Orientation.

You used the [Alt] (Win) or [option] (Mac) keyboard shortcut to create two copies of the square. You then used the buttons in the Align Objects section of the Align palette to reposition the frames with various alignments.

FIGURE D-22
Repositioning a copy

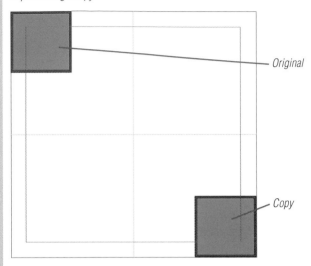

Original

Copy

FIGURE D-23
Repositioning a second copy

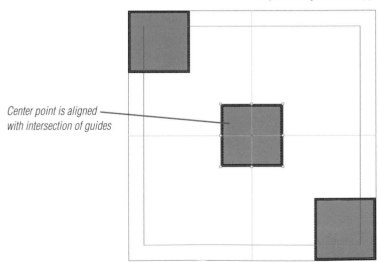

Center point is aligned
with intersection of guides

FIGURE D-24

Distributing objects evenly on the horizontal axis

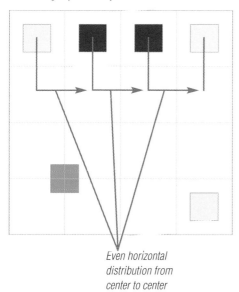

*Even horizontal
distribution from
center to center*

FIGURE D-26

Distributing 5 objects evenly on the vertical axis

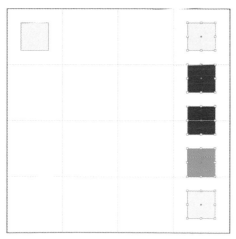

FIGURE D-25

Distributing objects evenly on the vertical axis

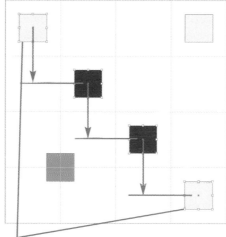

*Even vertical distribution
from center to center*

Distribute objects

1. Open ID D-2.indd, then save it as **Distribution**.

2. Select the top two yellow squares and the two red squares, then click the **Align top edges button** in the Align Objects section of the Align palette.

   The four objects are aligned at their top edges.

3. Click the **Distribute horizontal centers button** in the Distribute Objects section of the Align palette.

   The center points of the two red squares are distributed evenly on the horizontal axis between the center points of the two yellow squares, as shown in Figure D-24.

4. Click **Edit** on the menu bar, click **Deselect All**, select the top-left yellow square, select the two red squares, then select the bottom-right yellow square.

5. Click the **Distribute vertical centers button**, then compare your screen to Figure D-25.

6. Select the green square, the two red squares and the bottom yellow square, then click the **Align right edges button**.

7. Press and hold **[Shift]** then click the **top-right yellow square** to add it to the selection.

8. Click the **Distribute vertical centers button**.

   The center points of the five squares are distributed evenly on the vertical axis, as shown in Figure D-26.

9. Save your work, then close Distribution.

You spaced objects evenly on the horizontal or vertical axis.

INDESIGN D-13

STACK AND LAYER OBJECTS

What You'll Do

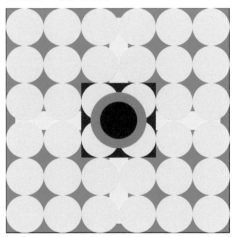

In this lesson, you will use commands to manipulate the stacking order of objects on the page, and you'll use the Layers palette to control how objects are layered.

Understanding the Stacking Order

The **stacking order** refers to how objects are "stacked." When you create multiple objects, it is important for you to remember that every object is on its own hierarchical level. For example, if you draw a square frame, and then draw a circle frame, the circle frame is automatically created one level in front of the square, whether or not they overlap. If they did overlap, the circle would appear in front of the square.

QUICKTIP

Use the word "level" when discussing the hierarchy of the stacking order, not the word "layer." Layers in InDesign are very different from levels in the stacking order.

You control the stacking order with the four commands on the Arrange menu. The Bring to Front command moves a selected object to the front of the stacking order. The Send to Back command moves a selected object to the back of the stacking order. The Bring Forward command moves a selected object one level forward in the stacking order, and the Send Backward command moves a selected object one level backward in the stacking order.

Using these four commands, you can control and arrange how every object on the page overlaps other objects.

Understanding Layers

The Layers palette, as shown in Figure D-27, is a smart solution for organizing and managing elements of a layout. By default, every document is created with one layer. You can create new layers and give them descriptive names to help you identify a layer's content. For example, if you were working on a layout that contained both text and graphics, you might want to create a layer for all of the text frames called Text and create another layer for all of the graphics called Graphics.

Why would you do this? Well, for one reason, you have the ability to lock layers in the Layers palette. Locking a layer makes its contents non-editable until you unlock it. In the example, you could lock the Text layer while you work on the graphic elements of the layout. By doing so, you can be certain that you won't make any inadvertent changes to the text elements. Another reason is that you have the ability to hide layers. You could temporarily hide the Text layer, thus allowing you to work on the graphics with a view that is unobstructed by the text elements.

You can also duplicate layers. You do so by clicking the Duplicate Layer command in the Layers palette menu or by dragging a layer on top of the Create new layer icon in the Layers palette. When you duplicate a layer, all of the objects on the original layer are duplicated and will appear in their same locations on the new layer.

Working with Layers

You can create multiple layers in the Layers palette—however many you need to organize your work. Figure D-28 shows the Layers palette with three layers. Notice the icon of a pencil with the red line through it on Layer 2. This icon, called the Toggles lock button, indicates that this layer cannot be edited. All objects on Layer 2 are locked. Clicking the Toggles lock button will unlock the layer.

Think of layers in the Layers palette as being three-dimensional. The topmost layer is the front layer; the bottommost layer is the back layer. Therefore, it follows logically that objects on the topmost layer are in front of objects on any other layer. Layers themselves are transparent. If you have a layer with no objects on it, you can see through the layer to the objects on the layers behind it.

Note that each layer contains its own stacking order. Let's say that you have three layers, each with five objects on it. Regardless of the stacking order of the top layer, all the objects on that layer are in front of any

FIGURE D-27
Layers palette

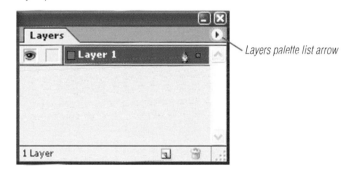

Layers palette list arrow

FIGURE D-28
Layers palette with three layers

Toggles visibility button (on state)

Toggles lock button (on state)

Toggles visibility button (off state)

Indicates current drawing layer icon

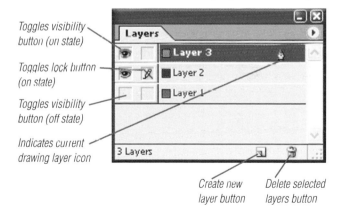

Create new layer button   *Delete selected layers button*

objects on the other layers. In other words, an object at the back of the stacking order of the top layer is still in front of any object on any layer beneath it.

One great organizational aspect of layers is that you can assign a selection color to a layer. When you select an object, its bounding box appears in the selection color of the layer that it is placed on, as shown in Figure D-29. You determine a layer's selection color by selecting the layer, clicking the Layers palette list arrow,

clicking Layer Options for the name of the selected layer, then choosing a new color from the Color menu. When you are working with a layout that contains numerous objects, this feature is a great visual aid for keeping track of objects and their relationships to other objects.

Manipulating Layers and Objects on Layers

Once you have created layers in a document, you have many options for manipulating objects on the layers and the layers

themselves. You can move objects between layers, and you can reorder the layers in the Layers palette.

Clicking a layer in the Layers palette to select it is called **targeting** a layer. The layer that you click is called the **target layer**. When you create a new object, the object will be added to whichever layer is targeted in the Layers palette. The pen tool icon next to a layer's name in the Layers palette is called the **Indicates current drawing layer icon**. This icon will help

FIGURE D-29
Assigning a selection color to a layer

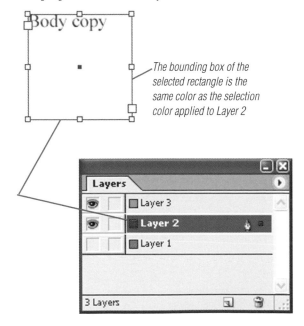

The bounding box of the selected rectangle is the same color as the selection color applied to Layer 2

Working with Frames

remind you that anything placed or drawn will become part of that layer.

You can select any object on the page, regardless of which layer is targeted. When you select the object, the layer that the object is on is automatically targeted in the Layers palette. Thus, by clicking an object, you know which layer it is on.

When an object is selected, a small button appears to the right of the name of the layer, as shown in Figure D-30. That small button, identified as the **Indicates selected items button**, represents the selected object (or objects). You can click and drag the Indicates selected items button and move it to another layer. When you do so, the selected object(s) moves to that layer. Therefore, you should never feel constrained by which layer you choose for an object; it's easy to move objects from one layer to another.

You can also change the order of layers in the Layers palette by dragging a layer up or down in the palette. As you drag, a heavy black line indicates the new position for the layer when you release the mouse. In Figure D-31, the Graphics Elements layer is being repositioned under the Text Elements layer.

Selecting Artwork on Layers

Let's say you have three layers in your document, each with six objects. That means your document has a total of 18 objects. If you apply the Select All command on the Edit menu, all 18 objects will be selected, regardless of which layer is targeted in the Layers palette.

If you want to select only the objects on a single layer, you must use a keyboard shortcut. Press and hold [Alt] (Win) or [option] (Mac), and then click the layer. Pressing and holding [Alt] (Win) or [option] (Mac) when clicking a layer selects all the objects on that layer.

FIGURE D-30

Indicates selected items button

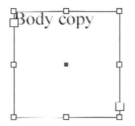

Button indicates selected items

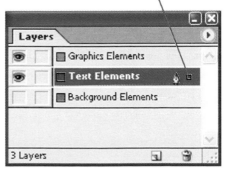

FIGURE D-31

Changing the order of two layers in the Layers palette

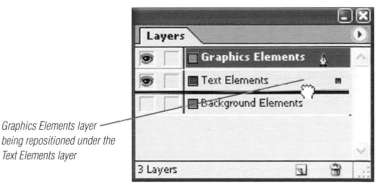

Graphics Elements layer being repositioned under the Text Elements layer

Use the Arrange commands to change the stacking order of objects

1. Open ID D-3.indd, then save it as **Stack and Layer**.

2. Press **[V]** to access the Selection Tool, then click the **yellow rectangle**.

3. Click **Object** on the menu bar, point to **Arrange**, then click **Bring Forward**.

   The yellow rectangle moves forward one level in the stacking order.

4. Click the **red square**, click **Object** on the menu bar, point to **Arrange**, then click **Bring to Front**.

5. Select both the yellow rectangle and the blue circle, click **Object** on the menu bar, point to **Arrange**, then click **Bring to Front**.

6. Click the **green circle**, click **Object** on the menu bar, point to **Arrange**, then click **Bring to Front**.

7. Select all, then click the **Align horizontal centers button** in the Align palette.

8. Click the **document window** to deselect all, click the **green circle**, click **Object** on the menu bar, point to **Arrange**, then click **Send Backward**.

   As shown in Figure D-33, the green circle moves backward one level in the stacking order, behind the blue circle.

You used the Arrange commands to manipulate the stacking order of four objects.

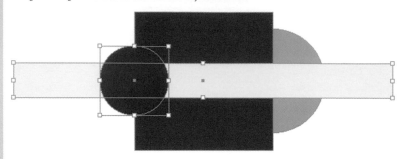

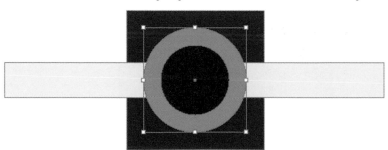

Layers palette with Layer 1

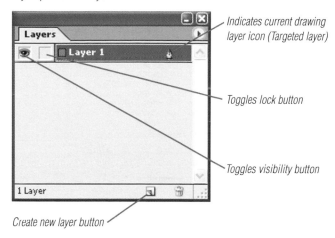

Indicates current drawing
layer icon (Targeted layer)

Toggles lock button

Toggles visibility button

Create new layer button

Create new layers in the Layers palette

1. Deselect all, click **Window** on the menu bar, then click **Layers**.

   As shown in Figure D-34, the Layers palette has one default layer named Layer 1.

   > **TIP** The default location for the Layers palette is to the right of the document window with the Layers, Pages, and Info tabs vertically aligned on the left of the palette.

2. Double-click **Layer 1** in the Layers palette.

   The Layer Options dialog box opens, which allows you to change settings for Layer 1, such as its name and selection color.

3. Type **Background** in the Name text box, then click **OK**.

4. Click the **Create new layer button** in the Layers palette, then double-click **Layer 2**.

5. Type **Circles** in the Name text box, click the **Color list arrow**, click **Orange**, then click **OK**.

6. Click the **Layers palette list arrow**, then click **New Layer**.

7. Type **Rectangles** in the Name text box, click the **Color list arrow**, click **Purple**, then click **OK**.

   Your Layers palette should resemble Figure D-35.

You renamed Layer 1, then created two new layers in the Layers palette.

Layers palette with three layers

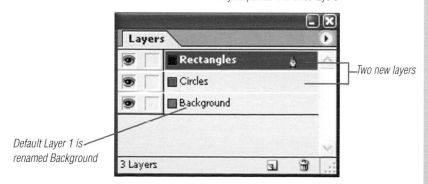

Two new layers

Default Layer 1 is
renamed Background

Position objects on layers

1. Press **[V]** to access the Selection Tool (if necessary), then click the **green circle**.

   As shown in Figure D-36, the Background layer is highlighted and the Indicates selected items button appears next to the Indicates current drawing layer icon.

2. Click and drag the Indicates selected items button up to the Circles layer.

   The green circle is moved to the Circles layer. The frame around the circle now appears orange, the selection color assigned to the Circles layer.

3. Select both the red square and the yellow rectangle, then drag the **Indicates selected items button** from the Background layer up to the Rectangles layer.

4. Click the **Toggles visibility button** 👁 on the Rectangles layer to hide that layer, then click 👁 on the Circles layer to hide that layer.

5. Click the **blue circle**, then drag the **Indicates selected items button** 🔲 from the Background layer up to the Circles layer.

   As shown in Figure D-37, you cannot move the circle to the Circles layer because it is hidden.

6. Press and hold **[Ctrl]** (Win) or ⌘ (Mac), then drag the **Indicates selected items button** 🔲 from the Background layer up to the Circles layer.

   The blue circle disappears because it is moved to the Circles layer, which is hidden.

   (continued)

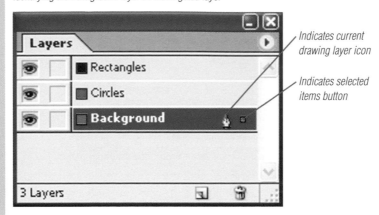

Indicates current drawing layer icon

Indicates selected items button

The selected object cannot be placed on a layer that is hidden

Layer not visible

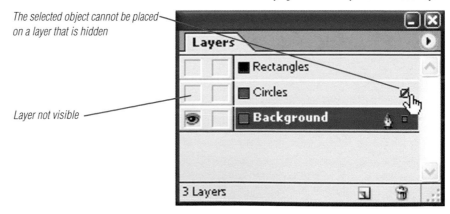

FIGURE D-38

Viewing a layered document

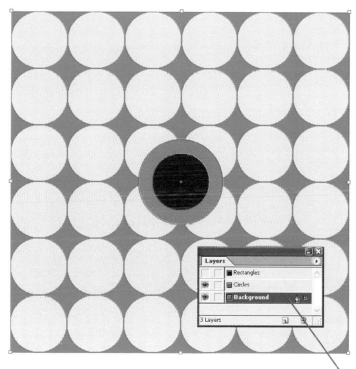

Circles pasted on Background layer

TIP Pressing and holding [Ctrl] (Win) or ⌘ (Mac) while you drag the Indicates selected items button allows you to place an object on a hidden or locked layer.

7. Click the **Background layer** in the Layers palette to target it, click the **Rectangle Tool** ▭, then draw a rectangle that is exactly the same size as the page.

   Because the Background layer was targeted in the Layers palette, the new object is positioned on the Background layer.

8. Click the **Fill button** in the Toolbox, click **Light Blue** in the Swatches palette, then remove any stroke if necessary.

9. Open ID D-4.indd, select all the objects on the page, click **Edit** on the menu bar, click **Copy**, then close ID D-4.indd.

10. Verify that the Background layer is still targeted in the Layers palette, click **Edit** on the menu bar, then click **Paste**.

    The objects are pasted onto the Background layer.

11. Click the **Toggles visibility button** 👁 on the Circles layer so that your Layers palette and page resemble Figure D-38.

You used the Layers palette to move selected objects from one layer to another. You targeted a layer, and then created a new object, which was added to that layer. You then pasted objects into a targeted layer.

Change the order of layers in the Layers palette

1. Deselect all, click the **Rectangles layer**, then click the **Toggles visibility button** ☐ in its off state in order to make the layer visible.

2. Using Figure D-39 as an example, drag the **Rectangles layer** down until you see a heavy black line below the Circles layer, then release your mouse.

   As shown in Figure D-40, because the Rectangles layer is now below the Circles layer, all the objects on the Rectangles layer are now beneath the objects on the Circles layer.

3. Click the **Selection Tool** ▶ , then click any of the light blue circles.

   The light blue circles are grouped, so when you click one, you select them all.

4. Click and drag the **Indicates selected items button** ▣ from the Background layer up to the Circles layer.

   Because it is the newest object on the Circles layer, the blue circles group is at the top of the stacking order on that layer.

5. Click **Object** on the menu bar, point to **Arrange**, then click **Send to Back**.

   As shown in Figure D-41, the blue circles group is sent to the back of the stacking order on the Circles layer. However, it is in front of the two rectangles, because their layer is beneath the Circles layer.

   (continued)

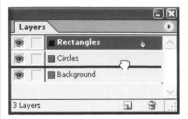

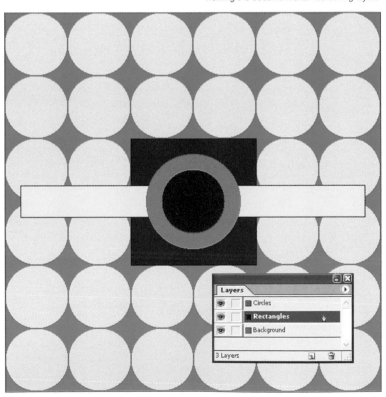

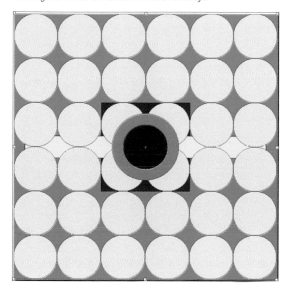

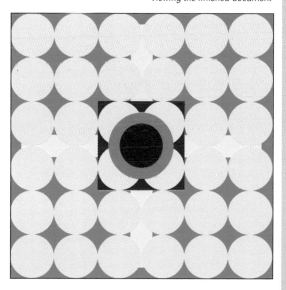

6. Click and drag the **Rectangles layer** down to the Create new layer button 🔳 in the Layers palette.

   A duplicate layer named Rectangles copy is created above the original Rectangles layer.

7. Press and hold **[Alt]** (Win) or **[option]** (Mac), then click the **Rectangles copy layer**.

   > TIP Press and hold [Alt] (Win) or [option] (Mac) when clicking a layer in the Layers palette to select all the objects on the layer.

8. Click the **center reference point** on the proxy in the Transform palette, type **90** in the Rotation Angle text box in the Transform palette, then press **[Enter]** (Win) or **[return]** (Mac).

9. Click outside the window to deselect all, press **[W]** to switch to Preview Mode, press **[V]** to access the Selection Tool, click the **red square**, click **Object** on the menu bar, point to **Arrange**, click **Bring to Front**, then deselect all so that your page resembles Figure D-42.

10. Save your work, then close Stack and Layer.

You changed the order of layers, noting the effect on the objects on the page. You also changed the stacking order of objects within layers. You duplicated a layer, and you learned a keyboard shortcut for selecting all the objects on a single layer.

WORK WITH GRAPHICS FRAMES

What You'll Do

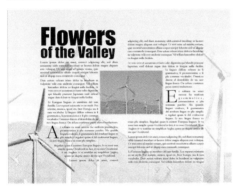

 In this lesson, you will create graphics frames, resize them, and manipulate graphics that you import into them.

Placing Graphics in a Document

The term **graphic** is pretty broad. In its most basic definition, a graphic is an element on the page that is not text. A simple square with a fill could be called a graphic. However, when you are talking about placing graphics in an InDesign document, the term graphic usually is referring to bitmap images or vector graphics. **Bitmap images** are images that consist of pixels created in a program, such as Adobe Photoshop. They can also be digital photos. Anything that has been scanned is a bitmap image. Vector graphics are usually illustrations created in and imported from drawing programs like Adobe Illustrator.

There are two essential methods for placing a graphic in a document. You can create a graphic placeholder frame using any of the three shape frame tools, shown in Figure D-43. Once you have created the frame and it is selected on the page, you use the Place command on the File menu to select the graphic you want to import into the document. The graphic will appear in the selected graphics frame.

You can also place a graphic without first creating a graphics frame. If you click the Place command and then select the graphic you want to import, you will see the loaded graphics icon when you float your cursor over the page. Click the loaded graphics icon on the page to place the graphic. The graphic will be placed on the page in a graphics frame whose top-left corner will be positioned at the location where you clicked the loaded graphics icon.

Which is the better method? It depends on what you want to do with the graphic. If the size and location of the graphics frame is important, it's probably better to create and position the frame first, then import the graphic and make it fit into the frame. If the size and location of the frame are negotiable, you might want to place the graphic anywhere in the layout and then modify its size and location.

Understanding the Difference Between the Graphics Frame and the Graphic

It is important that you understand that the graphics frame contains the graphic. Think of the graphics frame as a window through which you see the placed graphic. This understanding is important in cases where the graphics frame is smaller than the graphic that it contains. In this case, you can see only the areas of the graphic that can fit in the frame. The other areas of the graphic are still there, you just can't see them because they are outside of the frame.

Understanding the Difference Between the Selection Tool and the Direct Selection Tool

The discussion above is a clear signal that you must differentiate the graphics frame from the graphic itself. This differentiation is reflected in the Toolbox by the Selection Tool and the Direct Selection Tool. Specifically, the Selection Tool addresses the graphics frame while the Direct Selection Tool addresses the *contents* of the frame. Anything you want to do to the frame, you do with the Selection Tool selected. Anything you want to do to the contents—to the graphic itself—you do

with the Direct Selection Tool selected. This concept is the key to manipulating graphics within a graphics frame.

Figure D-44 shows a selected graphics frame which contains a placed graphic. Note that the frame was selected with the Selection Tool. The Transform palette shows the X and Y locations of the frame and the width and height of the frame.

Figure D-45 shows the same object, but this time it has been selected with the Direct Selection Tool, which is selected in the Toolbox. Note that the information in the Transform palette now refers to the graphic

FIGURE D-43

Three shape tools for creating graphics frames

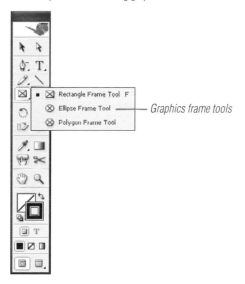

Graphics frame tools

FIGURE D-44

Selecting a graphics frame with the Selection Tool

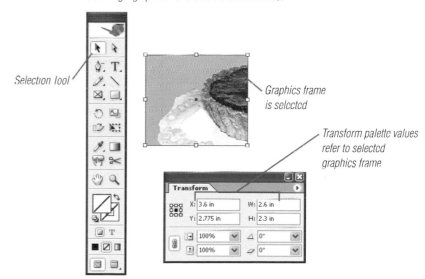

Selection tool

Graphics frame is selected

Transform palette values refer to selected graphics frame

itself, not the frame that contains it. Note too that the selection itself appears differently. The bright blue frame that is selected is called the bounding box. The **bounding box**—always rectangular—is the frame that defines the horizontal and vertical dimensions of the graphic. Finally note that even though you can see the entire bounding box, there are parts of the graphic that you can't see. That's because the graphic is being cropped by the graphics frame.

Hang on. There's a lot of information coming at you all at once here. Let's summarize the terminology and concepts. The graphics frame contains the graphic. The graphics frame determines how the graphic is cropped. When you click a graphic with the Selection Tool, the graphics frame is selected and the Transform palette displays the physical characteristics of the graphics frame.

When you click a graphic with the Direct Selection Tool, the graphic itself is selected. This selection is indicated by showing you the graphic's bounding box. The bounding box and the graphics frame are completely independent of one another.

They can be, and often are, different sizes. When you click the graphic with the Direct Selection Tool, the Transform palette describes the physical characteristics of the graphic itself.

QUICK**TIP**

When you click a graphic with the Direct Selection Tool, a small plus sign appears beside the X and Y values in the Transform palette, indicating that the X and Y locations refer to the graphic *within* the graphics frame.

FIGURE D-45

Selecting a graphic with the Direct Selection Tool

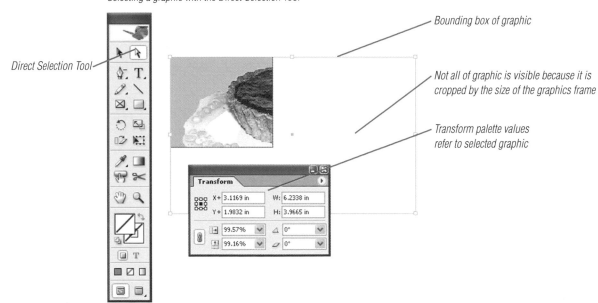

Direct Selection Tool

Bounding box of graphic

Not all of graphic is visible because it is cropped by the size of the graphics frame

Transform palette values refer to selected graphic

Working with Frames

Moving a Graphic Within a Graphics Frame

Once you understand that the Direct Selection Tool selects the graphic itself, it is easy to move a graphic within the graphics frame. When you click the graphic with the Direct Selection Tool, a hand icon appears, as shown in Figure D-46. If you drag the hand icon, you move the graphic within the frame. But wait... there's a better way to do it. Press and hold the hand icon until it turns into a black arrow, then drag the black arrow to move the graphic. When you do so, you see a ghosted image of the areas of the graphic that are outside the graphics frame, as shown in Figure D-47. The ghosted image is referred to as a **dynamic preview**.

Once you release your mouse, the graphic will be repositioned within the frame. Remember, though, that regardless of where you move the graphic within the frame, the frame crops the graphic.

Resizing a Graphic

When you select a graphic with the Direct Selection Tool, you can then resize the graphic within the frame. Changes that you make to the size of the graphic do not affect the size of the graphics frame.

One easy way to **scale**, or resize a graphic is to use the Transform palette. With the graphic selected, change the Scale X Percentage and the Scale Y Percentage values in the Transform palette, as shown in Figure D-48, to reduce or enlarge the graphic.

You can also use the Transform/Scale command on the Object menu to scale the graphic. Remember, when the graphic is selected with the Direct Selection Tool, only the graphic will be scaled when you use this command.

QUICKTIP

You can resize a graphics frame and the graphic simultaneously by pressing and holding [Ctrl][Shift] (Win) or [⌘][Shift] (Mac) while dragging the graphics frame bounding box handle.

QUICKTIP

When you select a graphics frame with the Selection Tool then resize the graphics frame using the Width and Height text boxes in the Transform palette, the graphic is resized with the frame.

FIGURE D-46
Moving the graphic within the graphics frame

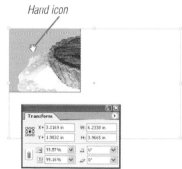

Hand icon

FIGURE D-47
Viewing the dynamic preview

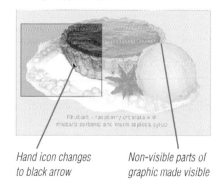

Hand icon changes to black arrow

Non-visible parts of graphic made visible

FIGURE D-48
Scaling a graphic using the Transform palette

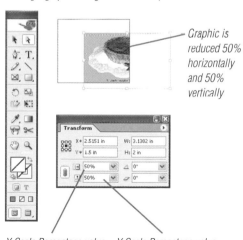

Graphic is reduced 50% horizontally and 50% vertically

X Scale Percentage value   Y Scale Percentage value

Using the Fitting Commands

"There must be an easier way to resize a graphic," you are thinking. You're right! While it's not difficult to select a graphic with the Direct Selection Tool and then scale it in the Transform palette, there are a lot of steps in the process.

For the quick solution, you can use the Fitting commands, located on the Object menu. The Fitting commands refer to the graphic as the content. The Fit Content to Frame command scales the content to fit the frame, and the Fit Frame to Content command scales the frame to fit the content. The Center Content command centers the graphic within the frame.

When you click the Fit Content to Frame command, the content is often distorted to fit the frame. For example, let's say that your content is a two inch square, and it's within a rectangular graphics frame. Applying the Fit Content to Frame command will distort the square's width to fit the full width of the rectangular frame, as shown in Figure D-49. You can easily restore the graphic to its normal proportions by clicking the Fit Content Proportionally command, which is the fourth Fitting command on the Object menu.

Wrapping Text Around an Imported Photoshop Graphic Saved with a Named Clipping Path

In Chapter C, you learned how to use the Text Wrap palette to wrap text around a bounding box using the Wrap around bounding box button. You can also wrap text around a graphic inside a graphics frame, as shown in Figure D-50.

The Text Wrap palette offers a number of methods for doing so. In this chapter, you will focus on wrapping text around an image that was saved with a named clipping path in Photoshop. Figure D-51 shows a Photoshop image with a clipping path drawn around a man. A **clipping path** is a graphic that you draw in Photoshop that outlines the areas of the image that you want to show when the file is placed in a layout program like InDesign. When you save the Photoshop file, you can name the clipping path and save it with the file.

FIGURE D-49
Using the Fit Content to Frame command can distort a graphic

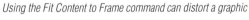
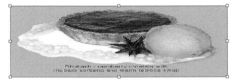

FIGURE D-50
Wrapping text around a graphic

The text is able to enter the graphics frame to wrap around the picture

FIGURE D-51
A Photoshop image with a clipping path

Clipping path created in Photoshop

When you place a graphic that has a named clipping path saved with it into your layout, InDesign is able to recognize the clipping path. With the graphic selected, click the Wrap around object shape button in the Text Wrap palette, click the Type list arrow in the Contour Options section of the palette, and then choose Photoshop Path, as shown in Figure D-52. When you do so, the Path menu will list all the paths that were saved with the graphic file (usually, you will save only one path with a file).

Choose the path that you want to use for the text wrap.

Remember, in every case, you can always manually adjust the resulting text wrap boundary. Though the clipping path is created in Photoshop, the text wrap itself is created in InDesign—and it is editable. As shown in Figure D-53, you can relocate the path's anchor points using the Direct Selection Tool. You can also use the Add Anchor Point and Delete Anchor Point

Tools to add or delete points to the path as you find necessary. Click the Add Anchor Point Tool anywhere on the path to add a new point, which gives you further control for manipulating the path. Click any anchor point with the Delete Anchor Point Tool to remove it. Changing the shape of the path changes how text wraps around the path.

FIGURE D-52

Choosing the Wrap around object shape button

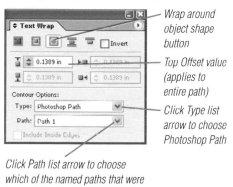

Wrap around object shape button

Top Offset value (applies to entire path)

Click Type list arrow to choose Photoshop Path

Click Path list arrow to choose which of the named paths that were saved with the Photoshop file that you want to use

FIGURE D-53

Manipulating the text wrap path

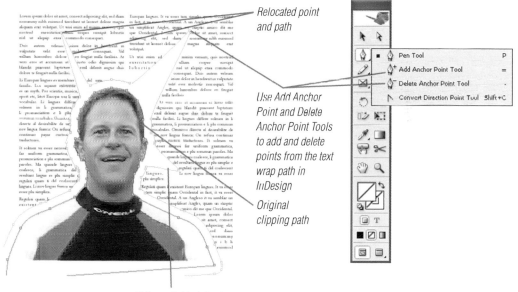

Relocated point and path

Use Add Anchor Point and Delete Anchor Point Tools to add and delete points from the text wrap path in InDesign

Original clipping path

Path created in InDesign

Place graphics in a document

1. Open ID D-5.indd, click **Fix Links Automatically**, click **No** in the next warning dialog box, then save it as **Flowers**.

2. In the Layers palette, click the **Toggles lock button** ☐ on the Text layer to lock the Text layer, as shown in Figure D-54.

   TIP When a layer is locked, the contents of the layer cannot be modified; this is a smart way to protect the contents of the layer from unwanted changes.

3. Click the **Background layer** to target it, click the **Rectangle Frame Tool** ⊠ , then draw a graphics frame in the center of the page that is approximately the size shown in Figure D-55. The bounding box of the graphics frame is orange because orange is the selection color applied to the Background layer.

4. Click **File** on the menu bar, click **Place**, navigate to the drive and folder where your Chapter D Data Files are stored, then double-click **Windmills Ghost.psd**. Because the frame was selected, the graphic is placed automatically into the frame, as shown in Figure D-56.

5. Click the **Selection Tool** ▶ , click anywhere to deselect the frame, click the **Toggles visibility button** 👁 on the Background layer to hide it, then click the **Images layer** to target it in the Layers palette.

6. Click **File** on the menu bar, click **Place**, navigate to the drive and folder where your Chapter D Data Files are stored, click **Windmills Color.psd**, then click **Open**.

   TIP You can also access the Place command by pressing [Ctrl][D] (Win) or ⌘[D] (Mac).

(continued)

FIGURE D-54
Locking the Text layer

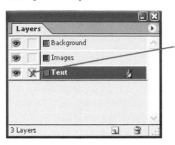

Toggles lock button

FIGURE D-55
Drawing a graphics frame

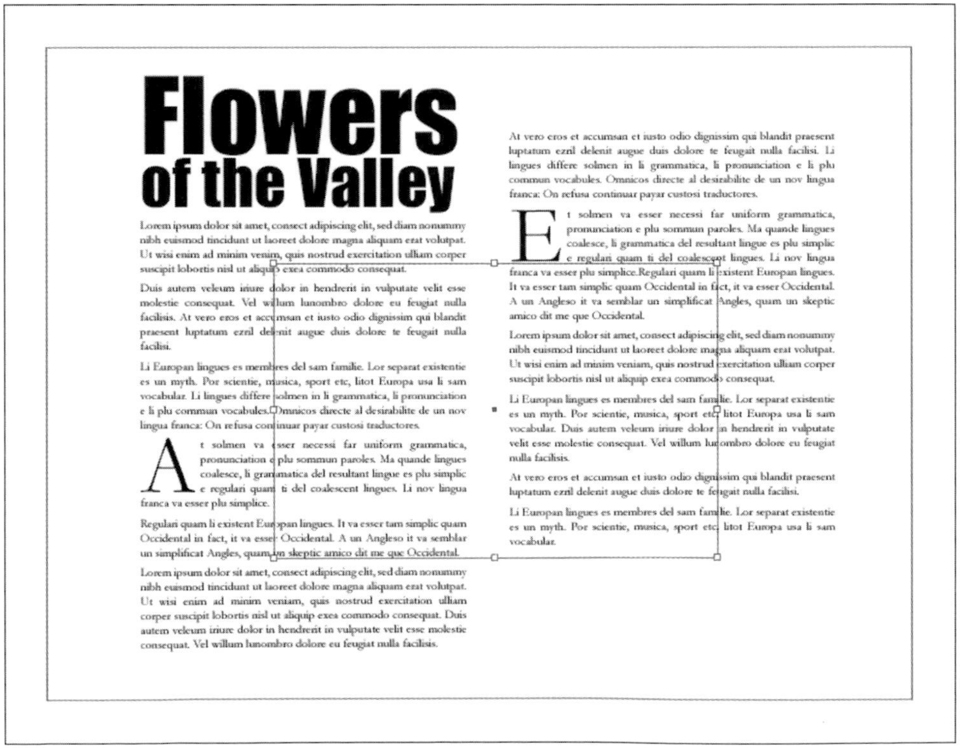

FIGURE D-56
Viewing the placed graphic

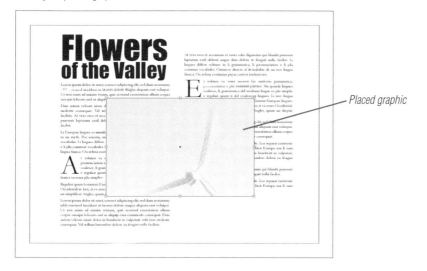

Placed graphic

FIGURE D-57
Viewing the graphic placed with the loaded graphics icon

Top-left corner of placed graphic located at same spot where loaded graphics icon was clicked

7. Position your cursor over the document.

   The cursor changes to the loaded graphics icon.

8. Click the **loaded graphics icon** on the F in the word Flowers.

   As shown in Figure D-57, the graphic is placed in a new graphics frame whose top-left corner is located where the loaded graphics icon was clicked.

You imported two graphics using two subtly different methods. You created a graphics frame, and then used the Place command to place a graphic in that frame. Then, you used the Place command to load a graphic file, and finally clicked the loaded graphics icon to create a new frame for the new graphic.

Move a graphic in a graphics frame

1. Hide the Images layer, show the Background layer, click the **Selection Tool**, then click the **Windmills Ghost.psd graphic**.

2. Click the **top-left reference point** on the proxy in the Transform palette.

3. Click the **Direct Selection Tool**, position the tool over the graphic, then click the graphic.

   When the Direct Selection Tool is over the graphic, the cursor changes to a hand icon.

4. Note the width and height of the graphic, as listed in the Transform palette.

   The graphic is substantially larger than the frame that contains it, thus there are many areas of the graphic outside the frame that are not visible through the frame.

(continued)

5. Press and hold the **hand icon** on the graphic until the hand icon changes to a black arrow, then drag inside the graphics frame, releasing your mouse when the windmill is centered in the frame, as shown in Figure D-58.

   The graphic moves within the frame, but the frame itself does not move. Note that the blue bounding box, now visible, is the bounding box for the graphic within the frame.

6. Click the **Selection Tool** , then click the graphic.

   The orange graphics frame appears and the blue bounding box of the graphic disappears. Note that the values in the Transform palette are again specific to the frame only.

7. Click and drag the **top-left selection handle** of the graphics frame so that it is aligned with the top-left corner of the document page.

   As shown in Figure D-59, the graphic within the frame does not change size or location.

8. Drag the **bottom-right corner** of the graphics frame so that it is aligned with the bottom-right corner of the document page.

   As the frame is enlarged, more of the graphic within the frame is visible.

9. Click the **Direct Selection Tool** , click the graphic, type **0** in the X+ text box in the Transform palette, type **0** in the Y+ text box, then press **[Enter]** (Win) or **[return]** (Mac).

   As shown in Figure D-60, the top-left corner of the graphic is aligned with the top-left corner of the frame.

You used the Direct Selection Tool and X+ and Y+ values in the Transform palette to move a graphic within a graphics frame.

FIGURE D-58
Viewing the graphic as it is moved in the frame

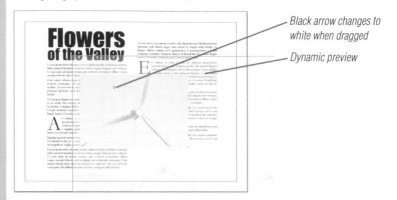

Black arrow changes to white when dragged

Dynamic preview

FIGURE D-59
Resizing the graphics frame

Top-left corner of bounding box

Resized frame

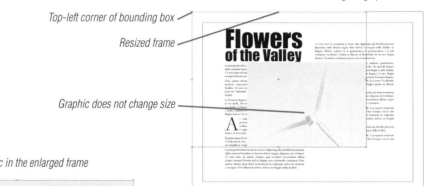

Graphic does not change size

FIGURE D-60
Viewing the entire graphic in the enlarged frame

Working with Frames

FIGURE D-61

Scaling a graphic

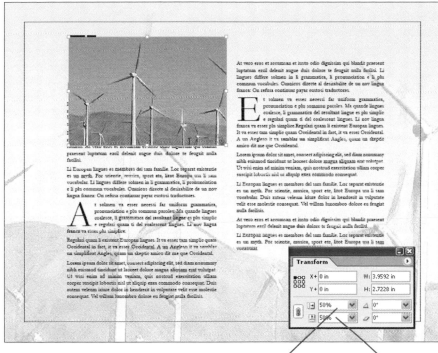

Scale X Percentage text box   Scale Y Percentage text box

1. Drag the **Background layer** below the Text layer in the Layers palette, then show the Images layer.

2. Press **[A]** to access the Direct Selection Tool, then click the **Windmills Color.psd graphic**.

3. Type **50** in the Scale X Percentage text box in the Transform palette, press **[Tab]**, type **50** in the Scale Y Percentage text box, then press **[Enter]** (Win) or **[return]** (Mac).

   The graphic is scaled 50% horizontally and 50% vertically, as shown in Figure D-61.

4. Press **[V]** to access the Selection Tool, then click the **Windmills Color.psd graphic**.

   The graphics frame was not resized with the graphic.

5. Click **Object** on the menu bar, point to **Fitting**, then click **Fit Frame to Content**.

6. Click the **top-left reference point** on the proxy in the Transform palette, then click the **Constrain proportions for scaling button** in the Transform palette.

7. With the frame still selected, type **4.5** in the X Location text box, type **3** in the Y Location text box, type **3.32** in the Width text box, type **2.125** in the Height text box, then press **[Enter]** (Win) or **[return]** (Mac).

(continued)

8. Press **[A]** to access the Direct Selection Tool, click the graphic, then note the Scale X Percentage and Scale Y Percentage text boxes in the Transform palette.

The graphic was scaled with the frame—it is no longer at 50% of its original size; the graphic has been distorted—its X scale percentage is larger than its Y scale percentage, as shown in Figure D-62.

TIP When you resize a graphics frame using the Width and Height text boxes in the Transform palette, the graphic is resized with the frame.

9. Click **Object** on the menu bar, point to **Fitting**, then click **Fit Content Proportionally**.

The Transform palette now shows that the X and Y scale percentages are the same.

10. Press **[V]**, then click the graphic.

11. Click **Object** on the menu bar, point to **Fitting**, then click **Fit Frame to Content**.

As shown in Figure D-63, the right edge of the frame moves left to fit to the right edge of the graphic.

You scaled a graphic using the Transform palette, noting that the graphics frame did not change with the scale. You then scaled the graphics frame with the Transform palette, noting that the graphic itself was also scaled—and distorted. Lastly, you used the Fitting command to fit the graphic proportionally to the new frame size.

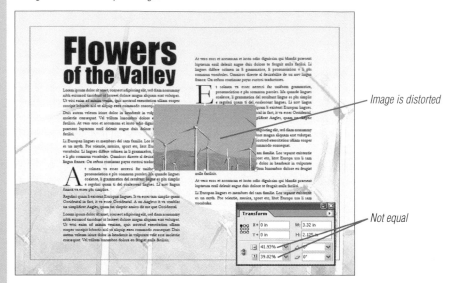

— Image is distorted

— Not equal

Wrapping text around a frame's bounding box

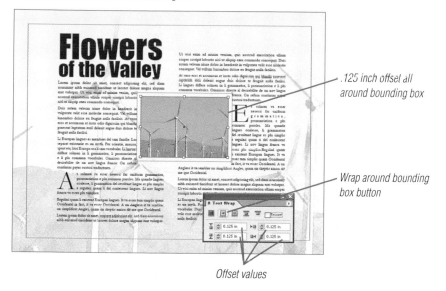

.125 inch offset all
around bounding box

Wrap around bounding
box button

Offset values

FIGURE D-65

Wrapping text around the graphic

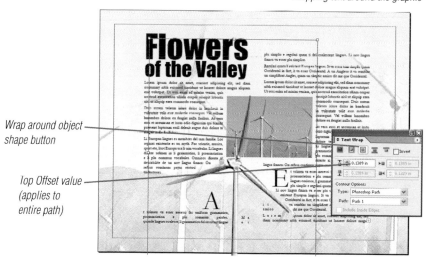

Wrap around object
shape button

Top Offset value
(applies to
entire path)

Wrap text around a graphic

1. Verify that the Selection Tool is selected, click the graphic, click the **Wrap around bounding box button** ▦ in the Text Wrap palette, type **.125** in all four of the Offset text boxes in the Text Wrap palette, then press **[Enter]** (Win) or **[return]** (Mac).

    Your page and Text Wrap palette should resemble Figure D-64.

2. Click anywhere to deselect all, press **[Ctrl][D]** (Win) or ⌘**[D]** (Mac), navigate to the drive and folder where your Chapter D Data Files are stored, then double-click **Windmills Silhouette.psd**.

3. Click the **loaded graphics icon** 🏿 on the F in the word Flowers.

    Windmills Silhouette.psd was saved with a clipping path named "Path 1" in Photoshop.

4. Click the **Wrap around object shape button** ▦ in the Text Wrap palette, click the **Type list arrow**, click **Photoshop Path**, then note that Path 1 is automatically listed in the Path text box.

    As shown in Figure D-65, the text wraps around the graphic's shape. The Text Wrap palette specifies a default offset of .1389 inches for the wrap.

    (continued)

5. Type **-1.79** in the X Location text box in the Transform palette, type **1.875** in the Y Location text box, then press **[Enter]** (Win) or **[return]** (Mac).

As shown in Figure D-66, because of the shape of the path around the graphic, one word appears in an odd position near the graphic.

6. Click the **Direct Selection Tool** , then click the graphic.

7. Click the **Delete Anchor Point Tool** , then click the anchor point circled in Figure D-67.

TIP The Delete Anchor Point Tool is hidden under the Pen Tool .

The point is deleted and the reshaped path leaves no room for the stray word.

(continued)

Noting a minor problem with the wrap

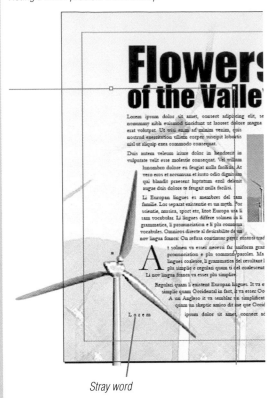

Stray word

Identifying the point to be deleted

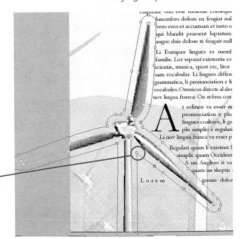

Click with Delete Anchor Point Tool

Working with Frames

FIGURE D-68

Resizing the graphics frame

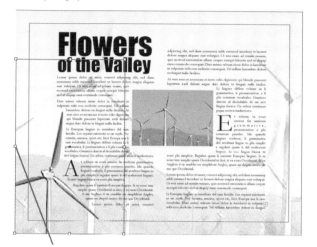

Drag handle right

FIGURE D-69

Viewing the completed document

8. Click the **Selection Tool** ➤, click the graphic, drag the **left-middle handle** of the bounding box to the right so that it abuts the left edge of the page, then drag the **bottom-middle handle** of the bounding box up so that it abuts the bottom of the page, as shown in Figure D-68.

   TIP You may need to reduce the page view to see the bottom handles on the bounding box.

9. Click the **pasteboard** to deselect the frame, press **[W]** to change to Preview Mode, then compare your work to Figure D-69.

10. Save your work, then close Flowers.

WORK WITH TEXT FRAMES

What You'll Do

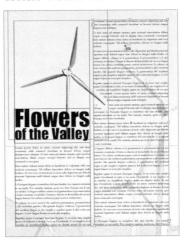

 In this lesson, you will explore options for autoflowing text through a document. You will also learn how to add column breaks to text.

Semi-Autoflowing Text

In Chapter C, you learned how to thread text manually—to make it flow from text frame to text frame. When you click the out port of one text frame with the Selection Tool, your cursor changes to the loaded text icon. When you click the loaded text icon in another text frame, text flows from the first frame to the second frame—and the cursor automatically changes back to the Selection Tool. That's great, but what if you wanted to keep manually threading text? Would you need to repeat the process over and over again?

This is where **semi-autoflowing** text comes in. When you are ready to click the loaded text icon in a text frame where you want text to flow, press and hold [Alt] (Win) or [option] (Mac) and then click the text frame. Text will flow into the text frame, but the loaded text icon will remain active—it will not automatically revert back to the Selection Tool. You can then thread text into another text frame. In a nutshell, semi-autoflowing text is a method for manually threading text through multiple frames.

Autoflowing Text

You can also **autoflow** text, which is a powerful option for quickly adding text to your document. Let's say that you create a six-page document and you specify that each page has three columns. When you create the document, the pages have no text frames on them—they're just blank, with columns and margin guides. To autoflow text into the document, you click the Place command and choose the text document that you want to import. Once you choose the document, your cursor changes to the loaded text icon. If you press and hold [Shift], the loaded text icon becomes the autoflow loaded text icon. When you click the autoflow loaded text icon in a column, InDesign creates text frames within column guides on that page and all subsequent pages, and flows the text into those frames.

Because you specified that each page has three columns when you created the document, InDesign will create three text frames in the columns on every page for the text to flow to. Figure D-70 shows a page with three text frames created by autoflowing text. Note that if you autoflow more text than the document can create, InDesign will add as many pages as necessary to autoflow all of the text. Note also that, if your document pages contain objects such as graphics, the text frames added by the autoflow will be positioned in front of the graphics already on the page.

As you may imagine, autoflowing text is a powerful option, but don't be intimidated by it. The text frames that are generated are all editable. You can resize them or delete them. Nevertheless, you should take a few moments to practice autoflowing text to get the hang of it. Like learning how to ride a bicycle, you can read about it all you want, but actually doing it is where the learning happens.

Inserting a Column Break

When you are working with text in columns, you will often want to move text from the bottom of one column to the top of the next. You do this by inserting a column break. A **column break** is a typographic command that forces text to the next column. The Column Break command is located within the Insert Break Character command on the Type menu.

FIGURE D-70

Three text frames created in columns by autoflowing text

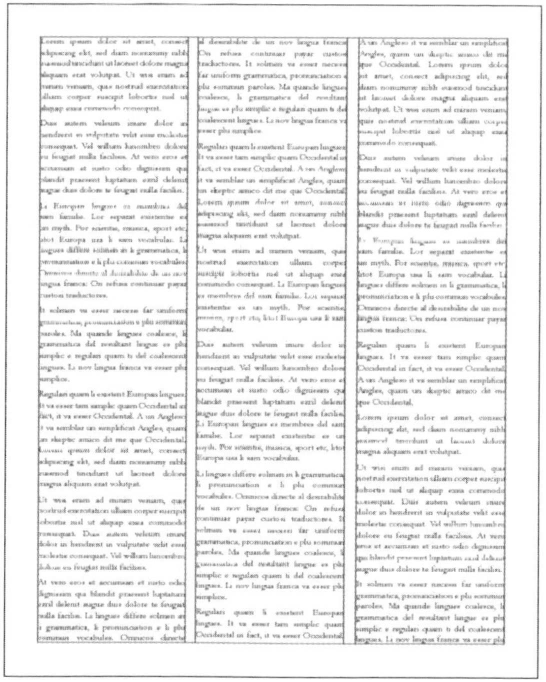

Using the Story Editor

InDesign CS has a great new feature called the Story Editor that makes it easier to edit text in complex documents. Imagine that you are doing a layout for a single magazine article. The text for the article is flowed through numerous text frames across 12 pages. Now imagine that you want to edit the text—maybe you want to proofread it or spell check it. Editing the text within the layout might be difficult— you'd have to scroll from page to page. Instead, you could use the Edit in Story Editor command on the Edit menu. This opens a new window, which contains all the text in a single file—just like a word processing document. Any changes that you make in the Story Editor window will be immediately updated to the text in the layout. It's a great feature!

In Figure D-71, the headline near the bottom of the first column would be better positioned at the top of the next column. By inserting a column break, you do exactly that, as shown in Figure D-72.

Inserting a "Continued on page..." Notation

When threading text manually or auto-flowing text, you will get to a point where text has filled all the text frames on the page and continues to another page. Usually, the text continues onto the next page—but not always. In many cases, the next page will be reserved for pictures or other publication elements, such as tables or graphs. When the reader gets to the bottom of the page of text, they need to know on which page the text is continued.

You can insert a "Continued on page..." notation to let the reader know where to go to continue reading.

If you've ever read a magazine or newspaper article, you are familiar with "Continued on page..." notations. In InDesign, a page continuation is formatted as a special character. Simply create a text frame, then type the words "Continued on page X." Select the X, then apply the Next Page Number command. The X changes to the page number of the page that contains the text frame that the text flows into. If for any reason you move pages within the Pages palette and page numbers change, the Next Page Number character will automatically update to show the page number where the text continues.

The Next Page Number command is located within the Insert Special Character command on the Type menu.

There's one important point you need to note when creating a "Continued on page..." notation. By definition, body copy will reach the end of a text frame on a given page and be continued on another page. At the end of the text frame on the first page, you will need to create a text frame to contain the "Continued on page..." notation. In order for the notation to work—for it to list the page where the text continues—the top edge of the text frame that contains the notation must be touching the frame that contains the body copy that is to be continued.

FIGURE D-71
Viewing text that needs a column break

FIGURE D-72
Viewing text after inserting a column break

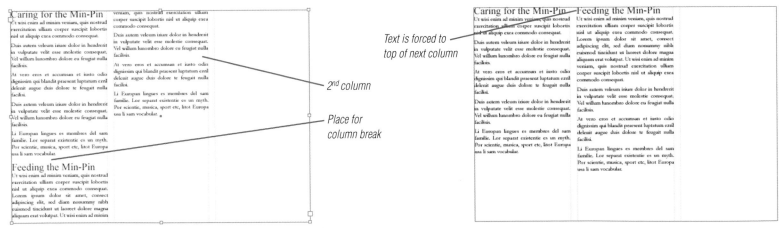

Text is forced to top of next column

2nd column

Place for column break

Creating a text frame using the loaded text icon

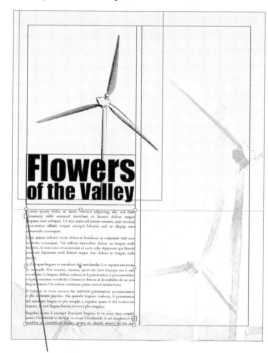

*Aligned with intersection
of margin and guide*

FIGURE D-74
Flowing text with the semi-autoflow loaded text icon

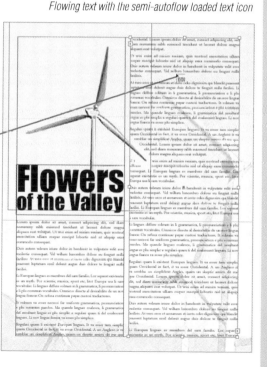

*Cursor remains
as loaded text
icon after text has
been flowed*

Autoflow text

1. Open ID D-6.indd, save it as **Autoflow**, then look at each page in the document.

    Other than the text frame that holds the headline on page 1, there are no text frames in the document.

2. Click the **Selection Tool** ▸, double-click the **page 1 icon** in the Pages palette, click **File** on the menu bar, click **Place**, navigate to the drive and folder where your Chapter D Data Files are stored, then double-click **Windmill text.doc**.

    The cursor changes to the loaded text icon.

3. Drag a text frame in the position shown in Figure D-73.

    Note that once you have drawn the frame, the loaded text icon automatically changes back to the Selection Tool.

4. Click the **out port** of the text frame, then position the loaded text icon over the right column on the page.

5. Press and hold **[Alt]** (Win) or **[option]** (Mac) so that your cursor changes to the semi-autoflow loaded text icon.

6. Still pressing and holding **[Alt]** (Win) or **[option]** (Mac), click the **top-left corner** of the right column, so that the text flows into the frame.

    Because you used the semi-autoflow loaded text icon, the cursor remains as a loaded text icon and does not revert back to the Selection Tool, as shown in Figure D-74.

(continued)

7. Double-click the **page 2 icon**, then click the **top-left corner** of the left column on the page.

   A new frame is created and text flows into the left column.

8. Click the **out port** of the new text frame on page 2, then position your cursor over the right column on page 2.

9. Press and hold **[Shift]**, note the change to the loaded text icon, then click the **top-left corner** of the second column.

   InDesign creates text frames within column guides on all subsequent pages. InDesign has added new pages to the document to accommodate the autoflow.

   You placed text by clicking and dragging the loaded text icon to create a new text frame. You flowed text using the semi-autoflow loaded text icon and the autoflow loaded text icon.

Reflow text

1. Double-click the **page 4 icon** in the Pages palette, then create a horizontal guide at 5.875 in.

2. Click the **left text frame** to select it, drag the **bottom-middle handle** of the text frame's bounding box up until it snaps to the guide, then do the same to the right text frame, so that your page resembles Figure D-75.

   The text is reflowed in the document.

3. Double-click the numbers **2-3** in the Pages palette to center the spread in the document window, click **View** on the menu bar, click **Show Text Threads**, then click the **right text frame** on page 2.

   (continued)

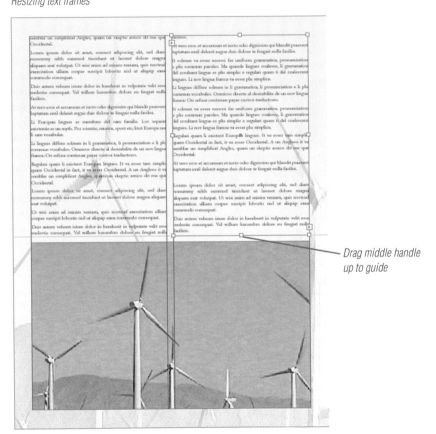

Drag middle handle up to guide

FIGURE D-76

Flowing text after deleting a text frame

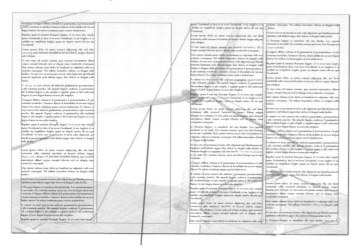

Text flow continues
between remaining
text frames

FIGURE D-77

Threading text to a new text frame

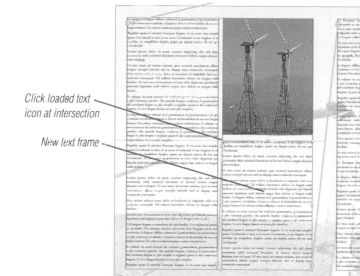

Click loaded text
icon at intersection

New text frame

4. With the right frame on page 2 still selected, press **[Delete]** (Win) or **[delete]** (Mac), then click the **text frame** remaining on page 2.

   As shown in Figure D-76, the text is reflowed from the second text frame on page 2 to the first text frame on page 3.

5. Press **[Ctrl][D]**(Win) or ⌘**[D]** (Mac), navigate to the drive and folder where your Chapter D Data Files are stored, then double-click **2 Windmills.psd**.

6. Click the **top-left corner** of the right column on page 2.

7. Create a horizontal guide at 5.375 in.

8. Click the **text frame** on page 2, then click the **out port**.

9. Click the intersection between the guide you created and the left edge of the right column, beneath the graphic.

   As shown in Figure D-77, text is now threaded through the new text frame.

You resized two text frames, noting that text was reflowed through the document. You deleted a text frame, then created a text frame, noting that text continued to flow through the document.

Add a column break

1. Double-click the **page 5 icon** in the Pages palette, then delete the two text frames on page 5.

2. Click **Layout** on the menu bar, click **Margins and Columns**, change the number of columns to 3, then click **OK**.

(continued)

3. Press **[Ctrl][D]**(Win) or **⌘[D]** (Mac), navigate to the drive and folder where your Chapter D Data Files are stored, then double-click **Sidebar Copy.doc**.

4. Drag the loaded text icon to create a text frame, as shown in Figure D-78.

5. Click **Object** on the menu bar, click **Text Frame Options**, change the number of columns to 3, then click **OK**.

6. Click the **Type Tool** T., then click the cursor before the W in Windmill Speeds.

7. Click **Type** on the menu bar, point to **Insert Break Character**, then click **Column Break**.

   The Windmill Speeds text is forced into the second column.

8. Click before the W in Windmill Productivity, click **Type** on the menu bar, point to **Insert Break Character**, then click **Column Break**.

   Your page should resemble Figure D-79.

You deleted two text frames on a page, then changed the number of columns on that page. You then placed text, formatted the text frame to have three columns, and finally used the Column Break command to create two new column breaks.

Creating a text frame with the loaded text icon

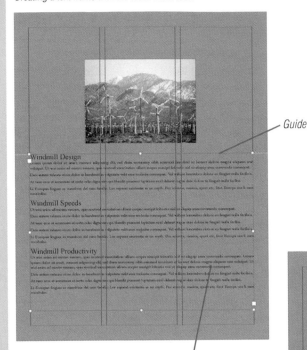

Guide

Text frame

Viewing the text frame with column breaks

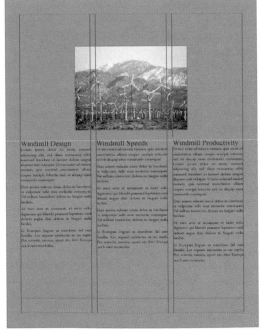

Working with Frames

FIGURE D-80

Creating a text frame for the page continuation notation

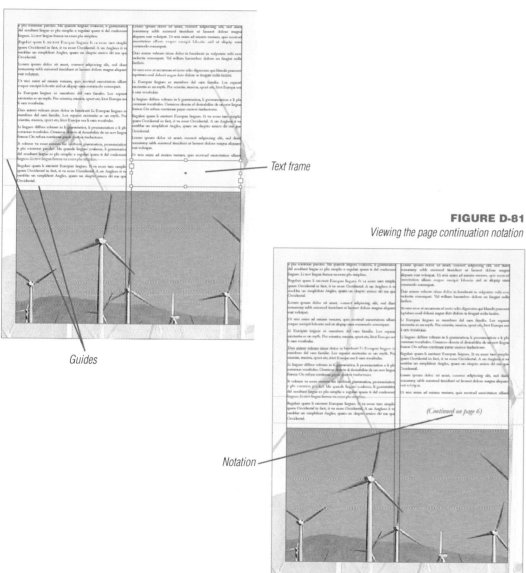

Text frame

Guides

FIGURE D-81

Viewing the page continuation notation

Notation

(Continued on page 6)

Insert a page continuation notation

1. Double-click the **page 4 icon** in the Pages palette, then create a horizontal guide at 5 in.

2. Click the **Selection Tool** ▶, click the text frame in the right column, then drag the bottom middle bounding box handle up until it snaps to the guide at 5 in.

3. Click the **Type Tool** T, then create a text frame between the two guides, as shown in Figure D-80.

   The two text frames both touch each other at the guide.

4. Click **Object** on the menu bar, click **Text Frame Options**, change the vertical justification to Center, then click **OK**.

5. Click inside the new text box, type **(Continued on Page X)**, click anywhere within the word Page, show the Paragraph Styles palette, then click the style named **Continued**.

6. Select the letter **X**, click **Type** on the menu bar, point to **Insert Special Character**, then click **Next Page Number**.

   The text now reads (Continued on Page 6), as shown in Figure D-81.

7. Click the **Selection Tool** ▶, click the **text frame** above the "Continued" text frame, then verify that the text does indeed continue on page 6.

8. Save your work, then close Autoflow.

You inserted a page continuation notation in the document.

Align and distribute objects on a page.

1. Open ID D-7.indd, then save it as **Dog Days**.
2. Click the Type Tool, then drag a text frame that fills the left column on the page.
3. Click the Selection Tool, press and hold [Shift][Alt] (Win) or [Shift][option] (Mac), then drag a copy of the text frame and position it in line with the right column.
4. Click the Rectangle Frame Tool, click anywhere on the page, type **1.5** in both the Width and Height text boxes, then click OK.
5. Click the top-left handle on the proxy in the Transform palette, type **0** in the X Location text box, type **0** in the Y Location text box, then press [Enter] (Win) or [return] (Mac).
6. Verify that the frame has no fill and no stroke.
7. Click Edit on the menu bar, click Step and Repeat, type **1** in the Repeat Count text box, type **9.5** in the Horizontal Offset text box, type **0** in the Vertical Offset text box, then click OK.
8. Select both graphics frames, click Edit on the menu bar, click Step and Repeat, type **1** in the Repeat Count text box, type **0** in the Horizontal Offset text box, type **7** in the Vertical Offset text box, then click OK.

9. Click the Rectangle Frame Tool, click anywhere in the left column, type **3** in both the Width and Height text boxes, click OK, then verify that the frame has no fill or stroke.
10. Click the Selection Tool, press and hold [Shift], click the top-left graphics frame, then click the top-right graphics frame so that three frames are selected.

FIGURE D-82
Completed Skills Review, Part 1

11. In the Align palette, click the Distribute horizontal centers button.
12. Deselect all, select the top-left and bottom-left graphics frames, select the 3" x 3" frame, click the Distribute vertical centers button, then compare your page to Figure D-82.

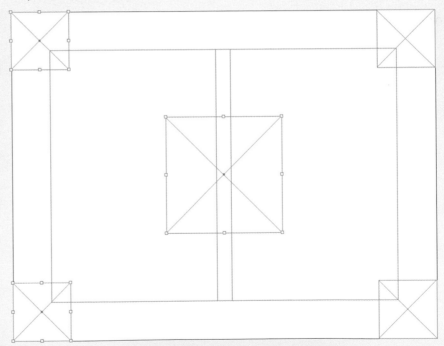

Stack and layer objects.

1. Click Window on the menu bar, then click Layers to show the Layers palette.
2. Double-click Layer 1, type **Background Graphic** in the Name text box, then click OK.
3. Click the Create new layer button in the Layers palette, double-click the new layer, type **Dog Pics** in the Name text box, then click OK.
4. Click the palette list arrow, click New Layer, type **Body Copy** in the Name text box, then click OK.
5. Click the Selection Tool, select the five graphics frames, then drag the Indicates selected items button from the Background Graphic layer up to the Dog Pics layer.
6. Select the two text frames, then drag the Indicates selected items button from the Background Graphic layer up to the Body Copy layer.
7. Verify that the Body Copy layer is targeted, select only the left text frame, click File on the menu bar, click Place, navigate to drive and folder where your Chapter D Data Files are stored, then double-click Skills Text.doc.
8. Select all the text, then click the Body Format style in the Paragraph Styles palette. (*Hint*: Click OK in the dialog box that follows if necessary).
9. Click the Selection Tool, click the out port of the left text frame, then click the loaded text icon anywhere in the right text frame.
10. In the Layers palette, drag the Body Copy layer down below the Dog Pics layer.
11. Save your work.

Work with graphics frames.

1. Click the Selection Tool, select the top-left graphics frame, press [Ctrl][D] (Win) or ⌘[D] (Mac), navigate to the drive and folder where your Chapter D Data Files are stored, then double-click Red 1.psd.
2. Select the top-right graphics frame, press [Ctrl][D] (Win) or ⌘[D] (Mac), navigate to the drive and folder where your Chapter D Data Files are stored, then double-click Black 1.psd.
3. Select the bottom-left graphics frame, press [Ctrl][D] (Win) or ⌘[D] (Mac), navigate to the drive and folder where your Chapter D Data Files are stored, then double-click Red 2.psd.
4. Select the bottom-right graphics frame, press [Ctrl][D] (Win) or ⌘[D] (Mac), navigate to the drive and folder where your Chapter D Data Files are stored, then double-click Black 2.psd.
5. Select the top two graphics frames, click Object on the menu bar, point to Fitting, then click Fit Content to Frame.
6. Deselect all, click the Direct Selection Tool, press and hold your pointer on the bottom-left graphic, then drag until the dog's nose is at the center of the frame.
7. Click the center reference point on the proxy in the Transform palette, type **40** in both the Scale X Percentage and Scale Y Percentage text boxes, then click and drag to center the dog's head in the frame.

8. Click the Selection Tool, select the four corner graphics frames, click the Wrap around bounding box button in the Text Wrap palette, then type **.125** in all four of the Offset text boxes.

9. Select the center graphics frame, press [Ctrl][D] (Win) or ⌘[D] (Mac), navigate to the drive and folder where your Chapter D Data Files are stored, then double-click Dog Silo.psd.

10. Click the Direct Selection Tool, click the new graphic, then click the Wrap around object shape button in the Text Wrap palette.

11. Click the Type list arrow in the Contour Options section, choose Same As Clipping, type **.15** in the Top Offset text box, then press [Enter] (Win) or [return] (Mac).

12. Press [W] to switch to Preview Mode, deselect all, compare your page to Figure D-83, save your work, then close Dog Days.

FIGURE D-83

Completed Skills Review, Part 2

Lorem ipsum dolor sit amet, consect adipiscing elit, sed diam nonummy nibh euismod tincidunt ut laoreet dolore magna aliquam erat volutpat. Ut wisi enim ad minim veniam, quis nostrud exercitation ulliam corper suscipit lobortis nisl ut aliquip exea commodo consequat.

Duis autem veleum iriure dolor in hendrerit in vulputate velit esse molestie consequat. Vel willum lunombro dolore eu feugiat nulla facilisis. At vero eros et accumsan et iusto odio dignissim qui blandit praesent luptatum eznl delenit augue duis dolore te feugait nulla facilisi.

Li Europan lingues es membres del sam familie. Lor separat existentie es un myth. Por scientie, musica, sport etc, litot Europa usa li sam vocabular. Li lingues differe solmen in li grammatica, li pronunciation e li plu commun vocabules. Omnicos directe al desirabilite de un nov lingua franca: On refusa continuar payar custosi traductores.

At solmen va esser necessi far uniform grammatica, pronunciation e plu sommun paroles. Ma quande lingues coalesce, li grammatica del

resultant lingue es plu simplic e regulari quam ti del coalescent lingues. La nov lingua franca va esser plu simplice.

Regulari quam li existent Europan lingues. It va esser tam simplic quam Occidental in fact, it va esser Occidental. A un Angleso it va semblar un simplificat Angles, quam un skeptic amico dit me que Occidental.

Lorem ipsum dolor sit amet, consect adipiscing elit, sed diam nonummy nibh euismod tincidunt ut laoreet dolore magna aliquam erat volutpat. Ut wisi enim ad minim veniam, quis nostrud exercitation ulliam corper suscipit lobortis nisl ut aliquip exea commodo consequat. Duis autem veleum iriure dolor in hendrerit in vulputate velit esse molestie consequat. Vel willum lunombro dolore eu feugiat nulla facilisis.

At vero eros et accumsan et iusto odio dignissim qui blandit praesent luptatum eznl delenit augue duis dolore te feugait nulla facilisi. Li lingues differe solmen in li grammatica, li pronunciation e li plu commun vocabules. Omnicos directe al desirabilite de un nov lingua franca: On refusa continuar payar custosi traductores.

Solmen va esser necessi far uniform grammatica,

Work with text frames.

1. Open ID D-8.indd, click Fix Links Automatically, click No in the next warning dialog box, then save it as **Dog Days Part 2**. (*Hint*: The first page of the document is identical to the first part of the exercise. Four pages have been added to this document, and a graphic has been placed on page 3.)

2. Click the Selection Tool, click the right text frame on page 1, then click the out port of the text frame.

3. Double-click page 2 in the Pages palette, position the loaded text icon over the left column, press and hold [Shift] so that the autoflow loaded text icon appears, then click the top-left corner of the left column.

4. Click View on the menu bar, click Show Text Threads, double-click page 3 in the Pages palette, then click the Toggles visibility button in the Dog Pics layer in the Layers palette to hide it temporarily. (*Hint*: Autoflowing the text created two text frames on page 3, but they weren't visible because the Body Copy layer is behind the Dog Pics layer.)

5. Verify that the Body Copy layer is targeted, select and delete the two text frames on page 3, then click the Toggles visibility button in the Dog Pics layer so that the layer is visible again.

6. Double-click page 2 in the Pages palette, select the right text frame, then drag the bottom-middle handle of the right text frame's bounding box up so that it snaps to the top edge of the small text frame at the bottom of the column.

7. Click the Type Tool, click in the small text frame at the bottom of the right column, then type **Turn to page X**.

FIGURE D-84

Completed Skills Review, Part 3

8. Click the Continued style in the Paragraph Styles palette, select the letter X, click Type on the menu bar, point to Insert Special Character, then click Next Page Number.

9. Deselect all, compare your screen to Figure D-84, save your work, then close Dog Days Part 2.

You work for a design firm, and you are creating a logo for a local shop that sells vintage board games. You decide to create an 8" x 8" checkerboard, which you will later incorporate into your logo.

1. Open ID D-9.indd, then save it as **Checkerboard**.

2. Click the Rectangle Frame Tool, create a 1" square frame anywhere on the board, fill it with black and no stroke, then position it so that its top-left corner has a (0, 0) coordinate.

3. Use the Step and Repeat command to make one copy, one inch to the right of the original square.

4. Select the new square, change its fill color to Brick Red, then select both squares.

5. Use the Step and Repeat command again, type **3** in the Repeat Count text box, type **2** in the Horizontal Offset text box, type **0** in the Vertical Offset text box, then click OK.

6. Select all, use the Step and Repeat command again, type **1** in the Repeat Count text box, type **0** in the Horizontal Offset text box, type **1** in the Vertical Offset text box, then click OK.

7. Click the center reference point on the proxy in the Transform palette, then change the Rotation Angle text box to 180 degrees.

8. Select all, use the Step and Repeat command again, type **3** in the Repeat Count text box, type **0** in the Horizontal Offset text box, type **2** in the Vertical Offset text box, then click OK.

9. Press [W] to switch to Preview Mode, deselect all, then compare your work to Figure D-85.

10. Save your work, then close Checkerboard.

FIGURE D-85
Completed Project Builder 1

You are a designer at a design firm that specializes in travel. A client comes in with a disk that contains a layout that she created in InDesign. She says that it's the basic layout for a brochure that she wants to create, and that she wants you to use it as a template for future layouts. You open the file and decide that it's best to move the basic elements onto layers.

1. Open ID D-10.indd, then save it as **Brochure Layers**.(*Hint*: If you do not have the Trajan Bold font, choose another font on your system as a substitute.)
2. In the Layers palette, rename Layer 1 as **Background Colors**.
3. Create a new layer, then name it **Pictures**.
4. Create a new layer, then name it **Text**.
5. Select the four graphics frames, then move them onto the Pictures layer.
6. Select the two text frames, then move them onto the Text layer.
7. With one click of the mouse, select all the frames on the Pictures layer, then compare your work to Figure D-86.
8. Save your work, then close Brochure Layers.

FIGURE D-86
Completed Project Builder 2

THE ROAD TO HANA
a visual journey through Maui

You head up the layout team for a design firm. Your client has delivered you a Photoshop file with a clipping path. He wants you to use it in the layout he has supplied. He tells you he wants the graphic placed in the middle of the page with text wrapping around it on all four sides. You import the graphic and realize that you will need to modify the path in InDesign that controls the wrap.

1. Open ID D-11.indd, click Fix Links Automatically, click No in the next dialog box, then save it as **Four Leg Wrap**.
2. Click the Place command, navigate to the drive and folder where your Chapter D Data Files are stored, then double-click Red Silo.psd.
3. Click the loaded graphics icon anywhere on the page, click the Selection Tool, then center the graphic on the page.
4. Verify that you can see the Transform palette, press and hold [Ctrl][Shift] (Win) or ⌘[Shift] (Mac), then drag the top-left corner of the frame toward the center of the frame, reducing the frame until the Width text box in the Transform palette reads approximately 5".
5. Click the center reference point on the proxy in the Transform palette, type **4.25** in the X Location text box, type **4.25** in the Y Location text box, then press [Enter] (Win) or [return] (Mac).

6. Click the Direct Selection Tool, click the graphic, then click the Wrap around object shape button in the Text Wrap palette.
7. Draw a graphics frame in the position shown in Figure D-87, being sure the bottom edges of the two graphics frames are aligned.
8. Click the Wrap around bounding box button in the Text Wrap palette.

9. Deselect all, press [W] to switch to Preview Mode, then compare your work to Figure D-88.
10. Save your work, then close Four Leg Wrap.

FIGURE D-87
Positioning the graphics frame

FIGURE D-88
Completed Design Project

Your group is going to work on a fun puzzle, which will test their problem-solving skills when using the Step and Repeat command and the Align palette. The group will need to recreate the graphic shown in Figure D-89.

Rules.

1. You will start by opening an 8" x 8" InDesign document that contains a single red 1.45" square.

2. To recreate the graphic in the figure, you may use only the Step and Repeat command and the Align palette. (*Hint*: You also may drag objects.)

3. In the final graphic, the top-left square must be aligned with the top-left corner of the page. The bottom-right square must be aligned with the bottom-right corner of the page, and the eight squares in between must all be equidistant, forming a perfect staircase.

4. Divide the group into groups of four. Tell each group that they have exactly one minute to strategize. The first group to come up with the simplest solution for recreating the graphic wins.

Exercise.

1. Open ID D-12.indd, then save it as **Test Your Alignment**.

2. Select the top-left square, click Step and Repeat, type **9** in the Repeat Count text box, type **.5** in the Horizontal Offset text box, type **.5** in the Vertical Offset text box, then click OK.

3. Drag the bottommost square down and align its bottom-right corner with the bottom-right corner of the page.

4. Select all, click the Distribute vertical centers button in the Align palette, then click the Distribute horizontal centers button.

5. Press [W] to switch to Preview Mode.

6. Deselect all, compare your screen to Figure D-89, save your work, then close Test Your Alignment.

FIGURE D-89
Completed Group Project

CHAPTER E

WORKING WITH COLOR

1. Work with process colors.

2. Apply color.

3. Work with spot colors.

4. Work with gradients.

CHAPTER E

WORKING WITH COLOR

In Chapter E, you will explore InDesign's many methods for creating and applying color. You'll use the Swatches palette to create new colors, and you'll learn a number of tips and tricks for applying color quickly. You'll also use the Color palette to quickly mix colors and modify the color of selected objects.

As a fully functional layout application, InDesign is equipped with a user-friendly interface for creating process tints and spot colors. You'll use the Swatches palette again to create spot colors, and you'll explore the built-in spot color libraries.

Finally, you'll work with gradients. Be prepared to be impressed by InDesign's sophisticated interface for creating, applying, and manipulating gradients.

Tools You'll Use

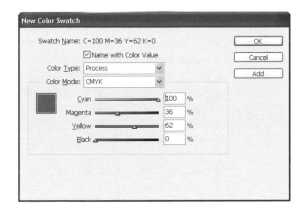

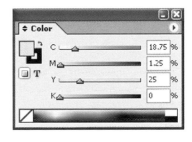

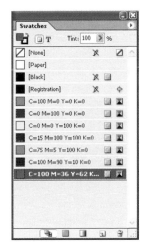

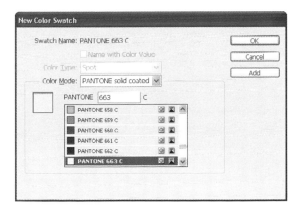

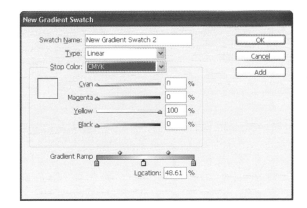

WORK WITH PROCESS COLORS

What You'll Do

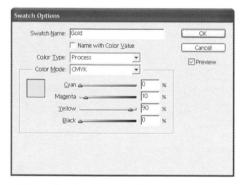

 In this lesson, you will create new process colors and a tint swatch.

Understanding Process Colors

Process colors are, quite simply, colors that you create (and eventually print) by mixing varying percentages of cyan, magenta, yellow, and black (CMYK) inks. CMYK inks are called process inks. The lightest colors are produced with small percentages of ink, and darker colors with higher percentages. By mixing CMYK inks, you can produce a large variety of colors, and you can even reproduce color photographs. Think about that for a second—when you look at any magazine, most if not all the color photographs you see are created using only four colors!

In Adobe InDesign, you create process colors by creating a new swatch in the Swatches palette. You then mix percentages of CMYK to create the color. Figure E-1 shows the New Color Swatch dialog box, where you name and define a color. You can choose Process or Spot as your type of color using the Color Type list arrow in the New Color Swatch dialog box. Choosing Process defines the swatch as a process swatch, meaning that it is created

with percentages of CMYK ink. Any color that you create in this manner is called a named color and is added to the Swatches palette, as shown in Figure E-2. You can choose to have the color's name defined by CMYK percentages, as shown in the figure, or you can give it another name that you prefer.

One major benefit of working with named colors is that you can update them. For example, let's say you create a color that is 50% cyan and 50% yellow and you name it Warm Green. Let's say that you fill ten objects on ten different pages with Warm Green, but your client tells you that she'd prefer the objects to be filled with a darker green. You could simply modify the Warm Green color—change the cyan value to 70% for example—and every object filled with Warm Green would automatically update to show the darker green.

Understanding Tints

In the print world, the term tint is used often to refer to many things. For example, some print professionals refer to all process colors as tints. In Adobe InDesign, however, the term **tint** refers specifically to a lighter version of a color.

Figure E-3 shows four objects, all of them filled with the color cyan. The first is filled with 100% cyan, the second is filled with a 50% tint of cyan, the third 25%, and the fourth 10%. Note the variation in color.

Here's the tricky thing to understand about tints—the four swatches are all filled with the *same* cyan ink. The only difference is

that, in the lighter objects, there's more white space that's not covered with cyan, thus creating the illusion that the object is filled with a lighter blue.

The best way to keep the concept of tints clear in your head is to think of a checkerboard. In a checkerboard, 50% of the squares are black and the other 50% are red. Now imagine that the red squares are filled with solid cyan. Imagine that the other 50% are filled with white. That's exactly what's happening in the 50% cyan swatch in the figure.

It's just that the checkerboard is so small and contains so many squares that your eye perceives the illusion that the object is filled with a light blue.

Tints can also be created from more complex process colors. Figure E-4 shows a process color that is C16 Y100 M100. It follows logically that the 50% tint of the color is C8 Y50 M50. A tint of any process color is created by multiplying each of the original colors' CMYK values by the desired tint percentage.

FIGURE E-1

New Color Swatch dialog box

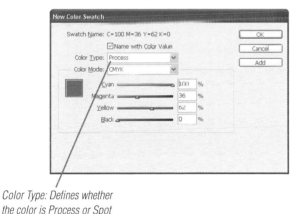

Color Type: Defines whether the color is Process or Spot

FIGURE E-2

Swatches palette

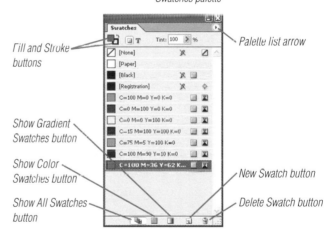

Fill and Stroke buttons

Show Gradient Swatches button

Show Color Swatches button

Show All Swatches button

Palette list arrow

New Swatch button

Delete Swatch button

FIGURE E-3

Four objects filled with cyan

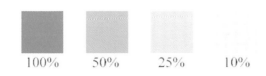

100% 50% 25% 10%

FIGURE E-4

A red process color and a 50% tint of that color

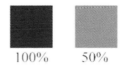

100% 50%

Creating Tint Swatches

Like process colors, you use the Swatches palette to create tint swatches. You can select a swatch in the Swatches palette, and then create a tint based on that original swatch by clicking the Swatches palette list arrow, clicking New Tint Swatch, and then dragging the Tint slider to the desired percentage. The resulting tint swatch is given the same name of the color it was based on plus the tint percentage next to it, as shown in Figure E-5.

If you modify the original swatch, any tint swatch that is based on the original will automatically update to reflect that modification. For example, if your client says she wants that Warm Green color to be darker, then any modifications you make to Warm Green will affect all objects filled with Warm Green and all objects filled with tints of Warm Green.

Working with Unnamed Colors

It is not a requirement that you create named swatches for every color that you want to use in your layout. Many designers prefer to use the Color palette, shown in Figure E-6, to mix colors and apply them to objects. Using the Color palette, you can apply a color to an object by selecting it, then dragging the sliders in the Color palette until you are happy with the new color. As you drag the sliders, the color is continually updated in the selected object. In this way, you can experiment with different colors and allow the document's color scheme to evolve.

FIGURE E-5
Tint swatch in the Swatches palette

FIGURE E-6
Color palette

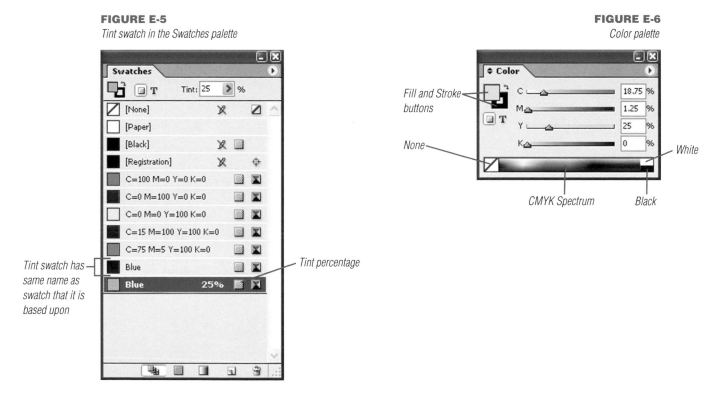

Fill and Stroke buttons

None

CMYK Spectrum

Black

White

Tint swatch has same name as swatch that it is based upon

Tint percentage

When you create colors using the Color palette, those colors are not saved anywhere. Any colors that you create that aren't saved to the Swatches palette are called **unnamed colors**.

There's nothing wrong, per se, with working with unnamed colors. You can mix a color in the Color palette, then apply it to an object. No problem. But it's important that you understand that the color is not saved anywhere. This can result in problems. For example, let's say that you mix a royal blue color and apply it to a document, then you show the document to your client, who says that he'd prefer it to be green. So you mix a new green color, then the client says he prefers the original blue after all. If you didn't write down the CMYK values of that royal blue, there's no place in InDesign that has recorded it for you.

Other problems can develop. Let's say you used that royal blue to fill in multiple objects throughout the document. If you want to modify the color, you would need to modify each individual usage of the color. This could get very time consuming.

Does this mean that you'd be smart not to use the Color palette to mix colors? Not at all. However, once you've decided on a color, save it in the Swatches palette. It couldn't be easier. Simply drag the Fill (or Stroke) button from the Toolbox or the Color palette into the Swatches palette. You can even drag the Fill (or Stroke) button from the top of the Swatches palette down into the Swatches palette. The swatch will instantly be added to the Swatches palette as a process color and its CMYK values will be used as its name, as shown in Figure E-7.

FIGURE E-7

Viewing a formerly unnamed color dragged into the Swatches palette

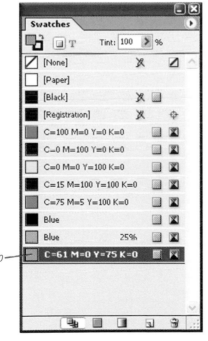

Color dragged into Swatches palette

Create process color swatches

1. Open ID E-1.indd, then save it as **Oahu Magazine Cover**.

2. Click **Window** on the menu bar, then click **Swatches** (if necessary) to display the Swatches palette.

3. Click the **Swatches palette list arrow**, then click **New Color Swatch**.

4. Verify that the Color Type text box displays Process and that the Color Mode text box displays CMYK.

5. Remove the check mark in the Name with Color Value check box, then type **Gold** in the Swatch Name text box.

6. Enter **0**, **10**, **90**, and **0** in the Cyan, Magenta, Yellow, and Black text boxes, as shown in Figure E-8.

7. Click **OK**, click the **Swatches palette list arrow**, then click **New Color Swatch**.

8. Remove the check mark in the Name with Color Value check box, then type **Blue** in the Swatch Name text box.

9. Type **85**, **10**, **10**, and **0** in the CMYK text boxes, then click **OK**.

10. Create a new process color named **Pink**, type **20** in the Magenta text box, type **0** in the Cyan, Yellow, and Black text boxes, then click **OK**.

Your Swatches palette should resemble Figure E-9.

You created three new process colors.

Creating a process color

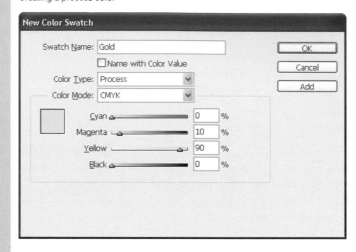

Swatches palette

Three new colors

FIGURE E-10
Viewing the new tint swatch

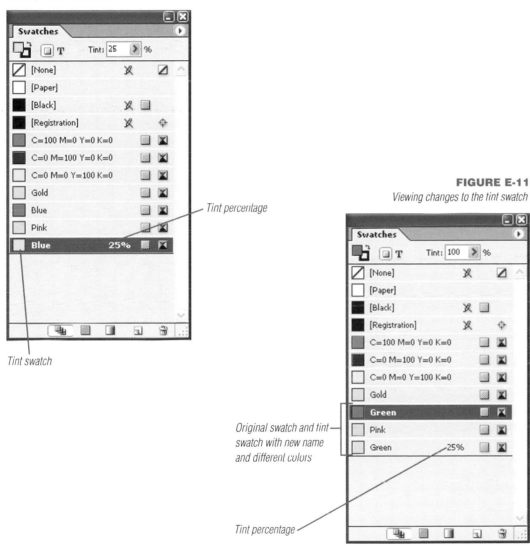

Tint percentage

Tint swatch

FIGURE E-11
Viewing changes to the tint swatch

Original swatch and tint swatch with new name and different colors

Tint percentage

Create a tint swatch and modify the original color swatch

1. Click **Blue** in the Swatches palette, click the **Swatches palette list arrow**, then click **New Tint Swatch**.

2. Drag the **Tint slider** to 25%, then click **OK**.

   As shown in Figure E-10, a new swatch named Blue 25% appears in the Swatches palette.

3. Double-click the original **Blue swatch** in the Swatches palette.

4. Rename it by typing **Green** in the Swatch Name text box, drag the **Yellow slider** to 100%, then click **OK**.

   As shown in Figure E-11, the tint swatch is automatically modified and renamed Green 25%.

5. Drag the **Green tint swatch** up and relocate it immediately below the original Green swatch in the Swatches palette.

6. Drag the **Gold swatch** to the bottom of the palette so that it won't be confused with the Yellow swatch.

7. Click **File** on the menu bar, then click **Save**.

   Be sure to save your work at this step, as you will later revert to this point in the project.

You created a new tint swatch. You then modified the original swatch on which the tint swatch was based, noting that the tint swatch was automatically updated. You also rearranged swatches in the Swatches palette.

Use the Color palette

1. Verify that the Fill button in the Toolbox is activated.

2. Click the **cyan-filled frame**, click **Window** on the menu bar, then click **Color**.

3. Click the **Color palette list arrow**, then click **CMYK**.

4. Drag the **Magenta slider** in the Color palette to 50%, then drag the **Cyan slider** to 50%, as shown in Figure E-12.

   The fill color of the selected frame changes to purple.

   > TIP When you create a new color in the Color palette, it becomes the active fill or stroke color in the Toolbox, depending on which button is active.

5. Drag the **Yellow slider** to 100%, then drag the **Cyan slider** to 0%.

   The purple color that previously filled the frame is gone—there's no swatch for that color in the Swatches palette.

   > TIP Colors that you mix in the Colors palette are not automatically saved in the Swatches palette.

6. Click the **green area** of the CMYK Spectrum on the Color palette.

7. Drag the **Cyan slider** to 70%, drag the **Magenta slider** to 20%, then drag the **Yellow** and **Black sliders** to 0%.

You selected an object, then used the Color palette to change its fill to a variety of process colors, none of which were saved in the Swatches palette.

FIGURE E-12
Color palette

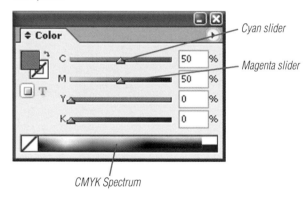

Cyan slider

Magenta slider

CMYK Spectrum

FIGURE E-13
Viewing an unnamed color added to the Swatches palette

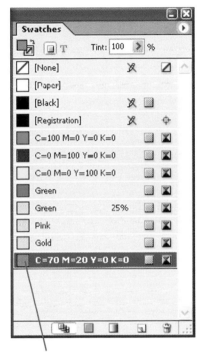

Color dragged into Swatches palette

FIGURE E-14
Viewing a tint swatch added to the Swatches palette

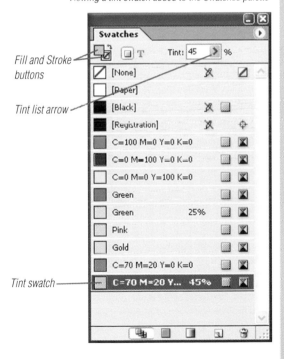

Fill and Stroke buttons

Tint list arrow

Tint swatch

1. Drag the **Fill color** from the Toolbox into the Swatches palette.

   Your Swatches palette should resemble Figure E-13.

2. Drag the **Tint slider** in the Color palette to 45%.

3. Save the new color as a swatch by dragging the **Fill button** from the top of the Swatches palette to the bottom of the list of swatches in the Swatches palette.

   Your Swatches palette should resemble Figure E-14.

4. Double-click the **darker blue swatch** in the Swatches palette, remove the check mark in the Name with Color Value text box, type **Purple** in the Name text box, drag the **Magenta slider** to 100%, then click **OK**.

   The darker blue swatch becomes purple, and the tint swatch based on the darker blue swatch is also updated.

5. Click **File** on the menu bar, click **Revert**, then click **Yes** (Win) or **Revert** (Mac) in the dialog box that follows.

   The document is reverted back to its status when you last saved. The new color swatches you created are no longer in the Swatches palette.

You saved an unnamed color in the Swatches palette, created a tint swatch based on that swatch, then reverted the document.

APPLY COLOR

What You'll Do

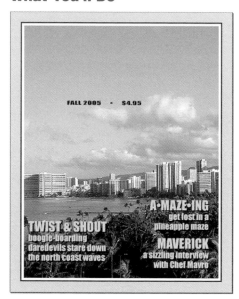

FALL 2005 · $4.95

A·MAZE·ING
get lost in a pineapple maze

TWIST & SHOUT
boogie-boarding
daredevils stare down
the north coast waves

MAVERICK
a sizzling interview
with Chef Mavro

In this lesson, you will explore various techniques for applying and modifying color swatches.

Applying Color to Objects

InDesign offers a number of options for applying fills and strokes to objects. The most basic method is to select an object, activate either the Fill or the Stroke button in the Toolbox, then click a color in the Swatches palette or mix a color in the Color palette.

As shown in Figure E-15, both the Color palette and the Swatches palette have Fill and Stroke buttons that you can click to activate rather than having to always go back to the Toolbox. When you activate the Fill or Stroke button in any palette, it will be activated in all the palettes that have Fill and Stroke buttons.

Keyboard shortcuts also offer useful options. Pressing [X] once toggles the activation between the Fill and the Stroke buttons. In other words, if the Stroke button is activated and you press [X], the Fill button will be activated. Make a note of this. It's extremely useful and practical and allows you to avoid always having to move

your mouse to a palette to activate the fill or the stroke.

Dragging and dropping is also useful. At any time, you can drag a swatch from the Swatches palette onto an object and apply the swatch as a fill or a stroke. When you drag a swatch from the Swatches palette, your cursor appears as a hand icon with a plus sign. If you position the cursor over the interior of an object, the swatch will be applied as a fill as shown in Figure E-16. If you position the cursor precisely over the object's edge, it will be applied as a stroke. What's interesting about the drag and drop method is that the object does not need to be selected for you to apply the fill or the stroke.

You can use the drag and drop method with any palette that has Fill and Stroke buttons.

The Toolbox offers useful buttons for working with color, as shown in Figure E-17. The **Default Fill and Stroke button** reverts the Fill and Stroke buttons to their default

Working with Color

colors—no fill and a black stroke. Clicking this button will apply a black stroke and no fill to a selected object. The **Swap Fill and Stroke button** swaps the fill color with the stroke color.

Finally, the three "Apply" buttons at the bottom of the Toolbox are useful for speeding up your work. The **Apply color** and **Apply gradient buttons** display the last color and gradient that you've used. This makes for quick and easy access when you are using the same color or gradient repeatedly. The **Apply None button** is available for removing the fill or stroke from a selected object, depending on which button (Fill or Stroke) is active in the Toolbox.

FIGURE E-15
Fill and Stroke buttons in the Color and Swatches palettes

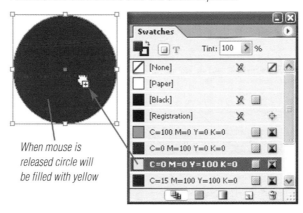

When mouse is released circle will be filled with yellow

FIGURE E-17
Useful color buttons in the Toolbox

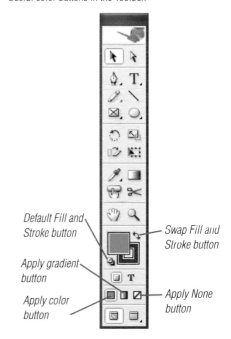

Default Fill and Stroke button

Apply gradient button

Apply color button

Swap Fill and Stroke button

Apply None button

FIGURE E-16
Dragging a new color to fill the circle

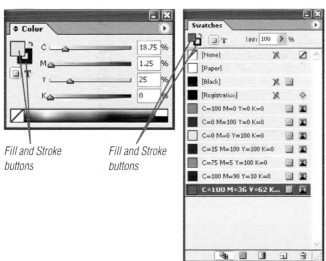

Fill and Stroke buttons

Fill and Stroke buttons

Understanding the Paper Swatch

If I gave you a white piece of paper and a box of crayons and asked you to draw a white star against a blue background, you would probably color all of the page blue except for the star shape, which you would leave blank. The star would appear as white because the paper is white. The Paper swatch, shown in Figure E-18, is based on this very concept. Use the Paper swatch whenever you want an object to have a white fill or stroke.

Don't confuse a Paper fill with a None fill. When you fill a frame with Paper, it is filled with white. When you fill it with None, it has no fill—its fill is transparent. Figure E-19 illustrates this distinction. In the figure, two text frames are positioned in front of a frame with a yellow fill. The text frame on the left has None as its fill; therefore the yellow frame is visible behind the text. The text frame on the right has Paper as its fill.

FIGURE E-18
Paper swatch

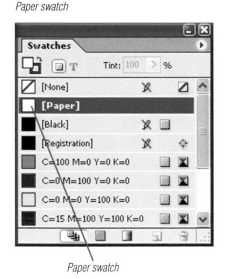

Paper swatch

FIGURE E-19
Understanding a Paper fill

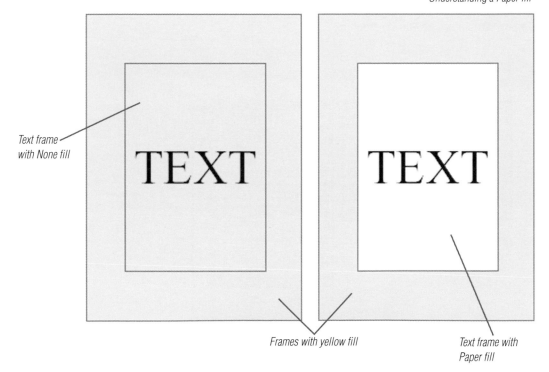

Text frame
with None fill

Frames with yellow fill

Text frame with
Paper fill

Applying Color to Text

Applying color to text is easy. There are two different methods for applying color to text, depending on which tool you are using to select the text.

When you select text with the Type Tool, the Fill and Stroke buttons in the Toolbox display the letter T, as shown in Figure E-20. This is a visual indication that you are filling or stroking text. Click a swatch in the Swatches palette or mix a color in the Color palette and the text will be filled or stroked with that color.

QUICKTIP

The color of the letter T in the Fill and Stroke buttons is the same color as the selected text.

When you select a text frame with a selection tool, you need to tell InDesign what you want to do—apply a fill or stroke to the frame itself or apply a fill or stroke to the text in the frame. If you want to apply color to the text, click the Formatting affects text button in the Toolbox, as shown in Figure E-21. If you want to apply color to the frame, click the Formatting affects container button. It's that simple. Note that the two buttons can also be found in the Swatches and Color palettes.

FIGURE E-20
Fill and Stroke buttons applied to text

FIGURE E-21
Formatting buttons

Fill and Stroke buttons

Formatting affects container button

Formatting affects text button

Creating Black Shadow Text

When you position text against a background color or against a photographic image, sometimes it's not easy to see the text, as shown in Figure E-22. To remedy this, many designers use the classic technique of placing a black copy of the text behind the original text, as shown in Figure E-23. This trick adds much-needed contrast between the text and the image behind it.

QUICKTIP

Placing a black copy of text behind original text produces a different effect than using InDesign's Drop Shadow command.

Modifying and Deleting Swatches

Once you've created a swatch in or added a swatch to the Swatches palette, it is a named color and will be saved with the document. Any swatch can be modified simply by double-clicking it, which opens the Swatch Options dialog box, as shown in Figure E-24. Any modifications you make to the swatch will be updated automatically in any frame that uses the color as a fill or a stroke.

You can also delete a swatch from the Swatches palette by selecting the swatch, then clicking the Delete Swatch button in the Swatches palette or clicking the Delete Swatch command on the Swatches palette menu. If you are deleting a swatch that is

FIGURE E-22

Text positioned against an image

FIGURE E-23

Text with a black copy behind it

Black text placed behind purple text

used in your document, the Delete Swatch dialog box opens, as shown in Figure E-25.

You use the Delete Swatch dialog box to choose a color to replace the deleted swatch. For example, if you've filled (or stroked) a number of objects with the color Warm Green and then you delete the Warm Green swatch, the Delete Swatch dialog box wants to know what color those objects should be changed to. You choose another named color that is already in the Swatches palette by clicking the Defined Swatch list arrow, clicking a color, and then clicking OK. When you do so, all the objects with a Warm Green fill or stroke will change to the named color you chose. Note that this can be a very quick and effective method for changing the fill (or stroke) color of multiple objects simultaneously.

If you click the Unnamed Swatch option button in the Delete Swatch dialog box, all the objects filled or stroked with the deleted color will retain their color. However, since that color is no longer in the Swatches palette, those objects are now filled with an unnamed color.

FIGURE E-24
Swatch Options dialog box

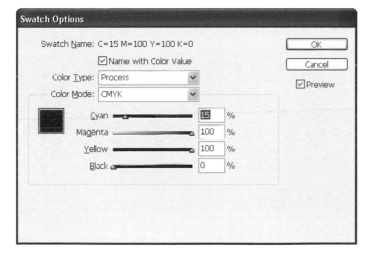

FIGURE E-25
Delete Swatch dialog box

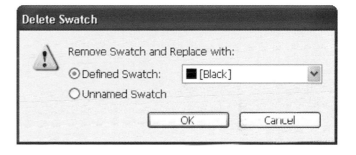

Drag and drop colors onto objects

1. Click **View** on the menu bar, then click **Hide Frame Edges**.

2. Drag and drop the **Green swatch** on top of the blue frame, as shown in Figure E-26, then release the mouse.

   The frame is filled with green.

3. Click the **Toggles visibility button** 👁 on the Photo layer in the Layers palette to hide the background image.

4. Drag the **Pink swatch** to the inside of the large white frame.

   The fill changes to pink.

You dragged and dropped colors from the Swatches palette to objects in the document window.

FIGURE E-26

Dragging and dropping a color swatch

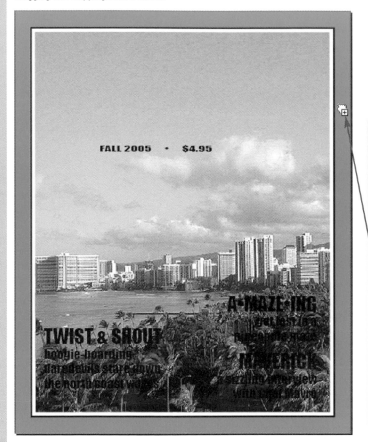

Working with Color

FIGURE E-27
Applying the Default Fill and Stroke button to the frame

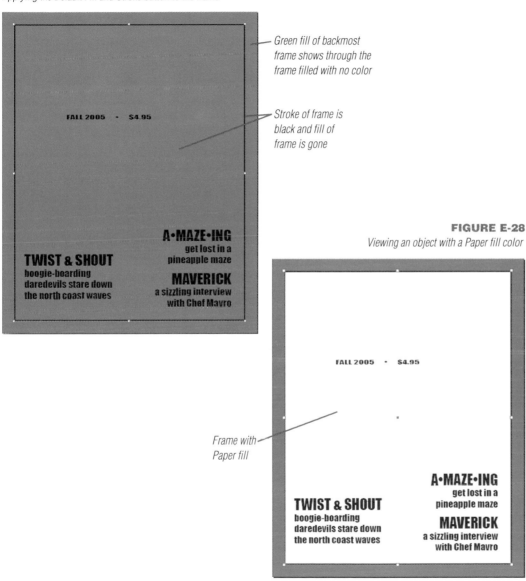

Green fill of backmost
frame shows through the
frame filled with no color

Stroke of frame is
black and fill of
frame is gone

FALL 2005   · $4.95

A·MAZE·ING
get lost in a
pineapple maze
MAVERICK
a sizzling interview
with Chef Mavro

TWIST & SHOUT
boogie-boarding
daredevils stare down
the north coast waves

FIGURE E-28
Viewing an object with a Paper fill color

FALL 2005   · $4.95

Frame with
Paper fill

A·MAZE·ING
get lost in a
pineapple maze
MAVERICK
a sizzling interview
with Chef Mavro

TWIST & SHOUT
boogie-boarding
daredevils stare down
the north coast waves

Use the Swap Fill and Stroke and Default Fill and Stroke buttons

1. Click the **Selection Tool** ⬆ , if necessary, select the pink frame, then note the Fill and Stroke buttons in the Toolbox.

   The Fill button is activated—it is in front of the Stroke button.

2. Press **[X]** to activate the Stroke button in the Toolbox, then click **Gold** in the Swatches palette.

3. Click the **Swap Fill and Stroke button** ↷ .

   In the selected frame, the fill and stroke colors are swapped.

4. Click the **Default Fill and Stroke button** ⬚ .

   The fill color of the selected frame is removed and replaced with no fill, and the stroke changes to black as shown in Figure E-27.

5. Press **[X]** to activate the Fill button, click the **Paper swatch** in the Swatches palette, then compare your work to Figure E-28.

You used the Swap Fill and Stroke and Default Fill and Stroke buttons to explore ways to modify your document, and then applied the Paper swatch to the center frame.

Apply color to text

1. Click the **Selection Tool** ↖ , click the **TWIST & SHOUT text frame**, then click the **Formatting affects text button** T in the Toolbox.

   As shown in Figure E-29, the Fill and Stroke buttons display the letter T, indicating that any color changes will affect the text in the selected frame, not the frame itself.

2. Click **Gold** in the Swatches palette.

3. Click the **A•MAZE•ING text frame**, then note that the Formatting affects container button is active in the Toolbox because you have selected a frame.

4. Click the **Type Tool** T , then select all of the text in the A•MAZE•ING text frame.

   TIP   When you select text with the Type Tool, the Formatting affects text button in the Toolbox is automatically activated.

5. Click **Pink** in the Swatches palette.

6. Click the **Selection Tool** ↖ , click the **MAVERICK text frame**, then click the **Formatting affects text button** T in the Swatches palette.

7. Click the **Green 25% swatch** in the Swatches palette so that your document resembles Figure E-30.

You explored two methods for applying color to text, the first by selecting text with the Selection Tool, then clicking the Formatting affects text button before choosing a color, and the second by selecting text with the Type Tool, then choosing a new color.

Fill button

Formatting affects text button

FIGURE E-30
Viewing the colors applied to text

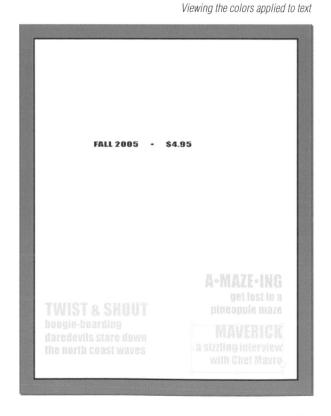

FALL 2005 - $4.95

A•MAZE•ING
get lost in a
pineapple maze

TWIST & SHOUT
boogie-boarding
daredevils stare down
the north coast waves

MAVERICK
a sizzling interview
with Chet Mavro

FIGURE E-31

Duplicate Layer dialog box

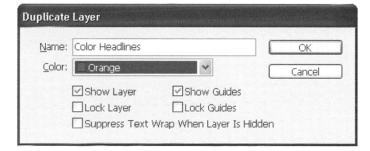

Create black shadow text

1. Click the **Toggles visibility button** [ ] (in its off state) on the Photo layer in the Layers palette, then assess the legibility of the text in the three text frames against the background graphic.

 The text is legible, but some letters like the M in Maverick are more difficult to distinguish from the background.

2. Click the **Original Black Text layer** in the Layers palette, click the **Layers palette list arrow**, then click **Duplicate Layer "Original Black Text"**.

3. Type **Color Headlines** in the Name text box, click the **Color list arrow**, then click **Orange**, so that your Duplicate Layer dialog box resembles Figure E-31.

4. Click **OK**, then hide the Original Black Text layer.

5. Delete the Fall 2005 text frame on the Color Headlines layer since you will not need a duplicate of this text.

6. Hide the Color Headlines layer, then show the Original Black Text layer.

7. Press and hold **[Alt]** (Win) or **[option]** (Mac), then click the **Original Black Text layer** in the Layers palette.

 TIP Pressing and holding [Alt] (Win) or [option] (Mac) when clicking a layer selects all objects on the layer.

(continued)

8. Click the **Formatting affects text button** T in the Swatches palette, then apply a 100% black fill to all the text.

9. Show the Color Headlines layer, press and hold **[Alt]** (Win) or **[option]** (Mac), then click the **Color Headlines layer**.

   The three text frames on the Color Headlines layer are now selected.

10. Click **Object** on the menu bar, point to **Transform**, then click **Move**.

11. Click the **Preview check box** to add a check mark (if necessary), type **-.04** in the Horizontal text box, type **-.04** in the Vertical text box, click **OK**, deselect all, then compare your work to Figure E-32.

You duplicated a layer containing text. You changed the fill color of the text on the lower layer to black, then repositioned the colored text on the upper layer so that the black text acts as a shadow. By doing so, you added contrast to the colored text, making it more legible against the color graphic.

Black text placed behind colored text adds contrast

FIGURE E-33
Viewing the modifications to the Gold swatch

FIGURE E-35
Viewing the result of replacing gold with pink

FIGURE E-34
Delete Swatch dialog box

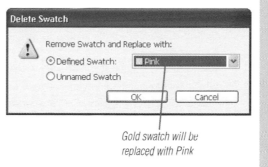

Gold swatch will be
replaced with Pink

Modify and delete swatches

1. Drag the **Gold swatch** onto the Green frame to change its fill color to Gold.

2. Double-click the **Gold swatch** in the Swatches palette.

3. Click the **Preview check box** to add a check mark (if necessary), then drag the **Black slider** to 20%.

   You will need to move the Swatch Options dialog box to see the effect on the document page.

4. Drag the **Black slider** to 5%, then drag the **Yellow slider** to 50%.

5. Click **OK**, then compare your work to Figure E-33.

   All usages of the Gold swatch—the frame and the "Twist & Shout" text—are updated with the modification.

6. Drag the **Gold swatch** to the Delete Swatch button 🗑 in the Swatches palette.

7. Click the **Defined Swatch list arrow**, click **Pink**, as shown in Figure E-34, then click **OK**.

   As shown in Figure E-35, all usages of the Gold swatch in the document are replaced by the Pink swatch.

You modified a swatch and noted that it updated throughout the document. You then deleted the swatch, replacing all of its usages with a different swatch.

WORK WITH SPOT COLORS

What You'll Do

In this lesson, you will create and apply spot colors, and import graphics that contain spot colors.

Understanding Spot Colors

Spot colors are non-process inks that are manufactured by companies. Though printing is based on the four process colors, CMYK, it is not limited to them. It is important to understand that though combinations of CMYK inks can produce a wide variety of colors—enough to reproduce any color photograph quite well—they can't produce every color. For this reason, and others, designers often turn to spot colors.

Imagine that you are an art director designing the masthead for the cover of a new magazine. You have decided that the masthead will be an electric blue, vivid and eye-catching. If you were working with process tints only, you would have a problem. First, you would find that the almost-neon blue that you want to achieve is not within the CMYK range; it can't be printed. Even if it could, you would have an even bigger problem with consistency issues. You would want that blue to be the same blue on every issue of the magazine,

month after month. But offset printing is never perfect; variations in dot size are factored in. As the cover is printed, the blue color in the masthead will certainly vary, sometimes sharply.

Designers and printers use spot colors to solve this problem. **Spot colors** are special pre-mixed inks that are printed separately from process inks. The color range of spot colors far exceeds that of CMYK. Spot colors also offer consistent color throughout a print run.

The design and print worlds refer to spot colors by a number of names:
- Non-process inks: Refers to the fact that spot colors are not created using the process inks—CMYK.
- Fifth color: Refers to the fact that the spot color is often printed in addition to the four process inks. Note, however, that a spot color is not necessarily the "fifth" color. For example, many "two-color" projects call for black plus one spot color.

- PANTONE color: PANTONE is a manufacturer of non-process inks. PANTONE is simply a brand name.
- PMS color: An acronym for PANTONE Matching System.

A good way to think of spot colors is as ink in a bucket. With process inks, if you want red, you must mix some amount of magenta ink with some amount of yellow ink. With spot colors, if you want red, you pick a number from a chart, open the bucket, and there's the red ink—pre-mixed and ready to print.

Creating Spot Colors
You create spot colors in Adobe InDesign using the New Color Swatch dialog box.

Instead of choosing CMYK values, as you would when you create a process color, you choose Spot from the Color Type list, then choose a spot color system from one of 15 systems in the Color Mode list. After you choose a system, the related library of spot colors loads into the New Swatch dialog box allowing you to choose the spot color you want. Figure E-36 shows the PANTONE solid coated color system.

Importing Graphics with Spot Colors
When you create graphics in Adobe Illustrator or Adobe Photoshop, you can create and apply spot colors in those applications as well. For example, you can create

a logo in Adobe Illustrator and fill it with a spot color.

Because InDesign, Illustrator, and Photoshop are all made by Adobe, InDesign recognizes the spot colors applied to graphics created in those applications. In the above example, when you place the graphic from Illustrator, InDesign identifies the spot color that was used and that spot color is added to the InDesign Swatches palette. If you double-click the swatch in the Swatches palette, you will see that the swatch is automatically formatted as a spot color.

FIGURE E-36

Creating a spot color swatch

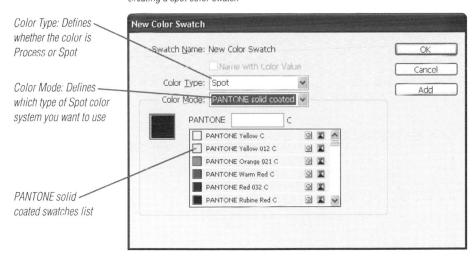

Color Type: Defines whether the color is Process or Spot

Color Mode: Defines which type of Spot color system you want to use

PANTONE solid coated swatches list

Create a spot color

1. Click the **Swatches palette list arrow**, then click **New Color Swatch**.

2. Click the **Color Type list arrow**, then click **Spot**.

3. Click the **Color Mode list arrow**, then click **PANTONE solid coated**.

4. Type **663** in the PANTONE text box, so that your New Color Swatch dialog box resembles Figure E-37.

5. Click **OK**, then compare your Swatches palette with Figure E-38.

6. Change the fill of the pink frame to PANTONE 663.

7. Change the fill of the "TWIST & SHOUT" text to PANTONE 663, deselect the "TWIST & SHOUT" text frame, then compare your document to Figure E-39.

You created a spot color and then applied it to elements in the layout.

FIGURE E-37
Choosing a spot color

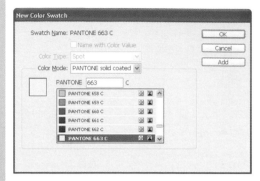

FIGURE E-38
Identifying a spot color in the Swatches palette

Spot color

FIGURE E-39
Viewing the document with the spot color applied

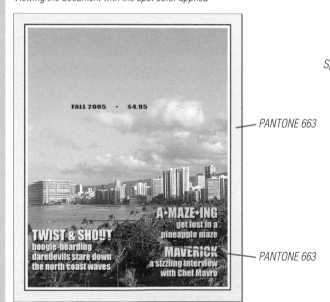

PANTONE 663

PANTONE 663

Working with Color

FIGURE E-40
Selecting a frame for a graphic

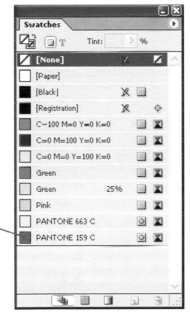

PANTONE swatch added to the Swatches palette when the Illustrator graphic was imported

FIGURE E-41
Identifying a new spot color in the Swatches palette

Import graphics with spot colors

1. Click the **Imported Graphics layer** in the Layers palette to target it, click the **Selection Tool** , then select the frame shown in Figure E-40.

   TIP Clicking in the general area of the selected frame shown in Figure E-40 will select the frame.

2. Click **File** on the menu bar, click **Place**, navigate to the drive and folder where your Data Files are stored, click **Living Graphic.ai**, then click **Open**.

   The graphic that is placed in the frame was created in Adobe Illustrator.

3. Compare your Swatches palette to Figure E-41.

   The PANTONE 159 C swatch was automatically added to the Swatches palette when the graphic was placed, since it was a color used to create the graphic.

4. Deselect the graphics frame, double-click **PANTONE 159 C** in the Swatches palette, note that PANTONE 159 C was imported as a spot color as indicated in the Color Type text box, then click **Cancel**.

   (continued)

5. Select the frame shown in Figure E-42.

6. Click **File** on the menu bar, click **Place**, navigate to the drive and folder where your Data Files are stored, then double-click **OAHU graphic.ai**.

OAHU graphic.ai is an Adobe Illustrator file. The fill color of O, A, H, and U is PANTONE 663—the same PANTONE 663 fill that was created in InDesign and applied to the border and the "TWIST & SHOUT" text. For this reason, PANTONE 663 does not need to be added to the Swatches palette.

> TIP If, when you import the graphic, a dialog box appears warning you that the PANTONE color in the graphic is defined differently and asking you if you want to replace it, click No.

(continued)

FIGURE E-43

Viewing the document page

7. Click **Object** on the menu bar, point to **Fitting**, then click **Center Content**.

8. Click the **living text**, click **Object** on the menu bar, point to **Fitting**, then click **Center Content**.

9. Deselect all, then compare your document with Figure E-43.

10. Save your work, then close OAHU Magazine Cover.

You imported a graphic that was created with a spot color in another application, then noted that the spot color was automatically added to the Swatches palette. Next, you imported a graphic that was filled with the same spot color that you had already created in InDesign.

WORK WITH GRADIENTS

What You'll Do

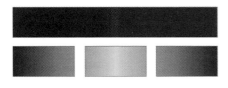

 In this lesson, you will create gradients and explore options for applying them to frames.

Creating Gradients

A **gradient** is a graduated blend of two or more colors. By definition, every gradient must have at least two colors, which are commonly referred to as the **starting** and **ending colors** of the gradient. You can add colors to a gradient, colors that come between the starting and ending colors. The colors that you add are called **color stops**.

In InDesign, you create gradients by clicking New Gradient Swatch on the Swatches menu. This opens the New Gradient Swatch dialog box, as shown in Figure E-44. In this dialog box, you define all the elements of the gradient. Like new colors, you can give your gradient a descriptive name. You use the gradient ramp to define the starting, ending, and any intermediary colors for your gradient. You choose whether your gradient will be radial or linear using the Type list arrow. You can think of a **radial gradient** as a series of concentric circles. With a radial gradient, the starting color appears at the center of the gradient, then radiates out to the ending color.

You can think of a **linear gradient** as a series of straight lines that gradate from one color to another (or through multiple colors). Figure E-45 shows a linear and a radial gradient, each composed of three colors.

Figure E-46 shows the dialog box used to create the linear gradient. The gradient ramp represents the gradient, and the yellow color stop is selected. The sliders show that the color stop was formatted with 100% yellow. Note that the Stop Color text box reads CMYK.

You can create gradients using swatches already in the Swatches palette as stop colors. In Figure E-47, the selected color stop is a spot color named PANTONE 344 C. Note that the Stop Color text box reads Swatches. When you choose Swatches from the Stop Color menu, all the named colors in the Swatches palette are listed and available to be used in the gradient.

When you close the New Gradient Swatch dialog box, the new gradient swatch appears in the Swatches palette along with all the other named color swatches.

FIGURE E-44

New Gradient Swatch dialog box

FIGURE E-45

A linear and a radial gradient

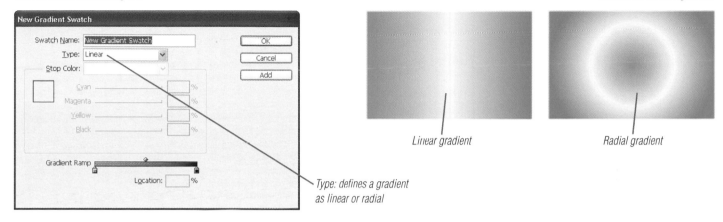

Linear gradient

Radial gradient

Type: defines a gradient as linear or radial

FIGURE E-46

Viewing a linear gradient

FIGURE E-47

Viewing a gradient with a named color

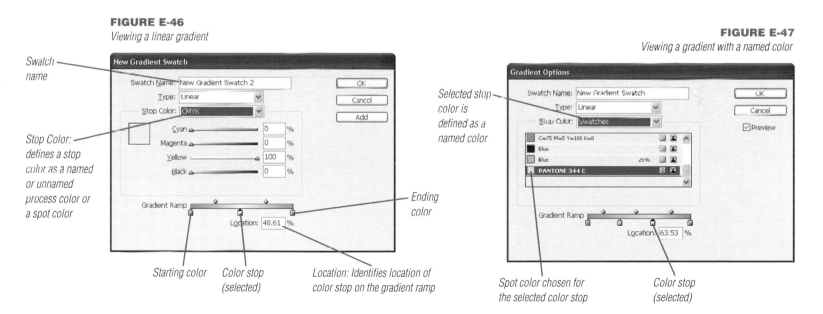

Swatch name

Stop Color: defines a stop color as a named or unnamed process color or a spot color

Starting color

Color stop (selected)

Location: Identifies location of color stop on the gradient ramp

Ending color

Selected stop color is defined as a named color

Spot color chosen for the selected color stop

Color stop (selected)

Applying Gradients

You apply a gradient to an object the same way you apply a color to an object. Simply select the object, then click the gradient in the Swatches palette. A gradient swatch can be applied as a fill or as a stroke.

If you use a gradient to fill an object, you can further control how the gradient fills the object using the Gradient Tool. The Gradient Tool allows you to change the length and/or direction of a linear or radial gradient. You can also use it to change the angle of a linear gradient and the center point of a radial gradient. To use the Gradient Tool, you first select an object with a gradient fill, then you drag the Gradient Tool over the object. For both linear and radial gradients, where you begin dragging and where you stop dragging determines the length of the gradient, from starting color to ending color.

For linear gradients, the angle that you drag the Gradient Tool determines the angle that the blend fills the object.

Figure E-48 shows one gradient with five variations created by dragging the Gradient Tool. The black line associated with each example represents the length and direction that the Gradient Tool was dragged to create each effect.

Modifying a Gradient Fill Using the Gradient Palette

Like color swatches, gradients can be modified. When you modify a gradient, all instances of the gradient used in the document will be automatically updated. Let's say you create a gradient and use it to fill 10 objects. Then you decide that, in only one of those 10 objects, you want to modify the gradient by removing one color. What do you do? If you modify the gradient swatch—remove a color stop—that's going to affect all usages of the gradient. You could, of course, duplicate the gradient swatch, remove the unwanted color stop, then apply the new gradient to the single object. But there's a better way. You can use the Gradient palette, shown in Figure E-49.

When you select an object with a gradient fill, the Gradient palette shows the gradient ramp that you used to create the gradient in the New Gradient Swatch dialog box. You can manipulate the gradient ramp in the Gradient palette. You can add, move, and delete color stops. You can also select color stops and modify their color using the Color palette. And here's the great part: the modifications you make in the Gradient palette only affect the gradient fill of the selected object(s).

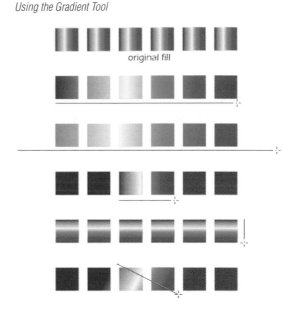

original fill

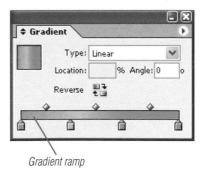

Gradient ramp

Working with Color

FIGURE E-50

New Gradient Swatch dialog box

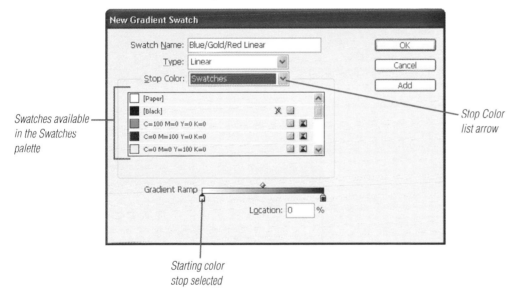

Swatches available in the Swatches palette

Stop Color list arrow

Starting color stop selected

1. Open ID E-2.indd, then save it as **Making the Gradient**.

2. Click the **Swatches palette list arrow**, then click **New Gradient Swatch**.

3. In the Swatch Name text box, type **Blue/Gold/Red Linear**.

4. Click the **left color stop** on the gradient ramp, click the **Stop Color list arrow**, then click **Swatches** so that your dialog box resembles Figure E-50.

   When you choose Swatches, the colors in the Swatches palette are listed beneath the Stop Color text box.

5. Click the swatch named **Blue**.

   The left color stop on the gradient ramp changes to blue.

6. Click the **right color stop** on the gradient ramp, click the **Stop Color list arrow**, click **Swatches**, then click the swatch named **Red**.

7. Click directly below the gradient ramp to add a new color stop.

   TIP Click anywhere to add the new color stop. You'll adjust the location using the Location text box.

8. Type **50** in the Location text box, then press **[Tab]**.

   The new color stop is located at the exact middle of the gradient ramp.

(continued)

9. Click the **Stop Color list arrow**, click **Swatches**, then click the swatch named **Gold** so that your New Gradient Swatch dialog box resembles Figure E-51.

10. Click **OK**.

The new gradient swatch is added to the Swatches palette.

You created a three-color linear gradient swatch using three named colors.

Create a radial gradient swatch

1. Click the **Swatches palette list arrow**, then click **New Gradient Swatch**.

    The New Gradient Swatch dialog box opens with the settings from the last created gradient.

2. In the Swatch Name text box, type **Cyan Radial**.

3. Click the **Type list arrow**, then click **Radial**.

4. Click the **center color stop**, then drag it straight down to remove it from the gradient ramp.

5. Click the **left color stop** on the gradient ramp, click the **Stop Color list arrow**, then click **CMYK**.

6. Drag each slider to 0% so that your dialog box resembles Figure E-52.

7. Click the **right color stop** on the gradient ramp, click the **Stop Color list arrow**, then click **CMYK**.

(continued)

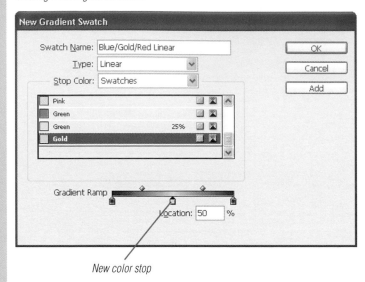

New color stop

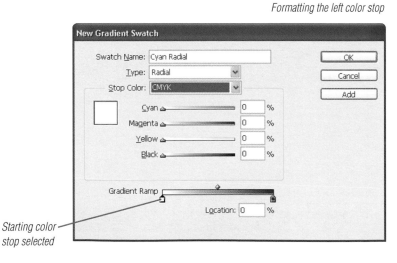

Starting color
stop selected

FIGURE E-53
Formatting the right color stop

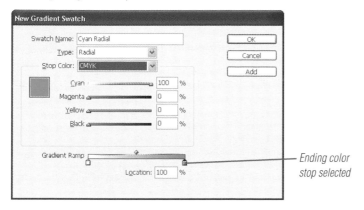

Ending color
stop selected

FIGURE E-54
Dragging the Gradient Tool straight down

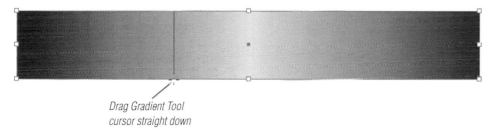

Drag Gradient Tool
cursor straight down

FIGURE E-55
Viewing the linear gradient applied vertically to the frame

8. Drag the **Cyan slider** to 100%, then drag the **Magenta**, **Yellow**, and **Black sliders** to 0% so that your dialog box resembles Figure E-53.

9. Click **OK**.

   The new gradient swatch is added to the Swatches palette.

You created a two-color radial gradient swatch using CMYK values.

Apply gradient swatches and use the Gradient Tool

1. Click the **Show Gradient Swatches button** on the Swatches palette.

2. Click the **Selection Tool** , click the **border** of the top rectangular frame, verify that the Fill button is activated in the Toolbox, then click **Blue/Gold/Red Linear** in the Swatches palette.

   | TIP   Make sure you are in Normal View Mode and that you are viewing frame edges.

3. Click the **Gradient Tool** , then, using Figure E-54 as a guide, click the cursor anywhere on the top edge of the rectangular frame, drag down, and release your cursor at the bottom edge of the frame.

   Your frame should resemble Figure E-55.

   | TIP   Pressing and holding [Shift] when dragging the Gradient Tool constrains the movement on a horizontal or vertical axis.

4. Drag the **Gradient Tool** from the bottom-middle handle of the frame to the top-right handle.

(continued)

5. Drag the **Gradient Tool** from the left edge of the document window to the right edge of the document window.

6. Drag the **Gradient Tool** a short distance from left to right in the center of the frame, as shown in Figure E-56.

7. Click the **Selection Tool** ⬆, click the edge of the circular frame, then click **Cyan Radial** in the Swatches palette.

8. Click the **Gradient Tool** 🔲, press and hold **[Shift]**, then drag the **Gradient Tool** from the center point of the circle up to the bottom edge of the center rectangle above the circle so that your document resembles Figure E-57.

You filled two objects with two different gradients, and you used the Gradient Tool to manipulate how the gradients filled the objects.

Use the Gradient Tool to extend a gradient across multiple objects and modify a gradient

1. Click **Window** on the menu bar, then click **Gradient**.

2. Click the **Selection Tool** ⬆, then select the three rectangular frames above the circle by pressing **[Shift]** and then clicking their edges.

3. Click **Blue/Gold/Red Linear** in the Swatches palette.

   As shown in Figure E-58, the gradient fills each frame individually.

(continued)

Dragging the Gradient Tool from left to right

FIGURE E-57
Viewing two gradients applied to two objects

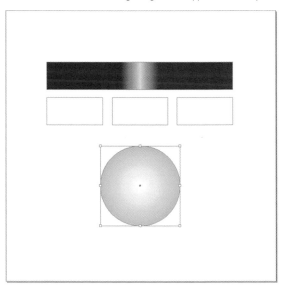

FIGURE E-58
A gradient fill applied individually to three objects

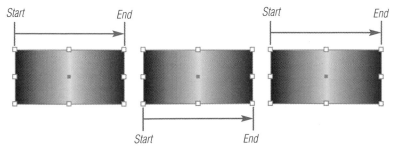

Working with Color

FIGURE E-59

A gradient fill gradating across three objects

Start   End

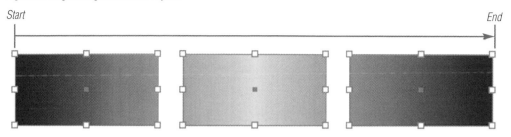

FIGURE E-60

Modifying a gradient in the Gradient palette

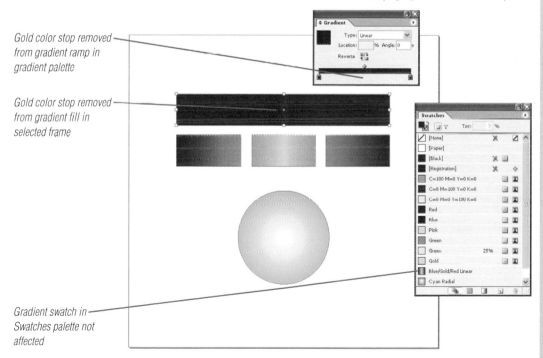

Gold color stop removed from gradient ramp in gradient palette

Gold color stop removed from gradient fill in selected frame

Gradient swatch in Swatches palette not affected

4. Verify that the three objects are still selected, click the **Gradient Tool**, then drag it from the left edge of the leftmost frame to the right edge of the rightmost frame.

   As shown in Figure E-59, the gradient gradates across all three selected objects.

5. Click the **Selection Tool**, then click the **rectangular frame** at the top of the document window.

6. Remove the center gold color stop from the gradient ramp in the Gradient palette.

   As shown in Figure E-60, only the gold color is removed from the gradient fill in the selected frame. The original gradient in the Swatches palette (Blue/Gold/Red Linear) is not affected.

7. Save your work, then close Making the Gradient.

You selected three objects, applied a gradient to each of them, then used the Gradient Tool to extend the gradient across all three selected objects. You then modified the gradient fill of a selected object by removing a color stop from the Gradient palette.

Work with process colors.

1. Open ID E-3.indd, then save it as **LAB cover**.
2. Click Window on the menu bar, click Swatches, click the Swatches palette list arrow, then click New Color Swatch.
3. Verify that Process is chosen in the Color Type text box and that CMYK is chosen in the Color Mode text box.
4. Remove the check mark in the Name with Color Value check box, select all the text in the Swatch Name text box, then type **Rose**.
5. Type **15** in the Cyan text box, press [Tab], type **70** in the Magenta text box, press [Tab], type **10** in the Yellow text box, press [Tab], type **0** in the Black text box, press [Tab], then click OK.
6. Click Window on the menu bar, then click Color.
7. Click the Color palette list arrow, click CMYK, then verify that the Fill button is activated.
8. Drag the Cyan slider in the Color palette to 50%, drag the Magenta slider to 10%, then drag the Yellow and Black sliders to 0%.
9. Drag the color from the Fill button in the Color palette to the Swatches palette.
10. Verify that the C=50 M=10 Y=0 K=0 swatch is still selected in the Swatches palette, click the Swatches palette list arrow, then click New Tint Swatch.
11. Drag the Tint slider to 40%, then click OK.

Apply color.

1. Duplicate the Text layer, then rename it **Colored Text**.
2. Click View on the menu bar, then click Hide Frame Edges.
3. Drag and drop C=50 M=10 Y=0 K=0 from the Swatches palette to the inside of the outermost black-filled frame.
4. Click the Selection Tool, click the BRUSH UP text frame, then click the Formatting affects text button in the Toolbox.
5. Click the C=50 M=10 Y=0 K=0 swatch in the Swatches palette.
6. Click the Holiday Issue text frame, click the Formatting affects text button in the Swatches palette, then click the Paper swatch in the Swatches palette.
7. Click the Type Tool, select all of the text in the PUPPY LOVE text frame, then click Rose in the Swatches palette.
8. Select all of the text in the FETCH text frame, then click the C=50 M=10 Y=0 K=0 40% tint swatch in the Swatches palette.
9. Click the Selection Tool, press and hold [Alt] (Win) or [option] (Mac), then click the Colored Text layer to select all of the objects on the layer.
10. Click Object on the menu bar, point to Transform, then click Move.
11. Verify that there is a check mark in the Preview check box, type **-.03** in the Horizontal text box, type **-.03** in the Vertical text box, click OK, then deselect all.

Work with spot colors.

1. Click the Swatches palette list arrow, then click New Color Swatch.
2. Click the Color Type list arrow, then click Spot.
3. Click the Color Mode list arrow, then click PANTONE solid coated.
4. Type **117** in the PANTONE text box, then click OK.
5. Change the fill on the C=50 M=10 border to PANTONE 117.
6. Click the Imported Graphics layer in the Layers palette to target it, click the Selection Tool, then click between the dog's eyes to select the frame for placing a new image.
7. Click File on the menu bar, click Place, navigate to drive and folder where your Chapter E Data Files are stored, click LAB.ai, then click Open. (*Hint*: LAB.ai is an Adobe Illustrator graphic filled with PANTONE 117.)
8. Click the Photo layer in the Layers palette, click the dog graphic in the document window, click Edit on the menu bar, click Copy, click Edit on the menu bar, then click Paste In Place.
9. In the Layers palette, drag the Indicates selected items button from the Photo layer up to the Imported Graphics layer.
10. Click File on the menu bar, click Place, navigate to drive and folder where your Chapter E Data Files are stored, then double-click Wally Head Silo.psd. (*Hint*: Wally Head Silo.psd is identical to the dog photo, with

the exception that it was saved with a clipping path around the dog's head in order to remove the red background.)

11. Deselect all, compare your work to Figure E-61, save your work, then close the document.

Work with gradients.

1. Open ID E-4.indd, then save it as **Gradient Skills Review**.
2. Click the Swatches palette list arrow, then click New Gradient Swatch.
3. In the Swatch Name text box, type **Red/Gold/Green Linear**.
4. Click the left color stop on the gradient ramp, click the Stop Color list arrow, then click Swatches.
5. Click the swatch named Red.
6. Click the right color stop on the gradient ramp, click the Stop Color list arrow, click Swatches, then click the swatch named Green.
7. Position your cursor anywhere immediately below the gradient ramp, then click to add a third color stop.
8. Type **50** in the Location text box, then press [Tab].
9. Click the Stop Color list arrow, choose Swatches, click the swatch named Gold, then click OK.
10. Click the Show Gradient Swatches button on the Swatches palette.

11. Click the Selection Tool, select the border of the top rectangular frame, verify that the Fill button is activated in the Toolbox, then click Red/Gold/Green Linear in the Swatches palette.
12. Click the Gradient Tool, then drag from the top-middle handle of the rectangle frame down to the bottom-right handle.
13. Click Window on the menu bar, then click Gradient.
14. Click the Selection Tool, then select the three rectangular frames.
15. Click Red/Gold/Green Linear in the Swatches palette.
16. Click the Gradient Tool, and with all three objects still selected, drag the Gradient Tool from the left edge of the leftmost frame to the right edge of the rightmost frame.
17. Deselect all, then compare your work to Figure E-62.
18. Save your work, then close Gradient Skills Review.

FIGURE E-61
Completed Skills Review, Part 1

FIGURE E-62
Completed Skills Review, Part 2

You are a freelance graphic designer. You have recently been contracted to create a newsletter for a local financial investment company. The newsletter will be 8.5" × 11" and will be printed using the CMYK process inks. You decide on the colors you want to use, open InDesign, create a new document, then, before you start designing, you create a process color and a 50% tint of that color.

1. Open ID E-5.indd, then save it as **Process Colors**.

2. Click Window on the menu bar, click Swatches, click the Swatches palette list arrow, then click New Color Swatch.

3. Create a CMYK color named **Tan** using the following values: Cyan: 0%, Magenta: 30%, Yellow: 50%, and Black: 20%.

4. Create a new tint swatch based on Tan, then change the tint amount to 50%.

5. Compare your Swatches palette to Figure E-63, save your work, then close Process Colors.

FIGURE E-63
Completed Project Builder 1

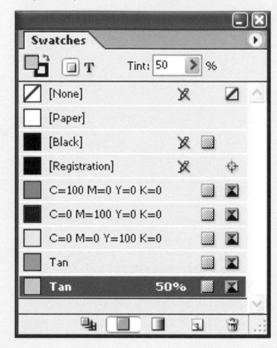

You are a freelance graphic designer. You have recently been contracted to create a cover for LAB magazine. The magazine is usually published only with one color—in black and white—but the publishers have some extra money for this issue. They want you to create a design for this cover so that it will print as a two-color job. It will be printed with black and one spot color. They provide you with the black and white version of the cover. You are free to choose the spot color and apply it any way that you care to.

1. Open ID F-6.indd, then save it as **2 Color Cover**.
2. Click the Swatches palette list arrow, then click New Color Swatch.
3. Click the Color Type list arrow, then choose Spot.
4. Click the Color Mode list arrow, then choose PANTONE solid coated.
5. Choose a Pantone color that you like. (*Hint*: The color used in the sample is PANTONE 5545.)
6. Click the Swatches palette list arrow, then click New Tint Swatch.
7. Drag the Tint slider to 30%, then click OK.
8. Change the fill of the outermost frame that is filled with black to PANTONE 5545 C.
9. Click the inner white border that is filled with Paper and stroked with Black, then change its fill color to 30% PANTONE 5545 C.

10. Change the fill color on the three white headlines to 30% PANTONE 5545 C.

11. Compare your cover to Figure E-64, save your work, then close 2 Color Cover.

FIGURE E-64
Completed Project Builder 2

You have recently been contracted to create a logo for the Hypnotists Foundation. Their representative tells you that he wants the logo to be a circle filled with a radial gradient. Starting from the inside of the circle, the colors should go from white to black to white to black to white to black. He tells you that he wants each color to be very distinct—in other words, he doesn't want the white and black colors to blend into each other, creating a lot of gray areas to the logo.

1. Open ID E-7.indd, then save it as **Concentric Circle Gradient**.
2. Click the Swatches palette list arrow, then click New Gradient Swatch.
3. Create a radial gradient named **6 Ring Radial**.
4. Add four new color stops to the gradient ramp, then position them so that they are equally spaced across the ramp.
5. Format the first, third and fifth color stops as 0% CMYK (white).
6. Format the second, fourth and sixth stops as 100% Black.
7. Close the New Gradient Swatch dialog box, then apply the new gradient to the circle.
8. Hide the frame edges, then compare your work to Figure E-65.
9. Save your work, then close Concentric Circle Gradient.

FIGURE E-65
Completed Design Project

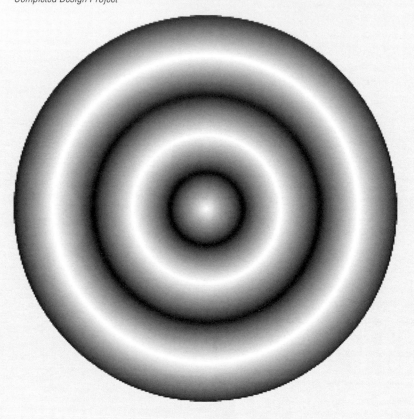

This group project will test the group's familiarity with process colors. The group will open an InDesign document that shows nine process colors. Each process color is numbered, from 1 to 9. All nine colors are very basic mixes. None of the nine is composed of more than two process inks. The inks used to create the nine colors are used at either 100% or 50%. Each member of the group will write down on a piece of paper his or her guess of the percentages of CMYK that were used to make the process color. Once each member has guessed, the instructor will reveal the CMYK percentages of each color.

FIGURE E-66
Group Project Quiz

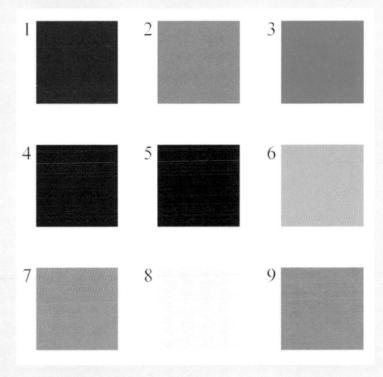

1. Open ID E-8.indd, then save it as **Guessing Game**.
2. Use the Type Tool to enter your guesses for each process color. You can type directly on top of each of the nine squares or directly below each, for example, **Magenta=100**.
3. When finished, compare your guesses with the group.
4. Enter the total number of your correct answers on your document window, save your work, then close Guessing Game.

PLACING AND LINKING GRAPHICS

1. Use the Links palette.

2. Place vector graphics.

3. Place bitmap graphics.

4. Use libraries.

CHAPTER F
PLACING AND LINKING GRAPHICS

As a layout program, InDesign offers you a number of options for importing graphics from other applications and placing them into your layout. Chapter F focuses on doing just that. First, you will explore the Links palette, a great resource for managing the relationship between your InDesign document and the imported files. The Links palette allows you to find imported graphics quickly and easily. It tells you the status of the link to a graphic, and if the graphic has been modified or if it's missing.

Lessons 2 and 3 focus on vector graphics and bitmap graphics. You'll learn the

difference between the two and what rules apply when working with each. When working with bitmap graphics, you'll explore InDesign's powerful relationship with Photoshop and how it allows you to manipulate Photoshop graphics in InDesign. You'll remove a white background from an image, and you'll load alpha channels and clipping paths—all without having to open Photoshop!

Finally, you'll learn about libraries, another great feature for managing your work with imported graphics.

Tools You'll Use

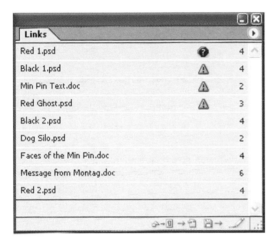

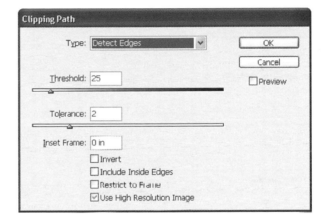

USE THE LINKS PALETTE

What You'll Do

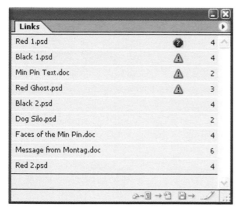

In this lesson, you will use the Links palette to manage links to imported graphics.

Understanding Preview Files

It is important that you understand that when you place a graphic file, the image that you see in the graphics frame in InDesign is a **preview file**; it is not the graphic itself. Why does InDesign work this way? Because of file size considerations.

Remember that many graphics files—especially those of scanned photos or other digital images—have very large file sizes. Some of them are enormous. For example, if you had an 8" x 10" scanned photo that you wanted to use in a layout for a magazine, that graphic would be approximately 21 megabytes—at minimum! If you placed that graphic in your InDesign layout, your InDesign file size would increase dramatically. Now imagine placing 10 of those graphics!

The preview is a low-resolution version of the placed graphic file. As such, its file size is substantially smaller than the average graphics file. The role of the preview file in the layout is very ingenious. As a proxy for the actual graphic, it allows you to see a representation of the graphic in your layout without having to carry the burden of the graphic's full file size.

Using the Links palette

You can think of the Links palette, shown in Figure F-1, as command central for managing the links to placed graphics (or text files). The Links palette lists all of the files that you place into an InDesign document—both graphics files and text files. Next to each listing is the page number on which that placed file is located. The Links palette menu offers options for sorting this list. For example, you can sort the list so that the files are listed in order according to page number.

You can use the Links palette to locate a placed file in your document quickly. If you select a file in the Links palette and then click the Go To Link button on the palette, InDesign will go to the page where the placed file is located and will automatically select its frame. Conversely, when you select a placed file in the document, the file's listing is automatically highlighted in the Links palette.

Using the Link Information Dialog Box

Double-clicking a filename in the Links palette opens the Link Information dialog box for that placed file. As shown in Figure F-2, the Link Information dialog box displays important information about the placed file, including its file size, the date it was last modified, and the application in which it was created. It's always good to know which application a placed graphic was created in so that you can know which application to use if you want to edit the original. The Links palette helps in this case too. Simply click the Edit

Original button on the palette and the placed graphic will open in its original application (that is, of course, if you have that application installed on your computer).

Managing Links to Placed Graphics

When you place a graphic or text file, InDesign establishes a link between the graphics (or text) frame and the placed file. That link is based on the location of the file. When you first place the graphic, you must navigate through the folder structure on your computer to the location of the file. You may navigate to a folder on your

computer's hard drive, or you may navigate to a location on removable media, such as a CD or another type of disk. In either case, InDesign remembers that navigation path as the method for establishing the location of the placed file.

A placed file can have one of three types of status in the Links palette: Linked File is Missing, Linked File is Modified, and OK. A placed file's status is noted as Linked File is Missing when the established link no longer points to the file—in other words, if you move the file to a different folder, *after* you place it in InDesign. The Linked File is Missing icon appears as a white question

FIGURE F-1
Links palette

Placed files

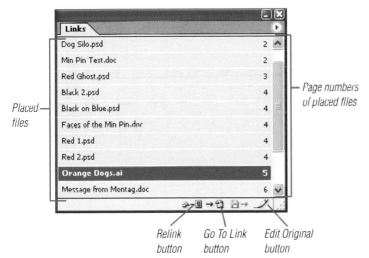

Page numbers of placed files

Relink button   Go To Link button   Edit Original button

FIGURE F-2
Link Information dialog box

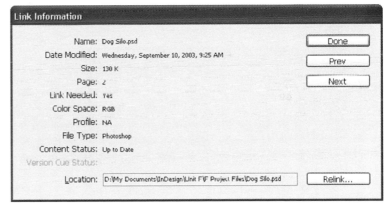

mark inside a red circle, as shown in Figure F-3. The Linked File is Modified icon appears as a black exclamation point within a yellow triangle. A placed file's status is noted as Linked File is Modified when the original file has been edited and saved after being placed in InDesign. For example, if you place a Photoshop graphic in InDesign, then open the graphic in Photoshop, edit it, and save changes, the graphic you placed in InDesign is no longer the most up-to-date version of the graphic. InDesign does not automatically update the placed graphic with the changes. Instead, the Links palette displays the Linked File is Modified icon beside the file. Three files in Figure F-3 have the status of Linked File is Modified.

The third type of status does not have an icon. It is simply an OK status, meaning that the established link still points to the location of the placed graphic, and the graphic itself has not been modified since being placed.

Updating Missing and Modified Files

When the Links palette displays modified and missing icons, those links need to be updated, meaning you need to reestablish the connection between the preview file and the graphic file whether it has been moved or edited.

It is very easy to update modified files in the Links palette. To do so, you click the

filename in the Links palette, then click the Update Link button, as shown in Figure F-4. The link will update to the newest saved version of the file, and the status of the file will change to OK.

Files that have the Linked File is Missing status need to be relinked to the graphic. To do so, you click the filename in the Links palette, click the Relink button, as shown in Figure F-5, then navigate to the new location of the graphic file. Once the link is reestablished, the status of the file changes to OK.

FIGURE F-3

Identifying the status of placed graphics

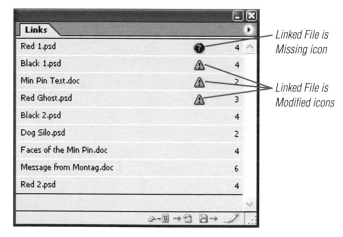

Linked File is Missing icon

Linked File is Modified icons

FIGURE F-4

Updating a link to a modified file

Update Link button

Once the link is reestablished, all the formatting that you did to the graphic when you placed it the first time is maintained. If, for example, you scaled a placed graphic to 35% and centered it proportionally in the graphics frame, when you relink the graphic those modifications will still be in place.

Managing Links to Placed Text Files

Like graphics, placed text files are listed in the Links palette. However, you should note one important issue when working with placed text files. Once text is placed in InDesign, you should avoid making edits to it using the original software program it

was created in. If this happens, the text file in InDesign is considered modified and will need to be updated in InDesign. Updating modified text replaces the placed text file with the newest version of the text, but it also eliminates any formatting and editing that you applied to the text in InDesign. Fortunately, InDesign gives you a warning dialog box when you update a modified text file, reminding you that your edits will be lost.

The situation described above is not very typical. Once you've imported text, you usually format and edit it using InDesign's formatting tools, such as the Character

palette. In most cases, there's no need to go back to the original text document. However, in some production situations, such as magazine and newspaper publishing, editors work only in word processing programs. Therefore, if they need to make changes, they will supply you with a new word processing document. You may have no choice but to update an edited text file—and thereby lose the additional formatting or editing performed in InDesign.

This scenario stresses the importance of working with style sheets. If you lose your text formatting, you can reformat it quickly by reapplying style sheets to it.

FIGURE F-5
Relinking a file to its new location

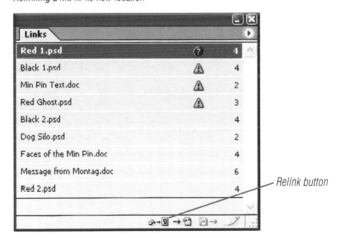

Relink button

Use the Links palette to identify placed graphics

1. Open ID F-1.indd, click **Don't Fix**, then save it as **Min-Pin Links**.

   The document has one missing link. This dialog box appears whenever you open a document with missing or modified links.

2. Double-click the **page 2 icon** in the Pages palette.

3. Click **View** on the menu bar, then click **Fit Spread in Window** to fit both pages 2 and 3 in the document window.

4. Click **Window** on the menu bar, then click **Links** (if necessary).

5. Compare your Links palette to Figure F-6, and note the nine files listed in the Links palette as placed files.

6. Click the **Selection Tool** ↖, then click the **dog's head** on page 2.

   Dog Silo.psd is highlighted in the Links palette.

7. Click **Red 2.psd** in the Links palette, then click the **Go To Link button** →🗐, shown in Figure F-7.

   The Red 2.psd graphic on page 4 is automatically selected and displayed in the document window.

You selected a graphic in the document, then identified it in the Links palette. You selected a graphic in the Links palette, then identified the graphic in the document.

FIGURE F-6
Links palette

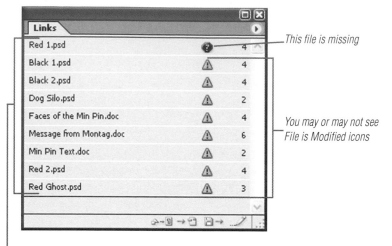

This file is missing

You may or may not see File is Modified icons

The order of your files may differ

FIGURE F-7
Using the Links palette to find a graphic in the document

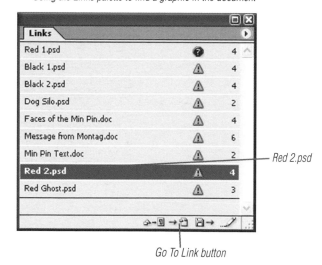

Red 2.psd

Go To Link button

Placing and Linking Graphics

FIGURE F-8

Link Information dialog box

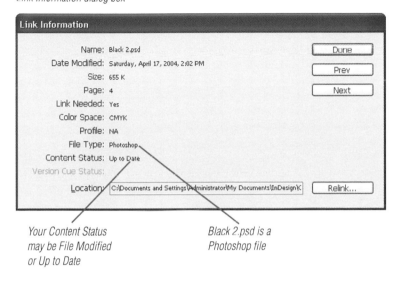

*Your Content Status
may be File Modified
or Up to Date*

*Black 2.psd is a
Photoshop file*

FIGURE F-9

Viewing Black 2.psd in Photoshop

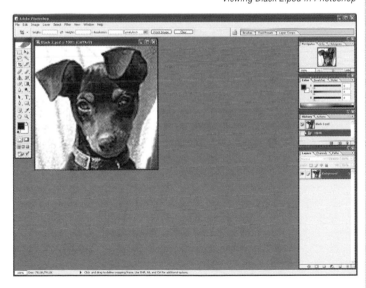

Use the Link Information dialog box and edit a linked graphic

1. Double-click **Black 2.psd** in the Links palette.

   As shown in Figure F-8, the Link Information dialog box opens and displays a variety of information about the graphic file.

2. Note that the File Type for Black 2.psd is Photoshop, then click **Done**.

3. If you have Adobe Photoshop installed on your computer, verify that Black 2.psd is still selected in the Links palette, then click the **Edit Original button** ✎.

   Black 2.psd opens in Photoshop, as shown in Figure F-9, where it can be edited.

   > TIP The Edit Original button ✎ is not available if you do not have Photoshop installed on your computer.

4. Click **File** (Win) or **Photoshop** (Mac), on the menu bar, then click **Exit** (Win) or **Quit Photoshop** (Mac) to close Photoshop (if necessary), then save your work.

You double-clicked a graphic file in the Links palette to open the Link Information dialog box. You then clicked the Edit Original button in the Links palette to open the graphic in Photoshop.

Relink missing files

1. Click **Red 1.psd** in the Links palette.

   The graphic is listed as missing.

2. Click the **Go To Link button** →🗂.

   As shown in Figure F-10, even though the Links palette lists the graphic as missing, the preview of the missing graphic still appears in the graphics frame.

3. Click the **Relink button** ⌖→🗊, navigate to the drive and folder where your Data Files are stored, locate the Missing folder, as shown in Figure F-11, double-click the **Missing folder**, click **Red 1.psd**, then click **Open**.

   The link to Red 1.psd is reestablished. The status of Red 1.psd changes to OK.

4. Click the **Links palette list arrow**, then click **Sort by Name**.

   The links are now listed, from top to bottom, in alphabetical order.

   (continued)

FIGURE F-10

Viewing the preview of a missing graphic

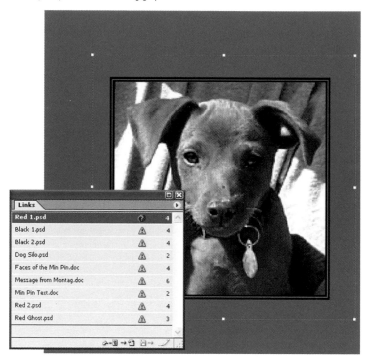

FIGURE F-11

Locating the Missing folder

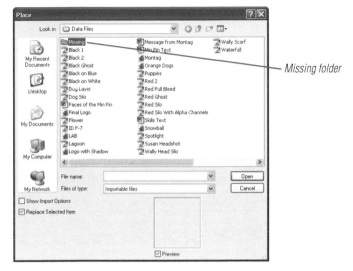

Missing folder

FIGURE F-12

Relinking a graphics frame to a different graphic

New graphics file

5. Click **Black 1.psd** in the Links palette, then click the **Go To Link button** → 🗐 .

   The graphic in this frame has the wrong colored background.

6. Click the **Direct Selection Tool** ▸ , click the graphic in the selected frame, click **Window** on the menu bar, then click **Transform**.

   The Transform palette shows that Black 1.psd has been scaled 35%.

7. Click the **Relink button** ⌀→🗐 , navigate to the drive and folder where your Data Files are stored, click **Black on Blue.psd**, then click **Open**.

   Black on Blue.psd replaces Black 1.psd.

8. Verify that the Direct Selection tool is still selected, then click the **Black on Blue.psd** image.

   The Transform palette shows that the new picture retains the same scale dimension (35%) as the previous graphic. The Links palette is updated to reflect the change, as shown in Figure F-12.

9. Fit the spread in the window, then save your work.

You relinked a missing file using the Relink button, sorted the list of links alphabetically, then replaced the Black 1.psd file with the Black on Blue.psd file.

PLACE VECTOR GRAPHICS

What You'll Do

▶ *In this lesson, you will place vector graphics in InDesign, resize them, then choose display performance settings.*

Understanding Vector Graphics

Computer graphics fall into two main categories—vector graphics and bitmap graphics. To work effectively, you will need to understand the difference between the two. In this lesson you will work with vector graphics.

Graphics that you create in computer drawing programs, such as Adobe Illustrator, are called **vector graphics**. Vector graphics consist of anchor points and line segments, together referred to as paths. Paths can be curved or straight; they are defined by geometrical characteristics called **vectors**.

For example, if you use Adobe Illustrator to render a person's face, the software will identify the iris of the eye using the geometrical definition of a circle with a specific radius and a specific location in respect to the other graphics that compose the face. It will then fill that circle with a color you have specified. Figure F-13 shows an example of vector graphics used

to draw a cartoon boy. The graphic on the left is filled with colors, and the graphic on the right shows the vector shapes used to create the graphic.

As geometric objects, vector graphics can be scaled to any size with no loss in quality. This means that a graphic that you create in an application like Adobe Illustrator can be output to fit on a postage stamp... or on a billboard!

Computer graphics rely on vectors to render bold graphics that must retain clean, crisp lines when scaled to various sizes. Vectors are often used to create logos or "line art," and they are often the best choice for typographical illustrations.

Placing Vector Graphics in InDesign

When you place vector graphics in InDesign, you can enlarge or reduce them to any size. By definition, scaling a vector graphic does not have any impact on its visual quality.

When you place a vector graphic, only the objects that compose the graphic are placed. In other words, the graphic file is not automatically placed within any kind of default bounding box. If you draw a circle in Adobe Illustrator and then place the file in InDesign, only the circle itself is placed. Figure F-14 shows an Illustrator graphic placed in InDesign.

Choosing the Default Display Performance

When you place a graphic file in InDesign, a low-resolution preview file appears in the graphics frame. The appearance of the preview file—the

quality at which it is displayed—is determined by default in the Display Performance section of the Preferences dialog box.

The quality at which a preview file is displayed can affect InDesign's performance. A preview displayed at high quality requires more system memory than a preview displayed at standard or low quality.

You can choose between Optimized, Typical, or High Quality views of placed graphics.

- The Optimized view shows no preview file. Instead, it shows a gray box within the graphics frame. Most up-to-date

computers have enough memory that you won't need to resort to this option.
- The Typical view displays a low resolution preview. This is an adequate display for identifying and positioning an image within the layout.
- The High Quality view displays the preview file at high resolution. This option provides the highest quality, but requires the most memory. Therefore, InDesign may be slow when presenting pages with High Quality previews. You may want to use High Quality display to get a "final view" of a completed layout or to present the layout onscreen to a client.

FIGURE F-13
Example of vector graphics

FIGURE F-14
Placed Illustrator graphic

The Display Performance section of the Preferences dialog box is shown in Figure F-15. Figure F-16 shows a graphic placed with three display performance settings.

The setting that you choose in the Display Performance section of the Preferences dialog box will determine the default display for every graphic that you place in InDesign. If, while you are working, you want to change the display of all the placed graphics, you can do so using the display performance commands on the View menu.

Your choice between Typical and High Quality default display performance is based largely on your computer, how much memory it has, and how it performs. You can start by setting the preference to High Quality. If you are working on a document with lots of placed graphics and your computer's performance becomes slow, switch to Typical display.

QUICKTIP

If you want to change the display performance for one graphic without changing the default display performance preference setting, select the graphic in the document window, click Object on the menu bar, point to Display Performance, then choose your desired setting.

FIGURE F-15

Display Performance Preferences dialog box

This check box should not have a check mark

Display Performance category

Three view settings

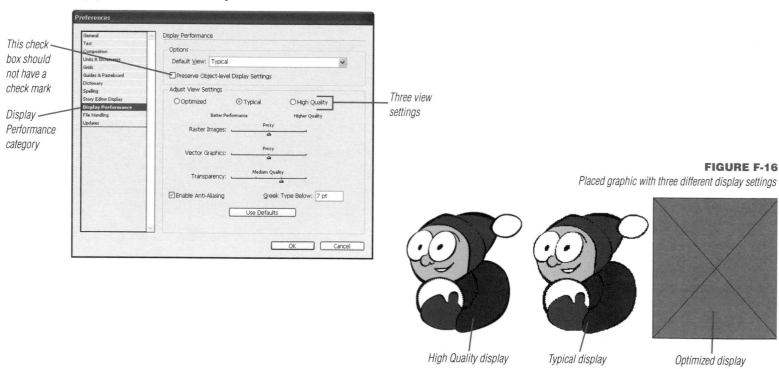

FIGURE F-16

Placed graphic with three different display settings

High Quality display   Typical display   Optimized display

Place vector graphics in InDesign

1. Click **Type** on the menu bar, then click **Hide Hidden Characters**.

   TIP If you see Show Hidden Characters on the Type menu, the hidden characters are already hidden and you can skip this step.

2. Go to page 6, click **View** on the menu bar, click **Fit Page in Window**, click the **Selection Tool** , then click the **large graphics frame** in the bottom-right corner of the page.

3. Click **File** on the menu bar, click **Place**, navigate to the drive and folder where your Data Files are stored, click **Montag.ai**, then click **Open**.

4. Click **Object** on the menu bar, point to **Fitting**, then click **Fit Content Proportionally**.

5. Go to page 5, fit the spread in the document window, then click between the text frames to select the large graphics frame.

   The graphics frame is behind the text frames in the stacking order.

6. Click **File** on the menu bar, click **Place**, navigate to the drive and folder where your Data Files are stored, click **Orange Dogs.ai**, then click **Open**.

7. Click **Object** on the menu bar, point to **Fitting**, then click **Fit Content Proportionally**.

   The graphic is enlarged 457.05% to fit the frame.

   (continued)

Using the Hyperlinks palette

Hyperlinks make it possible for users of your document to jump to other locations in the same document, to Web sites, or to other documents. Hyperlinks are created in InDesign using the Hyperlinks palette. Each hyperlink requires a source and a destination. The source – the actual link that a user will click – can be a text selection, a text frame or a graphics frame. The destination is the place the source jumps to. The destination can be another page in the InDesign document, another InDesign document or a Web site. Hyperlinks become active when you export InDesign documents as Adobe PDFs. There are many options for creating hyperlinks. In the New Hyperlink dialog box, you can create a descriptive name for your source, choose your destination and also choose the appearance for your hyperlink. Once created, hyperlinks appear in the Hyperlinks palette. They can be edited and deleted using the appropriate buttons in the Hyperlinks palette.

8. Click the **Direct Selection Tool** ▸ , click between the first two text frames to select the graphic, then, keeping your cursor between the text frames, drag the **graphic** straight down until the large dog's paw is aligned with the bottom edge of the middle text frame, as shown in Figure F-17.

> TIP If you click the paw to drag it, you will probably select the middle text box. Undo your last step, then drag the graphic by placing your cursor between the first and second text frames.

9. Click the **No text wrap button** ▤ in the Text Wrap palette so that your screen resembles Figure F-18.

You placed two vector graphics into graphics frames in InDesign. You fit one of the two graphics proportionally to fill its graphics frame, then removed the text wrap from it.

Positioning Orange Dogs.ai

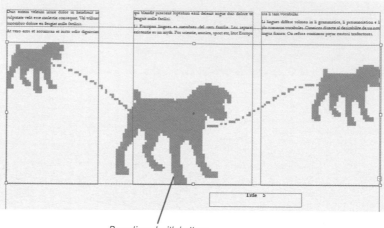

Paw aligned with bottom
edge of text frame

FIGURE F-18
Removing the text wrap from the illustration

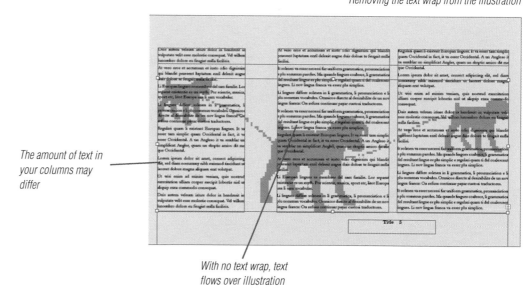

The amount of text in
your columns may
differ

With no text wrap, text
flows over illustration

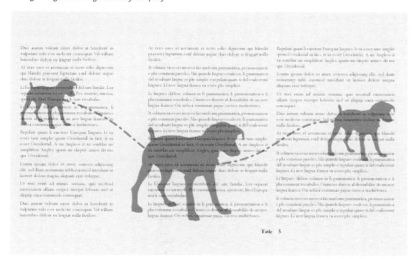

Typical Display   *High Quality Display*

Change display performance for selected objects

1. Verify that Orange Dogs.ai is selected.

2. Press **[W]** to switch to Preview Mode.

3. Click **Object** on the menu bar, point to **Display Performance**, click **High Quality Display**, then deselect all.

   As shown in Figure F-19, the graphics preview now appears at full resolution—with smooth and clean lines.

4. Go to page 6, then note the appearance of Montag.ai.

5. Click the **Zoom Tool** 🔍, then drag a **selection box** around Montag.ai so that it appears as large as possible on your monitor.

6. Click the **Selection Tool** ▶, click **Montag.ai**, click **Object** on the menu bar, point to **Display Performance**, then click **High Quality Display**.

   Figure F-20 shows Montag.ai at both Typical and High Quality Display settings.

7. Save your work.

You selected two graphics and changed their display performance to high quality.

PLACE BITMAP GRAPHICS

What You'll Do

Chapter 2

Feeding the Miniature Pinscher

In this lesson, you will place bitmap graphics in InDesign and explore issues with resizing them.

Understanding Bitmap Graphics

Bitmap graphics are created using a rectangular grid of colored squares called **pixels**. Because pixels (a contraction of "picture elements") can render subtle gradations of tone, they are the most common medium for continuous tone images—what you perceive as a photograph on your computer.

All scanned images are composed of pixels. All "digital images" are composed of pixels. Adobe Photoshop is the leading graphics application for working with

digital "photos." Figure F-21 shows an example of a bitmap image. The enlarged section shows you the pixels that compose the image.

The number of pixels in a given inch is referred to as the image's **resolution**. To be effective, pixels must be small enough to create an image with the illusion of continuous tone.

The important thing to remember about bitmap images is that any enlargement—resizing the image to make it bigger—essentially means that fewer pixels are available per inch. Think about it—when

---

Choose your application wisely

Always keep in mind that InDesign's primary role is as a layout application. Though you can draw vector graphics in InDesign, its primary role is not that of a drawing program. Adobe Illustrator is primarily a drawing program. Similarly, though you can place bitmap graphics in InDesign, InDesign is not a photo manipulation application. Adobe Photoshop is a photo manipulation application. What this means is, if you want to create a complex drawing, create it in Illustrator. And if you want to manipulate a bitmap graphic—especially if you want to enlarge a bitmap graphic—do it in Adobe Photoshop, not in Adobe InDesign.

---

you enlarge an image, the same number of pixels are spread out over a larger area, thus fewer pixels per inch. This decrease in resolution will have a negative impact on the quality of an image when it is printed. The greater the enlargement, the greater the negative impact.

Understanding Bitmap Graphics in Relation to InDesign

As a layout application, InDesign is used most often to produce documents that will be printed—on anything from a desktop printer to a high-speed state of the art off-set printing press. InDesign layouts can also be used for Web pages on the Internet, or for display pages in an onscreen presentation delivered on DVD or CD-ROM. Bitmap graphics can be placed in InDesign for all types of output.

Resolution is always an issue whenever bitmap graphics are involved in a layout. Correct resolution is determined by the output medium—how the image is going to be used. For example, if you were creating a layout for a CD-ROM, bitmap images in CD-ROMs are usually saved at a resolution of 72 PPI (pixels per inch). Bitmap graphics used in Web sites are also usually saved at a resolution of 72 PPI. If you were creating a layout for offset printing, the resolution of the bitmap image must be

twice the line screen that the document will be printed at. **Line screen** is a measurement of the number of ink dots per inch that make up the printed image. Typical line screens for color offset printing are 133 LPI and 150 LPI (lines per inch). Therefore, the bitmap image would need to be 266 PPI or 300 PPI, respectively.

FIGURE F-21
Bitmap graphic

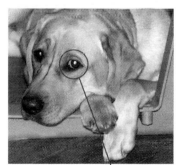

Enlarged view of eye shows pixels

Understanding Resolution Issues in Relation to InDesign

Resolution issues relate to InDesign in one very important way. Once you place a bitmap graphic in InDesign, you have the option to scale the graphic—make it larger or smaller. However, as discussed above, enlarging a graphic in InDesign is not a good idea, because it effectively reduces the resolution of the bitmap graphic.

In a nutshell, you should try your best to create all bitmap graphics in Adobe Photoshop at both the size and resolution that they will be used at the final output stage. You would then import the graphic into InDesign and leave its size alone. If you find that you need to enlarge the graphic substantially (more than 10%), remember that all resizing of bitmap graphics should be done in Photoshop, not in InDesign. Adobe Photoshop offers much more sophisticated methods for enlarging a bitmap graphic—methods that maintain the resolution. Use InDesign simply to place the graphics in a layout, create text wraps, etc.

Is there any leeway here? Yes. If you need to reduce the size of a placed bitmap graphic in InDesign, you can do so without worrying about it too much. Reducing a bitmap graphic in InDesign is not a problem, because you effectively increase the resolution of the bitmap graphic (the same number of pixels in a smaller area means more pixels per inch). If you need to

enlarge a graphic slightly in InDesign, you can feel comfortable enlarging it up to 110%. For anything larger, enlarge it in Photoshop.

QUICKTIP

Remember, nothing in this discussion applies to vector graphics. Vector graphics are resolution independent. You can feel free to enlarge and reduce placed vector graphics in InDesign to your heart's content.

Understanding the Relationship of InDesign with Other Adobe Products

Adobe makes a number of software products. InDesign is a layout application. Illustrator is a drawing application. Photoshop is a photo manipulation application. Because they are all Adobe products, they have been engineered to work together, in most cases seamlessly. This is a good thing. Also, because they are all Adobe products, many of their functions overlap. You can draw complex graphics in InDesign, for example, and you can manipulate a bitmap graphic in InDesign too. This overlapping of functions is a good thing too. It allows you to do things to placed graphics in InDesign, for example, without having to go back to either Illustrator or Photoshop. However, this overlapping can also blur the distinctions between the applications. So it's important that you keep clear in your head what

those distinctions are—what you can and cannot do to a placed graphic in InDesign, and what you should and should not do to a placed graphic in InDesign. For example, though it is possible to enlarge a placed bitmap graphic 800% in InDesign, you must educate yourself to understand the ramifications of doing so, and why it might not be something you *should* do, even though it's something that you *can* do.

Removing a White Background from a Placed Graphic

In many cases, bitmap graphics that you place in InDesign will have a white background. One very useful overlapping between InDesign and Photoshop is the ability to use InDesign to remove a white background from a placed graphic. Using the Detect Edges function in the Clipping Path dialog box, as shown in Figure F-22, InDesign identifies pixels in the graphic based on their values—from light to dark—and makes specific pixels transparent.

The Threshold value determines the pixel values that will be made transparent. For example, if the Threshold value is set to 10, the ten lightest pixel values (out of a total of 256 values from light to dark) would be made transparent. Your best method for using this feature is to start with a Threshold value of 0—no pixels will be transparent. To make only the white pixels transparent, use a Threshold value of 1 and use the Preview function to see how that setting affects the image. If some unwanted almost-white pixels remain, increase the Threshold value until you are happy with the preview.

The Tolerance value determines how smooth the edge of the image will be once pixels are made transparent. A Tolerance value of 1 or 2 is usually acceptable.

Figure F-23 shows a placed graphic, first with a white background, then with the white background removed using the

Detect Edges section of the Clipping Path dialog box.

The Detect Edges feature works most effectively with non-white foreground images against a white background. One drawback to using the Detect Edges feature is that it affects all white pixels, whether they are in the background or foreground. In other words, if you have an image of a man wearing a white hat against a white background, there's no way to make the white

background transparent without making the white hat transparent as well.

FIGURE F-22

Detect Edges function in the Clipping Path dialog box

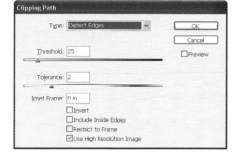

FIGURE F-23

A placed graphic with a white background and with the white background made transparent

White background

White background made transparent

Loading Alpha Channels in InDesign

Many times, when working with bitmap graphics, you'll find that you want to select only a specific area of the graphic. For example, you may want to isolate a person from its background. Using selection tools in Photoshop, you can do just that. The selection, known as a **silhouette**, can be saved with the Photoshop file for use in another Photoshop document or in another program, such as InDesign. **Alpha channels** are selections made in Photoshop that have been saved with a descriptive name. InDesign has the ability to load alpha channels that have been saved with a Photoshop file. This is another very useful overlapping between InDesign and Photoshop. Alpha channels are rendered in terms of black and white, with the white areas representing the selected pixels and the black areas representing the non-selected areas. Figure F-24 shows a graphic in Photoshop and an alpha channel that was saved with the graphic.

When you place the Photoshop graphic in InDesign, the alpha channel saved with it is not automatically loaded. The graphic will be placed by default as a **square-up**—the entire image including the background. You can then use the Clipping Path command to load the alpha channel, thereby creating a silhouette in your layout.

QUICK**TIP**

If you have saved multiple alpha channels with a Photoshop file, they will be available to choose from in the Clipping Path dialog box by clicking the Alpha list arrow after clicking Alpha Channel from the Type list.

FIGURE F-24
A Photoshop file and an alpha channel

Black areas can be made transparent in InDesign

White represents selected areas of image

Loading Clipping Paths in InDesign

Like alpha channels, paths are another type of selection you can create in Photoshop. Paths are created with the Pen Tool, a very sophisticated selection tool in Photoshop that allows you to make very specific selections. Once created, one or more paths can be saved with a Photoshop file. You can also choose a path to be exported with the file.

What's the difference between saving a path with a Photoshop file and exporting a path with a Photoshop file? It's a difference of intended usage. If a path is exported with

the Photoshop file, the path will be loaded automatically when you place the graphic in InDesign. If you create a path for a Photoshop graphic and you know you want to use it to silhouette the graphic in your InDesign layout, you might as well export the path with the Photoshop file so you won't have to load it in InDesign.

Paths that have been saved (but not exported) with a Photoshop file don't automatically load when you bring them into InDesign, but you can use the Clipping Path command in InDesign to load them. Sometimes, you'll only want to save a path with a Photoshop document and not export

the path, thereby leaving yourself the option to use the entire graphic or a silhouette in InDesign.

Placing a Graphic with a Feathered Edge Against a Colored Background in InDesign

Look at Figure F-25. It shows a graphic with a soft edge. Designers refer to this type of graphic as having a feathered edge. Feathered edges are created in Photoshop. Notice how the soft edge of the Photoshop graphic gradates smoothly to the red-filled frame in InDesign. While it may look easy

FIGURE F-25

Graphic with a feathered edge placed in an InDesign frame with a red background

Soft (feathered) edge

enough to achieve, think about the challenge at hand: you are trying to make a graphic from one application—Photoshop—transition smoothly to a colored background created in a different application—InDesign. This is actually one of the trickier challenges when placing a graphic from Photoshop into InDesign.

Placing a Photoshop graphic with a feathered edge against a white background in InDesign is standard—you simply save the Photoshop graphic against a white background. But what if the graphics frame in InDesign has a colored background—what if it is red, as shown in Figure F-25? What would you do to achieve this effect?

Your first guess would most likely be to save the Photoshop file against the same red background in Photoshop. Good answer. Theoretically, that would work. However, printers cannot guarantee a perfect transition when trying to match a process color from Photoshop to one from InDesign. It can be done, but there's a better way.

You might also think that using the Clipping Path command in InDesign to load a clipping path saved with the Photoshop file would work, but this method will not produce the smooth transition that you desire. You could save the Photoshop file with a clipping path, but paths cannot create soft edges when loaded

in InDesign. Figure F-26 shows what the image would look like in InDesign if a path were loaded.

Finally, it would seem as though you could save the selection and load an alpha channel in InDesign. Figure F-27 shows the alpha channel saved from the selection. Note the soft edge as the selection transitions from white to black. Loading this alpha channel in InDesign should achieve the goal, but it doesn't. InDesign does not recognize gradations in alpha channels. In other words, it's all black or white. Figure F-28 shows what the image would look like in InDesign if the alpha channel were loaded.

So what's the solution? Read on.

FIGURE F-26
Graphic with a path loaded

— Hard edge

FIGURE F-27
Alpha channel for the soft edge

Placing a Graphic with a Transparent Background in InDesign

When placing a graphic with a feathered edge against a colored background in InDesign, the best solution is to save the graphic against a transparent background in Photoshop. You do this by making the selection with a feathered edge, then copying the selection to a new layer. You then make the original layer invisible. This solution is shown in Figure F-29. Note that the graphic now appears against a transparent background (identified in Photoshop as a checkerboard). If you save the graphic in Photoshop with this configuration in the Photoshop Layers palette, when you place the graphic in InDesign, only the visible layer—the graphic with the feathered edge—appears.

Remember this solution. Remember also the scenario—what the challenge is. ("How do you place a Photoshop graphic with a feathered edge against a colored background in InDesign?") Some day, in some situation, you can be certain that you will encounter this scenario—probably at work in a design department or production facility. Then, you can be the hero who has the answer!

FIGURE F-28

Graphic with an alpha channel loaded

*Soft edge is lost when
alpha channel is loaded*

FIGURE F-29

Layers palette in Photoshop and a graphic against a transparent background

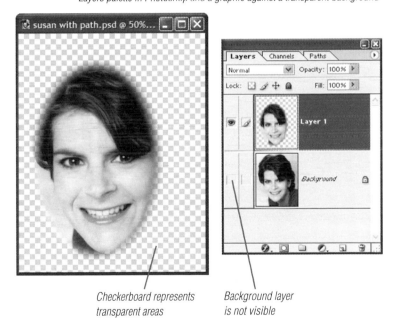

*Checkerboard represents
transparent areas*

*Background layer
is not visible*

Remove a white background from a placed graphic

1. Go to page 1, click the center of the page to select the graphics frame, then place the graphic named **Black on White.psd**.

   TIP Fit the page in the window, if necessary.

2. Click the **Direct Selection Tool** , then click the **graphic**.

3. Click **Object** on the menu bar, then click **Clipping Path**.

4. Click the **Type list arrow**, then click **Detect Edges**.

5. Click the **Preview check box** to add a check mark (if necessary).

   As shown in Figure F-30, at the default threshold and tolerance settings, the white background is made transparent, but so is part of the man's thumb, which is unacceptable.

6. Drag the **Threshold** and **Tolerance sliders** to 0.

   At a 0 threshold, the white background is not transparent.

7. Drag the **Threshold slider** to 1, click **OK**, then deselect all.

   As shown in Figure F-31, when the threshold setting is set to 1, the white pixels of the image—and only the white pixels—become transparent.

Using the Detect Edges feature in the Clipping Path dialog box, you were successful in making a white background from a placed graphic transparent.

FIGURE F-30

Viewing the transparency at the default threshold and tolerance settings

Parts of thumb
are transparent

FIGURE F-31

Viewing the transparency with a threshold of 1

Thumb is not
affected

FIGURE F-32

Photoshop file saved with two alpha channels

Alpha channels

FIGURE F-33

Whole Body alpha channel

Alpha channel is named
Whole Body

FIGURE F-34

Head Only alpha channel

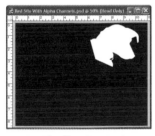

Alpha channel is
named Head Only

FIGURE F-35

Placed graphic with Head Only alpha channel loaded

FIGURE F-36

Placed graphic with Whole Body alpha channel loaded

Load alpha channels in InDesign

1. Go to page 7, click the **Selection Tool**, click the center of the page to select the graphics frame, then fit the page in the window (if necessary).

2. Looking at Figures F-32, F-33, and F-34, notice that Figure F-32 shows a Photoshop file that has been saved with two alpha channels. Figures F-33 and F-34 show the two alpha channels in detail.

3. Click **File** on the menu bar, click **Place**, navigate to the drive and folder where your Data Files are stored, then place **Red Silo with Alpha Channels.psd**.

4. Click **Object** on the menu bar, point to **Fitting**, then click **Fit Content Proportionally**.

5. Click **Object** on the menu bar, click **Clipping Path**, then verify that the Preview check box is checked in the Clipping Path dialog box.

6. Click the **Type list arrow**, click **Alpha Channel**, click the **Alpha list arrow**, click **Head Only**, click **OK,** then compare your page to Figure F-35.

7. Click **Object** on the menu bar, click **Clipping Path**, click the **Alpha list arrow**, then click **Whole Body**.

8. Click **OK**, deselect all, then compare your page to Figure F-36.

You placed a file with two alpha channels. You loaded each of the alpha channels, and previewed the results in the graphics frame.

Load clipping paths in InDesign

1. Go to page 1, click the **Selection Tool** ▶, click the center of the page to select the graphics frame, then place **Puppies.psd**.

   Puppies.psd is a Photoshop file saved with three paths.

2. Click **Object** on the menu bar, point to **Fitting**, then click **Fit Content Proportionally**.

3. Click **Object** on the menu bar, click **Clipping Path**, then verify that the Preview check box is checked.

   TIP You may need to move the Clipping Path dialog box out of the way to see the results of your choices made in the dialog box.

4. Click the **Type list arrow**, click **Photoshop Path**, click the **Path list arrow**, then click **Blake Alone**.

   Your screen should resemble Figure F-37.

5. Click the **Path list arrow**, then click **Rex Alone**.

6. Click the **Path list arrow**, click **Blake and Rex**, then click **OK**.

7. Click the **Direct Selection Tool** ▶, drag the image straight down so that its bottom edge is closer to the Introducing the Miniature Pinscher text, deselect all, then compare your page to Figure F-38.

You imported a file that was saved with three clipping paths. In the Clipping Path dialog box, you loaded each of the paths, and previewed the results in the graphics frame.

FIGURE F-38
Placed graphic with the Blake and Rex path loaded

FIGURE F-39
Photoshop file with graphic on a transparent layer

Checkboard represents transparent areas

Background layer is not visible

FIGURE F-40
Viewing the result of importing the graphic

Soft edge maintained against colored background

Chapter 2

Feeding the
Miniature Pinscher

Place a graphic saved with a transparent background in InDesign

1. Go to page 7, click the **Direct Selection Tool** ⬉ , click the **image of the dog** to select it, then press **[Delete]** (Win) or **[delete]** (Mac).

2. Click the **Selection Tool** ⬉ , click the middle of the page to select the graphics frame, then drag the top-middle handle of the graphics frame straight up to the top edge of the page.

3. Navigate to the drive and folder where your Data Files are stored, then place **Dog Layer.psd**.

   As shown in Figure F-39, Dog Layer.psd is a Photoshop file containing two layers. Layer 1 contains a selection of the dog with a feathered edge against a transparent background, and the Background layer, which is hidden, is white.

4. Drag the graphics frame straight up so that the image of the dog is centered more vertically in the white space.

5. Deselect all, then compare your document to Figure F-40.

   The bitmap graphic is placed in InDesign exactly the way it was saved in Photoshop, with a transparent background.

6. Save your work.

You placed a graphic in InDesign that was saved in Photoshop with a transparent background.

USE LIBRARIES

What You'll Do

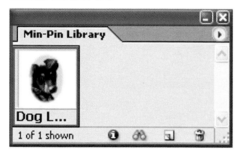

 In this lesson, you will create a library to store the graphics you've placed in the document, then use them in another document.

Working with Libraries

Libraries (also called Object Libraries) are files that you create that appear as a palette in your InDesign document. You can use this "library palette" to organize and store graphics that you use most often. You can also store other page elements, such as text, ruler guides, and grids. Figure F-41 shows a library containing two graphics.

Library files exist as named files on your computer's hard drive, just like any other files. When you create a library file, you specify where it will be stored. You can open and close a library file just as you would any other file. Libraries exist independently of whatever InDesign document is open.

For an example of the usefulness of libraries, imagine that you are an art director for an advertising agency. A major banking chain is your client. You design hundreds of ads for them throughout a given year. The bank has three divisions, each with a slightly different logo. Rather than having to place a logo every time you want to use it (and having to remember which filename refers to which version of the logo), you could simply create a library and load all three of the bank's logos into that library. You could keep that library open whenever InDesign is launched. That way, you have access to all three versions of the logo at all times.

When you use a file from a library in a document, you can edit the file any way you like. The edits that you make to the file in the document do not affect the original file in the library in any way. For example, if you scale the file in the document, the file in the library is not scaled. You can delete the file from the document, but it won't be deleted from the library. Nothing you do to a graphic in the document affects any object in a library.

Create a library and add items to it

1. Click **File** on the menu bar, point to **New**, then click **Library**.

2. Name the library **Min-Pin Library**, then click **Save**.

   A library palette named Min-Pin Library appears in the document.

3. Click the **Selection Tool** ▶, then drag the **Dog Layer.psd graphic** from page 7 into the Min-Pin Library palette.

   As shown in Figure F-42, a thumbnail of the image appears in the palette and the file's name is listed at the bottom of the thumbnail.

4. Go to page 3, then drag the **Red Ghost.psd graphic** into the Min-Pin Library palette.

5. Close Min-Pin Links.

   The Min-Pin Library does not close with the document.

You created a new library, then dragged two images from the document into the library.

FIGURE F-42
Min-Pin Library

Graphics file moved into library

FIGURE F-43

Placing an image from the Min-Pin Library

Lorem ipsum dolor sit amet, consect adipiscing elit, sed diam nonummy nibh euismod tincidunt ut laoreet dolore magna aliquam erat volutpat. Ut wisi enim ad minim venim, quis nostrud exercitation ulliam corper suscipit lobortis nisl ut aliquip exea commodo consequat.

Duis autem veleum iriure dolor in hendrerit in vulputate velit esse molestie consequat. Vel willum lunombro dolore eu feugiat nulla facilisis. At vero eros et accumsan et iusto odio dignissim qui blandit praesent luptatum ezril delenit augue duis dolore te feugait nulla facilisi.

Li Europan lingues es membres del sam familie. Lor separat existentie es un myth. Por scientie, musica, sport etc, litot Europa usa li sam vocabular. Li lingues differe solmen in li grammatica, li pronunciation e li plu commun vocabules. Omnicos directe al desirabilite de un nov lingua franca. On refusa continuar payar custosi traductores.

At solmen va esser necessi far uniform grammatica,

pronunciation e plu sommun paroles. Ma quande lingues coalesce, li grammatica del resultant lingue es plu simplic e regulari quam ti del coalescent lingues. Li nov lingua franca va esser plu simplice.

Regulari quam li existent Europan lingues. It va esser tam simplic quam Occidental in fact, it va esser Occidental. A un Angleso it va semblar un simplificat Angles, quam un skeptic amico dit me que Occidental.

Lorem ipsum dolor sit amet, consect adipiscing elit, sed diam nonummy nibh euismod tincidunt ut laoreet dolore magna aliquam erat volutpat. Ut wisi enim ad minim veniam, quis nostrud exercitation ulliam corper suscipit lobortis nisl ut aliquip exea commodo consequat. Duis autem veleum iriure dolor in hendrerit in vulputate velit esse molestie consequat. Vel willum lunombro dolore eu feugiat nulla facilisis.

At vero eros et accumsan et iusto odio dignissim qui blandit praesent luptatum ezril delenit augue duis dolore te feugait nulla facilisi. Li lingues differe solmen in li grammatica, li pronunciation

1. Open ID F-2.indd, click **Fix Links Automatically**, navigate to the Missing folder to locate Red 1.psd, open Red 1.psd, then save the file as **Library Test**.

   > TIP   Do not be concerned if some of the files show the Linked File is Modified icon in the Links palette.

2. Drag **Dog Layer.psd** from the Min-Pin Library palette onto the document page.

3. Display the Links palette (if necessary).

   Dog Layer.psd is listed in the Links palette.

4. Center the graphic on the page, display the Text Wrap palette, then click the **Wrap around object shape button** 🔘 (if necessary).

5. Type **.5** in the Top Offset text box in the Text Wrap palette, deselect all, switch to Preview Mode (if necessary), then compare your document to Figure F-43.

6. Save your work, then close Library Test.

You dragged a graphic from the Min-Pin Library to the Library Test document.

Use the Links palette.

1. Open ID F-3.indd, click Don't Fix, then save the document as **Program Cover**. (*Hint*: Do not be concerned if some of the files show the Linked File is Modified or Linked File is Missing icons in the Links palette.)
2. Click the Normal View Mode button in the Toolbox (if necessary).
3. Click the Selection Tool, click the spotlight graphic on page 1, then note that the graphic's name is highlighted in the Links palette.
4. Click Final Logo.ai in the Links palette, then click the Go To Link button.
5. Click susan.psd in the Links palette, then click the Go To Link button.
6. Click the Relink button, navigate to the Missing folder, click susan.psd, then click Open.
7. Click the graphics frame with susan.psd, click Object on the menu bar, point to Fitting, then click Fit Content Proportionally.

8. Go to page 1, fit the page in the window, then click the center of the spotlight oval to select the empty graphics frame.

Place vector and bitmap graphics.

1. Click File on the menu bar, click Place, navigate to your Data Files folder, click Logo with Shadow.ai, then click Open.
2. Press [W] to switch to Preview Mode.
3. Click Object on the menu bar, point to Display Performance, click High Quality Display, then deselect all.
4. Go to page 2, then click the graphic named susan.psd.
5. Click the Zoom Tool, then zoom in on the graphic so that you are viewing it at 400%.
6. Click Object on the menu bar, point to Display Performance, then click High Quality Display.
7. Click Object on the menu bar, then click Clipping Path.

8. Click the Type list arrow, then click Detect Edges.
9. Verify that there is a check mark in the Preview check box.
10. Drag the Threshold slider to 40, then click OK.
11. With susan.psd still selected, click Object on the menu bar, then click Clipping Path.
12. Click the Type list arrow, then click Alpha Channel.
13. Click the Alpha list arrow, then click Head Silhouette Only.
14. Drag the Threshold slider to 1, verify that the Tolerance slider is set to 2, then click OK.
15. With susan.psd still selected, click Object on the menu bar, then click Clipping Path.
16. Click the Type list arrow, click Photoshop Path, then click OK.
17. Deselect all, then fit the page in the window.

Use libraries.

1. Click File on the menu bar, point to New, then click Library.
2. Name the library **Susan Library**, then click Save.
3. Click the Selection Tool, then drag the susan.psd graphic from page 2 into the Susan Library palette.
4. Drag Final Logo.ai from page 2 into the Susan Library palette.
5. Go to page 1, drag Logo with Shadow.ai into the Susan Library palette, then drag Spotlight.psd into the Susan Library palette.
6. Resize the Susan Library palette so that you can see all four graphics, then compare your page to Figure F-44.
7. Save your work, then close Program Cover.

FIGURE F-44

Completed Skills Review

You are a designer at a local studio. A client has delivered an Adobe Illustrator graphic for you to place in an InDesign document. She says she wants you to place it with a text wrap, then show her the results on your monitor.

1. Open ID F-4.indd, click Don't Fix in the alert dialog box, then save it as **Snowball**. (*Hint*: Do not be concerned if the Min Pin Text.doc file shows the Linked File is Modified icon in the Links palette.)
2. Click the Normal View Mode button in the Toolbox (if necessary).
3. Select the graphics frame in the center of the page, then place the file Snowball.ai.
4. Fit the content proportionally in the graphics frame.
5. Click the Wrap around object shape button in the Text Wrap palette, click the Type list arrow in the Text Wrap palette, then click Detect Edges.
6. Click Object on the menu bar, point to Display Performance, then click High Quality Display.
7. Deselect all, then switch to Preview Mode.
8. Save your work, compare your page to Figure F-45, then close Snowball.

FIGURE F-45
Completed Project Builder 1

You work for a print production service bureau. You have just been given a new job—to print 10 color copies of a supplied file. You open the file and decide that you need to update the links before printing the copies.

1. Open ID F-5.indd, click Don't Fix, then save the file as **Hawaii Links**.
2. Click the Preview Mode button in the Toolbox (if necessary).
3. Click the link for Tree coverage.psd that is on page 1, then click the Go To Link button.
4. Click the Relink button, navigate to the Missing folder in your Data Files folder, click Tree coverage.psd, then click Open.
5. Relink Tree coverage.psd that is on page 2.
6. Relink the remaining files in the Links palette, if necessary.
7. Compare your Links palette to Figure F-46.
8. Save your work, then close Hawaii Links.

FIGURE F-46
Completed Project Builder 2

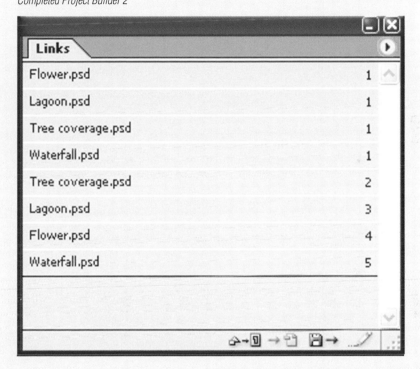

You are designing a cover for LAB magazine. You run into a problem. The way the
cover photograph has been shot, the dog's
face is hidden behind the magazine's title.
You open the photograph in Photoshop,
then create a path around the dog's head.

1. Open ID F-6.indd, click Fix Links
   Automatically, then save it as **Lab Cover**.
2. Click the Normal View Mode button in the
   Toolbox (if necessary).
3. Verify that guides are showing.
4. Click the Selection Tool, click the photograph, copy it, click Edit on the menu bar,
   then click Paste in Place.
5. Place the file Wally Head Silo.psd.
   (*Hint*: When the new graphic is placed, it
   will look exactly the same as the previous
   graphic.)
6. Click Object on the menu bar, then click
   Clipping Path.
7. Click the Type list arrow, click Photoshop
   Path, then click OK.
8. Click Object on the menu bar, point to
   Arrange, then click Send Backward.
9. Deselect all, click View on the menu bar,
   point to Display Performance, then click
   High Quality Display.
10. Click View on the menu bar, click Hide
    Guides, then compare your page to
    Figure F-47.
11. Save your work, then close Lab Cover.

FIGURE F-47
Completed Design Project

GROUP PROJECT

In this group project, one member of the group will demonstrate how to save a graphic in Photoshop with a transparent background and then place it against a colored background in InDesign.

Note: This project requires that both Photoshop and InDesign are available on the computer being used for the demonstration.

1. Start Photoshop, open ID F-7.psd, then save it as **Soft Circle**.
2. Display the Layers palette (if necessary).
3. Click the Elliptical Marquee Tool, press and hold [Shift], then create a circle that is approximately the diameter of a compact disc on top of the flower. (*Hint*: The Elliptical Marquee Tool may be hidden beneath the Rectangular Marquee Tool.)
4. Click Select on the menu bar, click Feather, type **16**, then click OK.
5. Click Edit on the menu bar, click Copy, click Edit on the menu bar, then click Paste.
6. In the Layers palette, click the Indicates layer visibility button (eye) on the Background layer to make the Background layer invisible. (*Hint*: Your Photoshop window should resemble Figure F-48.)
7. Save your work click OK, in the Photoshop Format Options dialog box (if necessary), close Soft Circle, then close Photoshop.
8. Start InDesign, open ID F-8.indd, then save it as **Soft Circle Layout**.
9. Click the Normal View Mode button in the Toolbox (if necessary).
10. Place Soft Circle.psd in the graphics frame at the center of the page.
11. Click Object on the menu bar, point to Fitting, then click Fit Content to Frame.
12. Click Object on the menu bar, point to Display Performance, then click High Quality Display.
13. Deselect all, press [W], then compare your page to Figure F-49.

FIGURE F-48
Soft Circle.psd

FIGURE F-49
Completed Group Project

CHAPTER G

CREATING GRAPHICS

1. Use the Pen Tool.

2. Reshape frames and apply stroke effects.

3. Work with polygons and compound paths.

4. Work with advanced text features, corner effects, and drop shadows.

CHAPTER G
CREATING GRAPHICS

By now, you are aware that InDesign is a sophisticated layout program, but you may be surprised to find out that it is a cool little graphics program as well. You can use the Pen Tool to create any shape, which is why it's often called "the drawing tool." More precisely, the Pen Tool is a tool for drawing straight lines, curved lines, polygons, and irregularly shaped objects. The challenges of the Pen Tool are finite if you study its features. Like most else in graphic design (and in life!), mastery comes with practice. So make it a point to learn Pen Tool techniques. And use the Pen Tool often, even if it's just to play around making odd shapes.

In addition to the Pen Tool, you can create simple shapes with the Rectangle, Ellipse, and Polygon Tools, and then reshape them using the Direct Selection Tool. You can also apply corner effects—like rounded corners—drop shadows, and stroke effects. If you're into typography, you can use the Type on a Path Tool to position type on any path. You can even wrap it around a circle!

So sit down and get ready to have fun with Chapter G. It's back to the drawing board!

Tools You'll Use

Pen tools

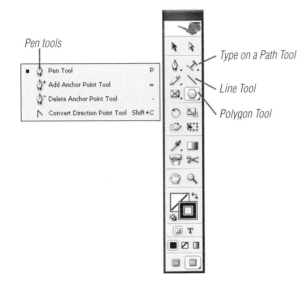

- Pen Tool   P
- Add Anchor Point Tool =
- Delete Anchor Point Tool -
- Convert Direction Point Tool Shift+C

Type on a Path Tool

Line Tool

Polygon Tool

Stroke

Weight: 10 pt   Cap:

Miter Limit: 4   x   Join:

Align Stroke:

Type:

Start: None

End: None

Gap Color: [None]

Gap Tint: 100%

Corners: Adjust dashes and gaps

12 pt

dash   gap   dash   gap   dash   gap

Polygon Settings

Number of Sides: 6   OK

Star Inset: 0%   Cancel

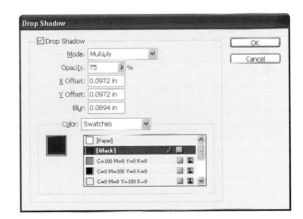

Drop Shadow

☑ Drop Shadow   OK

Mode: Multiply   Cancel

Opacity: 75 %

X Offset: 0.0972 in

Y Offset: 0.0972 in

Blur: 0.0694 in

Color: Swatches

[Paper]

[Black]

C=100 M=0 Y=0 K=0

C=0 M=100 Y=0 K=0

C=0 M=0 Y=100 K=0

USE THE PEN TOOL

What You'll Do

In this lesson, you will use the Pen Tool to create a complex vector graphic.

Understanding the Pen Tool

You use the Pen Tool to create **paths**—straight or curved lines. Paths, which consist of anchor points and line segments, are created by clicking the Pen Tool on the page. Each time you click the Pen Tool, you create an anchor point. Line segments automatically fall into place between every two anchor points. You start off by creating one anchor point, then creating another at a different location. Once the second anchor point is created, a line segment is automatically placed between the two anchor points, as shown in Figure G-1. The number of anchor points and line segments you'll need depends on the type of object you are creating.

QUICKTIP

The Pen Tool can also be found in both Adobe Illustrator and Adobe Photoshop. In Illustrator, as in InDesign, the Pen Tool is used to draw—to create shapes. In Photoshop, the Pen Tool is most often used to create clipping paths to silhouette images.

You can create open paths or closed paths with the Pen Tool. The letter U, or a simple straight line, are both good examples of open paths. An **open path** is a path whose end points are not connected. You can think of a circular object, such as a melon or the letter O, as examples of closed paths. **Closed paths** are continuous lines that do not contain end points. In fact, when you create a closed path, you end your drawing at the same point where you started it by clicking the Pen Tool on the first anchor point. Figure G-2 shows examples of open and closed paths.

Notice that in this example, some paths are filled with color. You can apply fills and strokes to paths. In general, you will seldom want to fill an open path. Usually, when a path is open, you will want only to apply a stroke to it.

Choose None for a fill when you are drawing with the Pen Tool, then add a fill after you close your path. If you have a fill color selected while you draw, the fill color will create a new fill each time you add an anchor point, which can be very distracting.

Drawing Straight Segments with the Pen Tool

Drawing straight segments with the Pen Tool is easy. Simply click with the Pen Tool, then click again in a new location and your first straight segment appears. Straight segments are connected by **corner points**—

anchor points that create a corner between the two segments. Figure G-3 shows a simple path drawn with five anchor points and four segments.

Pressing and holding [Shift] constrains the Pen Tool to create either straight lines or diagonal lines at 45 degrees.

Reconnecting to a Path

There will be times when you are working with the Pen Tool that you will become

disconnected from the path. This often happens when you stop drawing, change tools to do something else, then go back to the Pen Tool. When you create a new anchor point, you will be surprised that it stands alone—no path segment connects it to the path you made previously.

Whenever you need to reconnect to a path, simply position the Pen Tool over the path's end point until a diagonal line appears beside the Pen Tool. Then, click the end point. You have successfully reconnected to the path and can continue drawing.

FIGURE G-1

Creating paths with the Pen Tool

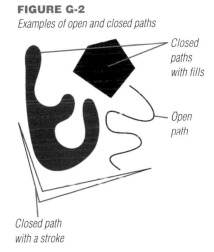

First anchor point

Third anchor point

Line segment created between second and third anchor points

Line segment created between first and second anchor points

Second anchor point

Click here to create fourth anchor point

FIGURE G-2

Examples of open and closed paths

Closed paths with fills

Open path

Closed path with a stroke

FIGURE G-3

Elements of a path composed of straight segments

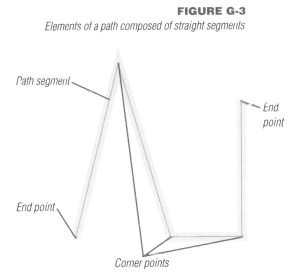

Path segment

End point

End point

Corner points

Adding Anchor Points and Using the Direct Selection Tool

Perfection is an unnecessary goal when you are using the Pen Tool. Anchor points and line segments can be moved and repositioned. New points can be added and deleted. Use the Pen Tool to create the general shape that you have in your mind. Once the object is complete, you can use the Direct Selection Tool to perfect—or tweak—the points and paths. "Tweaking" a finished object—making small, specific improvements—is always part of the drawing process.

To use the Direct Selection Tool, make sure your path is deselected, then click the path with the Direct Selection Tool. The anchor points, which normally contain a solid fill color, appear hollow or empty. This means that you can use the Direct Selection Tool to move each anchor point independently.

Simply click an anchor point, then drag it to a new location. You can also use the Direct Selection Tool to move a line segment independently.

When the Pen Tool is positioned over a line segment, it automatically changes to the Add Anchor Point Tool. Click the path and an anchor point will be added, which you can use to manipulate the path further.

Deleting Anchor Points

When the Pen Tool is positioned over an existing anchor point, it automatically changes to the Delete Anchor Point Tool. Click the anchor point to delete it from the path. When you delete an anchor point, the two segments on both sides of it are joined as one new segment. The Delete Anchor Point Tool will delete a point from the path without breaking the path into two paths. This is very different from selecting an

anchor point and using the Cut command or the Delete key to delete it. If you do so, the two line segments on both sides of it are also deleted, thus creating a break in your path.

Drawing Curved Segments with the Pen Tool

So far you have learned about creating straight paths. You can also draw curved paths with the Pen Tool. To draw a curved path, click an anchor point, then click and drag the Pen Tool when creating the next point. A curved segment will appear between the new point and the previous point.

Anchor points that connect curved segments are called **smooth points**. A smooth point has two **direction lines** attached to it. Direction lines determine the arc of the curved path, depending on their direction and length. Figure G-4 shows a curved

FIGURE G-4

A smooth point and direction lines

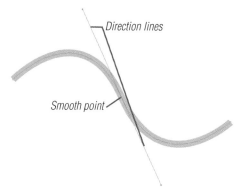

Direction lines

Smooth point

Creating Graphics

path made from three smooth points. Since the center point is selected, you can see the two direction lines attached to it.

Changing the Shape of a Path Using Direction Lines

Using the Direct Selection Tool, you can manipulate the direction lines of a smooth point. When you do this, you alter the arc of both segments attached to the point, always maintaining a smooth transition through the anchor point. Simply click the point that you want to modify, then drag the **direction handle**—the round blue circle at the top of the direction line—in a new direction or to shorten or elongate it.

When two segments are joined at a **corner point**, the two segments can be manipulated independently. A corner point can join two straight segments, one straight segment and one curved segment, or two curved segments. That corner point would have zero, one, and two direction lines, respectively.

Figure G-5 compares smooth points and corner points and shows how direction lines define the shape of a path.

Converting Anchor Points

Direction lines work in tandem. When you move one, the other one also moves. This is often very useful when making curved paths. However, in some cases, you will want to move one direction line independently of the other, especially when creating or tracing a path that abruptly changes direction.

The Convert Direction Point Tool "breaks" a smooth point's direction lines and allows you to move one independently of the other. When you do so, the smooth point is converted to a corner point that now joins two unrelated curved paths. Once the direction lines are broken, they remain broken. You can manipulate them independently with the Direct Selection Tool; you no longer need the Convert Direction Point Tool to do so.

FIGURE G-5
Smooth points, corner points, and direction lines

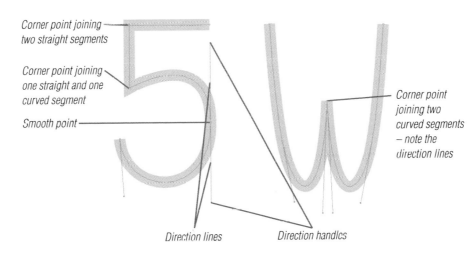

Corner point joining two straight segments

Corner point joining one straight and one curved segment

Smooth point

Corner point joining two curved segments – note the direction lines

Direction lines

Direction handles

The Convert Direction Point Tool can also be used to change corner points to smooth points and smooth points to corner points. To convert a corner point to a smooth point, click the Convert Direction Point Tool on the anchor point, then drag the pointer. As you drag, new direction lines appear, as shown in Figure G-6.

To convert a smooth point to a corner point, simply click the Convert Direction Point Tool on the smooth point. The direction lines disappear and the two attached paths become straight paths, as shown in the center object in Figure G-7.

Note the rightmost object in Figure G-7. If you drag a direction line with the Convert Direction Point Tool, the point is automatically converted from a smooth point to a corner point. Therefore, the direction line you are dragging moves independently from the other direction line.

FIGURE G-6
Converting a corner point to a smooth point

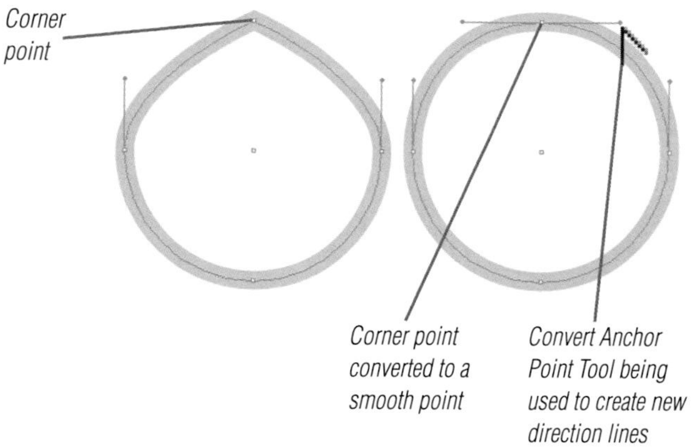

FIGURE G-7
Converting a smooth point to a corner point

Corner point

Corner point converted to a smooth point

Convert Anchor Point Tool being used to create new direction lines

Smooth point

Smooth point converted to a corner point

Dragging direction line converts smooth point to corner point

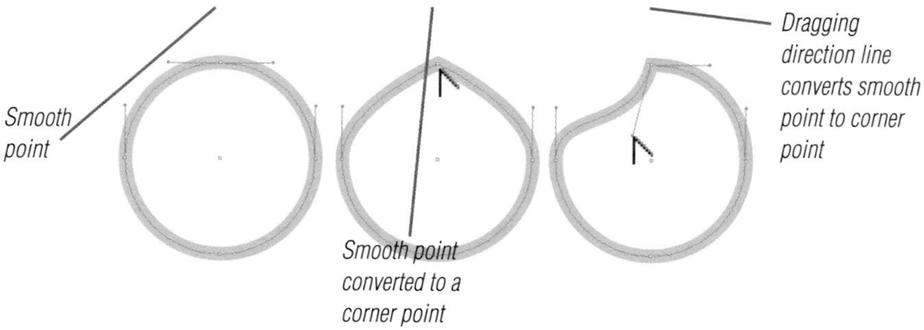

FIGURE G-8

Drawing straight paths

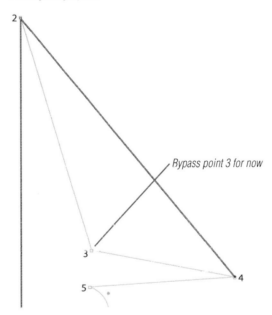

Bypass point 3 for now

Create straight segments

1. Open ID G-1.indd, then save it as **Halloween Witch**.

2. Click **View** on the menu bar, point to **Display Performance**, then click **High Quality Display** (if necessary).

3. In the Toolbox, set the Fill button to None and the Stroke button to black.

4. Click the **Zoom Tool** 🔍 , then draw a selection box around the bottom half of the witch template.

5. Verify that Layer 2 is targeted in the Layers palette, click the **Pen Tool** ✒ , then click the center of the purple star at the bottom-right corner of the witch template.

   TIP The Pen Tool may be hidden behind the Add Anchor Point Tool ✒⁺ , the Delete Anchor Point Tool ✒⁻ , or the Convert Direction Point Tool ⌐ .

6. Press and hold **[Shift]**, then click **point 1** by clicking the small white square next to it.

   TIP As you proceed, click the small white square next to each consecutive number.

   Pressing and holding [Shift] constrains the Pen Tool to create either straight lines or diagonal lines at 45 degrees.

7. Press **[Spacebar]** to access the Hand Tool, then click and drag the document window using the Hand Tool to scroll to the top of the witch's hat.

8. Press and hold **[Shift]**, then click **point 2**.

9. Release [Shift], bypass point 3, then click **point 4**, so that your screen resembles Figure G-8.

You created straight segments with the Pen Tool.

Add an anchor point to a path

1. Position the Pen Tool 𝄐 over the path between point 2 and point 4.

   TIP When the Pen Tool is positioned directly over a path, it changes to the Add Anchor Point Tool.

2. Click anywhere on the path between the two points.

   An anchor point is added where you clicked.

3. Click the **Direct Selection Tool** ▶ , click the **new anchor point**, then drag it to point 3, so that your path resembles Figure G-9.

   TIP Only the Direct Selection Tool allows you to select a single point on a path.

4. Click the **Pen Tool** 𝄐 , then click **point 5**.

   An anchor point is created, but it is not joined to the existing path.

5. Click **Edit** on the menu bar, then click **Undo Add New Item**.

   The stray anchor point is removed.

6. Click **point 4** with the Pen Tool to reconnect with the path, then click **point 5**.

   TIP To reconnect to an open path, simply click the end point with the Pen Tool.

7. Click **point 5**, then drag a **direction line** to the center of the yellow star, so that your screen resembles Figure G-10.

   This path has made an abrupt change in direction. The new direction line points in the direction that the path will go in order to draw the next segment.

You added an anchor point to the path, then repositioned it. You then reconnected to the path, which allowed you to continue drawing.

INDESIGN G-10

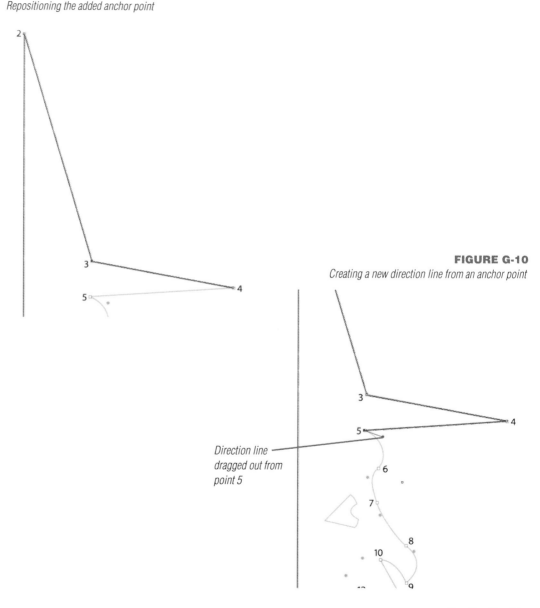

Direction line dragged out from point 5

FIGURE G-11
Viewing four curved segments

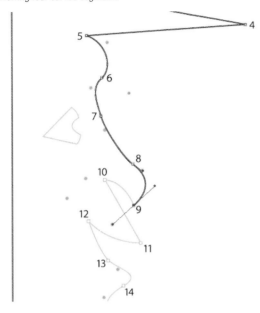

FIGURE G-13
Viewing the path between points 8 and 9

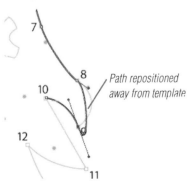

Path repositioned
away from template

FIGURE G-12
Viewing the path between points 9 and 10

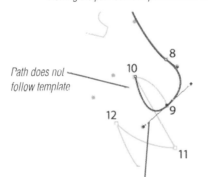

Path does not
follow template

Direction line from point 9 does
not point toward point 10

Lesson 1   Use the Pen Tool

Create curved segments

1. Position the Pen Tool 🖊 over point 6, then click and drag a **direction line** to the next yellow star.

2. Position the Pen Tool over point 7, then click and drag a **direction line** to the next yellow star.

3. Position the Pen Tool over point 8, then click and drag a **direction line** to the next yellow star.

4. Position the Pen Tool over point 9, then click and drag a **direction line** to the yellow star between points 12 and 11, so that your screen resembles Figure G-11.

You created four curved segments.

Use the Convert Direction Point Tool to change directions while drawing

1. Click the **Pen Tool** 🖊 on point 10.

   As shown in Figure G-12, the path does not follow the template because the direction line on point 9 points in a different direction.

2. Click the **Direct Selection Tool** ▸, then drag the **direction line** from point 9 to position the path properly between points 9 and 10.

   As shown in Figure G-13, because the direction lines are joined by the same anchor point, manipulating the path between points 9 and 10 also repositions the path between points 8 and 9.

3. Click **Edit** on the menu bar, then click **Undo Modify Path**.

(continued)

4. Click the **Convert Direction Point Tool** 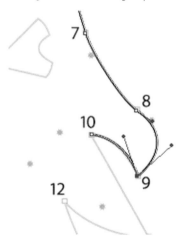, then drag the **direction line** from point 9 to position the path properly between points 9 and 10.

   As shown in Figure G-14, the Convert Direction Point Tool allows you to alter the path between points 9 and 10 without affecting the path between points 8 and 9.

5. Click the **Pen Tool**, click **point 10** to reconnect to the path, then click **point 11**.

6. Position the Pen Tool over point 12, then click and drag a **direction line** to the yellow star above it.

   The direction line does not point toward the next point—point 13.

7. Click **point 12** with the Pen Tool.

   Clicking a point with the Pen Tool removes the direction line.

8. Position the Pen Tool over point 13, then click and drag a **direction line** to the yellow star.

   (continued)

FIGURE G-14
Viewing the results of altering the path with the Convert Direction Point Tool

FIGURE G-15

Viewing the finished drawing

9. Position the Pen Tool over point 14, then click and drag a **direction line** to the yellow star.

10. Using the same skills used in Steps 6 through 9, create points 15 through 18.

11. Click the **starting anchor point** (on the purple star) to close the path.

12. Click the **Swap Fill and Stroke button**  in the Toolbox, fit the page in the window, then hide Layer 1 in the Layers palette.

13. Save your work, compare your page to Figure G-15, then close Halloween Witch.

You finished drawing a closed path. You used the Convert Direction Point Tool to change direction while drawing.

RESHAPE FRAMES AND APPLY STROKE EFFECTS

What You'll Do

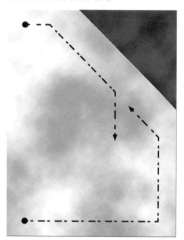

 In this lesson, you will use the Pen Tool to reshape frames and create stroke effects, including dashed line patterns.

Reshaping Frames

The Toolbox offers a number of tools for creating basic shapes. The graphics frame tools include the Rectangle, Polygon, and Ellipse; you can also use the regular Rectangle, Polygon, and Ellipse tools. The objects that you create with any of these tools can be modified using the Direct Selection Tool or the Pen Tool.

When you select an object, the appearance of the object will differ depending on which of the two selection tools is selected in the Toolbox. Figure G-16 shows the appearance of the same object when the Selection Tool and the Direct Selection Tool are active in the Toolbox.

When the Selection Tool is selected, you'll see the object's bounding box. The bounding box includes eight handles, which you can manipulate to change the object's size.

When you click the Direct Selection Tool, the object's bounding box disappears and is replaced by its path. You can select and move anchor points or path segments along the path. Figure G-17 shows a rectangle

Using the rectangle tools

The Toolbox contains two tools for creating rectangles: the Rectangle Frame Tool and the Rectangle Tool. What is the difference, you may ask? The surprising answer is that there really is no difference. Both create rectangular shaped objects. Both can be filled and stroked with color. Both can contain a placed graphic. About the only distinction between the two is that the Rectangle Frame Tool is considered one of the graphics frames tools and is used for placing graphics in, whereas the Rectangle Tool creates rectangles that are meant to be used as simple illustrations. However, as stated above, both can be filled and stroked, and both can contain placed graphics.

Creating Graphics

reshaped by using the Direct Selection Tool. Figure G-18 shows that, when the Selection Tool is activated, the reshaped object is once again positioned within its bounding box.

When an object is selected, clicking the Pen Tool has the same effect as clicking the Direct Selection Tool—the eight handles disappear and are replaced by anchor points. Just as with any other path, you can use the Pen Tool to add or delete anchor points to give you further control for reshaping an object. Figure G-19 shows the same object reshaped with three added anchor points.

Remember, when the Direct Selection Tool or the Pen Tool is active in the Toolbox, any selected object is essentially a path, composed of anchor points and path segments, and able to be manipulated like any other path. This means that, using the Direct Selection Tool or the Pen Tool, the basic objects that you create with the shape tools—rectangles, ellipses, and polygons—can be reshaped into anything that your imagination can dream up!

FIGURE G-16
Viewing a selected object

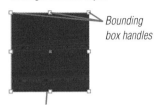 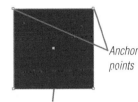

Bounding box handles

Anchor points

Appearance of selected object when Selection Tool is active

Appearance of selected object when Direct Selection Tool is active

FIGURE G-17
A reshaped rectangle

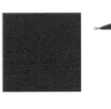

Anchor points may be moved independently

FIGURE G-18
A reshaped rectangle with the Selection Tool activated

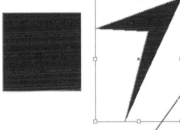

Bounding box

FIGURE G-19
A rectangle reshaped with three added anchor points

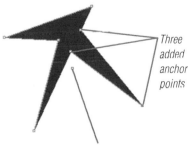

Three added anchor points

Center point

Defining Strokes

Color that you apply to a path is called a stroke. Once you've applied a stroke to a path, you can manipulate characteristics of the stroke using the Stroke palette. There, you can adjust the weight or thickness of the stroke. You have options for changing the design of the stroke, such as making it a dotted line instead of a solid line. You can format the stroke as a dashed stroke, and you can apply end shapes to the stroke, such as arrowheads and tail feathers.

Defining Joins and Caps

Once you've applied a stroke to a path, you should decide upon joins and caps for the path. Make a note of this, because your choice for joins and caps can have a subtle but effective impact on your illustration. However, these are attributes that many designers forget about or just plain ignore—to the detriment of their work.

Joins define the appearance of a corner point when a path has a stroke applied to it. There are three types of joins: miter, round, and bevel. The miter join, which produces pointed corners, is the default. The round join produces rounded corners, and the bevel join produces squared corners. Figure G-20 shows examples of all three joins.

Sometimes, it is hard to see which type of join is being used. The greater the weight of the stroke, the more apparent the join will be.

Caps define the appearance of end points when a stroke is added to a path. The Stroke palette offers three types of caps: butt, round, and projecting. Butt caps produce squared ends and round caps produce rounded ends. Generally, round caps are more appealing to the eye. The projecting cap applies a squared edge that extends the anchor point at a distance that is one-half the weight of the stroke. With a projecting cap, the weight of the stroke is equal in all directions around the line. The projecting cap is useful when you align two anchor points at a right angle, as shown in Figure G-21.

Joins and caps are subtle features, but they are effective. Note the different appearances of the three heads in Figure G-22. Note the round caps vs. the bluntness of the butt caps, especially visible on the character's nose. Note, too, the corners of the character's mouth, which are sharp with miter joins, rounded with round joins, and blunt with bevel joins.

FIGURE G-20
Three types of joins

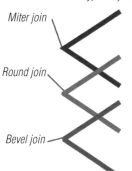

Miter join

Round join

Bevel join

FIGURE G-21
Viewing projecting caps

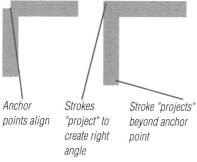

Anchor points align

Strokes "project" to create right angle

Stroke "projects" beyond anchor point

FIGURE G-22
Viewing different effects with different joins and caps

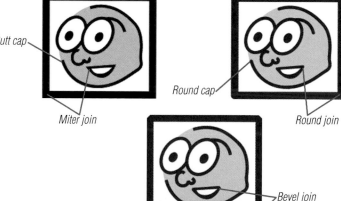

Butt cap

Miter join

Round cap

Round join

Bevel join

Creating Graphics

Defining the Miter Limit

The miter limit determines when a miter join will be squared off to a beveled edge. The miter is the length of the point, from the inside to the outside, as shown in Figure G-23. The length of the miter is not the same as the stroke weight. When two stroked paths are at an acute angle, the length of the miter will greatly exceed the weight of the stroke, which results in an extreme point that can be very distracting.

The default miter limit is 4, which means that when the length of the miter reaches 4 times the stroke weight, it will automatically be squared off to a beveled edge. Generally, you will find the default miter limit satisfactory, but be conscious of it when you draw objects with acute angles, such as stars or triangles.

Creating a Dashed Stroke

Dashed strokes, which are created and formatted using the Stroke palette, are strokes that consist of a series of dashes and gaps. You define the dash sequence for a dashed stroke by entering the lengths of the dashes and the gaps between them in the dash and gap text boxes in the Stroke palette. You can create a maximum of three different sized dashes separated by three different sized gaps. The pattern you establish will be repeated across the length of the stroke. Figure G-24 shows a dashed stroke and its formatting in the Stroke palette.

FIGURE G-23

Understanding miters and miter limits

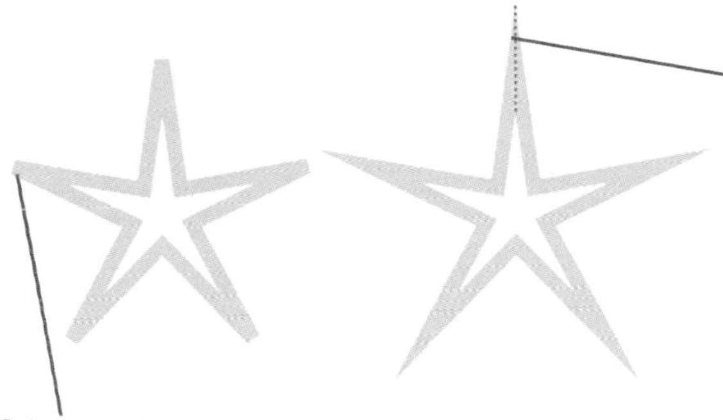

FIGURE G-24

Formatting a dashed stroke

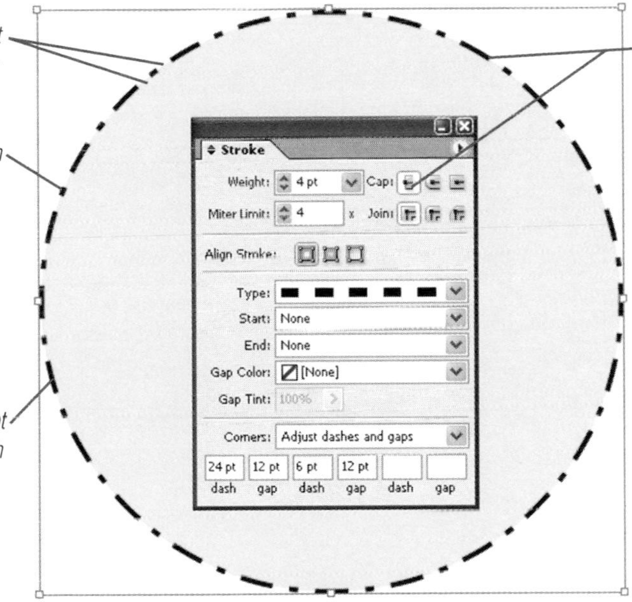

Measurement of miter

Point reduced to a beveled edge

12 pt gaps

6 pt dash

24 pt dash

Dashes have butt caps

Reshape a frame using the Direct Selection Tool and Pen Tool

1. Open ID G-2.indd, then save it as **Halloween Invitation**.

2. Click the **Selection Tool** ▶ , click the **Orange Clouds.tif graphic**, copy it, click **Edit** on the menu bar, then click **Paste in Place**.

   A duplicate frame and graphic is placed directly in front of the original.

3. Place Blue Clouds.tif, from the location where your Chapter G Data Files are stored, in the new frame.

4. Click the **Direct Selection Tool** ▶ .

5. Drag the **top-right corner point** toward the center so that it is in approximately the location shown in Figure G-25.

6. Click **Edit** on the menu bar, then click **Undo Move**.

7. Click the **Pen Tool** ♧ , then add an anchor point on the top path of the frame, where it intersects with the burgundy guide.

8. Add an anchor point on the right path of the frame, where it intersects with the burgundy guide.

   Your page should resemble Figure G-26.

9. Position the Pen Tool over the top-right corner point.

   The Pen Tool becomes the Delete Anchor Point Tool ♧ .

10. Click the **top-right corner point** to delete it.

    Your screen should resemble Figure G-27.

You used the Pen Tool to reshape a graphics frame.

FIGURE G-25
Moving the top-right corner point independently

FIGURE G-26
Viewing two added anchor points

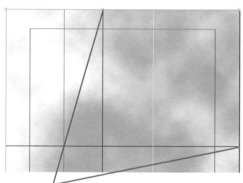

Added anchor points

FIGURE G-27
Viewing the results of deleting an anchor point

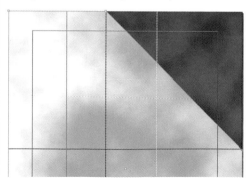

FIGURE G-28

Creating a rectangle

Path positioned
on margin guides

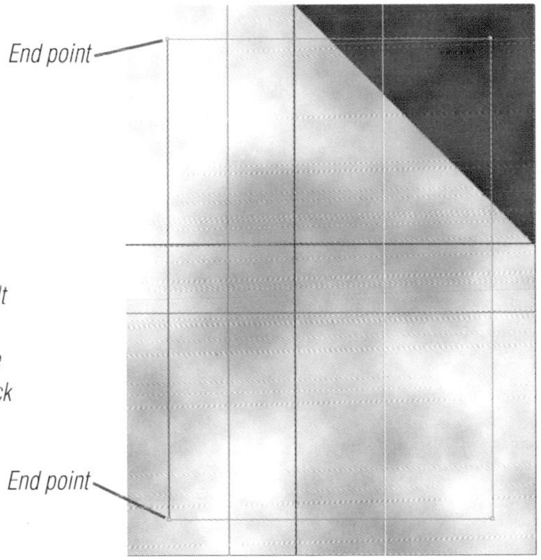

FIGURE G-30

Viewing the path

Clicking the Default
Fill and Stroke
button changes the
stroke color to black

FIGURE G-29

Viewing the results of deleting the added anchor point

End point

End point

Reshape a frame into an open path

1. Verify that None is selected for both the fill and stroke colors in the Toolbox, click the **Rectangle Tool** ▢, then create a rectangle that snaps to the inside of the four margin guides, as shown in Figure G-28.

2. Click the **Pen Tool** ✎, then add an anchor point anywhere on the left segment of the frame.

3. With the new anchor point still selected, click **Edit** on the menu bar, then click **Cut**.

   As shown in Figure G-29, when the anchor point is cut, the two segments connected to it are also deleted.

4. Click the **Default Fill and Stroke button** ▣ in the Toolbox.

5. Click **Window** on the menu bar, then click **Stroke**.

6. Click the **Weight list arrow** in the Stroke palette, then click **4 pt**.

7. Using the Pen Tool, add an anchor point on the top path of the frame, where it intersects with the blue guide.

8. Add an anchor point on the right path of the frame, where it intersects with the blue guide.

9. Click the **Delete Anchor Point Tool** ✎, then click the **top-right anchor point**.

   Your screen should resemble Figure G-30.

You created a simple rectangle, then reshaped it into an open path.

Use the Stroke palette to add end shapes to a path

1. Click the **Preview Mode button** 🔲, in the Toolbox, click the **Selection Tool** ▶, then click the **black-stroked path**.

   | TIP All objects, even open paths, are selected within a rectangular bounding box.

2. Click the **Start list arrow** in the Stroke palette, then click **CircleSolid**.

   | TIP Click the Stroke palette list arrow, then click Show Options, if necessary.

3. Click the **End list arrow**, click **CircleSolid**, then compare your page to Figure G-31.

4. Click the **Normal View Mode button** 🔲, click the **Pen Tool** ✒, then position it over the location where the diagonal section of the black path intersects with the yellow guide.

5. When you see the Pen Tool change to the Add Anchor Point Tool ✒⁺, click.

6. Add another anchor point where the black path intersects with the horizontal burgundy guide.

7. Add a third new anchor point approximately halfway between the two new anchor points.

8. Deselect all, click the **Direct Selection Tool** ▶, select only the anchor point you added in Step 7, click **Edit** on the menu bar, then click **Cut**.

   Your page should resemble Figure G-32.

9. Deselect all, click the **Selection Tool** ▶, click the top black path, click the **Pen Tool** ✒, float it over the anchor point where the top black path intersects with the yellow guide, then stop when a diagonal line appears beside the Pen Tool.

   (continued)

CircleSolid
end shapes

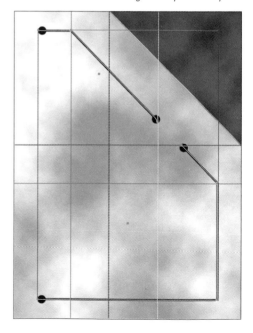

FIGURE G-33

Adding a triangle end shape to an extended path

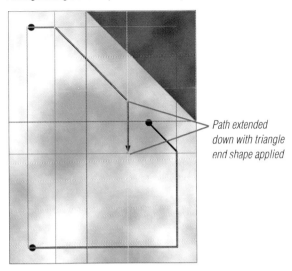

Path extended
down with triangle
end shape applied

FIGURE G-35

Viewing dashed strokes

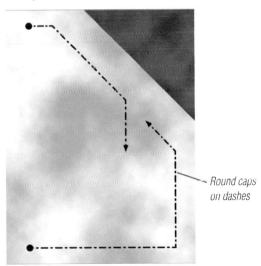

Round caps
on dashes

The diagonal line indicates that the Pen Tool
is being used to reconnect to the path.

10. Click the **Pen Tool** 🖋 on the anchor point,
press and hold **[Shift]**, then click where the
yellow guide intersects with the blue guide.

11. In the Stroke palette, click the **Start list
arrow**, then click **Triangle**.

Your page should resemble Figure G-33.

12. Click the **Selection Tool** 🔺, select the bottom black path, click the **End list arrow**, then
click **Triangle**.

*You added end shapes to a path, split the path,
then noted that the end shapes were applied to the
two new paths.*

FIGURE G-34

Formatting a dashed stroke

Dash and
gap sizes

Create a dashed stroke

1. Click **View** on the menu bar, then click **Hide
Guides**.

2. Click the **Selection Tool** 🔺, then select
both **black paths**.

3. Click the **Type list arrow** in the Stroke
palette, then click **Dashed**.

4. Type **14**, **8**, **3**, and **8** in the dash and gap text
boxes in the Stroke palette, as shown in
Figure G-34.

5. Click the **Round Cap button** 🗀 in the
Stroke palette, deselect, then compare your
page to Figure G-35.

*You used the Stroke palette to format a path with a
dashed stroke using round caps.*

WORK WITH POLYGONS AND COMPOUND PATHS

What You'll Do

In this lesson, you will work with polygons and use them to create compound paths and inline graphics.

Creating Polygons

The Toolbox offers the Polygon Tool and the Polygon Frame Tool for creating multi-sided objects, such as triangles, pentagons, hexagons, etc. You can place graphics into objects you create with either tool.

To determine how many sides you want your polygon to be, double-click the tool to open the Polygon Settings dialog box, as shown in Figure G-36. If, for example, you enter 5 in the Number of Sides text box and then click OK, when you click and drag with the Polygon Tool selected, you will create a perfect pentagon.

FIGURE G-36
Polygon Settings dialog box

The Star Inset setting allows you to use the Polygon Tool or the Polygon Frame Tool to create star shapes. The greater the Star Inset percentage, the more acute and longer the points of the star will be, as shown in Figure G-37. The number entered in the Number of Sides text box determines the number of points on the star.

Creating Compound Paths

Imagine you were going to use the Pen Tool to trace the outline of a doughnut. You would draw an outer circle for the dough-nut itself, then an inner circle to define the doughnut hole. Then, you would want to

FIGURE G-37
Comparing different star inset percentages

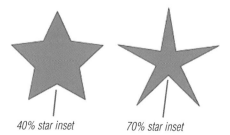

40% star inset   70% star inset

format the two paths so that the inner circle "cuts a hole" in the outer circle.

You create **compound paths** when you want to use one object to cut a hole in another object. In the above example, you would select both circles and then apply the Compound Path command. Figure G-38 shows an example of the result. Note that you can see the blue square through the hole in the gold circle.

Once compounded, the two paths create one object.

Compound paths are not only used for the practical purpose of creating a hole. When you work with odd or overlapping shapes, the Compound Path command can produce results that are visually interesting and can be used as design elements, as shown in Figure G-39.

Using Polygons as Inline Frames

Inline frames are objects that you create and use as text characters within a block of text. Figure G-40 shows a red star used as an inline frame to make a block of text appear more eye-catching.

Inline frames flow with the text as though it were a text character. For example, when you edit the text, the inline frame will flow forward or backward with the rest of the text.

Inline frames can be used for practical purposes. For example, if you were designing a form that required check boxes, you could create a simple rectangle and then use it as an inline frame wherever you needed a check box to appear.

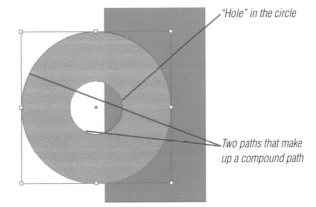

"Hole" in the circle

Two paths that make up a compound path

A "hole" is created where the letter overlaps the circle

FIGURE G-40
Viewing inline frames

Our annual Summer Sale ★ begins on Tuesday ★ Get huge discounts ★ from many of your favorite departments.

Inline frame

Create polygons, circles, and lines

1. In the Toolbox, set the fill color to black and the stroke color to None, then double-click the **Polygon Tool** ⬡ in the Toolbox.

   TIP The Polygon Tool may be hidden beneath the Rectangle Tool, or the Ellipse Tool.

2. Type **8** in the Number of Sides text box, type **70** in the Star Inset text box, then click **OK**.

3. Drag anywhere on the page to create a polygon of any size.

4. In the Transform palette, verify that the center reference point on the proxy is selected, type **1.25** in both the Width and Height text boxes, press **[Enter]** (Win) or **[return]** (Mac), then position the polygon in the top-right corner of the page, as shown in Figure G-41.

5. Deselect the polygon, change the fill color in the Toolbox to yellow, click the **Ellipse Tool** ◯ , then position your cursor at the center of the black star polygon.

6. Press and hold **[Shift][Alt]** (Win) or **[Shift][option]** (Mac), then drag a circle approximately the size shown in Figure G-42.

   TIP Pressing and holding [Alt] (Win) or [option] (Mac) allows you to draw a circle from its center. Pressing and holding [Shift] constrains the shape to a perfect circle.

7. Click the **Selection Tool** � , click the **pasteboard** to deselect all, click the **Swap Fill & Stroke button** ↰ in the Toolbox, click the **Stroke button** to activate it, then change the weight in the Stroke palette to 4 pt and the type to Solid.

(continued)

FIGURE G-41
Positioning the polygon

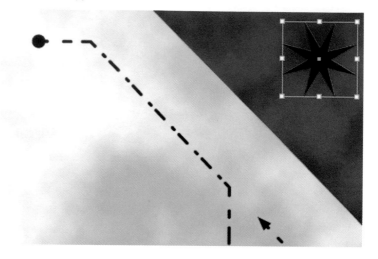

FIGURE G-42
Drawing the circle

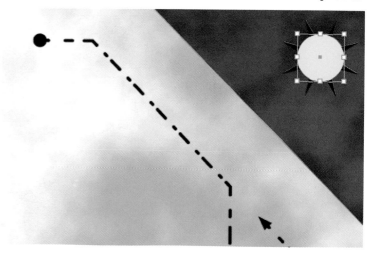

FIGURE G-43
Drawing the line

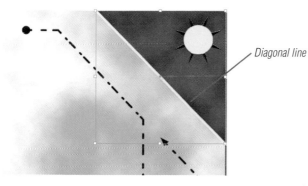

Diagonal line

FIGURE G-45
Viewing the witch polygon with the placed graphic and black stroke

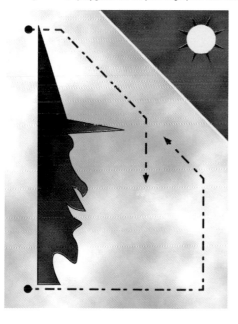

FIGURE G-44
Positioning the witch polygon

8. Click the **Line Tool** ⟍, position your cursor on the top edge of the page where the orange clouds graphic meets the blue clouds graphic, then drag a **diagonal line** along the base of the orange clouds triangle, as shown in Figure G-43.

You created an eight-pointed polygon, a circle, and a line.

Place graphics in polygons

1. Open the Halloween Witch file that you created, select the witch graphic, copy it, click **Window** on the menu bar, click **Halloween Invitation.indd**, click **Edit** on the menu bar, then click **Paste**.

2. Position the witch polygon in the location shown in Figure G-44.

3. Click **File** on the menu bar, click **Place**, navigate to the drive and folder where your Chapter G Data Files are stored, then double-click **Orange Clouds.tif**.

4. Click the **Swap Fill & Stroke button** ↰ in the Toolbox, change the stroke weight to 2 pt, then deselect.

   Your page should resemble Figure G-45.

5. Select the star polygon, then place the Blue Clouds.tif graphic in it.

   TIP When you place a graphic into a polygon that has a fill, the fill remains, even though it may not be visible because of the placed graphic.

6. Click **Object** on the menu bar, point to **Fitting**, then click **Fit Content to Frame**.

(continued)

Lesson 3   Work with Polygons and Compound Paths

7. Change the fill color of the star polygon to None, deselect, then compare your page to Figure G-46.

8. Select the small ten-pointed polygon in the pasteboard, then place Orange Clouds.tif into it.

9. Click **Object** on the menu bar, point to **Fitting**, then click **Fit Content to Frame**.

You placed three graphics into three polygons.

Create compound paths

1. Click the **Selection Tool** , select the yellow "eye" polygon on the pasteboard, click **Object** on the menu bar, point to **Arrange**, then click **Bring to Front**.

2. Position the eye above the witch polygon as shown in Figure G-47.

3. Verify that the eye polygon is still selected, press **[Shift]**, then click the **witch polygon** so that both polygons are selected.

4. Click **Object** on the menu bar, point to **Compound Paths**, then click **Make**.

   As shown in Figure G-48, the eye polygon becomes a "hole" in the witch polygon through which you can see the Blue Clouds.tif graphic.

5. Select both the yellow circle and the star polygons in the top-right corner of the page.

6. Click **Object** on the menu bar, point to **Compound Paths**, click **Make**, then deselect all.

   Your page should resemble Figure G-49.

You created two compound paths.

FIGURE G-46
Viewing two graphics placed in polygons

Blue Clouds.tif placed into the star polygon

Orange Clouds.tif placed into "witch" polygon

FIGURE G-48
Creating a compound path

"Eye" polygon creates a hole in the "witch" polygon when compounded

FIGURE G-47
Positioning the "eye" polygon

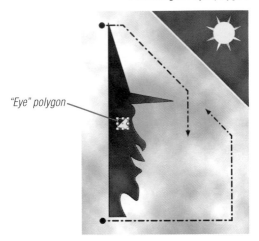

"Eye" polygon

FIGURE G-49
Viewing two compound paths

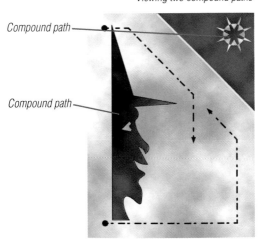

Compound path

Compound path

FIGURE G-50
Placing the inline frame

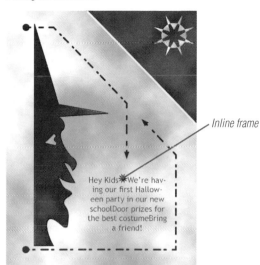

Inline frame

FIGURE G-52
Viewing three inline frames

FIGURE G-51
Selecting the inline frame

The inline frame
is selected as are
the spaces before
and after it

1. Drag the **Text layer** to the top of the Layers palette.

2. Select the **ten-pointed polygon** in the pasteboard, click **Edit** on the menu bar, then click **Cut**.

3. Click the **Type Tool** **T.**, click between the words Kids and We're, then paste.

    As shown in Figure G-50, the polygon is pasted into the block of text.

4. Press **[Spacebar]** to create a space after the inline frame, position your cursor before the graphic, then press **[Spacebar]** to create a space before the graphic.

5. Select the space, the graphic, and the space after the graphic, as shown in Figure G-51.

6. In the Character palette, type **-3** in the Baseline Shift text box, then press **[Enter]** (Win) or **[return]** (Mac).

    The inline frame is positioned more inline with the text.

7. With the space-graphic-space still selected, click **Edit** on the menu bar, then click **Copy**.

8. Click between the words school and Door, then paste.

9. Click between the words costume and Bring, then paste.

10. Select the words "We're having", then type **It's**.

    As shown in Figure G-52, when the text is edited, the inline graphics reflow with the text.

You used a polygon as an inline frame within a block of text.

WORK WITH ADVANCED TEXT FEATURES, CORNER EFFECTS, AND DROP SHADOWS

What You'll Do

In this lesson, you will position type on a line, convert type to outlines, and apply drop shadows and corner effects to graphics.

Positioning Type on a Line

Once you've created an object—a line or a polygon—the Type on a Path Tool allows you to position text on the outline of the object. Simply float the Type on a Path Tool over the path until a plus sign appears beside the cursor, then click the path. A blinking cursor appears, allowing you to begin typing.

Figure G-53 shows text positioned on a path. Whenever you position text on a path, a default start, end, and center bracket are created. Drag the start bracket with either of the selection tools to move the text along the path.

If you drag the center bracket across the path, the text will flow in the opposite direction, as shown in Figure G-54.

> **QUICKTIP**
>
> The center bracket is small and often difficult to see amid the letters.

FIGURE G-53
Text positioned on a path

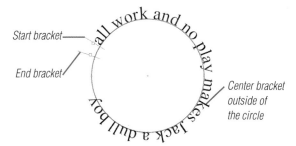

Start bracket

End bracket

Center bracket outside of the circle

FIGURE G-54
Reversing the direction of the text

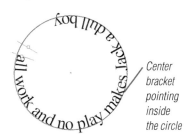

Center bracket pointing inside the circle

Once the text is entered, you can edit the text just as you would in a text frame. You can also modify the path. For example, if you modify the curve of the ellipse, the text will flow with the new shape.

One key design technique that many designers use in conjunction with text on a line is a baseline shift. You can use the Baseline Shift text box in the Character palette to make the text float above or below the path. Figure G-55 shows text floating above the path of the ellipse.

Converting Text to Outlines

After you create text in InDesign, you can convert the text to outlines. When text is converted to outlines, each character is converted to a closed path and shares the same characteristics of all paths. As shown in Figure G-56, the individual characters—which were once text—are now individual paths.

Why would you do this? One good reason is that when you convert text to outlines, you can place graphics into the outlines, as shown in Figure G-57. You do this using the Place command or the Paste Into command.

The ability to convert text to paths is a powerful feature. Beyond allowing you to use text as a frame for graphics, it makes it possible to create a document with text and *without* fonts. This can save you time in document management when sending files to your printer, and it can circumvent potential problems with missing fonts.

FIGURE G-55
Viewing text with a positive baseline shift value applied

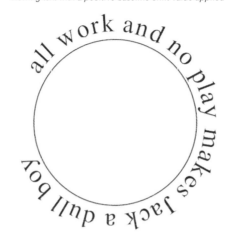

FIGURE G-56
Text converted to outlines

Text shapes drawn with anchor points and line segments

FIGURE G-57
Placing a graphic in outlined text

Blue stroke applied to paths

Does this mean that you should always convert all of your text in all of your documents to outlines? No. For quality purposes, it is best for text—especially small text such as body copy—to remain formatted as text as opposed to outlines. However, converting to outlines can be a good choice when you've used a typeface that you suspect your professional output house doesn't have. Rather than send them the font, you could choose simply to convert the text to outlines. Remember though, this is an option for larger text, like headlines, and is not recommended for body copy.

Applying Corner Effects

The Corner Effects command is a simple solution for modifying the corner points of polygons. With the Corner Effects command, you can, for example, change a rectangle's pointed corners to rounded corners. Figure G-58 shows various corner effects applied to a rectangle. When working in the dialog box, be sure to click the Preview option. Then you can experiment with different sizes, which will yield different corner effects.

Applying a Drop Shadow

A **drop shadow** is a soft-edged graphic behind another graphic that appears as though it is the shadow of the graphic. The Drop Shadow command on the Object menu makes it simple to create effective drop shadows.

FIGURE G-58
Viewing corner effects

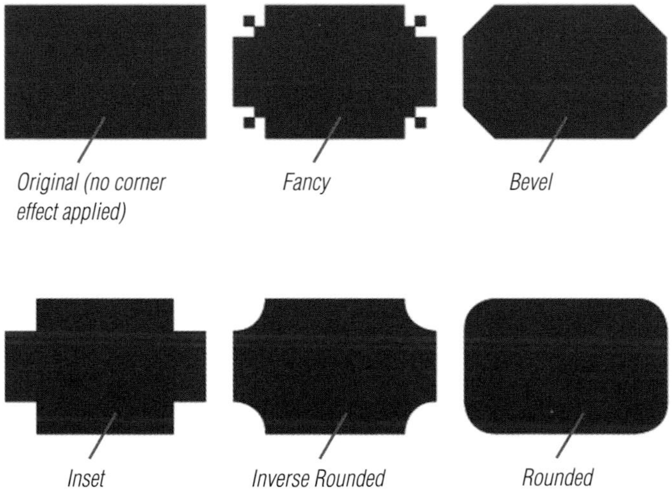

Original (no corner effect applied)

Fancy

Bevel

Inset

Inverse Rounded

Rounded

To apply a drop shadow, simply select any graphic, then click the Drop Shadow command to open the Drop Shadow dialog box, as shown in Figure G-59. Click the Drop Shadow check box to activate the drop shadow.

The dialog box contains six parameters for specifying the appearance of the drop shadow.

- Mode allows you to choose how the shadow appears in relation to other objects or colors behind it. Generally speaking, you will use Multiply mode most often. With Multiply mode, the shadow mimics a shadow in the real world—it is transparent and darkens anything it overlaps.

- Opacity controls how opaque the shadow is. The higher the opacity, the more opaque the shadow is. The lower the opacity, the less opaque the shadow is.

- The X and Y Offset settings control the distance—on the X axis and Y axis, respectively—that the shadow is from the selected object.

- Blur affects the width of the feathered edge of the selection. The greater the blur value, the more feathered—and less distinct—the edge will be.

- Color allows you to choose the color for the shadow.

FIGURE G-59

Drop Shadow dialog box

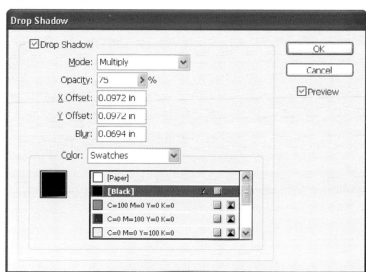

Position type on a line

1. Click the **Selection Tool** ![arrow], then click the **yellow diagonal line**.

2. Click the **Type on a Path Tool** ![icon], then position your cursor over the yellow line until a plus sign appears beside the cursor.

3. Click the **yellow line**.

   A blinking type cursor appears.

4. Type the word **happy** in lower-case letters, as shown in Figure G-60.

5. Double-click **happy**, change the font to Impact, change the font size to 60 pt, then change the fill color to Paper in the Swatches palette.

6. Click the **Selection Tool** ![arrow], then click the text.

   The Fill button in the Toolbox changes to None, and the Stroke button changes to yellow, because these are the attributes of the line that the type is positioned on, not the type itself.

7. Change the stroke color to None.

8. Position the word happy as shown in Figure G-61.

9. Press and hold **[Shift][Alt]** (Win) or **[Shift][option]** (Mac), then drag a copy of the word happy into the blue area beneath the orange triangle.

10. Click the **Type on a Path Tool** ![icon], double-click **happy**, then type **halloween**.

11. Click the **Selection Tool** ![arrow], then position the word halloween as shown in Figure G-62.

You used the Type on a Path Tool to position text on a diagonal line. You then created a copy of the text to create another word on the identical angle.

FIGURE G-60
Typing the word happy

Text on path

FIGURE G-61
Positioning the word happy

FIGURE G-62
Positioning the word halloween

FIGURE G-63

Viewing text converted to paths

FIGURE G-64

Viewing graphics pasted into text outlines

Convert text to outlines

1. Click the **Selection Tool**, then select the "happy" text.
2. Click **Type** on the menu bar, then click **Create Outlines**.
3. Select the "halloween" text.
4. Click **Type** on the menu bar, then click **Create Outlines**.
5. Click the **Direct Selection Tool**.

   Figure G-63 shows that the halloween text has been converted to nine paths.

You converted text to outlines.

Place graphics into outlines

1. Deselect all, click the **Selection Tool**, then click the word **happy**.
2. Click **File** on the menu bar, click **Place**, navigate to the drive and folder where your Data Files are stored, then place Blue Clouds.tif.
3. Click **Object** on the menu bar, point to **Fitting**, then click **Fit Content to Frame**.
4. Deselect all, click the **Selection Tool**, click the **Orange Clouds.tif** graphic visible in the triangle in the top-right corner, click **Edit** on the menu bar, then click **Copy**.
5. Click the word **halloween**, click **Edit** on the menu bar, then click **Paste Into**.
6. Click **Object** on the menu bar, point to **Fitting**, click **Fit Content to Frame**, deselect all, then compare your page to Figure G-64.

You used two methods for using a graphic to fill text outlines. You placed a graphic into text outlines, then pasted a graphic into text outlines.

Apply drop shadows

1. Click the **Selection Tool** ↖ , then select the compound path in the top-right corner of the orange triangle.

2. Click **Object** on the menu bar, then click **Drop Shadow**.

3. Click the **Drop Shadow check box**, then click **OK**.

   Your page should resemble Figure G-65.

4. Select both words happy and halloween, click **Object** on the menu bar, then click **Drop Shadow**.

5. Click the **Drop Shadow check box**, then click the **Preview check box**.

   TIP Move the Drop Shadow dialog box if it is blocking your view of happy halloween.

   (continued)

FIGURE G-65
Viewing a drop shadow created with default settings

Drop shadow

Creating Graphics

FIGURE G-66

Viewing the completed project

6. Click **Blue** in the Color box.

7. Change the Opacity to 40%.

8. In the X Offset text box, type a **minus sign** before the current number so that the offset is a negative number, then click **OK**.

9. Apply a 1 pt blue stroke to the letters, deselect, then compare your page to Figure G-66.

10. Save your work, close Halloween Invitation, then close Halloween Witch.

You applied a drop shadow using the default settings in the Drop Shadow dialog box. You then formatted and applied drop shadows to two text outlines. You also applied a stroke to text outlines that contain placed graphics.

Reshape frames.

1. Open ID G-3.indd, then save it as **Garden Party**.
2. Click the top edge of the frame containing the ghosted image with the Direct Selection Tool, then drag the top middle anchor point down to the first horizontal light blue guide.
3. Click the Pen Tool, position it over the bottom edge of the frame, then click to add an anchor point at the 3" mark on the horizontal ruler.
4. Deselect all, click the Direct Selection Tool, click one edge of the frame to select the frame, then select the new anchor point.
5. Click Edit on the menu bar, then click Cut.

Use the Pen Tool.

1. Click the Pen Tool, position the Pen Tool over the bottom-left anchor point of the frame until a diagonal line appears beside the Pen Tool, then click the anchor point.
2. Moving up and to the right, click the intersection of the pink vertical guide and the orange horizontal guide. (*Hint*: The intersection of the pink vertical guide and the orange horizontal guide is at the 1" mark on the horizontal ruler.)
3. Moving down and to the right, click where the next vertical guide intersects with the bottom of the page.
4. Repeat Steps 2 and 3 until your image matches Figure G-67, then click the anchor point in the bottom-right corner to close the path.

Work with polygons and compound paths.

1. Deselect all, then click the Default Fill and Stroke button in the Toolbox.
2. Click the Ellipse Tool, then position your cursor at the intersection of the cyan guide and the center pink guide.
3. Press and hold [Alt] (Win) or [option] (Mac), then click.
4. Type **1.65** in the Width text box, type **1.65** in the Height text box, then click OK.
5. Click the Selection Tool, press and hold [Shift], then select the frame that contains the Garden Party Screen graphic. (*Hint*: Both the circle and the frame should be selected.)
6. Click Object on the menu bar, point to Compound Paths, then click Make.
7. Select the text in the pasteboard, click Object on the menu bar, point to Arrange, click Bring to Front, then position it as shown in Figure G-68.
8. Click the Selection Tool, click the compound path, then add a 1 pt black stroke to the path.

Apply stroke effects.

1. Click the Ellipse Tool, then position your cursor at the intersection of the cyan guide and the center pink guide.
2. Press and hold [Shift][Alt] (Win) or [Shift][option] (Mac), then drag a circle that is the width of two columns.
3. Change the stroke color to magenta by clicking C=0 M=100 Y=0 K=0 in the Swatches palette, then change the stroke weight to 3 pt.
4. Click the Pen Tool, then click to add an anchor point in the two locations where the circle intersects with the black diagonal lines.

FIGURE G-67
Skills Review, Part 1

FIGURE G-68
Skills Review, Part 2

5. Click the Direct Selection Tool, deselect all, select only the top anchor point of the larger circle, click Edit on the menu bar, then click Cut. (*Hint*: Your screen should resemble Figure G-69.)

6. Click the Start list arrow in the Stroke palette, then click Barbed.

7. Click the End list arrow, then click CircleSolid.

8. Click the Type list arrow, then click Dashed.

9. Type **12** in the first dash text box, type **8** in the first gap text box, type **4** in the second dash text box, then type **8** in the second gap text box.

10. Click the Round Cap button in the Stroke palette.

Work with advanced text features, corner effects, and drop shadows.

1. Click the Ellipse Tool, position your cursor at the intersection of the cyan guide and the center pink guide, press and hold [Alt] (Win) or [option] (Mac), then click.

2. Type **3.25** in the Width text box, type **3.25** in the Height text box, then click OK.

3. Click the Pen Tool, then click to add an anchor point in the two locations where the largest circle intersects with the black diagonal lines.

4. Click the Direct Selection Tool, deselect all, select the top anchor point of the new circle, click Edit on the menu bar, then click Cut.

5. Click the Selection Tool.

6. Click the Type on a Path Tool, position it over the circle so that a plus sign appears beside the cursor, then click the path at approximately 9 o'clock.

7. Type **We're having a garden party! You're invited!**.

8. Select all of the text, change the font to Trajan, then change the horizontal scale to 50%.

9. Change the font size to 32 pt, then change the baseline shift to -8 pt.

10. Click the Direct Selection Tool, then move the start bracket on the left until the text is evenly distributed.

11. Click the Selection Tool, then change the stroke color to None.

Apply corner effects and a drop shadow.

1. Select the polygon that contains the Garden Party Screen.psd graphic.

2. Click Object on the menu bar, then click Corner Effects.

3. Click the Effect list arrow, then click Fancy.

4. Type **.25** in the Size text box, then click OK.

5. Click Object on the menu bar, then click Drop Shadow.

6. Click the Drop Shadow check box.

7. Change the Opacity value to 90.

8. Change the X Offset value to 0, change the Y Offset value to .125, then click OK.

9. Deselect all, click View on the menu bar, then click Hide Guides.

10. Save your work, compare your screen to Figure G-70, then close Garden Party.

FIGURE G-69
Skills Review, Part 3

FIGURE G-70
Completed Skills Review

Creating Graphics

You are a freelance designer, and you have just created an invitation for a Halloween party that features a black cat. Your client tells you that she loves the blue clouds and the orange clouds in the background, but she thinks the cat and its yellow eyes are "too flat." She says that she'd prefer that the cat and the eyes had texture.

1. Open ID G-4.indd, then save it as **Black Cat**.
2. Click the Selection Tool, select the cat, then change the fill color to None.
3. Place the file named Gray Clouds.tif.
4. Press and hold [Shift], then select the left eye, so that both the cat and the left eye are selected.
5. Create a compound path from the cat and the left eye objects.
6. Press and hold [Shift], then select the right eye, so that both the cat and the right eye are selected.
7. Create a compound path from the cat and the right eye objects.
8. Drag the circle from the pasteboard and position it so that it covers both of the cat's eyes.
9. Click Object on the menu bar, point to Arrange, then click Send Backward.
10. With the frame still selected, use the arrow keys to position the circle behind the cat's head in a way that you think is best, save your work, then compare your screen to Figure G-71.
11. Close Black Cat.

FIGURE G-71
Completed Project Builder 1

You are designing an advertisement for a travel magazine. The ad will promote tourism for a small island in the Caribbean named Lagoon Key. Unfortunately, the company you are working with doesn't have a huge budget. They've sent you only one photo. You decide to combine the photo with type to create a more complex design.

1. Open ID G-5.indd, then save it as **Lagoon**.
2. Click the Selection Tool, click the text, click Type on the menu bar, then click Create Outlines.
3. Click File on the menu bar, click Place, then place the Color Lagoon.psd file.
4. Click Object on the menu bar, point to Fitting, then click Fit Content to Frame.
5. Change the fill color to None, click View on the menu bar, then click Hide Frame Edges (if necessary).
6. Click Object on the menu bar, then click Drop Shadow.
7. Click the Drop Shadow check box, click the Green swatch in the Color section, then click OK.
8. Apply a 1 pt black stroke to the text outlines, then deselect all.
9. Save your work, compare your screen to Figure G-72, then close Lagoon.

FIGURE G-72
Completed Project Builder 2

You have been contracted to design an ad for Bull's Eye Barbecue. They supply you with their logo. You decide to position their name on a circle that surrounds the logo.

1. Open ID G-6.indd, then save it as **Bull's Eye**.
2. Click the Selection Tool, then click the black stroked circle that surrounds the logo.
3. Click the Type on a Path Tool, position it over the selection until a plus sign appears beside the cursor.
4. Click the path at approximately the 10 o'clock point.
5. Type **BULL'S EYE BARBECUE**, select the text, change the font to Garamond, then change the type size to 62 pt.
6. Click the Selection Tool, change the stroke color to None, then save your work.
7. Compare your screen to Figure G-73, then close Bull's Eye.

FIGURE G-73
Completed Design Project

In this Group Project, the group will work individually and then compare results. The project concerns drop shadows. In this case, the group will place a drop shadow behind white text, positioned against a white background. The shadow will be the only element that defines the white text. Therefore, the design and position of the drop shadow will play a critical role. The exercise is designed to get members of the group to spend time experimenting with the options in the Drop Shadow dialog box.

1. Open ID G-7.indd, then save it as **Everest**.
2. Click the Selection Tool, then click the center of the page to select the text frame.
3. Click Object on the menu bar, then click Drop Shadow.
4. Click the Drop Shadow check box and the Preview check box.
5. Change the X Offset value to 0.
6. Change the Y Offset value to .3.
7. Click the Color list arrow, click CMYK, then manipulate the color sliders to create at least three different colors for the shadow.

8. Experiment with at least three different X and Y Offset values.
9. Experiment with at least three different Blur values.
10. Decide on the formatting you like, then apply it by clicking OK.

FIGURE G-74
Sample Group Project

11. Save your work, then compare your work with the work of other members of the group.
12. Compare your work with Figure G-74, then close Everest.

WORKING WITH TRANSPARENCY

1. Colorize a grayscale image.

2. Work with opacity and feathering.

3. Work with blending modes.

4. Apply transparency to placed graphics.

CHAPTER H

WORKING WITH TRANSPARENCY

In Chapter G, you explored InDesign's features for drawing and creating graphics. Chapter H extends that exploration to InDesign's Transparency palette. Adobe's decision to include the Transparency palette as a feature of InDesign makes the application a sophisticated graphics utility as well as a top-notch layout program.

With the Transparency palette, InDesign offers you the ability to manipulate the appearance of graphics in ways that were once exclusive to Photoshop. Now you can manipulate a graphic's opacity in InDesign. You can also apply blending modes to InDesign graphics and to graphics you place from Photoshop or Illustrator.

In addition to the Transparency palette, the Feather command gives you the option to create soft edges on InDesign frames. You can even use the Swatches palette in combination with the selection tools to colorize a grayscale image that you place in InDesign. So keep your wits about you when you're working in Chapter H—you might forget yourself and think you're working in Photoshop, but remember, it's InDesign!

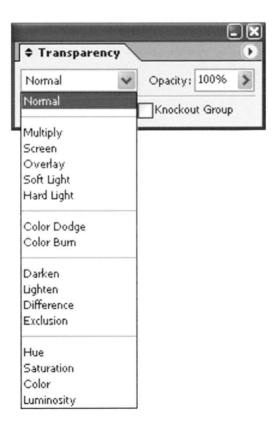

COLORIZE A GRAYSCALE IMAGE

What You'll Do

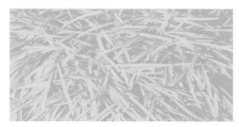

 In this lesson, you will explore techniques for colorizing both the light and dark areas of a placed grayscale image.

Defining a Grayscale Image

A grayscale image is a digital image reproduced using only one color. In most cases, that color is black. The image is reproduced using 256 shades of black—from light to dark. Thus, the term grayscale has become synonymous with a black and white image.

In Photoshop, grayscale is a color mode, just like RGB or CMYK. When you convert a file from RGB or CMYK mode to grayscale mode, the image appears as black and white. Figure H-1 shows two Photoshop files, one in CMYK mode and one in grayscale mode. When this book was printed, the CMYK image was printed using all four process inks; the grayscale image was printed using only black ink.

Colorizing Grayscale Images in InDesign

When you place a grayscale image from Photoshop in InDesign, you can apply InDesign swatches to it to colorize the graphic. You have the option of applying one swatch color to the light areas of the graphic—the **highlights**—and another to the dark areas—the **shadows**.

To colorize the light areas, select the graphics frame with the Selection Tool and then apply a fill color to the frame. The highlights of the grayscale graphic will change to the fill color. Figure H-2 shows a grayscale graphic in which the highlights have been colorized with yellow.

To colorize the dark areas of the graphic, you must select the graphic with the Direct Selection Tool. Once the graphic is selected, clicking a swatch in the Swatches palette colorizes the dark areas of the graphic. Figure H-3 shows the same graphic with a red swatch applied to the dark areas.

FIGURE H-1

A CMYK and a grayscale image

FIGURE H-2

Colorizing the light areas of a placed grayscale graphic

Light areas appear yellow

FIGURE H-3

Colorizing the dark areas of a placed grayscale graphic

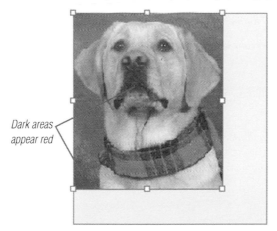

Dark areas appear red

Colorize the light areas of a grayscale graphic

1. Open ID H-1.indd, then save it as **Transparency**.

2. Click the **Selection Tool** ![selection tool], then select the graphics frame.

3. Display the Swatches palette (if necessary), verify that the Fill button is active in the Toolbox, then click the **yellow swatch** (C=0 M=0 Y=100 K=0) in the Swatches palette.

   As shown in Figure H-4, all of the white areas of the graphic become transparent and show the yellow fill applied to the graphics frame.

4. Click the **Tint list arrow** in the Swatches palette, then drag the **Tint slider** to 50%.

   The yellow areas are lightened.

5. Click the **Direct Selection Tool** ![direct selection tool], then click the **graphic** to select it.

6. Click **Edit** on the menu bar, then click **Cut**.

   The image is cut from the frame, but the frame remains with the 50% yellow background.

7. Make the Soft Blades layer visible in the Layers palette, then click the **Soft Blades layer** to target it.

8. Click the **Selection Tool** ![selection tool], then select the graphics frame.

(continued)

FIGURE H-4
Colorizing white areas of a placed graphic

FIGURE H-5
Colorizing light areas of a placed graphic

Working with Transparency

Applying Navy to the graphic

FIGURE H-7
Applying Grassy Green to the graphic

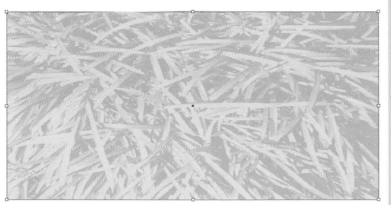

9. Click **Grassy Green 45%** in the Swatches palette.

As shown in Figure H-5, the lighter the areas of the graphic, the more the green background color shows through.

By applying a background fill to a frame, you created the effect that the light transparent areas of the grayscale graphic in the frame changed to that fill color.

Colorize the dark areas of a grayscale graphic

1. Click the **Direct Selection Tool** ▯ , then select the graphic.

2. Click **Navy** in the Swatches palette.

As shown in Figure H-6, the dark areas of the image change from black to navy.

> **TIP** When the Direct Selection Tool is activated and a graphic is selected, fills apply to the dark areas of a placed grayscale graphic.

3. Click **Grassy Green** in the Swatches palette, then compare your work to Figure H-7.

You selected a grayscale graphic, then changed its dark areas to a color in the Swatches palette.

WORK WITH OPACITY AND FEATHERING

What You'll Do

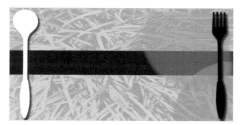

 In this lesson, you will use the Transparency palette to manipulate the opacity of InDesign objects and you'll use the Feather command to apply a soft edge to objects.

Manipulating Opacity

The term **opacity** is derived from the word opaque. An object that is opaque is neither transparent nor translucent—it can't be seen through. In InDesign, you manipulate an object's opacity in the Transparency palette, shown in Figure H-8.

By default, objects that you create in InDesign are created at 100% opacity—they are opaque. The more you decrease their opacity using the Transparency palette, the more see-through they become. Figure H-9 shows three circles with different opacity values.

As shown in Figure H-10, you can manipulate the opacity of graphics that you place in InDesign. You should also note that, if you manipulate the opacity of a graphic in Adobe Illustrator or Adobe Photoshop, InDesign will recognize and preserve that opacity setting when the graphic is placed in InDesign.

Applying a Feathered Edge

The Feather command, found on the Object menu, allows you to apply a feathered edge to a selected object. Applying a feather creates the effect that the object has a soft edge. Figure H-11 shows three circles created with InDesign's Ellipse Tool. The first circle does not have feathered edges. The other two have feathered edges.

Feathering is a form of transparency, because the feather effect is created by making the edge increasingly transparent. Note that in the figure, the rightmost circle's edge appears to be equal parts blue and yellow. This effect is created by making the circle's edge increasingly transparent.

If you place a graphic in a frame with a feathered edge, the graphic too will be feathered. Figure H-12 shows the same graphic placed in the three circles.

FIGURE H-8
Transparency palette

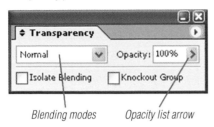

Blending modes   Opacity list arrow

FIGURE H-9
Three circles with different opacity values

100% opacity

50% opacity   25% opacity

FIGURE H-10
Dog graphic at 50% opacity

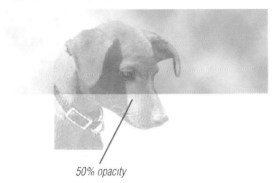

50% opacity

FIGURE H-11
Three different edges

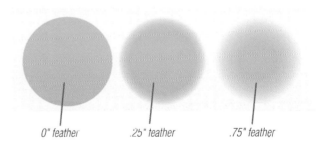

0" feather   .25" feather   .75" feather

FIGURE H-12
Graphics take on a frame's edge formatting

0" feather   .75" feather

.25" feather

Change the opacity of InDesign objects

1. Click **View** on the menu bar, point to **Display Performance**, then click **High Quality Display**.

   If you choose to do these lessons at the Typical Display setting, your graphics may appear noticeably different from the figures.

2. Make the InDesign Objects layer visible in the Layers palette, then click the **InDesign Objects layer** to target it.

3. Click **Window** on the menu bar, then click **Transparency**.

4. Click the **Selection Tool** , then select the dark orange object.

5. Click the **Opacity list arrow** in the Transparency palette, then drag the **slider** to 55%.

6. Select the blue semi-circle, click the **Opacity list arrow**, then drag the **slider** to 60%.

7. Deselect, then compare your work to Figure H-13.

FIGURE H-13

Viewing the reduced opacity of two objects

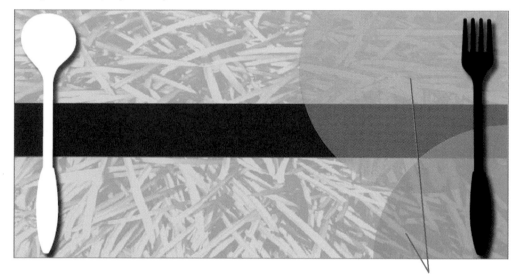

Reduced opacity

Working with Transparency

1. Select the blue semi-circle, click **Object** on the menu bar, then click **Feather**.

2. Click the **Feather check box**, type **.125** in the Feather Width text box, accept the default Diffused option in the Corners text box, then click **OK**.

   The edge of the blue semi-circle now appears soft.

3. Select the orange object, click **Object** on the menu bar, then click **Feather**.

4. Click the **Feather check box**, type **.375** in the Feather Width text box, then click **OK**.

5. Deselect, then compare your work to Figure H-14.

You applied different sized feathered edges to two objects.

FIGURE H-14

Viewing feathered edges applied to two objects

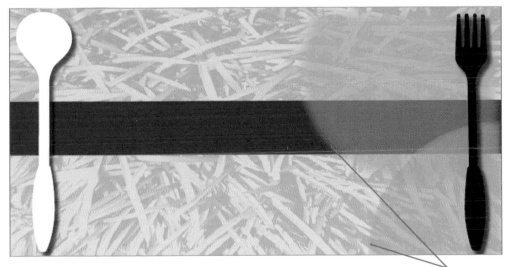

Feathered edges

WORK WITH BLENDING MODES

What You'll Do

 In this lesson, you will apply various blending modes to InDesign objects and note their effect.

Understanding Blending Modes

If InDesign objects are created with 100% opacity by default, it follows logically that when you overlap one object with another, the bottom object will be hidden behind the top object where they overlap. One option that you have to manipulate this relationship is to reduce the opacity of the top object.

Another option you have is to apply a blending mode to the top object. **Blending modes** allow you to create different transparency and color effects where two or more objects overlap.

The Transparency palette offers 15 blending modes, shown in Figure H-15. Some blending modes, such as Multiply, are very practical—they can be used to produce very common effects. Others, such as

Difference, produce more extreme effects and are therefore not used as often.

Blending modes work by comparing the colors in the overlapping graphics and then running those colors through a mathematical algorithm to produce an effect. You could investigate the algorithm of each of the blending modes, but your efforts might be better spent elsewhere. Instead, blending modes are almost always used on an experimental basis. Even when you understand the algorithm of how the mode works, it's not possible to memorize the effect that each blending mode will produce in every case. This is because the effect will be different with every overlapping object. Therefore, it's best to play around with blending modes. Experiment until you find an effect that works well with the objects you are blending.

Using the Multiply Blending Mode

Of the 15 blending modes, one in particular deserves special attention. **Multiply** is a practical and useful blending mode; be sure to familiarize yourself with it. When Multiply is applied to an object, the object becomes transparent but retains its color. You can think of the effect as that of overlapping magic markers. Figure H-16 shows an effect created by multiplying various InDesign objects.

There are two very important features of the Multiply blending mode that you must memorize: when you apply the Multiply blending mode, any white areas of a graphic become transparent and any black areas remain black.

FIGURE H-15

Blending modes in the Transparency palette

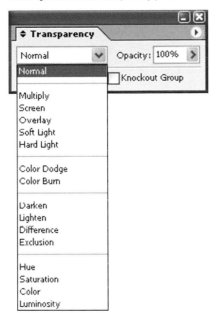

FIGURE H-16

Applying the Multiply blending mode

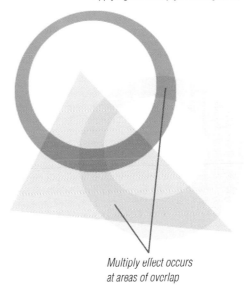

Multiply effect occurs at areas of overlap

Apply the Multiply blending mode

1. Select the blue rectangle, click the **Blending mode list arrow** in the Transparency palette, then click **Multiply**.

   As shown in Figure H-17, the rectangle becomes transparent and darkens the graphic it overlaps.

2. Select both the orange and blue circular objects, click the **Blending mode list arrow** in the Transparency palette, then click **Multiply**.

3. Click **Edit** on the menu bar, click **Undo Set Transparency Attributes**, click **Edit** on the menu bar, then click **Redo Set Transparency Attributes**.

4. Repeat Step 3 so that you can compare the difference in the transparency when the objects are multiplied with the background graphic versus when they are transparent simply because of reduced opacity.

   TIP When you are done comparing, be sure that the two objects remain with the Multiply blending mode applied.

5. Select the spoon, click **Object** on the menu bar, then click **Drop Shadow**.

6. Note that the blending mode of the drop shadow is already specified as Multiply, then click **Cancel**.

   The drop shadow is transparent because its blending mode was specified as Multiply when created; this applies only to the drop shadow, not to the spoon graphic.

   (continued)

FIGURE H-17

Applying the Multiply blending mode to the blue rectangle

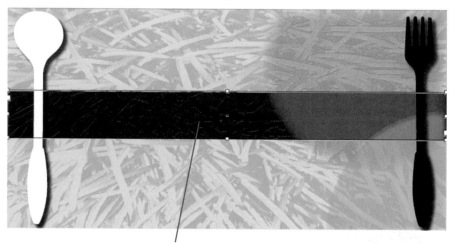

Transparent

FIGURE H-18

Applying the Multiply blending mode to an object with a white (Paper) fill

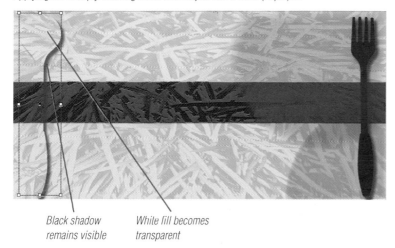

Black shadow
remains visible

While fill becomes
transparent

FIGURE H-19

Viewing the effect of changing the fill color of objects with the Multiply blending mode

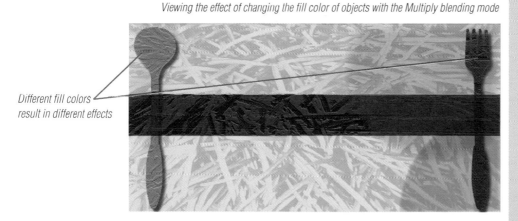

Different fill colors
result in different effects

7. Click the **Blending mode list arrow** in the Transparency palette, then click **Multiply**.

As shown in Figure H-18, the spoon disappears because a white fill (Paper) becomes completely transparent when multiplied.

8. With the spoon still selected, click **Wood** in the Swatches palette.

9. Select the fork, then change the blending mode to Multiply.

There is no visible change, because black multiplied with any other color remains black.

10. Change the fill color of the fork to Red, deselect the fork, then compare your work to Figure H-19.

You applied the Multiply blending mode to various InDesign objects.

Experiment with various blending modes

1. Select both the spoon and the fork, then change the blending mode to Screen.

   As shown in Figure H-20, the colors change and the drop shadow disappears, because black always becomes transparent when the Screen blending mode is applied.

   > TIP   The Screen blending mode always lightens the overlapping areas of objects.

2. Change the blending mode of the spoon and the fork to Overlay.

   In this case, the effect of the Overlay blending mode is similar to Screen, but it produces a richer color and the drop shadow reappears.

3. Change the blending mode to Hard Light.

4. Change the blending mode to Soft Light.

   > TIP   The Soft Light blending mode often produces an effect that is similar to but fainter than the Hard Light mode.

5. Change the blending mode to Color.

   The resulting effect is the combination of the hue and saturation values of the spoon and the fork with the brightness values of the background object (the green-colored graphic).

   (continued)

FIGURE H-20

Viewing the Screen blending mode applied to the spoon and fork

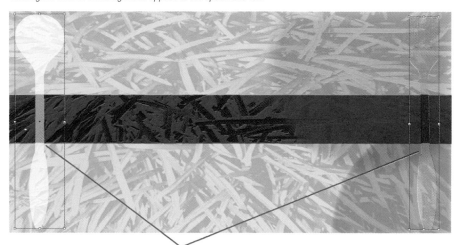

Drop shadows drop out

FIGURE H-21

Viewing the results of applying various blending modes

6. Change the blending mode to Darken.

   Areas of the background object that are lighter than the foreground objects change to the color of the foreground objects. Areas of the background object that are darker than the foreground objects do not change.

7. Make the Text layer visible on the Layers palette, click the **Selection Tool** ▶, then click the **Chefs on Safari** text on the page.

8. Change the blending mode of the Chefs on Safari text to Overlay.

   The object becomes much darker because of the dark blue object behind the text.

9. Change the blending mode to Hard Light, deselect, then compare your work to Figure H-21.

You applied various blending modes to objects and noted their effects.

APPLY TRANSPARENCY
TO PLACED GRAPHICS

What You'll Do

▶ *In this lesson, you will apply various blending modes to placed graphics in InDesign and note their effect.*

Applying Transparency to Placed Graphics

When you place graphics from other applications like Photoshop or Illustrator in InDesign, you can manipulate their opacity in InDesign. Manipulating the opacity of a placed graphic offers you the ability to create interesting relationships, as shown in Figure H-22. It's also a great solution when you want to use a graphic behind a block of text, as shown in Figure H-23.

You can also apply blending modes to placed graphics. The Multiply blending mode is very useful with placed graphics, because it makes all white areas of a graphic transparent. Thus, Multiply is often a good solution for removing the white background of a placed graphic.

FIGURE H-22
Reducing opacity of placed graphics

Figure H-24 shows the Multiply blending mode being applied to a placed graphic with a white background.

Remember the two essential rules when working with the Multiply blending mode: when a black color is multiplied with any other color, the result is black; when white is multiplied with any color, white always becomes transparent. Figure H-25 is an excellent example of these two rules.

The Screen blending mode works as the inverse of the Multiply mode. With the Screen mode, black areas become transparent and white areas remain white. Figure H-26 shows an example.

FIGURE H-23

Positioning text in front of a placed graphic

FIGURE H-24

Removing a white background with the Multiply mode

White background
becomes transparent

FIGURE H-25

Image 1 multiplied with Image 2 results in Image 3

FIGURE H-26

Image 1 screened with Image 2 results in Image 3

Placing Graphics into Transparent Frames

When you place a graphic into a frame, the graphic takes on any transparency effects that were applied to the frame. Figure H-27 shows a frame that is multiplied and has a feathered edge. Figure H-28 shows a graphic placed into that frame.

Selecting Overlapping Frames

When you create even slightly complex layouts, many objects on the page will overlap. When a layout contains many overlapping objects, it can become challenging to select the backmost objects in the stacking order. Rather than move the topmost objects to access the objects behind them, you can simply "click through" the topmost objects to select the objects behind them. Select any of the top objects, press and hold [Ctrl] (Win) or ⌘ (Mac), then click the top object again. This will select the object behind it in the stacking order, as if you "clicked through" the top object. Use this method to select any object positioned behind any other objects.

FIGURE H-27
Frame with transparency applied

*Multiply blending mode
and feather applied*

FIGURE H-28
Graphic placed into a transparent frame

*Multiply blending mode
and feather applied*

FIGURE H-29

Viewing the placed graphic with the Color blending mode applied

Color blending
mode applied

FIGURE H-30

Applying the Multiply blending mode to a placed graphic with a white background

White background
becomes
transparent

1. Make the Pink Flowers layer visible, click the **Selection Tool** ▶ (if necessary), then click the **flowers graphic**.

   TIP   Be sure that you select the flowers graphic and not the "take a wok on the wild side" text.

2. Change the blending mode to Screen.

3. Change the blending mode to Overlay.

4. Change the blending mode to Color, deselect, then compare your work to Figure H-29.

5. Make the Whisk layer visible, then click the **whisk graphic**.

6. Change the blending mode to Multiply.

   As shown in Figure H-30, the white background becomes transparent because white always becomes transparent when multiplied.

7. With the whisk graphic still selected, click the **Opacity list arrow** on the Transparency palette, then drag the **slider** to 70%.

You applied various blending modes to placed graphics in InDesign, then changed the opacity of one of the graphics.

Selecting overlapping graphics

1. Verify that the Selection Tool is selected, then click the **handle of the red fork**.

   The fork is selected.

2. Press and hold **[Ctrl]** (Win) or ⌘ (Mac), then click the **handle of the red fork** in the same place.

   The blue object behind the fork is selected.

   > TIP Pressing and holding [Ctrl] (Win) or ⌘ (Mac) allows you to select objects behind other overlapping objects.

3. Press and hold **[Ctrl]** (Win) or ⌘ (Mac), then click the **fork** in the same place.

   The Pink Flowers graphic is selected.

4. Press and hold **[Ctrl]** (Win) or ⌘ (Mac), then click the **fork** in the same place.

   The green background graphic is selected.

5. Click the **Opacity list arrow** in the Transparency palette, then drag the **slider** to 80%.

   By decreasing the opacity of the green graphic, the 50% yellow fill applied to the graphics frame behind it becomes more visible.

6. Press and hold **[Ctrl]** (Win) or ⌘ (Mac), then click the **fork** in the same place.

   The frame with the 50% yellow fill is selected.

7. Click the **Tint list arrow** in the Swatches palette, then drag the **slider** to 75% so that your page resembles Figure H-31.

You used a keyboard command to select objects behind overlapping objects.

FIGURE H-31
Viewing the tint change of the backmost graphic

Area appears
more yellow

FIGURE H-32
Viewing the transparency of a placed graphic

Graphic is transparent

FIGURE H-33
Viewing a placed graphic in a frame with transparency and a feathered edge

Feathered
cdgc

Placing graphics into transparent frames

1. Make the Illustrator Graphics layer visible.

2. Verify that the Selection Tool ⬉ is selected, then select the blue circular object.

3. Place the graphic named Octopus.ai from the location where your Data Files are stored, then compare your work to Figure H-32.

   The placed graphic is multiplied at 60% because that is the blending mode applied to the blue object.

4. Click **Object** on the menu bar, point to **Fitting**, then click **Fit Content to Frame**.

5. Select the orange circular object, place the graphic named Lava Rocks.psd from the location where your Data Files are stored, click **Object** on the menu bar, point to **Fitting**, then click **Fit Content to Frame**.

6. Deselect, then compare your work to Figure H-33.

   I ike the frame, the graphic is multiplied at 55% opacity. The graphic fades with the frame's feathered edge.

7. Select the blue circular object, then change the blending mode to Screen.

You placed graphics into transparent frames, noting that the graphics themselves took on the same transparency as the frames.

Apply transparency to placed Illustrator graphics

1. Select the Goblets.ai graphic to the right of the Octopus graphic, then note its transparency setting in the Transparency palette.

   As shown in Figure H-34, the graphic's blending mode is set to Normal even though it appears to be multiplied. The Multiply blending mode was applied to the graphic in Illustrator.

   TIP InDesign recognizes and preserves any transparency that is applied and saved with an Illustrator file.

2. In the Transparency palette, change the blending mode to Multiply.

   The graphic is darkened.

3. Select the black Illustrator graphic named Octopus.ai, then change the blending mode to Overlay.

   (continued)

FIGURE H-34

Viewing a placed graphic with transparency applied in its native application

Graphic appears
to be multiplied

Graphic is not
multiplied in InDesign

4. Select the Chefs on Safari text, then change its blending mode to Screen.

5. Deselect, then compare your work to Figure H-35.

6. Save your work, then close Transparency.

You modified the transparency on two placed Illustrator graphics, one of which had transparency applied to it in Illustrator.

FIGURE H-35
Viewing the completed project

Colorize a grayscale image.

1. Open ID H-2.indd, then save it as **Old Photo**.
2. Click the Selection Tool, then select the graphics frame.
3. Click Mustard in the Swatches palette.
4. Click the Tint list arrow in the Swatches palette, then drag the slider to 70%.
5. Click the Direct Selection Tool, then select the graphic.
6. Click Plum in the Swatches palette.

Work with opacity and feathering.

1. Make the Rectangles layer visible, click the Selection Tool, then select the green rectangle.
2. Click the Opacity list arrow in the Transparency palette, then drag the slider to 50%.

3. Select the red rectangle, click the Opacity list arrow, then drag the slider to 30%.
4. Make the Ovals layer visible, click the Selection Tool, then select the left oval.
5. Click Object on the menu bar, then click Feather.
6. Click the Feather check box, type **.25** in the Feather Width text box, then click OK.
7. Select the right oval, then repeat Steps 5 and 6.

Work with blending modes.

1. Select the green rectangle.
2. Click the Blending mode list arrow in the Transparency palette, then choose Overlay.
3. Select the red rectangle.

4. Click the Blending mode list arrow in the Transparency palette, then choose Multiply.
5. Make the Black Box layer visible, click the Selection Tool, then select the black frame.
6. Click the Opacity list arrow in the Transparency palette, then drag the slider to 45%.
7. Select both blue ovals, change the blending mode to Screen, then deselect all.

Apply transparency to placed graphics.

1. Select the left oval, then place the file named Old Photo.psd.
2. Click the Direct Selection Tool, select the graphic, click Edit on the menu bar, then click Copy.

3. Select the right oval with the Direct Selection Tool.
4. Click Edit on the menu bar, then click Paste Into.
5. Click the Selection Tool, then select the left oval.
6. Click the Blending mode list arrow in the Transparency palette, then choose Hard Light.
7. Change the blending mode to Luminosity, then save your work.
8. Deselect all, compare your screen to Figure H-36, then close Old Photo.

FIGURE H-36
Completed Skills Review

Working with Transparency

For your dad's birthday, you've decided to give him a framed photo of his mother— an old photo from when she was young. You scan in the old photo, retouch it to remove the damage as a result of it being placed in a drawer for years, then save it as a grayscale image. You import it into InDesign, then decide that it looks too stark in black and white. Rather than go back to Photoshop, you choose to colorize it in InDesign.

1. Open ID H-3.indd, then save it as **Colorize**.
2. Click the Selection Tool, select the graphics frame, then click Orange in the Swatches palette.
3. Click the Direct Selection Tool, click the graphic again, then click Brown in the Swatches palette.
4. Click the Selection Tool, then click the graphic again.
5. Click the Tint list arrow in the Swatches palette, then drag the Tint slider to 15%.
6. Deselect, then save your work.
7. Compare your work to Figure H-37, then close Colorize.

FIGURE H-37
Completed Project Builder 1

You run a small graphics business out of your home. A friend comes to you with an old photo of her grandmother. She wants to put it in a 3½" × 5" frame. She tells you that she wants you to create a soft oval effect for the photo.

1. Open ID H-4.indd, then save it as **Vignette**.
2. Click the Selection Tool, select the frame, then fill it with the Tan swatch.
3. With the frame still selected, click the Ellipse Tool, position your cursor over the center point of the selected frame, press and hold [Alt] (Win) or [option] (Mac), then click.
4. Type **3** in the Width text box, type **4.5** in the Height text box, then click OK.
5. Verify that the ellipse you just created has no fill or stroke.
6. Click Object on the menu bar, then click Feather.
7. Click the Feather check box, type **.75** in the Feather Width text box, then click OK.
8. Place the file named Portrait.psd from the drive and folder where your Data Files are stored.
9. Click the Direct Selection Tool, then center the woman's face in the oval.
10. Click View on the menu bar, click Hide Frame Edges (if necessary), then compare your work to Figure H-38.
11. Deselect all, save your work, then close Vignette.

FIGURE H-38
Completed Project Builder 2

Your client has opened a coffee shop near your home office. She doesn't have a big budget for purchasing artwork, so she's asked you to create some digital art to hang on her walls. She gives you an old photo and tells you she wants you to use it to create "something old and modern at the same time."

1. Open ID H-5.indd, then save it as **Granny Warhol**.
2. Make the Photos layer visible, then select the top-left graphics frame.
3. Change the blending mode to Multiply.
4. Select the top-right graphics frame, then change the blending mode to Screen.
5. Select the bottom-left graphics frame, then change the blending mode to Hard Light.
6. Select the bottom-right graphics frame, then drag the Opacity slider to 30%.
7. Press and hold [Alt] (Win) or [option] (Mac), then click the Background layer in the Layers palette to select the four colored squares behind the photos.
8. Double-click the Rotate Tool, type **90** in the Angle text box, then click OK.
9. Save your work, deselect all, compare your work to Figure H-39, then close Granny Warhol.

FIGURE H-39
Completed Design Project

This group project will focus on coloriz-ing grayscale graphics in InDesign. Your group will split up into groups of four. Each group will open an InDesign file containing the same graphic duplicated four times on four different pages. The project calls for each group to colorize each of the four graphics differently. The groups may use only the colors already available in the Swatches palette. Once done, the groups will compare their work with the other groups.

As an alternative, if the group wants to add some competition to the project, determine beforehand four categories that the groups can strive for when col-orizing. For example, each group may try to create the best example in each of the following four categories: most subtle, most appealing, most eye-catching, most outlandish.

1. Open ID H-6.indd, then save it as **Colored Flowers**.

2. Experiment with changing the color of the light areas of all four graphics.
3. Experiment with changing the color of the dark areas of all four graphics.
4. Decide on final combinations for each of the four graphics.
5. Save your work, compare your work to the four possibilities shown in Figure H-40, then close Colored Flowers.

FIGURE H-40
Completed Group Project

CHAPTER

WORKING WITH TABS AND TABLES

1. Work with tabs.

2. Create and format a table.

3. Format text in a table.

4. Place graphics in a table.

CHAPTER I
WORKING WITH TABS AND TABLES

InDesign offers many great options for creating charts and tables. The Tabs palette is an excellent resource with a sophisticated interface. You use tabs to position text at specific horizontal locations within a text frame, and you use the Tabs palette to determine the placement of those tabs.

In addition to tabs, an important component to any layout application is the ability to create tables. By setting up data in rows and columns, tables are an efficient method for communicating large amounts of information. InDesign provides excellent options for creating tables quickly and easily—in fact, it provides both a Table palette and an entire Table menu!

Tools You'll Use

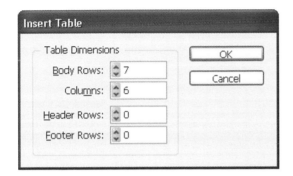

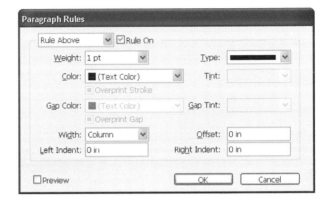

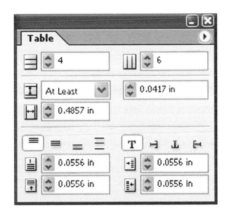

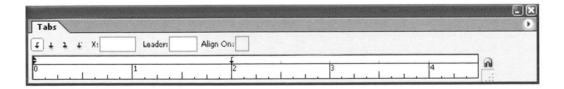

WORK WITH TABS

What You'll Do

Dancewear Sales - 2003				
Product	**# Purchased**	**#Sold**	**Best Color**	**Profit**
T-Shirts	50	45	White	$950.00
Sweatshirts	100	100	Navy	$1500.00
Leotards	200	150	White	$725.00
Tap Shoes	20	2	n/a	$60.50

In this lesson, you will use the Tabs palette to position text at specific horizontal positions within a frame.

Using Tabs

You use **tabs** to position text at specific horizontal locations within a text frame. Figure I-1 shows a simple layout created using tabs. The heading "Column 2" and the five items beneath it are all aligned in the left-justified tab shown in the tab ruler of the Tabs palette.

Note that the left edge of the white ruler in the Tabs palette is aligned with the left edge of the text frame. This alignment occurs by default when you select a text frame and open the Tabs palette. The alignment of the text frame with the Tabs palette makes it easier to note the horizontal position of text within a frame. For example, in the same figure, you can see at a glance that Column 2 is positioned two inches in from the left edge of the text frame.

If you scroll up or down, or resize the page or the text frame, the text frame will no longer be aligned with the Tabs palette. To realign the two, simply click the Position Palette above Text Frame button on the Tabs palette. The Tabs palette will move to realign itself with the text frame.

Once text has been aligned on a tab, moving the tab moves the text as well. In Figure I-2, the tab has been moved right to 2.5" and the left edge of the text is also aligned at that position. The text does not need to be selected to be moved. Simply moving the tab moves the text.

To delete a tab from the tab ruler, simply drag it off the tab ruler, and then release your mouse.

Using Different Tab Alignments

The Tabs palette offers four types of tab buttons for aligning text—Left-Justified Tab, Center-Justified Tab, Right-Justified Tab, and Align to Decimal Tab. To create a tab in the tab ruler, you can click a tab button, then click a location in the tab ruler or click a tab button, then enter a location in the X text box in the Tabs palette.

In Figure I-3, the second column of text is aligned with a left-justified tab. Note that the tab is selected in the tab ruler—it is highlighted with blue. When a tab is selected, its horizontal location is indicated in the X text box. This tab is positioned at 2.25.

In Figure I-4, the tab has been changed to a center-justified tab. Its horizontal location remains unchanged; however, now the center points of the text are aligned at the 2.25" mark.

FIGURE I-1
Tabs palette

FIGURE I-2
Moving a tab

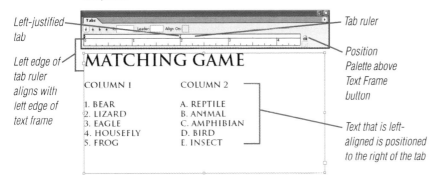

Left-justified tab

Left edge of tab ruler aligns with left edge of text frame

Tab ruler

Position Palette above Text Frame button

Text that is left-aligned is positioned to the right of the tab

Tab moved to 2.5"

Text moves with tab

FIGURE I-3
Using the Left-Justified Tab button

FIGURE I-4
Using the Center-Justified Tab button

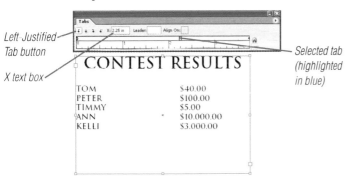

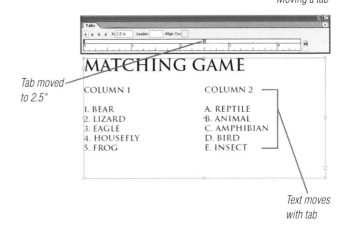

Left-Justified Tab button

X text box

Selected tab (highlighted in blue)

Center-Justified Tab button

Text is centered beneath center-aligned tab

In Figure I-5, the position of the tab has again not changed, but its alignment has changed to a right-justified tab. Notice that the lines of text are all aligned on the right.

In Figure I-6, the tab alignment has been changed to an align-to-decimal tab. The decimal points of each number in the column are aligned at the 2.25" mark. Clearly, this tab is a good choice when working with numbers.

When you use the align-to-decimal tab, you can align text with characters other than a decimal point, such as an asterisk or a dollar sign. As shown in Figure I-7, by clicking the Align to Decimal Tab button, then typing a $ in the Align On text box, the column is aligned on the dollar sign.

FIGURE I-5
Using the Right-Justified Tab button

FIGURE I-6
Using the Align to Decimal Tab button

FIGURE I-7
Using the Align On text box in the Tabs palette

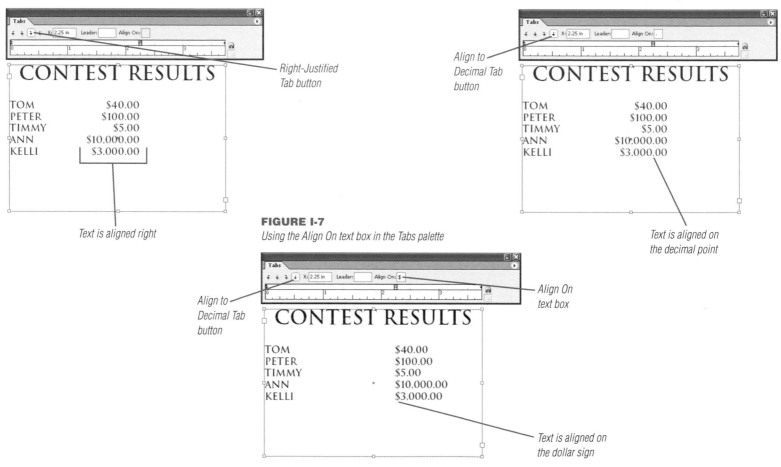

Right-Justified Tab button

Text is aligned right

Align to Decimal Tab button

Text is aligned on the decimal point

Align to Decimal Tab button

Align On text box

Text is aligned on the dollar sign

Using Text Insets

When you enter text in a text frame, **text insets** determine how far from the edge of the frame the text is positioned—how far it is *inset* into the frame. Text insets can be entered for all four sides of a text frame—top and bottom, left and right. For example, a .5" text inset means that text will be inset one-half inch on all four sides of a frame.

In Figure I-8, a heavy black rule has been added to the text frame. The addition of the rule makes the position of the text visually unpleasing—the text is too close to the top and the left edges of the frame.

Text inset values are entered in the Text Frame Options dialog box. In Figure I-9, a .25" text inset has been added to the top and left sides of the frame. Note the light blue line that indicates the top and left margins of the text within the text frame.

QUICKTIP

When you use tabs in a text frame that has a text inset, the tab ruler aligns itself with the text inset line—the light blue line—not the left edge of the text frame.

FIGURE I-8
Applying a rule creates the need for a text inset

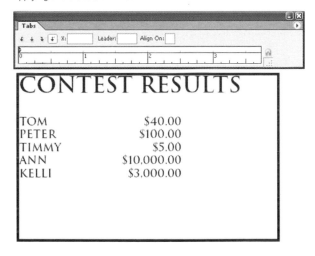

FIGURE I-9
Applying a text inset to the top and left sides of the text frame

.25" text inset top and left

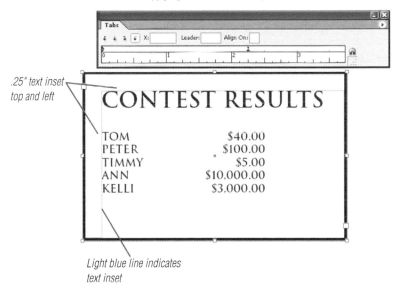

Light blue line indicates text inset

Adding Rules above or below Paragraphs

Many times, you will want to add a horizontal rule above or below a line (or lines) of text. InDesign regards rules above and below text as paragraph attributes—in other words, they are part of the text formatting. If you resize the text—let's say you make it larger—the rule increases however much is necessary to continue underlining the text. If you move the text, the rule moves with it.

Rules for text are defined in the Paragraph Rules dialog box, shown in Figure I-10. This dialog box allows you to specify a number of attributes for the rule, including its color and its weight. This is where you also specify whether the rule is positioned above or below the text.

When you apply a rule below text, the rule is positioned by default at the baseline of the text. Often, you will find this to be visually unpleasing. Figure I-11 shows text with a rule positioned at its baseline.

Generally speaking, a rule below looks best when it is slightly below the baseline. Use the Offset text box in the Paragraph Rules dialog box to accomplish this. When the rule is defined as a Rule Below, a positive offset value moves the rule *down* from the baseline.

Rule offsets are best specified in points. A **point** is 1/72 of an inch. This small increment allows you to be very specific when positioning a rule. For a rule below, a two- or three-point offset value is usually best. Figure I-12 shows the same rule with a three-point offset.

QUICKTIP

If your ruler units are set to inches, you can still enter values as points. Simply type p before a value to specify it as points. For example, if you want to specify a six-point offset value, type p6 in the Offset text box.

FIGURE I-10
Paragraph Rules dialog box

Paragraph Rules
Rule Above
Rule On
Weight: 1 pt
Type:
Color: (Text Color)
Tint:
Overprint Stroke
Gap Color: (Text Color)
Gap Tint:
Overprint Gap
Width: Column
Offset: 0 in
Left Indent: 0 in
Right Indent: 0 in
Preview
OK
Cancel

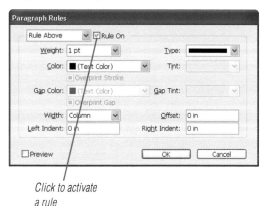

Click to activate a rule

FIGURE I-11
Rule below, at the baseline

Rule positioned with a zero offset value

CONTEST RESULTS
TOM $40.00
PETER $100.00
TIMMY $5.00
ANN $10,000.00
KELLI $3,000.00

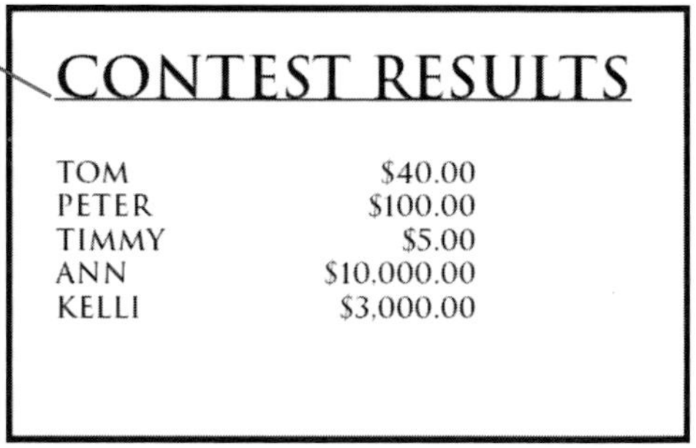

FIGURE I-12
Rule below, with a 3-point offset

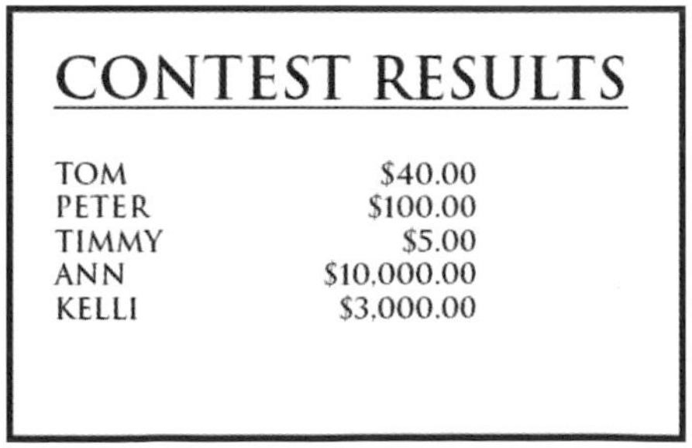

CONTEST RESULTS
TOM $40.00
PETER $100.00
TIMMY $5.00
ANN $10,000.00
KELLI $3,000.00

FIGURE I-13

Insetting text

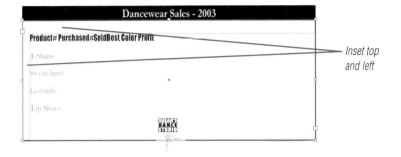

Inset top
and left

**Set a text inset and
insert tabs**

1. Open ID I-1.indd, then save it as **Tabs**.

2. Click the **Selection Tool** ▶, click the **blue
   text**, click **Object** on the menu bar, then click
   Text Frame Options.

3. In the Inset Spacing section, type **.25** in
   the Top text box, type **.125** in the Left text
   box, click **OK**, then compare your work to
   Figure I-13.

4. Click **Type** on the menu bar, then click **Tabs**.

   As shown in Figure I-14, the left edge of the
   tab ruler (not the left edge of the Tabs
   palette) is automatically aligned with the left
   edge of the text inset so that the measurements in the ruler exactly match the text.

5. Click the **Type Tool** T, select all of the
   text in the frame, then click the **Left-
   Justified Tab button** ↓ in the Tabs palette
   (if necessary).

6. Position your cursor in the white space in
   the top third of the tab ruler—just above the
   numbers—then click and drag until the X
   text box reads 1 in, as shown in Figure I-15.

7. Repeat Step 6 to create a new tab at 2".

   │ TIP To delete a tab from the tab ruler,
   │ simply drag it straight up and release
   │ your mouse.

8. Click anywhere in the tab ruler to the right of
   the second tab to add a third tab.

   The third tab remains selected, and its horizontal location is displayed in the X text box.

   (continued)

FIGURE I-14

Tabs palette

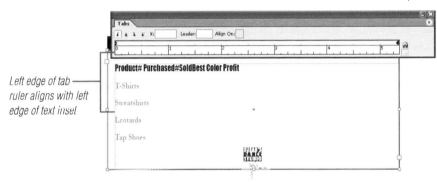

Left edge of tab
ruler aligns with left
edge of text inset

FIGURE I-15

Adding a tab to the tab ruler

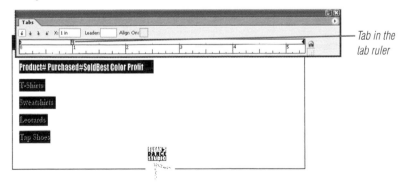

Tab in the
tab ruler

Lesson 1   Work with Tabs

INDESIGN I-9

9. Double-click the value in the X text box, type **3**, then press **[Enter]** (Win) or **[return]** (Mac).

  The third tab is moved to the 3" mark.

10. Using either of the two methods from the above steps, add a new tab at 4", then compare your work to Figure I-16.

You inset text from the top and left margins in the Text Frame Options dialog box. You then selected all the text in the frame and set four left-justified tabs at 1" intervals.

Enter text using tabs

1. Click the **Type Tool** T., click to the left of the first # sign in the first line of text, then press **[Tab]**.

2. Tab the remaining text in the first line so that your page resembles Figure I-17.

3. Click to the right of the word T-Shirts, press **[Tab]**, then type **50**.

4. Press **[Tab]**, type **45**, press **[Tab]**, type **White**, press **[Tab]**, then type **$950**.

  Your page should resemble Figure I-18.

5. Using the same method, enter the information shown in Figure I-19 so that your page matches the figure.

  Note that, now that the text is entered, the text is not centered in the frame—there is a large gap to the right of the last column.

6. Select all of the text, click **Object** on the menu bar, click **Text Frame Options**, change the Left inset value to **.5**, then click **OK**.

  (continued)

FIGURE I-16
Adding the fourth tab

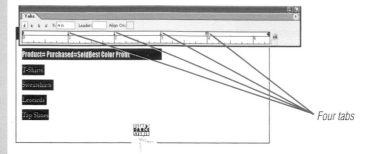

Four tabs

FIGURE I-17
Tabbing the first line of text

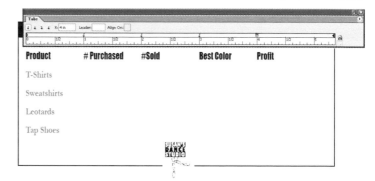

FIGURE I-18
Entering tabbed values for the first product line

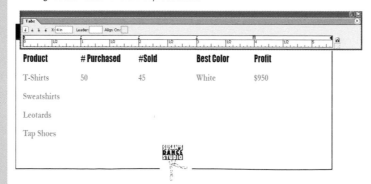

FIGURE I-19
Entering tabbed values for the remaining products

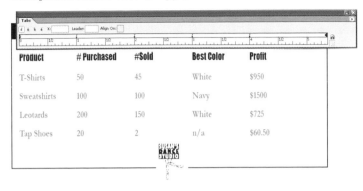

FIGURE I-20
Increasing the left inset

FIGURE I-21
Changing a left-justified tab to a center-justified tab

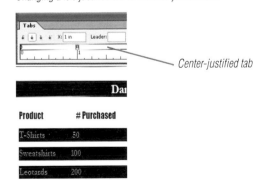

Center-justified tab

Everything shifts to the right and the tabs remain spaced at 1" intervals. As shown in Figure I-20, the left edge of the tab ruler is no longer aligned with the left edge of the text inset.

7. Click the **Position Palette above Text Frame button** .

   The left edge of the tab ruler realigns itself with the left edge of the text inset.

You used tabs to enter text at specific horizontal locations. You modified the left text inset value, noting that the 1" tab intervals were not affected.

Change type of tabs and location of tabs

1. Drag the **Tabs palette** straight up so that the entire document is visible, then select all of the blue text.

2. Click the **first tab** at the 1" location in the tab ruler to select it.

3. Click the **Center-Justified Tab button** .

   As shown in Figure I-21, the tab changes to a center-justified tab and the first column of text is now centered at the 1" mark.

4. With the first tab in the tab ruler still highlighted, double-click the value in the X text box, type **1.375**, then press **[Enter]** (Win) or **[return]** (Mac).

   The first column is now centered at the 1.375" mark.

5. Click the **second tab** to highlight it, click the **Center-Justified Tab button** , then relocate the tab to 2.3".

(continued)

6. Click the **third tab** to highlight it, click the **Center-Justified Tab button** ↓, then relocate the tab to 3.25".

7. Click the **fourth tab** to highlight it, click the **Align to Decimal Tab button** ↓, then relocate the tab to 4.25".

8. Select only the "# Sold" text in the top row, then relocate its tab to 2.1".

9. Type **.00** after $950, $1500 and $725.

10. Click **Edit** on the menu bar, click **Deselect All**, save your work, then compare your page with Figure I-22.

> TIP Be sure to save your work, because you will revert to this point after the next set of steps.

You selected tabs, changed them to different types of tabs, then moved tabs in the tab ruler.

Apply tab leaders and rules

1. Select all of the blue text, then click the **first tab** in the tab ruler to highlight it.

2. Type a **period (.)** in the Leader text box in the Tabs palette, press **[Enter]** (Win) or **[return]** (Mac), then deselect all.

   As shown in Figure I-23, the period is used as a character that connects the product listings to the first tab.

3. Select all of the blue text, click the **second tab** in the tab ruler, type a **period** (.) in the Leader text box, press **[Spacebar]**, then press **[Enter]** (Win) or **[return]** (Mac).

   Using the space creates a more open dot pattern.

(continued)

FIGURE I-22
Viewing reformatted tabs

Dancewear Sales - 2003				
Product	**# Purchased**	**#Sold**	**Best Color**	**Profit**
T-Shirts	50	45	White	$950.00
Sweatshirts	100	100	Navy	$1500.00
Leotards	200	150	White	$725.00
Tap Shoes	20	2	n/a	$60.50

Working with Tabs and Tables

FIGURE I-23
Using a period as a tab leader

FIGURE I-24

Viewing various characters as tab leaders

FIGURE I-25

Choosing attributes for the rule below

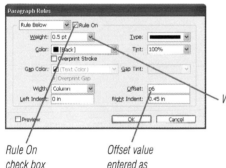

Weight list arrow

Rule On
check box

Offset value
entered as
six points

FIGURE I-26

Viewing the finished chart

4. Click the **third tab** in the tab ruler, type an **asterisk (*)** in the Leader text box, then press **[Enter]** (Win) or **[return]** (Mac).

5. Click the **fourth tab** in the tab ruler, type a **hyphen (-)** in the Leader text box, press **[Enter]** (Win) or **[return]** (Mac), then compare your work to Figure I-24.

6. Click **File** on the menu bar, click **Revert**, then click **Yes** (Win) or **Revert** (Mac).

7. Select all of the text, click the **Paragraph palette list arrow**, then click **Paragraph Rules**.

8. Click the **list arrow** at the top of the dialog box, click **Rule Below**, then click the **Rule On check box**.

9. Choose the settings shown in Figure I-25 to format the rule, click **OK**, then deselect all.

    Note that in the Offset text box, the intended six-point offset is specified as p6. When your cursor leaves the Offset text box, the value is displayed as inches.

10. Select only the top line of text, click the **Paragraph palette list arrow**, click **Paragraph Rules**, click the **Weight list arrow**, click **1 pt**, then click **OK**.

11. Deselect all, save your work, compare your page to Figure I-26, then close Tabs.

You used the Leader text box in the Tabs palette to set various characters as tab leaders. You used the Paragraph Rules dialog box to apply a rule below the rows of text in the text frame.

CREATE AND FORMAT A TABLE

What You'll Do

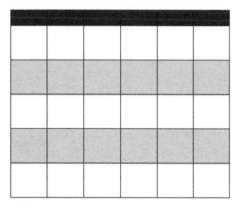

 In this lesson, you will create a table and apply fills and strokes.

Working with Tables

An important component to any layout application, **tables** are an efficient method for communicating large amounts of information. Tables consist of rectangles in horizontal **rows** and vertical **columns**. Each rectangle is called a **cell**. Figure I-27 shows an example of a table.

The first important thing to note about tables is that InDesign regards them as text. Tables can only be created within a text frame. When you edit a table, you do so with the Type Tool. If you select a table with the Selection Tool, you can only modify the text frame, not the contents of the table cells in the text frame.

Creating Tables

The first step in creating a table is to create a text frame. Once you've created the text frame, the Insert Table dialog box, shown in Figure I-28, allows you to specify the number of rows and the number of columns for the table. When you create the table, it always appears in a default layout, as shown in Figure I-29. Note that the width of the cells is determined by the number of columns and the width of the text frame. In other words, the default width of the cells is the width of the text frame divided by the number of cells.

Formatting Tables

The Table palette, shown in Figure I-30, is command central for manipulating a table. Even after you create the table, you can modify the number of rows and columns using the Table palette.

Once you have created the table, you then determine the width of the columns and the height of the rows. Columns and rows in a table do not have to have the same width and height. Individual columns can have varying widths, and individual rows can have varying heights. Column widths and row heights determine the size of the cells that they create.

You can determine the size of all the cells in a table simultaneously by selecting them all and entering values in the Table palette. You can also select a single column and specify a width for that column only, or select a single row and specify a height for that row only.

Figure I-31 shows the default table modified with different row heights. The top row is .5" high. The other rows are all 1.625" high.

QUICKTIP

Long tables may continue over many pages in your document. To repeat information from the top or bottom row each time the table is divided, you can use headers or footers.

Headers and footers can be specified in the Insert Table dialog box at the time that you create the table, or you can convert existing rows to header or footer rows using the Convert Rows To Header or Footer commands on the Table menu.

QUICKTIP

You can import a table from a Microsoft Word or Excel document using the Place command. The imported data appears in an InDesign table.

FIGURE I-27
An example of an InDesign table

State	Founded	Area	Capital	Pop	Flag
CONNECTICUT	1788	5,544 sq/mi	Hartford	3,405,000	
MASSACHUSETTS	1788	10,555 sq/mi	Boston	6,349,000	
NEW HAMPSHIRE	1788	9,351 sq/mi	Concord	1,235,000	
RHODE ISLAND	1790	1,545 sq/mi	Providence	1,048,00	
VERMONT	1791	9,615 sq/mi	Montpelier	608,000	
MAINE	1820	35,387 sq/mi	Augusta	1,274,000	

FIGURE I-28
Insert Table dialog box

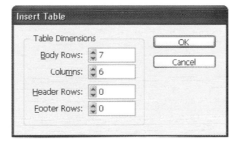

FIGURE I-29
Default table layout

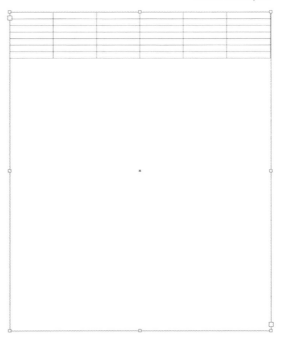

Lesson 2   Create and Format a Table

Applying Strokes and Fills to a Table

Adding color to a table can do wonders in terms of making the table more visually interesting and can improve the impact of the information you are trying to convey. You can apply strokes to the cells of the table, thereby controlling the color and the weight of the lines that make up the table grid.

You apply strokes and fills to a table just as you would to other InDesign objects. You can select a single cell, multiple cells, or an entire row or column. Remember, you use the Type Tool to select elements of a table. You can then use the Swatches palette to add a fill color or to apply a stroke color, and the Stroke palette to modify the weight of the strokes.

You can also use the Table menu to apply fills and strokes. In addition, the Table menu provides options for alternating fills by row or column. Alternating fills is a technique that is often used to make tables more visually interesting and easy to read. Figure I-32 shows the table with fills using two colors that alternate every other row.

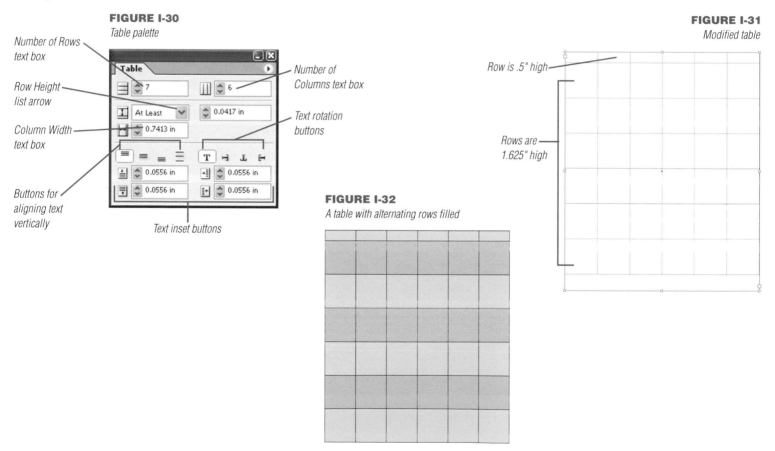

FIGURE I-30
Table palette

Number of Rows text box

Row Height list arrow

Column Width text box

Buttons for aligning text vertically

Number of Columns text box

Text rotation buttons

Text inset buttons

FIGURE I-32
A table with alternating rows filled

FIGURE I-31
Modified table

Row is .5" high

Rows are 1.625" high

Working with Tabs and Tables

FIGURE I-33
Insert Table dialog box

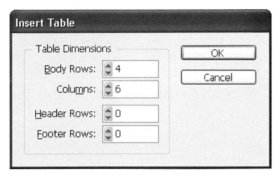

Create a table and change the number of rows

1. Open ID I-2.indd, then save it as **Table**.

2. Close all open palettes except for the Toolbox, click the **Type Tool** T. , then create a text frame that snaps to all four margin guides.

3. Click **Table** on the menu bar, then click **Insert Table**.

4. Type **4** in the Body Rows text box, then type **6** in the Columns text box, as shown in Figure I-33.

5. Click **OK**, click **Window** on the menu bar, point to **Type & Tables**, then click **Table**.

6. Click the **up arrow** next to the Number of Rows text box three times, so that there are seven rows in the table, as shown in Figure I-34.

You created a table, then used the Table palette to increase the number of rows in the table.

FIGURE I-34
Modifying the table with the Table palette

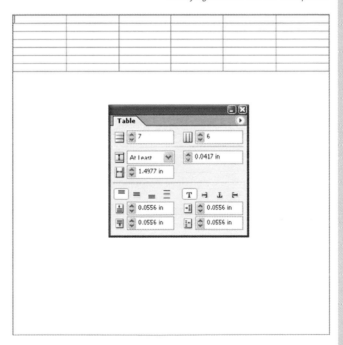

Set a table's size

1. Position your cursor over the second cell in the first column, then click and drag to select all of the rows except the top row, as shown in Figure I-35.

2. Click the **Row Height list arrow** in the Table palette, then click **Exactly**.

3. Type **1.4** in the text box next to the Row Height text box, press **[Enter]** (Win) or **[return]** (Mac), then compare your work to Figure I-36.

4. Position your cursor over the left edge of the top cell in the first row so that a heavy black arrow appears pointing to the right.

5. Click once to select the top row, as shown in Figure I-37.

6. Click the **Row Height list arrow** in the Table palette, then click **Exactly**.

(continued)

FIGURE I-35
Selecting multiple rows

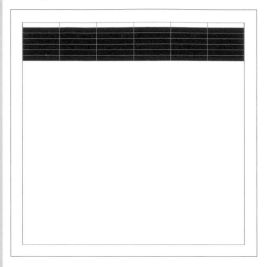

FIGURE I-36
Setting the height of selected rows

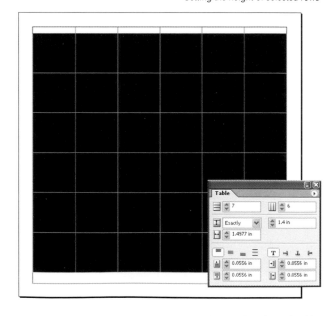

Working with Tabs and Tables

FIGURE I-37

Selecting a single row

FIGURE I-38

Setting the height of the top row

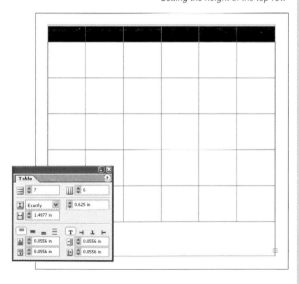

7. Type **.625** in the text box next to the Row Height text box, press **[Enter]** (Win) or **[return]** (Mac), then compare your work to Figure I-38.

The bottom row disappears and an overset text icon appears in the bottom-right corner of the text frame, indicating that there is no longer enough room in the text frame to hold all the rows in the table.

8. Position your cursor over the left edge of the second row so that a heavy black arrow appears pointing to the right.

9. Click to select the second row, click the **Table palette list arrow**, point to **Delete**, then click **Row**.

The row is deleted, and the overset text icon disappears because all six rows now fit in the text frame.

You selected six rows and entered a value for their height in the Table palette. You selected only the top row, then entered a different value for its height. You then deleted a row so that all rows could fit in the text frame.

Apply strokes to a table

1. Position your cursor over the top-left corner of the table so that a black diagonal arrow appears, as shown in Figure I-39, then click to select the entire table.

2. Click **Table** on the menu bar, point to **Cell Options**, then click **Strokes and Fills**.

3. Click the **Weight list arrow** in the Cell Options dialog box, then click **2 pt**.

4. Click the **Color list arrow**, then click **Navy**.

5. Click **OK**, then click the pasteboard to deselect all.

6. Click **View** on the menu bar, click **Hide Guides**, click **View** on the menu bar again, click **Hide Frame Edges** (if necessary), then compare your work to Figure I-40

You selected all the cells of the table, then applied strokes.

FIGURE I-39
Preparing to select the entire table

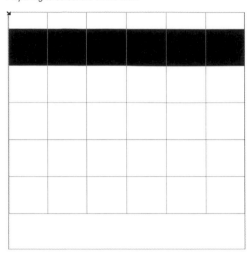

FIGURE I-40
Viewing strokes applied to cells

FIGURE I-41

Applying alternating fills

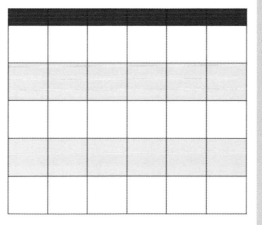

FIGURE I-42

Changing the fill color of the first row

Apply fills to a table

1. Position your cursor over the top-left corner of the table so that a black diagonal arrow appears, then click once to select the entire table.

2. Click **Table** on the menu bar, point to **Table Options**, then click **Alternating Fills**.

3. Click the **Alternating Pattern list arrow**, then click **Every Other Row**.

4. Click the **first Color list arrow** on the left side of the dialog box, click **Black**, type **20** in the Tint text box, then click **OK**.

5. Click the pasteboard to deselect all, then compare your table to Figure I-41.

6. Select the entire top row, click **Table** on the menu bar, point to **Cell Options**, then click **Strokes and Fills**.

7. Click the **Color list arrow** in the Cell Fill section of the dialog box, click **Red**, type **100** in the Tint text box, then click **OK**.

8. Click the pasteboard to deselect all, then compare your table to Figure I-42.

You applied a fill to three rows simultaneously by using the Alternating Fills command. You then changed the fill color of the first row.

FORMAT TEXT IN A TABLE

What You'll Do

restaurant	signature	chef	review	hours	info
SHAME ON THE MOON		Bill Cohen	"The fish selection is imaginative and varied. Be sure to sample from the chef's seafood tasting menu on Thursday nights."	5-10	dress to impress late night menu entertainment
BLAME IT ON MIDNIGHT		Ann Mahoney	"The pasta menu is Mahoney's secret weapon. The fettucine en brodo is rivaled only by the tortellini, which was simply a marvel."	3-11	children's menu take out
THE BLACK SWAN		Kelli Jacob	"With all of the incredible seafood specialty dishes, one might overlook the succulent beef and veal selections. That would be a tragedy."	4-11	dress to impress entertainment pre-theater menu
CHEZ BLAKE		Tim Brodt	"The juxtaposition of textures is stunning. My favorite was a crunchy crab salad served on a smooth lime gelée."	4-10	children's menu
THE GROOVE POD		Peter Panik	"Peter Panik is a culinary master of the unexpected."	5-11	late night menu children's menu

 In this lesson, you will explore options for formatting and positioning text within tables.

Entering Text in a Table

Because InDesign regards tables as text—tables are always in text frames—entering text in a table is simple and straightforward. With the Type Tool selected, simply click in a cell and begin typing. Press [Tab] to move from column to column. You can also use the arrow keys to move from cell to cell in any direction.

You can select text in a cell and modify it using the features in the Character palette, just as you would in a regular text frame.

When you enter text in a cell, by default it is aligned to the left edge of the cell. You can select the text and change its alignment—center it, justify it, etc.—using the alignment buttons in the Paragraph palette.

By default, text that you enter in a cell is aligned vertically to the top of the cell. To modify this, you use the vertical alignment buttons in the Table palette, shown in Figure I-43. Figure I-44 shows text in a table that is centered both horizontally and vertically.

Modifying a Table to Fit Text

Once you have entered text into a table, you will often find that you need to edit the table to better fit the text. Sometimes the rows will not be tall enough to contain all the text, and sometimes the column won't be wide enough. In Figure I-45, for example, the left column is too narrow for the state names—note that four of them are broken by hyphens. However, the second column is more than wide enough to contain the four-digit dates. Wouldn't it be great if you could quickly reduce the size of the second column and increase the size of the first?

Fortunately, InDesign makes it very easy to modify the height of a row or the width of a column. One way to do this is to select the row or column and enter a greater height or width value in the Table palette. Another option is simply to drag a cell border left or right to decrease or increase the width. Similarly, you can drag a cell border up or down to decrease or increase the height of a row.

In Figure I-46, the width of the first column has been increased by dragging the cell border to the right. Note the double arrow that appears when you position your cursor over a cell border. Note too that increasing the width of the first column increased the width of the entire table. If you wanted to return the table to its original width, you could decrease the width of another column. In Figure I-47, the width of the second column has been reduced.

The ability to change the size of cells in this manner is a very powerful option.

Being able to modify the table "by hand" allows you to experiment until the table looks the way you want it to look. If you didn't have this option, you'd need to enter different values into the Table palette, through trial-and-error guess work.

FIGURE I-43
Vertical alignment buttons

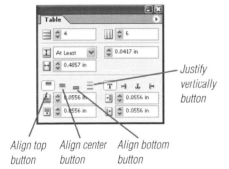

Justify
vertically
button

Align top
button

Align center
button

Align bottom
button

FIGURE I-44
Text centered horizontally and vertically

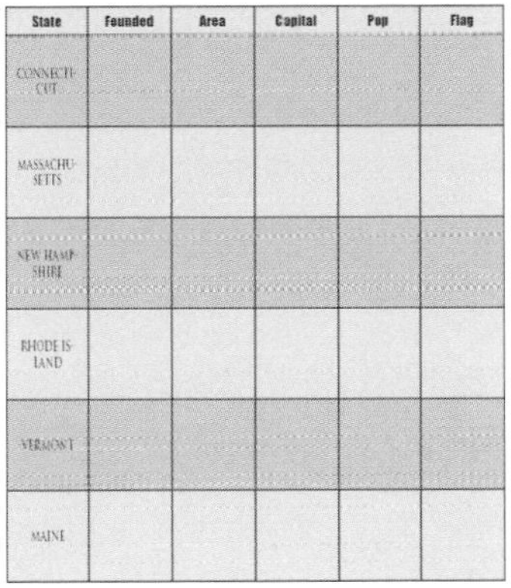

FIGURE I-45
Noting a column that is too narrow

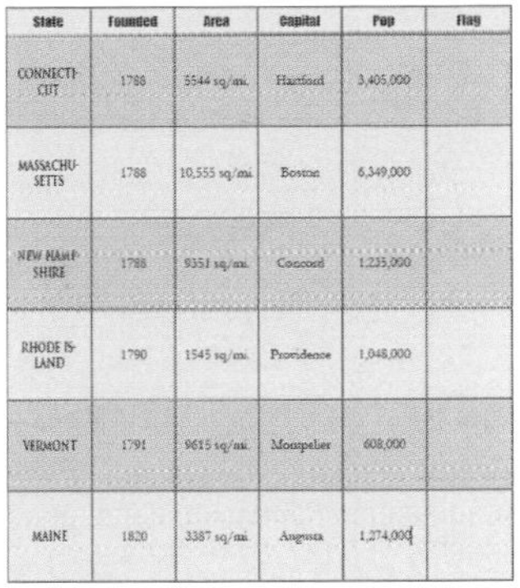

FIGURE I-46
Increasing the width of a column

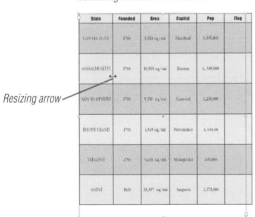

Resizing arrow

FIGURE I-47
Decreasing the width of a column

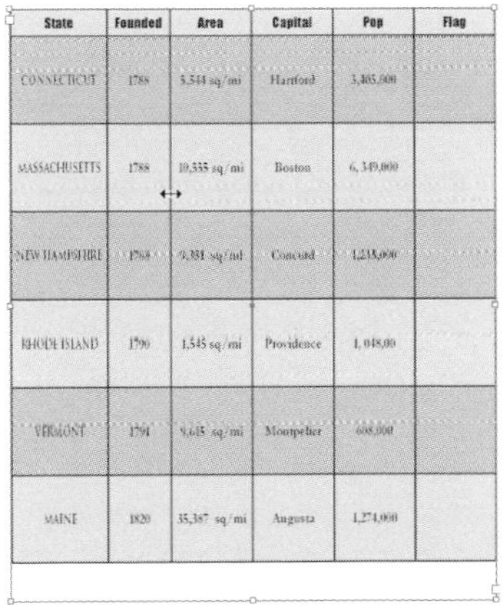

Insetting Text Within a Cell

The cell inset text boxes in the Table palette, shown in Figure I-48, allow you to control the text inset for all four sides of the cell. With the default inset of .0556 in, a block of text would appear as shown in Figure I-49. Note how on the left and right, the text is very close to the vertical borders of the cell, whereas there's a lot of "air" above and below. The reason the top and bottom margins are larger is because there's not enough text to take up more vertical space. The result is that the text appears to "fight" the cell, as though it doesn't fit properly.

Figure I-50 shows the same block of text with the left and right inset values increased to .1875 in. Note the improvement in appearance.

FIGURE I-48

Cell inset text boxes

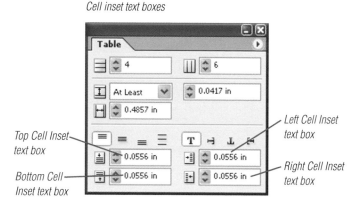

Top Cell Inset text box

Bottom Cell Inset text box

Left Cell Inset text box

Right Cell Inset text box

FIGURE I-49

Text with a default cell inset

> Lorem ipsum dolor sit amet, consect adipiscing elit, sed diam nonummy nib euismod tincidunt ut laoreet dolore magna.

FIGURE I-50

Text with increased right and left cell inset values

> Lorem ipsum dolor sit amet, consect adipiscing elit, sed diam nonummy nib euismod tincidunt ut laoreet dolore magna.

FIGURE I-51

Entering text into a table

restaurant	signature	chef	review	hours	info
Shame on the Moon					
Blame it on Midnight					
The Black Swan					
Chez Blake					
The Groove Pod					

Enter text in a table

1. Click the **Type Tool** T. (if necessary), click in the top-left cell, then type **restaurant**.

2. Press **[Tab]**, then type **signature**.

3. In the remaining four cells of the top row, type **chef**, **review**, **hours**, and **info**.

4. Click in the first cell of the second row, then type **Shame on the Moon**.

5. Press ↓, then type **Blame it on Midnight**.

6. Press ↓, then type **The Black Swan**.

7. Press ↓, then type **Chez Blake**.

8. Press ↓, type **The Groove Pod**, then compare your table to Figure I-51.

You entered text into the cells of a table.

Format text in a table

1. Position your cursor over the left edge of the first cell in the top row so that a black arrow appears pointing right, then click once to select the entire row.

   TIP The Type Tool must be selected in order for the black arrow to appear, so that you can select an entire row or column.

2. Show the Swatches palette, click the **Formatting affects text button** T , then click **Paper**.

   The text changes to a white fill.

3. Show the Character palette, change the font to Impact, then change the font size to 18 pt.

4. Click anywhere in the first cell of the second row, then drag down to select all of the cells in the first column (except the top cell).

5. Show the Character Styles palette, then click **Restaurant Name**.

6. Position your cursor over the top-left corner of the table so that a black diagonal arrow appears, then click to select the entire table.

7. Click the **Align center button** ≣ in the Paragraph palette.

8. Click the pasteboard to deselect all, use soft returns to remove the hyphen in BLAME IT ON MIDNIGHT, then compare your table to Figure I-52.

9. Save your work, then close Table.

You modified the font, the font size, and the alignment of text in a table. You also applied a character style to selected text in a table.

FIGURE I-52

Formatting text in a table

restaurant	signature	chef	review	hours	info
SHAME ON THE MOON					
BLAME IT ON MIDNIGHT					
THE BLACK SWAN					
CHEZ BLAKE					
THE GROOVE POD					

FIGURE I-53

Table with all text centered vertically and horizontally

restaurant	signature	chef	review	hours	info
SHAME ON THE MOON		Bill Cohen	*"The fish selection is imaginitive and varied. Be sure to sample from the chef's seafood tasting menu on*	5-10	dress to impress late night menu entertainment
BLAME IT ON MIDNIGHT		Ann Mahoney	*"The pasta menu is Mahoney's secret weapon. The fettucine en brodo is rivaled only by the tortellini,*	3-11	children's menu take out
THE BLACK SWAN		Kelli Jacob	*"With all of the incredible seafood specialty dishes, you might overlook the succulent beef and*	4-11	dress to impress entertainment pre-theater menu
CHEZ BLAKE		Tim Brodt	*"The juxtaposition of textures is stunning. My favorite was a crunchy crab salad served on a smooth*	4-10	children's menu
THE GROOVE POD		Peter Panik	*"Peter Panik is a culinary master of the unexpected."*	5-11	late night menu children's menu

Position text vertically within a cell

1. Open ID I-3.indd, verify that you are in Normal View Mode, then save it as **Table Complete**.

   This table has the exact formatting of the table you created up to this point. The only thing that is different is that more text has been added to the cells, a "key" graphic has been placed below the table, and icons are on the pasteboard.

2. Select the top row of cells, then click the **Align bottom button** ≡ in the Table palette.

3. Click anywhere in the "Blame it on Midnight" cell, then click the **Justify vertically button** ≡.

4. Position your cursor over the top-left corner of the table until a black diagonal arrow appears, then click to select the entire table.

5. Click the **Align center button** ≡ in the Table palette.

6. Deselect all, then compare your work to Figure I-53.

You used the align buttons in the Table palette to format how text is positioned vertically within a cell.

Lesson 3 Format Text in a Table

Adjust column widths and cell insets

1. Click **View** on the menu bar, then click **Show Guides**.

2. Note the "review" text in the fourth column.

   | TIP   Red circles in cells indicate that the cell content is too big to fit in the cell.

3. Position your cursor over the navy blue vertical cell border that separates the "hours" column from the "info" column so that a double arrow appears, as shown in Figure I-54.

4. Click and drag the **arrow** left, so that the vertical cell border is aligned with the green vertical guide, as shown in Figure I-55.

   The width of the "hours" column is reduced. The width of the "info" column is not reduced; it merely moves with the "hours" column.

5. Position your cursor over the navy blue vertical cell border to the right of the "review" column so that a double arrow appears.

   (continued)

FIGURE I-54
Positioning the cursor over a column rule

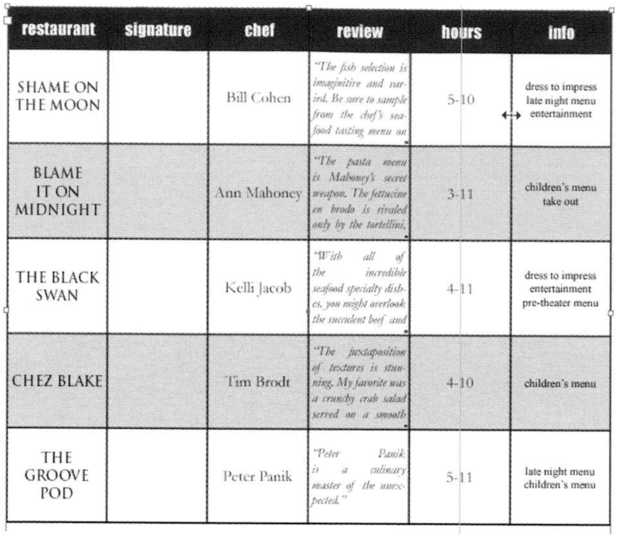

FIGURE I-55
Reducing the width of a column

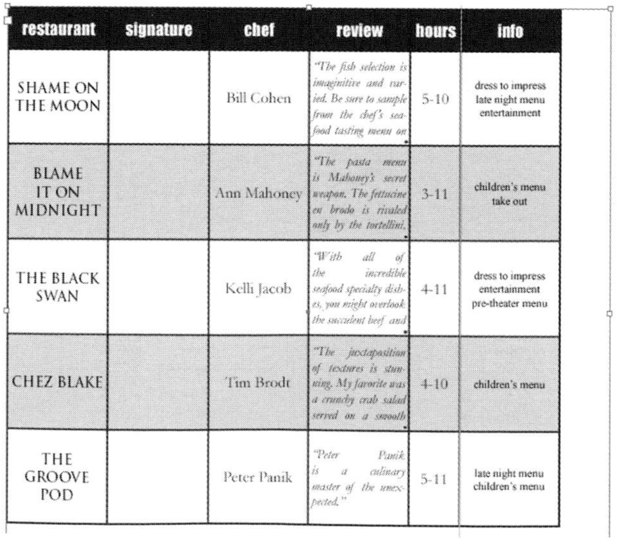

FIGURE I-56

Increasing the width of a column

6. Click and drag the **arrow** right until the right edge of the "review" column is aligned with the green guide, as shown in Figure I-56.

7. Select only the five cells containing reviews.

8. In the Table palette, increase the Left Cell Inset value to .125, then increase the Right Cell Inset value to .125.

9. Deselect all, click **View** on the menu bar, click **Hide Guides**, then compare your table to Figure I-57.

You decreased the width of one column and increased the width of another in order to fit text. You also increased the left and right cell insets so that the text was not too close to the vertical rules.

FIGURE I-57

Viewing the edited table

PLACE GRAPHICS IN A TABLE

What You'll Do

restaurant	signature	chef	review	hours	info
SHAME ON THE MOON		Bill Cohen	"The fish selection is imaginative and varied. Be sure to sample from the chef's seafood tasting menus on Thursday nights."	5-10	
BLAME IT ON MIDNIGHT		Ann Mahoney	"The pasta menu is Mahoney's secret weapon. The fettuccine en brodo is rivaled only by the tortellini, which was simply a marvel."	3-11	
THE BLACK SWAN		Kelli Jacob	"With all of the incredible seafood specialty dishes, you might overlook the succulent beef and veal selections. That would be a tragedy."	4-11	
CHEZ BLAKE		Tim Brodt	"The juxtaposition of textures is stunning. My favorite was a crunchy crab salad served on a smooth lime gelee."	4-10	
THE GROOVE POD		Peter Panik	"Peter Panik is a culinary master of the unexpected."	5-11	

 In this lesson, you will insert graphics into table cells using the Place command and the Copy and Paste commands.

Placing Graphics in a Table

InDesign makes it easy to place a graphic into a cell in a table. One simple method is to simply click your cursor in the cell and then use the Place command to choose and place the graphic.

If the graphic you place is too large to fit in the cell, a red circle will appear in the bottom-right corner of the cell. Your only options are to increase the size of the cell or decrease the size of the graphic.

Figure I-58 shows a table with six graphics placed in the rightmost column.

If you've entered text into a table, you have the option of replacing text with graphics. Remember, InDesign regards tables as text. Thus, graphics in tables function as inline graphics—they are just like any other text element. Many designers, when they are building tables, will simply type a graphic's name in a cell as a placeholder. They will place the graphics in the pasteboard for later use. Then, when they're finished editing the table, they replace the text with the graphics.

You replace text in a cell with a graphic the same way you add inline graphics to a block of text. Select the graphic in the pasteboard with the Selection Tool, copy it, select the text in the cell with the Type Tool, then paste the graphic. The graphic will flow with any other text that is in the cell. This is a very powerful option. It allows you to place both text and graphics in a single cell!

FIGURE I-58

Placing graphics in a table

State	Founded	Area	Capital	Pop	Flag
CONNECTICUT	1788	5,544 sq/mi	Hartford	3,405,000	
MASSACHUSETTS	1788	10,555 sq/mi	Boston	6, 349,000	
NEW HAMPSHIRE	1788	9,351 sq/mi	Concord	1,235,000	
RHODE ISLAND	1790	1,545 sq/mi	Providence	1, 048,00	
VERMONT	1791	9,615 sq/mi	Montpelier	608,000	
MAINE	1820	35,387 sq/mi	Augusta	1,274,000	

Place graphics in a table

1. Click in the second cell of the second row.

2. Place the file named Sole.tif from the location where your Data Files are stored.

3. Click in the second cell of the third row.

4. Place the file named Crab salad.tif, then compare your work to Figure I-59.

5. Click the **Selection Tool** ▸, select the Crab Salad.tif graphic, click **Object** on the menu bar, then click **Clipping Path**.

6. Click the **Type list arrow**, click **Alpha Channel**, then click **OK**.

7. Using the same methods and moving downward in the second column, place the following graphics: Striped bass.tif, Gnocchi.tif, and Tuna.tif.

8. Select the Gnocchi.tif graphic, click **Object** on the menu bar, then click **Clipping Path**.

9. Click the **Type list arrow**, click **Alpha Channel**, click **OK**, then compare your table to Figure I-60.

You used the Place command to place graphics in cells.

Replace text with graphics

1. Click the **Selection Tool** ▸, click the **moon graphic** in the pasteboard, click **Edit** on the menu bar, then click **Copy**.

   TIP The "moon" graphic is the top-left graphic on the pasteboard.

(continued)

FIGURE I-59
Placing two graphics

FIGURE I-60
Placing five graphics

FIGURE I-61

Replacing two lines of text with graphics

restaurant	signature	chef	review	hours	info
SHAME ON THE MOON		Bill Cohen	"The fish selection is imaginitive and varied. Be sure to sample from the chef's seafood tasting menu on Thursday nights."	5-10	dress to impress / entertainment
BLAME IT ON MIDNIGHT		Ann Mahoney	"The pasta menu is Mahoney's secret weapon. The fettucine en brodo is rivaled only by the tortellini, which was simply a marvel."	3-11	children's menu take out
THE BLACK SWAN		Kelli Jacob	"With all of the incredible seafood specialty dishes, you might overlook the succulent beef and veal selections. That would be a tragedy."	4-11	dress to impress entertainment pre-theater menu
CHEZ BLAKE		Tim Brodt	"The juxtaposition of textures is stunning. My favorite was a crunchy crab salad served on a smooth lime gelee."	4-10	children's menu
THE GROOVE POD		Peter Panik	"Peter Panik is a culinary master of the unexpected."	5-11	children's menu

FIGURE I-63

Completing the table

restaurant	signature	chef	review	hours	info
SHAME ON THE MOON		Bill Cohen	"The fish selection is imaginitive and varied. Be sure to sample from the chef's seafood tasting menu on Thursday nights."	5-10	
BLAME IT ON MIDNIGHT		Ann Mahoney	"The pasta menu is Mahoney's secret weapon. The fettucine en brodo is rivaled only by the tortellini, which was simply a marvel."	3-11	
THE BLACK SWAN		Kelli Jacob	"With all of the incredible seafood specialty dishes, you might overlook the succulent beef and veal selections. That would be a tragedy."	4-11	
CHEZ BLAKE		Tim Brodt	"The juxtaposition of textures is stunning. My favorite was a crunchy crab salad served on a smooth lime gelee."	4-10	
THE GROOVE POD		Peter Panik	"Peter Panik is a culinary master of the unexpected."	5-11	

Lesson 4   Place Graphics in a Table

FIGURE I-62

Placing three graphics in a cell

2. Click the **Type Tool** T, then select the "late night menu" text in the top cell of the info column.

3. Click **Edit** on the menu bar, then click **Paste**.

4. Select the "late night menu" text in the bottom cell of the info column, click **Edit** on the menu bar, then click **Paste**.

   Your table should resemble Figure I-61.

5. Click the **Selection Tool**, click the **tie graphic** in the pasteboard, copy it, then click the **Type Tool** T.

6. Triple-click **dress to impress** in the top cell of the info column to select the line of text, then paste.

   The tie graphic replaces the text; the moon graphic and tie graphic are on the same line.

7. Click the **Selection Tool**, click the **music graphic** in the pasteboard, copy it, click the **Type Tool** T, select the "entertainment" text in the top cell of the info column, then paste.

   The top cell in your info column should resemble Figure I-62.

8. Using the same method, replace all the text in the info column with corresponding icons so that your table resembles Figure I-63.

   TIP   Use the key below the table to identify the icon that corresponds with the text.

9. Save your work, then close Table Complete.

You replaced selected text elements with graphics.

Work with tabs.

1. Open ID I-4.indd, then save it as **Tab Review**.
2. Click the Selection Tool, click the text frame that contains the data, click Object on the menu bar, then click Text Frame Options.
3. In the Inset Spacing section, type **.25** in the Top text box, type **.25** in the Left text box, then click OK.
4. Click the Type Tool, then select all of the text.
5. Click Type on the menu bar, then click Tabs.
6. Click the Left-Justified Tab button in the Tabs palette (if necessary).
7. Position your cursor in the white space in the top third of the ruler—just above the numbers—then click and drag until the X text box reads 1 in.
8. Using the same method, create a new tab at 2.25".
9. Click anywhere to the right of the second tab to add a third tab.
10. Select the measurement in the X text box, type **3**, then press [Enter] (Win) or [return] (Mac).
11. Click the Type Tool to the left of the first # sign in the first line of text, then press [Tab].
12. Click the Type Tool to the left of the second # sign, then press [Tab].
13. Click the Type Tool to the left of the word Profit, then press [Tab].
14. Using the same tabs, tab the text on the next four lines.
15. Select all of the text, click Object on the menu bar, click Text Frame Options, change the Left inset to .5, then click OK.
16. Click the Position Palette above Text Frame button in the Tabs palette.
17. Select only the bottom four rows of text.
18. Click the first left-justified tab at 1" in the tab ruler to select it.
19. Type **1.4** in the X text box, then press [Enter] (Win) or [return] (Mac).
20. Click the second left-justified tab at 2.25" in the tab ruler to select it.
21. Type **2.4** in the X text box, then press [Enter] (Win) or [return] (Mac).
22. Click the third left-justified tab at 3" in the tab ruler to select it.
23. Click the Align to Decimal Tab button in the Tabs palette.
24. Type **3.2** in the X text box, then press [Enter] (Win) or [return] (Mac).
25. With the four rows of text still selected, click the first tab in the tab ruler to highlight it.
26. In the Leader text box, type a period followed by a space, then press [Enter] (Win) or [return] (Mac).
27. Click the second tab in the tab ruler to highlight it.

28. In the Leader text box, type a period followed by a space, then press [Enter] (Win) or [return] (Mac).
29. Click the third tab in the tab ruler to highlight it.
30. In the Leader text box, type a period followed by a space, then press [Enter] (Win) or [return] (Mac).
31. Select all of the text, click the Paragraph palette list arrow, then click Paragraph Rules.
32. Click the list arrow at the top of the dialog box, click Rule Below, then click the Rule On check box.
33. Choose the same settings shown in Figure I-64 to define the rule, then click OK.
34. Deselect all, close the Tabs palette, then compare your page to Figure I-65.
35. Save your work, then close Tab Review.

FIGURE I-64

Paragraph Rules dialog box

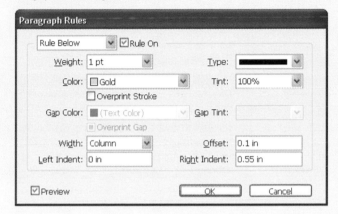

FIGURE I-65

Completed Skills Review, Part 1

Lemonade Stand Sales

Salesperson	# Pitchers Made	# Sold	Profit
Charlie	30	15	$150.00
Angela	37	27	$270.00
Christie	20	20	$200.00
Peter	20	7	$70.00

Create and format a table.

1. Open ID I-5.indd, then save it as **Table Review**.
2. Close all open palettes except for the Toolbox, click the Type Tool, then create a text frame that snaps to all four margin guides.
3. Click View on the menu bar, then click Hide Guides.
4. Click Table on the menu bar, then click Insert Table.
5. Type **7** in the Body Rows text box, then type **6** in the Columns text box.
6. Click OK, click Window on the menu bar, point to Type & Tables, then click Table.
7. Position your cursor over the second cell in the first column, then click and drag to select all of the rows except the top row.
8. Click the Row Height list arrow in the Table palette, then click Exactly.
9. Type **1.625** in the text box next to the Row Height text box, then press [Enter] (Win) or [return] (Mac).
10. Position your cursor over the left edge of the top cell in the first row so that a heavy black arrow appears pointing to the right.
11. Click once to select the top row.
12. Click the Row Height list arrow in the Table palette, then click Exactly.
13. Type **.5** in the text box next to the Row Height text box, then press [Enter] (Win) or [return] (Mac).

14. Position your cursor over the top-left corner of the table so that a black diagonal arrow appears.
15. Click once to select the entire table.
16. Click Table on the menu bar, point to Cell Options, then click Strokes and Fills.
17. Click the Weight list arrow, then click 2 pt.
18. Click the Color list arrow, click Black, then click OK.
19. Click Table on the menu bar, point to Table Options, then click Alternating Fills.
20. Click the Alternating Pattern list arrow, then click Every Other Row.
21. Click the first Color list arrow on the left side of the dialog box, click Gold, then type **100** in the Tint text box.
22. Click the second Color list arrow on the right side of the dialog box, click Navy, type **20** in the Tint text box, then click OK.
23. Select the top row of cells, click Table on the menu bar, point to Cell Options, then click Strokes and Fills.
24. In the Cell Fill area, click the Color list arrow, click Navy, type **100** in the Tint text box, then click OK.

Format text in a table.

1. Click the Type Tool in the top-left text box, then type **State**.
2. Press [Tab], then type **Founded**.
3. In the remaining four cells of the top row, type **Area**, **Capital**, **Pop**, and **Flag**.

4. Click in the first cell of the second row, then type **Connecticut**.
5. Press ↓, then type **Massachusetts**.
6. Press ↓, then type **New Hampshire**.
7. Press ↓, then type **Rhode Island**.
8. Press ↓, then type **Vermont**.
9. Press ↓, then type **Maine**.
10. Position your cursor over the left edge of the first cell in the top row so that a black arrow appears pointing right, then click to select the entire row.
11. Show the Swatches palette, click the Formatting affects text button, then click Paper.
12. Show the Character palette, change the font to Impact, then change the font size to 18 pt.
13. Click anywhere in the first cell of the second row, then drag down to select all of the cells in the first column (except the top row).
14. Show the Character Styles palette, then click Names.
15. Position your cursor over the top-left corner of the table so that a black diagonal arrow appears, then click to select the entire table.
16. Click the Align center button in the Paragraph palette.
17. Save your work, then close Table Review.
18. Open ID I-6.indd, then save it as **Table Review Completed**.
19. Select the top row of cells, then click the Align bottom button in the Table palette.

20. Click anywhere in the "Connecticut" cell, then click and drag to select the bottom six rows.
21. Click the Align center button in the Table palette.
22. Click View on the menu bar, then click Show Guides (if necessary).
23. Position your cursor over the vertical cell border that separates the first two columns so that a double arrow appears.
24. Click and drag the arrow right, so that the vertical cell border is aligned with the green vertical guide.
25. Position your cursor over the vertical cell border that separates the second and third columns so that a double arrow appears.
26. Click and drag the arrow left, so that the vertical cell border is aligned with the red vertical guide.
27. Position your cursor over the vertical cell border that separates the fifth and sixth columns so that a double arrow appears.
28. Click and drag the arrow left, so that the vertical cell border is aligned with the blue vertical guide.
29. Position your cursor over the right edge of the table, then drag right until the right edge of the table is aligned with the margin guide.

Place graphics in a table.

1. Click in the sixth cell of the second row.
2. Place the file named CT State Flag.tif from the location where your Chapter I Data Files are stored.
3. Click in the next cell down.
4. Place the file named MA State Flag.tif.

5. Using the same method and moving downward in the column, place the following graphics: NH State Flag.tif, RI State Flag.tif, VT State Flag.tif, ME State Flag.tif.
6. Deselect all, hide guides, then compare your table with Figure I-66.
7. Save your work, then close Table Review Completed.

FIGURE I-66
Completed Skills Review, Part 2

State	Founded	Area	Capital	Pop	Flag
CONNECTICUT	1788	5,544 sq/mi	Hartford	3,405,000	
MASSACHUSETTS	1788	10,555 sq/mi	Boston	6,349,000	
NEW HAMPSHIRE	1788	9,351 sq/mi	Concord	1,235,000	
RHODE ISLAND	1790	1,545 sq/mi	Providence	1,048,00	
VERMONT	1791	9,615 sq/mi	Montpelier	608,000	
MAINE	1820	35,387 sq/mi	Augusta	1,274,000	

You are a designer at a manufacturer of games. A junior designer has e-mailed you a chart that she created, showing the winners of a recent promotion. You note immediately that the chart is not well designed. You decide to make improvements before showing it to your boss.

1. Open ID I-7.indd, then save it as **Contest Redesign**.
2. Select the headline only, then click the Align center button in the Paragraph palette.
3. Select all of the text in the frame, click Object on the menu bar, then click Text Frame Options.
4. In the Inset Spacing section, type **.25** in the Top text box, then click OK.
5. Select only the five rows of text (not the headline).
6. Click Type on the menu bar, then click Tabs.
7. Click the left-justified tab already in the Tab ruler to select it, then click the Align to Decimal Tab button.
8. Select the contents of the X text box, type **2.75**, then press [Enter] (Win) or [return] (Mac).
9. Click the Tab ruler approximately at the 2" mark to add a new tab.
10. Change the tab to a left-justified tab.

11. Select the contents of the X text box, type **.5**, then press [Enter] (Win) or [return] (Mac).
12. Click your cursor to the left of the first name, then press [Tab].

13. Tab the remaining four names, close the Tabs palette, then compare your work to Figure I-67.
14. Save your work, then close Contest Redesign.

FIGURE I-67
Completed Project Builder 1

CONTEST RESULTS

T. JONES	$40.00
P. HELENEK	$100.00
T. BRODT	$5.00
A. MAHONEY	$10,000.00
K. JACOB	$3,000.00

Your company has recently held a sales contest. You are in charge of showing the contest results. One of your staff designers has e-mailed you a chart showing the results and says it's "ready to go." You feel that the chart looks a bit stark, so you decide to add rules to it.

1. Open ID I-8.indd, then save it as **Contest Rules**.
2. Select the five lines of text, then increase the leading to 20 pts.
3. Click the Paragraph palette list arrow, then click Paragraph Rules.
4. Click the Rule On check box, type **.25** in the Left Indent text box, type **.25** in the Right Indent text box, type **p5** in the Offset text box, then click OK.
5. Select only the first row of text (T. Jones), click the Paragraph palette list arrow, then click Paragraph Rules.
6. Click the Rule Below list arrow, choose Rule Above, then click the Rule On check box.
7. Type **.25** in the Left Indent text box, type **.25** in the Right Indent text box, type **p15** in the Offset text box, then click OK.
8. Save your work, compare your chart to Figure I-68, then close Contest Rules.

FIGURE I-68
Completed Project Builder 2

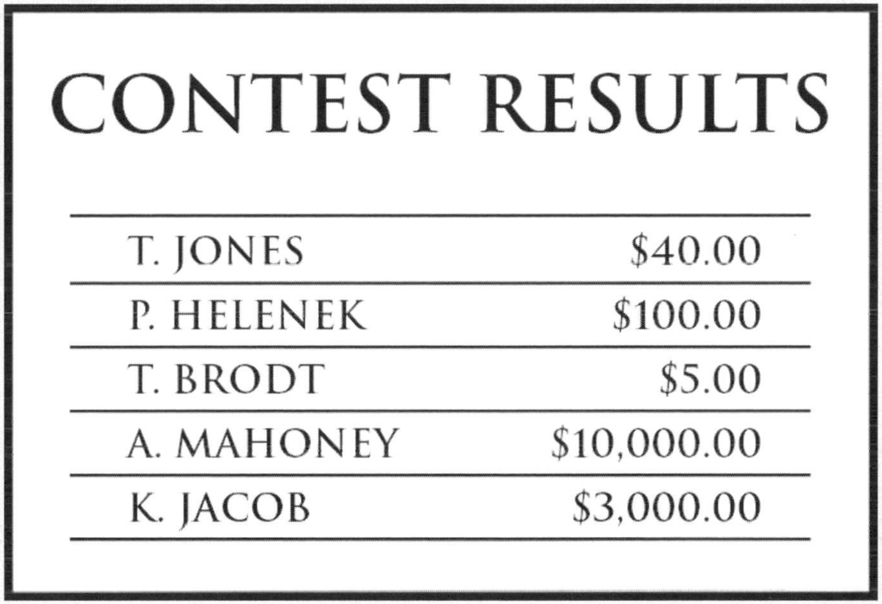

CONTEST RESULTS	
T. JONES	$40.00
P. HELENEK	$100.00
T. BRODT	$5.00
A. MAHONEY	$10,000.00
K. JACOB	$3,000.00

You are a freelance designer. Your client has given you a table she created in InDesign and has asked you to "give it some life." You open the file and decide that it needs color and some reformatting.

1. Open ID I-9.indd, then save it as **Mountain Table**.
2. Select all of the cells in the table, change their height to exactly .75 in, then change their width to exactly 2 in.
3. Center all the text horizontally and vertically.
4. Change the cell strokes to 2 pt. Navy.
5. Apply alternating fills of 20% Navy and 20% Green.
6. Change the fill on the top row to 100% Navy.
7. Change the top row of text to 22 pt. Impact.
8. Change the fill on the top row of text to Paper.
9. Select all of the text in rows 2 through 6, then change the type size to 22 pt.
10. Deselect all, then compare your work to Figure I-69.
11. Save your work, then close Mountain Table.

FIGURE I-69
Completed Design Project

Mountain	State	Height	First Scaled
Mount Jefferson	Utah	6288 ft.	1937
Mount Rustic	Colorado	7789 ft.	1933
Mount Green	Massachusetts	4953 ft.	1877
Bear Mountain	California	5784 ft.	1899
Goat Mountain	New Hampshire	6235 ft.	1910

In this project, each member of the group will build a chart from scratch, using tabs. The group will create a chart based on supplied information. Each group member is free to choose the size of the chart and any colors, rules, tab leaders, or text formatting that might make the chart more visually pleasing. The chart will be based on the following information:

1. Create a new InDesign document, then save it as **Holiday Chart**.

   The title of the chart is: **Annual Holiday Fund Raiser**.

   Five students sold five different products during the holiday raffle. The sales information is as follows:
   - Karen sold 100 lollipops at a retail cost of 25 cents per unit, for a total net revenue of $25.00.
   - Jimmy sold 45 lapel pins at a retail cost of $2 per unit, for a total net revenue of $90.00.
   - Billy sold 30 candles at a retail cost of $2.50 per unit, for a total net revenue of $75.00.
   - Susan sold 10 rolls of mints at a retail cost of 50 cents per unit, for a total net revenue of $5.00.
   - Michael sold 20 calendars at a retail cost of $10 per unit, for a total net revenue of $200.00.

FIGURE I-70
Sample Group Project

2. Once each member of the group has finished building the chart, they should compare their work with Figure I-70.
3. Save your work, then close Holiday Chart.

Annual Holiday Fund Raiser

Sales Person	Product	Number Sold	Retail Cost	Net Revenue
Karen	Lollipops	100	$.25	$25.00
Jimmy	Lapel Pins	45	$2.00	$90.00
Billy	Candles	30	$2.50	$75.00
Susan	Mints	10	$.50	$5.00
Michael	Calendars	20	$10.00	$200.00

MAKING BOOKS, TABLES OF CONTENTS, AND INDEXES

1. Create a book file.

2. Organize a book file.

3. Create a table of contents.

4. Create an index.

CHAPTER 1
MAKING BOOKS, TABLES OF CONTENTS, AND INDEXES

Imagine that you've created a number of InDesign documents, each of which is meant to be a chapter in a book. InDesign's Book feature allows you to combine and collate all of those separate documents into one book with continuous pagination. Want to switch the order of chapters? Feel free! The Book palette allows you to reorganize at will, and it will automatically repaginate your book every time you make a change.

This is a very cool feature. But InDesign's automatic table of contents and index features will really wow you! With a click of a button, InDesign examines all the documents in the Book palette, identifies text items that you've saved with specific paragraph styles, then sorts those text items into a table of contents or an index, complete with page numbers.

In the early days of desktop publishing, the ability to cut and paste text within an electronic document was revolutionary. Play around with InDesign's automatic table of contents and index features and you'll be amazed at how far we've come!

Tools You'll Use

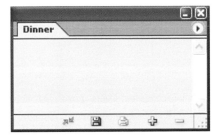

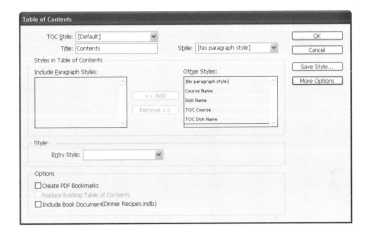

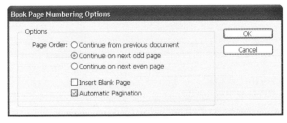

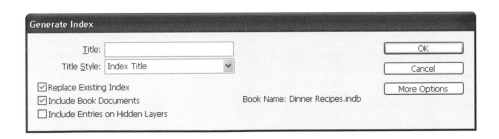

CREATE A BOOK FILE

What You'll Do

 In this lesson, you will create a book file and add documents to create a book.

Creating a Book File

In Adobe InDesign, a **book** is a collection of two or more InDesign documents, which are paginated as a single book. For example, you can collect three 10-page documents as a single 30-page book.

Creating a book is similar to creating a document—you use the New command on the File menu; however, you choose Book instead of Document. A book is an individual InDesign file, like a library file, and when opened, it appears as a palette. Figure J-1 shows an open book file.

> **QUICKTIP**
>
> Unlike InDesign documents, which have a filename extension of .indd (InDesign document), book files have a filename extension of .indb (InDesign book).

Adding Documents to a Book Palette

To create a book, you add InDesign documents to the Book palette. When you do so, the documents are paginated as though they were one book. For example, adding five 20-page documents would create a book that is paginated from 1-100. Figure J-2 shows a Book palette after four documents have been added. Note the page ranges next to each document name.

It is important that you understand that the documents themselves are being modified when they are added to the Book palette. For example, if you add two 20-page documents to the Book palette, the second document in the palette will be paginated from page 21-40. This change will take place in the document as well.

Though originally the two documents were paginated from page 1-20, if you opened the second document and looked at the Pages palette, the page range in the document will have changed to 21-40. This is why it is a very good idea to save backup copies of original documents before adding them to a Book palette. You never know when you might need to go back to the original document.

Double-clicking a document in the Book palette opens the document. When a document is open, the Book palette shows the Document is open icon, as shown in Figure J-3.

FIGURE J-1
An opened book file

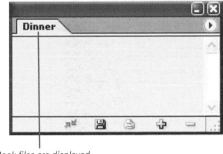

Book files are displayed as palettes

FIGURE J-2
Viewing documents in the Book palette

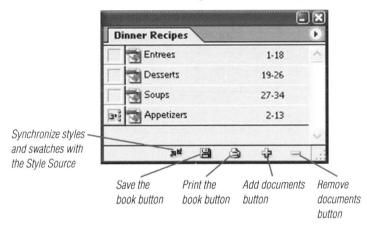

Synchronize styles and swatches with the Style Source

Save the book button   Print the book button   Add documents button   Remove documents button

FIGURE J-3
Book palette showing an open document

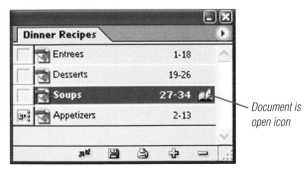

Document is open icon

Create a book file

1. Open ID J-1.indd, save it as **Toy Breeds**, then close the document.

   You will view each document that will become part of the book to familiarize yourself with the book content.

2. Open ID J-2.indd, save it as **Herding Breeds**, then close the document.

3. Open ID J-3.indd, save it as **Terrier Breeds**, then close the document.

4. Open ID J-4.indd, save it as **Hound Breeds**, then close the document.

5. Open ID J-5.indd, save it as **Sport Breeds**, then close the document.

6. Click **File** on the menu bar, point to **New**, then click **Book**.

7. Name the new file **Dog Breeds**, then click **Save**.

   As shown in Figure J-4, a Book palette appears with a single tab named Dog Breeds. This palette is the book file.

You viewed each document that will be used in the book, then created a new book file.

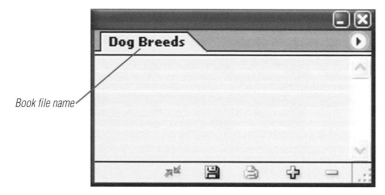

Book file name

Adding a document to the Book palette

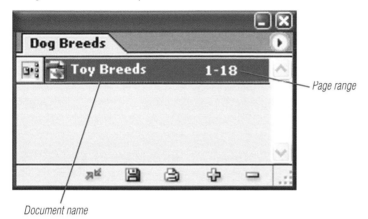

Page range

Document name

Dog Breeds book with five documents added

Continuous pagination

Add documents to a book file

1. Click the **Book palette list arrow**, then click **Add Document**.

2. Navigate to the drive and folder where your Data Files are stored, click **Toy Breeds.indd**, then click **Add** (Win) or **Open** (Mac).

   As shown in Figure J-5, the document is listed in the Book palette along with its page range.

3. Click the **Add documents button** ⊕ in the Book palette, then add the document named Herding Breeds.indd.

4. Using either of the two methods outlined above, add the following documents in the following order: Terrier Breeds.indd, Hound Breeds.indd, Sport Breeds.indd.

   As shown in Figure J-6, the Book palette contains five documents and the pagination is continuous for a total of 106 pages in the book.

5. Click the **Save the book button** 🖫 in the Book palette.

You added five documents to the Book palette to create a book with 106 pages.

ORGANIZE A BOOK FILE

What You'll Do

In this lesson, you will modify both the order and the page range of documents in the Book palette.

Manipulating the Order of Documents in a Book File

When you add documents to a book file, the documents are repaginated as you add them. However, you can reorder the documents at any time simply by dragging them up or down in the Book palette. Figure J-7 shows four documents in the Dinner Recipes book reordered into the sequence of a meal, with appetizers first and desserts last.

When you reorder documents in the Book palette, the documents are repaginated accordingly—in both the palette and the documents themselves.

Modifying the Page Range of Documents

Typically, the documents that you add to a Book palette will start on page 1 in their original incarnation. In other words, if you add five documents, each would have originally been numbered starting with page 1. Page 1 is always a right-hand page.

As discussed previously, documents are repaginated when added to a book file. This can create left-hand page/right-hand page issues. For example, let's say you add two documents. Originally, the first is paginated with pages 1-11. The second is paginated with pages 1-12. Therefore, each begins on a right page. However, once both are added to a book file, the second document will be paginated with pages 12-23. This means that the first page of the second document is now a left-hand page.

This may or may not be a problem. If it is a problem, you will want to repaginate the document so that it once again begins on a right-hand page. To do so, access the Book Page Numbering Options dialog box, shown in Figure J-8, from the Book palette menu. This dialog box allows you to manipulate how documents are paginated as they are added to the book file.

In the above example, you would select the second document and then click the Continue on next odd page option button.

This forces the next document to begin on the next odd page in the book. Thus, the second document once again begins on a right-hand page.

This method works on all documents in the Book palette *except* the first document, because the first document is not "continued" from any other document. In a book file, the first document starts on a right-hand page 1 by default. If you want it to start on an even left-hand page, you need to use a different method. Double-clicking the page numbers of a document in the Book palette opens both the document and the Document Page Numbering Options dialog box. You can use this dialog box to define the document start page as, say, page 2, as shown in Figure J-9. Now the first document begins on an even left-hand page.

FIGURE J-7
Reordering documents

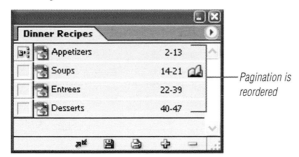

Pagination is reordered

FIGURE J-8
Book Page Numbering Options dialog box

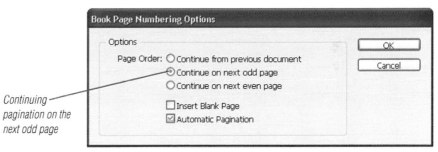

Continuing pagination on the next odd page

FIGURE J-9
Document Page Numbering Options dialog box

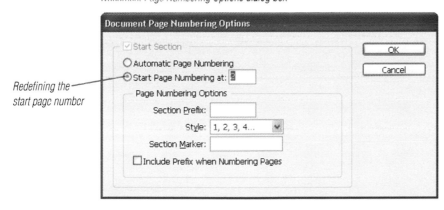

Redefining the start page number

Manipulate the order of documents

1. Note the order of documents in the Book palette.

   For this project, each document will be a chapter in the book. You want the chapters to flow in alphabetical order.

2. Drag **Toy Breeds** down to the bottom of the list.

   TIP When you move a document in the list, a black horizontal line appears to denote its new location.

   As shown in Figure J-10, when Toy Breeds is moved to the bottom of the list, the page range is renumbered—Toy Breeds now appear on pages 89-106.

3. Rearrange the list so that it is in alphabetical order, as shown in Figure J-11.

4. Double-click **Toy Breeds** in the Book palette.

   TIP Double-clicking the name of a document in the Book palette opens the InDesign document.

5. Click **Window** on the menu bar, then click **Pages** (if necessary).

   Manipulating a document in the Book palette affects the actual document. The Pages palette in Toy Breeds.indd lists the document pages as 89-106.

6. Close Toy Breeds.

You modified the order of documents in the Book palette, noting the changes in page range. You opened one of the documents and noted that the changes made in the Book palette directly affected the document.

FIGURE J-10
Moving Toy Breeds to the bottom of the list

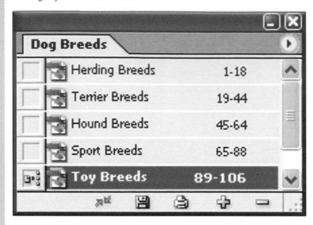

FIGURE J-11
Reordering the list into alphabetical order

Alphabetical order—

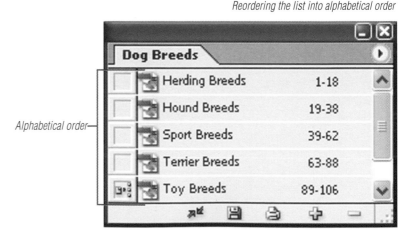

Making Books, Tables of Contents, and Indexes

FIGURE J-12

Changing the page range of four chapters

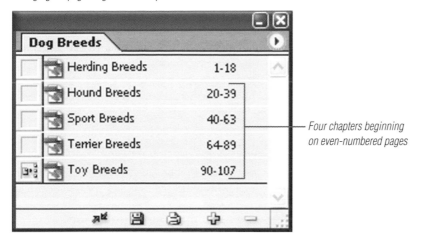

— Four chapters beginning
on even-numbered pages

FIGURE J-13

Changing the start page of the first chapter

Begins on page 2 —

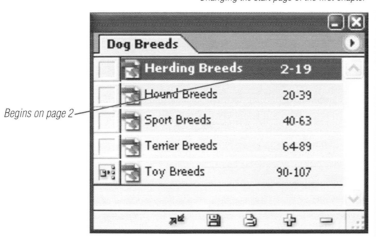

Modify the page range of documents

1. Click the **Book palette list arrow**, then click **Book Page Numbering Options**.

   You will designate the first page of every chapter to appear on a left page—an even page number.

2. Click the **Continue on next even page option button**, then click **OK**.

   As shown in Figure J-12, all chapters except the first now begin on an even-numbered page.

3. In the Book palette, double-click the **page numbers** for Herding Breeds.

   > TIP Double-clicking the page numbers in the Book palette opens both the document and the Document Page Numbering Options dialog box.

4. Click the **Start Page Numbering at option button**, type **2** in the text box, then click **OK**.

   The first page of the document is now an even-numbered left-hand page, which is part of a two-page spread.

5. Save the change, close Herding Breeds, then note the page range in the Book palette.

   As shown in Figure J-13, the book now begins on page 2 and ends on page 107, with all chapters beginning on an even-numbered left-hand page.

6. Click the **Save the book button** 🖫 in the Book palette.

You modified the page range of the book so that every chapter begins on a left-hand even-numbered page.

CREATE A TABLE OF CONTENTS

What You'll Do

 In this lesson, you will create a table of contents based on the documents in the book file.

Using Paragraph Styles to Create a Table of Contents

When you create a table of contents (TOC) for a book, it is generated from information contained within the documents that make up the book. Specifically, the entries in the TOC are text items from the documents that are formatted with specific paragraph styles.

Here's how it works: Let's say that you've created four documents that you want to collate into a recipe book. You want the title of every recipe—from all four documents—to be listed in the TOC. To make this happen, you must format the title of each recipe with the same paragraph style.

When you collate the four documents in the book file and then generate a TOC, InDesign searches through all four of the documents and locates all the text elements that were formatted with the paragraph style that you specified. In this example, that would be all the recipe titles. InDesign then copies all of those text elements into a TOC format. It lists all of the text elements and the pages on which they appear in the book. Isn't that an ingenious solution?

Loading Paragraph Styles

Now that you understand how InDesign uses paragraph styles to create a TOC, you need to understand how to manage paragraph styles properly. Remember, paragraph styles must be consistent for every document that has been added to the book.

The best method for assuring consistent paragraph styles is to load them between documents. This couldn't be easier. Once you've created the first document to be used in the book, create the second document, then use the Load Paragraph Styles command in the Paragraph Styles palette menu. You use this command to import the paragraph styles from the first document into the second document. Now, both documents access the same paragraph styles.

Do this for the remaining documents for the book, and you can be confident that all of the paragraph styles are consistent for all of the documents that make up the book.

Maintaining Consistent Styles Between Documents in a Book

In Figure J-14, note the Indicates the Style Source icon to the left of Entrees. This means that InDesign regards the paragraph styles in the Entrees document as the master paragraph styles. In other words, the paragraph styles in the three other documents should be consistent with those in Entrees.

By default, the first document that you add to the Book file is designated as the style source.

You can select documents in the Book palette and then use the Synchronize Selected Documents command in the palette menu to synchronize styles. When you do so, InDesign automatically searches all the paragraph styles in the selected files and compares them to those in the style source document. If InDesign finds paragraph styles in any of the selected documents that are not consistent with the style source document, it will modify those styles so that they do match, thus insuring consistency throughout the book.

This is a great feature. However, you should note that in most cases, you should not need to use it. Creating a TOC requires foresight and planning. By the time that you add documents into a book file, if you've done your work properly, all your paragraph styles should be consistent. You should not need to rely on the Synchronize Selected Documents command.

FIGURE J-14
Indicates the Style Source icon

Indicates the Style
Source icon

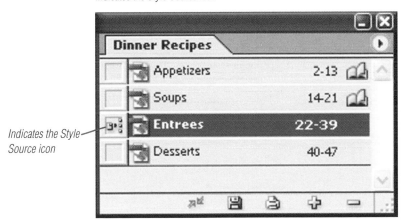

Generating a Table of Contents

A table of contents is an individual InDesign document that you add to the Book palette to become part of the book. When creating the TOC document, it is critical that you carefully choose the same document-setup specifications that were used to create the other documents in the book, such as page size, orientation, etc. Once you have created the TOC document, add it to the Book palette. Figure J-15 shows a TOC document added as page 1 in the Dinner Recipes book file.

Once you've added the TOC document to the Book palette, you must then load the paragraph styles used in the other documents in the book. The only way that the TOC document can access the paragraph styles necessary to create the TOC is to have those paragraph styles loaded into the TOC document itself. Simply use the Load Paragraph Styles command in the Paragraph Styles palette.

The Table of Contents dialog box, shown in Figure J-16, is command central for creating a TOC. Once you have loaded the paragraph styles, they will be available in the Other Styles box. Choose which styles you want the TOC to use by adding them to the Include Paragraph Styles box.

One last thing: Be sure to check the Include Book Document check box in the dialog box. This tells InDesign to use the documents in the book file as the basis for the TOC.

When you click OK, the TOC is generated. Your cursor will appear as the loaded text icon. Simply click it in the TOC document and it will flow the TOC data.

FIGURE J-15

TOC document in the Book palette

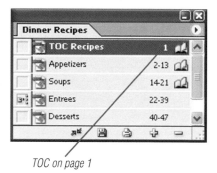

TOC on page 1

FIGURE J-16

Table of Contents dialog box

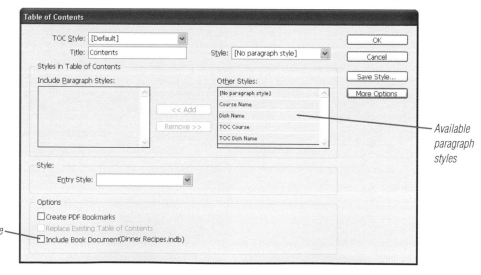

Available paragraph styles

Check to include documents in open book file

Reformatting Paragraph Styles

In most cases, the paragraph styles from which you generate your TOC will not be appropriate for the TOC layout. In the case of the recipe example, the recipe headlines were formatted as 24-pt. headlines. As shown in Figure J-17, this size is too large for TOC entries.

You have a number of options for formatting TOC entries. Once you generate the TOC, you can reformat the text any way you see fit or you can modify the paragraph styles in the TOC document only.

For a third solution, you can also create new paragraph styles in the TOC document that are more appropriate for the layout. Any new paragraph styles that you create will be listed in the Table of Contents dialog box.

In the Style section of the Table of Contents dialog box, you can use the new paragraph styles to modify the appearance of the loaded paragraph styles. In Figure J-18, the loaded Course Name paragraph style is being modified by the TOC Course paragraph style (note the Entry Style text box).

Here's the concept in a nutshell. A TOC is created based on text that is formatted with specific paragraph styles in the documents that make up a book. Sometimes, those paragraph styles are not appropriate for the TOC layout—they're too big or too small, etc. To correct this, you can create new paragraph styles in the TOC document only. Those new paragraph styles will be listed in the Table of Contents dialog box, where you can use them to modify the loaded paragraph styles.

Figure J-19 shows the same data reformatted with two new paragraph styles.

FIGURE J-17

TOC formatted with loaded paragraph styles

FIGURE J-18

Modifying a loaded paragraph style

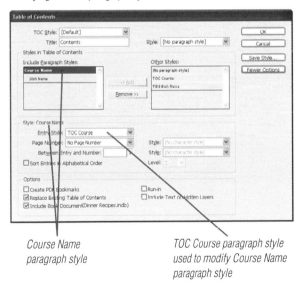

Course Name paragraph style

TOC Course paragraph style used to modify Course Name paragraph style

FIGURE J-19

TOC with reformatted paragraph styles

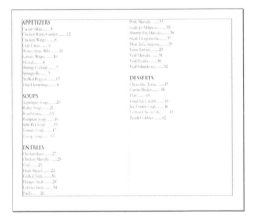

Identify and load paragraph styles for a TOC

1. Double-click **Toy Breeds** in the Book palette to open the document.

2. Click **Window** on the menu bar, point to **Type & Tables**, then click **Paragraph Styles**.

3. Click the **Type Tool T.**, then click to place your cursor anywhere in the TOY BREEDS headline on Page 1.

   The Paragraph Styles palette identifies the style applied to TOY BREEDS as Section Name.

4. Click to place your cursor in the Silky Terrier headline on Page 2.

   The Paragraph Styles palette identifies this style as Breed Name.

5. Close Toy Breeds.

6. Open ID J-6.indd, then save it as **TOC**.

7. Click the **Paragraph Styles palette list arrow**, then click **Load Paragraph Styles**.

8. Open **Toy Breeds**.

   As shown in Figure J-20, the Breed Name and Section Name styles are added to the Paragraph Styles palette.

9. Click **File** on the menu bar, then click **Save**.

You opened a document and examined which text elements were formatted with paragraph styles. You then opened a document that will be used as the TOC and loaded the paragraph styles from the first document.

FIGURE J-20
Loading paragraph styles

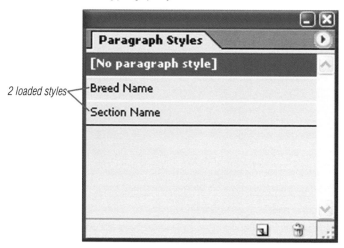

2 loaded styles

FIGURE J-21

Moving TOC to the top of the list

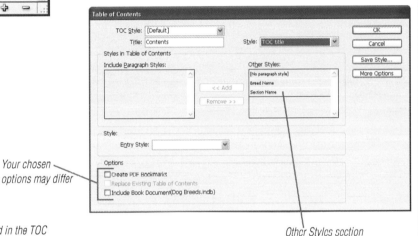

—Document is open icon

FIGURE J-22

Table of Contents dialog box

Your chosen —
options may differ

FIGURE J-23

Adding two styles to be used in the TOC

Other Styles section

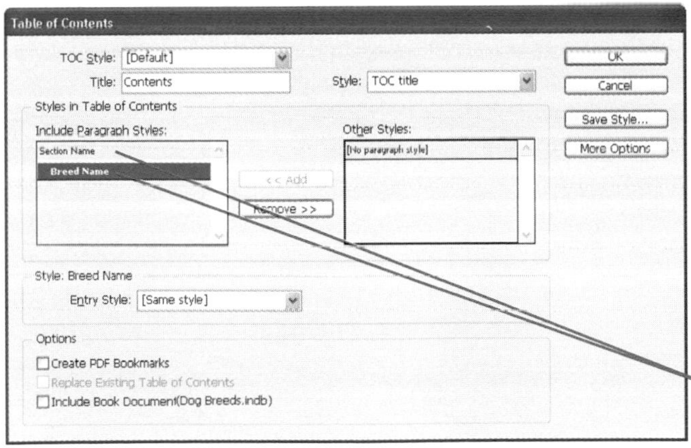

Two styles added
for use in the TOC

1. With TOC still open, click the **Add documents button** ➕ in the Book palette, then add TOC to the book.

   TOC is added to the bottom of the list.

2. Drag TOC to the top of the list so that your Book palette resembles Figure J-21.

   TIP When a document is open, the Document is open icon appears next to the document name in the Book palette.

3. Click **Layout** on the menu bar, then click **Table of Contents**.

4. Verify that the Title text box reads Contents, click the **Style list arrow**, then choose **TOC title** so that your dialog box resembles Figure J-22.

   TIP TOC title is a style loaded by default.

5. In the Styles in Table of Contents section, note that the two styles you loaded are listed in the Other Styles section.

6. Click **Section Name**, then click **Add**.

   Section Name is now listed under Include Paragraph Styles.

7. Double-click **Breed Name**.

   Breed Name is now listed beneath Section Name, as shown in Figure J-23.

   TIP Double-clicking a style is an alternative to using the Add button.

(continued)

8. In the Options section, click the **Include Book Document(Dog Breeds.indb) check box**.

This check box tells InDesign to create the TOC from the Dog Breeds book.

> TIP This step is very easy to forget. Make a mental note of it.

9. Click **OK**.

10. Position your cursor over the top-left corner of the margin guides, then click.

Your page should resemble Figure J-24. The information loaded correctly, but the paragraph styles used in the original documents are too large for this page.

You specified the two paragraph styles that will be used in the TOC, then loaded the TOC into a text frame.

Create paragraph styles for a TOC

1. Click the **Paragraph Styles list arrow**, then click **New Paragraph Style**.

2. Name the new style **TOC Section**, click **Basic Character Formats**, click the **Font Family list arrow**, click **Trajan**, click the **Font Style list arrow**, click **Bold**, click the **Size list arrow**, then click **14**.

3. Click **Indents and Spacing**, type **.2** in the Space Before text box, then click **OK**.

4. Click the **Paragraph Styles list arrow**, then click **New Paragraph Style**.

(continued)

Contents

HERDING BREEDS 2

English Sheepdog 3

Pembroke Welsh Corgi 4

Australian Cattle Dog 5

Bearded Collie 6

Australian Shepherd 7

FIGURE J-25
Two new paragraph styles

FIGURE J-26
Reformatting the Section Name paragraph style with the TOC Section paragraph style

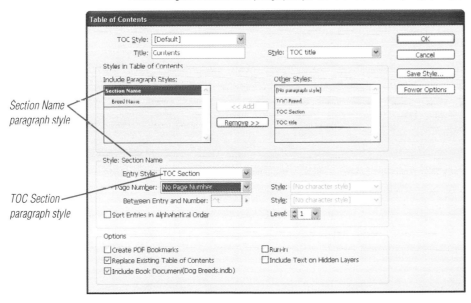

5. Name the new style **TOC Breed**, click **Basic Character Formats**, click the **Font Family list arrow**, click **Garamond**, click the **Size list arrow**, click **10**, then click **OK**.

Your Paragraph Styles palette should resemble Figure J-25.

You created two new paragraph styles for the TOC.

Reformat a table of contents

1. Click **Layout** on the menu bar, then click **Table of Contents**.

2. In the Include Paragraph Styles section, click **Section Name**.

The third section of the dialog box now reads Style: Section Name.

3. Click the **Entry Style list arrow**, then click **TOC Section**.

The Section Name paragraph style will be reformatted with the TOC Section paragraph style.

4. Click the **More Options button**.

5. In the Style: Section Name section, click the **Page Number list arrow**, then click **No Page Number**.

Your dialog box should resemble Figure J-26.

(continued)

6. In the Include Paragraph Styles section, click **Breed Name**.

   The third section of the dialog box now reads Style: Breed Name.

7. Click the **Entry Style list arrow**, click **TOC Breed**, click the **Page Number list arrow**, then click **After Entry**.

8. Select all of the text in the **Between Entry and Number text box**, then type .... (ten periods).

9. Click the **Sort Entries in Alphabetical Order check box**, then verify that the Replace Existing Table of Contents check box is checked.

   Your dialog box should resemble Figure J-27.

10. Click **OK**.

   TIP You may see an Information dialog box stating that the table of contents has been updated successfully.

   (continued)

FIGURE J-27

Reformatting the Breed Name paragraph style with the TOC Breed paragraph style

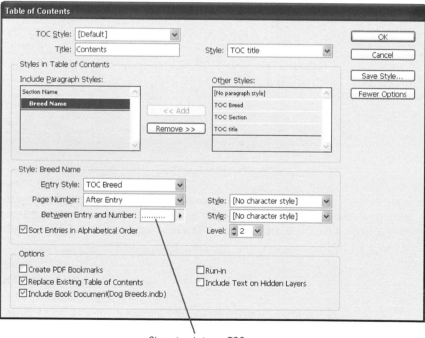

Characters between TOC entry and page number

FIGURE J-28

Viewing the reformatted TOC

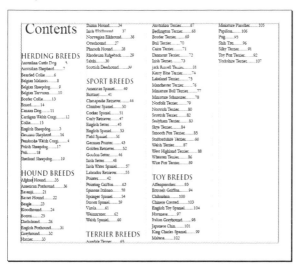

11. Click the **Selection Tool** , click the text frame on the page, click **Object** on the menu bar, click **Text Frame Options**, change the number of columns to 4, then click **OK**.

Your page should resemble Figure J-28.

12. Use any text formatting techniques you wish to improve the layout of the TOC, then save your work.

Figure J-29 shows the TOC with an improved text layout and a graphic placed behind the text.

You reformatted the imported paragraph styles with other styles you created that were appropriate for the TOC layout.

FIGURE J-29

Viewing a sample layout for the TOC

Contents

HERDING BREEDS
Australian Cattle Dog.....5
Australian Shepherd.....7
Bearded Collie.....6
Belgian Malinois.....8
Belgian Sheepdog.....9
Belgian Tervuren.....10
Border Collie.....13
Briard.....14
Canaan Dog.....11
Cardigan Welsh Corgi.....12
Collie.....15
English Sheepdog.....3
German Shepherd.....16
Pembroke Welsh Corgi.....4
Polish Sheepdog.....17
Puli.....18
Shetland Sheepdog.....19

HOUND BREEDS
Afghan Hound.....35
American Foxhound.....36
Basenji.....21
Basset Hound.....22
Beagle.....23
Bloodhound.....24
Borzoi.....25
Dachshund.....26
English Foxhound.....31
Greyhound.....32

Harrier.....33
Ibizan Hound.....34
Irish Wolfhound.....37
Norwegian Elkhound.....38
Otterhound.....27
Pharaoh Hound.....28
Rhodesian Ridgeback.....29
Saluki.....30
Scottish Deerhound.....39

SPORT BREEDS
American Spaniel.....51
Brittany.....41
Chesapeake Retriever.....44
Clumber Spaniel.....52
Cocker Spaniel.....53
Curly Retriever.....45
English Setter.....48
English Spaniel.....54
Field Spaniel.....56
German Pointer.....43
Golden Retriever.....46
Gordon Setter.....49
Irish Setter.....50
Irish Water Spaniel.....57
Labrador Retriever.....47
Pointer.....42
Pointing Griffon.....63
Spinone Italiano.....58
Springer Spaniel.....55
Sussex Spaniel.....59

Vizsla.....61
Weimaraner.....62
Welsh Spaniel.....60

TERRIER BREEDS
Airedale Terrier.....65
Australian Terrier.....67
Bedlington Terrier.....68
Border Terrier.....69
Bull Terrier.....70
Cairn Terrier.....71
Dandie Terrier.....72
Irish Terrier.....73
Jack Russell Terrier.....81
Kerry Blue Terrier.....74
Lakeland Terrier.....75
Manchester Terrier.....76
Miniature Bull Terrier.....77
Miniature Schnauzer.....78
Norfolk Terrier.....79
Norwich Terrier.....80
Scottish Terrier.....82
Sealyham Terrier.....83
Skye Terrier.....84
Smooth Fox Terrier.....85
Staffordshire Terrier.....66
Welsh Terrier.....87
West Highland Terrier.....88
Wheaten Terrier.....86
Wire Fox Terrier.....89

TOY BREEDS
Affenpinscher.....93
Brussels Griffon.....94
Chihuahua.....100
Chinese Crested.....103
English Toy Spaniel.....104
Havanese.....97
Italian Greyhound.....98
Japanese Chin.....101
King Charles Spaniel.....99
Maltese.....102
Miniature Pinscher.....105
Papillon.....106
Pug.....95
Shih Tzu.....96
Silky Terrier.....91
Toy Fox Terrier.....92
Yorkshire Terrier.....107

CREATE AN INDEX

What You'll Do

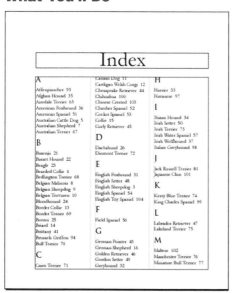

 In this lesson, you will create an index based on the documents in the book file.

Creating Index Entries

Index entries are specified within the documents that make up the book and are saved with the documents. Specifying index entries is easy to do. Simply select the text that you want to be used as an index entry, then click the Create a new index entry button in the Index palette. The selected text will be added to the Index palette, as shown in Figure J-30.

Generating an Index

An Index is an individual InDesign document that you add to the Book palette to become part of the book. This will usually be a one- or two-page document. As with the TOC document, it is critical that you carefully choose the same document-setup specifications that were used to create the other documents in the book. Once you have created the index document, add it to the Book palette.

Once you've added the index document to the Book palette, click the Generate index button in the Index palette, shown in Figure J-31. This opens the Generate Index dialog box, shown in Figure J-32. As its name implies, this dialog box generates the index based on the index entries saved with the documents that compose the book. Be sure to check the Include Book Documents check box before clicking OK.

FIGURE J-30

Creating an index entry

Selected text

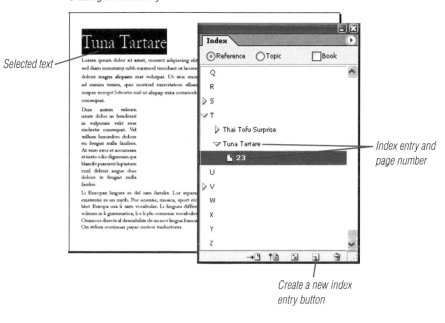

Index entry and
page number

Create a new index
entry button

FIGURE J-31

Generate index button

Generate index button

FIGURE J-32

Generate Index dialog box

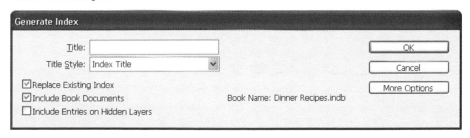

Generating a Cross-reference Index Entry

Creating an index is a linguistic challenge. One of your greatest challenges will be to anticipate the way a reader will search the index for specific topics. For example, if you have written a book on recipes, you might have an index entry for Bouillabaisse. That seems pretty straightforward, but you would also need to anticipate that some of your readers would go to the F section of your index looking for Bouillabaisse. F, you ask? Yes, F, for Fish Stew.

In this example, you could simply create an index entry for Fish Stew with the page number for Bouillabaisse. However, for consistency reasons, it would be better to create a cross-reference. You do this in the New Cross-reference dialog box, shown in Figure J-33. You create this cross-reference entry in the document itself, when you create the other index entries. When you click OK, a new entry will be created, as shown in Figure J-34.

FIGURE J-33
New Cross-reference dialog box

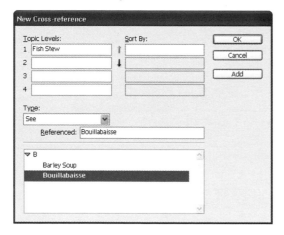

FIGURE J-34
Cross-reference index entry

F

Fish Stew. See Bouillabaisse

Flan 43

Fried Ice Cream 45

Cross-referenced

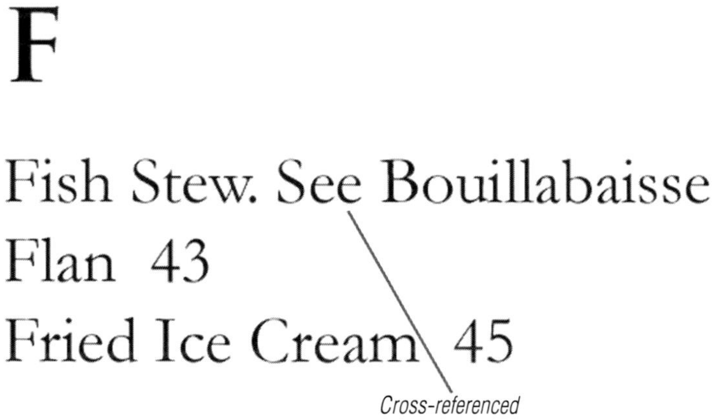

Sorting Index Entries

Once you've created individual index entries for specific topics in your document, you may want to sort specific entries together under a new topic. For example, you might have three separate index entries for Veal Marsala, Chicken Marsala, and Port Marsala. However, your reader might go to the "M" section of your index looking for the word "Marsala." For that reason, you would want an index entry that reads "Marsala Dishes" and lists the three Marsala dishes and their page numbers.

To do this, you must create a new index entry for Marsala Dishes. Go to the page for the first Marsala dish—in this example, that's Chicken Marsala—then click your cursor in the headline. Click the Create a new index entry button in the Index palette, which opens the New Page Reference dialog box. As shown in Figure J-35, Marsala Dishes is entered in the number 1 text box and Chicken Marsala is entered in the number 2 text box. When you click OK, a new entry appears in the "M" section for Marsala Dishes with Chicken Marsala listed beneath it, as shown in Figure J 36. Repeat this process for Veal Marsala and Pork Marsala, and your Index palette will resemble Figure J-37.

When you save changes to the document and generate the index, the listing will appear as shown in Figure J-38.

FIGURE J-35

Sorting an index entry

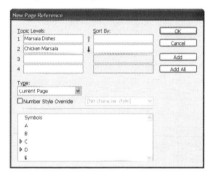

FIGURE J-36

Chicken Marsala is listed under Marsala Dishes

New entry with page number

FIGURE J-37

Three sorted entries in the Index palette

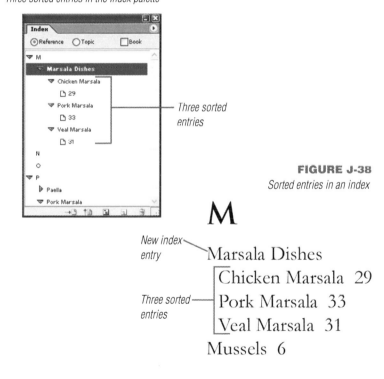

Three sorted entries

FIGURE J-38

Sorted entries in an index

M

New index entry

Marsala Dishes

Three sorted entries

⌐Chicken Marsala 29
├Pork Marsala 33
└Veal Marsala 31

Mussels 6

Create an index entry

1. In the Book palette, double-click **Toy Breeds**.

2. Click **Window** on the menu bar, point to **Type & Tables**, then click **Index**.

3. Click the **triangles** in the Index palette to explore the index entries that have already been created.

   An index entry has been created for every breed in the document except the breed on page 91, Silky Terrier.

4. In the Pages palette, double-click **page 91** to center it in the window, click the **Type Tool** **T.**, then select the Silky Terrier headline.

   | TIP   Be sure that the Index palette is visible, and that you can see the "S" section.

5. Click the **Create a new index entry button** in the Index palette.

   When text is selected, clicking this button opens the New Page Reference dialog box. When nothing is selected, clicking this button will open the New Cross-reference dialog box.

6. Note that the Type text box lists Current Page, click **OK**, then compare your Index palette to Figure J-39.

   An entry for Silky Terrier on page 91 is added to the Index palette.

7. Click **File** on the menu bar, click **Save**, then close Toy Breeds.

You created an index entry.

FIGURE J-39
New entry in the Index palette

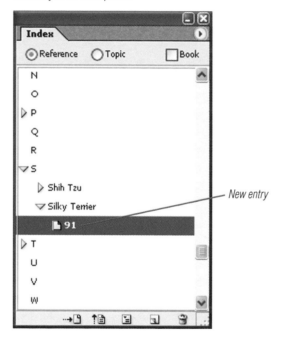

New entry

Generate Index dialog box

Generate Index

Title:

Title Style: [Index Title]

☐ Replace Existing Index
☑ Include Book Documents
☐ Include Entries on Hidden Layers

Book Name: Dog Breeds.indb

[OK]
[Cancel]
[More Options]

Generate an index

1. Open ID J-7.indd, then save it as **Index**.

2. Click the **Add documents button** ✚ on the Dog Breeds Book palette, then add Index.

   > TIP Index should be added at the bottom of the list. If it appears elsewhere, drag it to the bottom of the list.

3. Click the **Generate index button** 🔳 in the Index palette.

4. Delete the text in the Title text box.

   The title "Index" already exists in a text frame in the Index document.

5. Remove the check mark in the Replace Existing Index check box, then click the **Include Book Documents check box** so that your Generate Index dialog box resembles Figure J-40.

6. Click **OK**, position the loaded text cursor over the top-left corner of the text frame on page 108, click, then compare your spread to Figure J-41.

   The index is generated based on all the index entries created in each of the five documents. Note that Silky Terrier is listed on page 91 in the "S" section.

7. Click **File** on the menu bar, then click **Save**.

8. Click the **Save the book button** 💾 in the Book palette.

You generated an index based on all the index entries in the five documents.

Generating an index

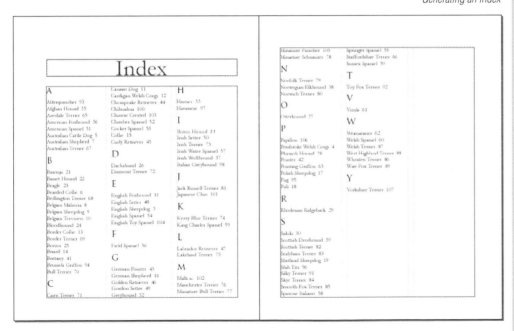

Create index cross-references

1. Double-click **Toy Breeds** in the Book palette.

2. Click the **Index palette list arrow**, then click **New Cross-reference**.

3. In the Topic Levels section, type **Min-Pin** in the number 1 text box.

4. Click the **Type list arrow**, then click **See**.

5. In the large white box at the bottom, scroll to the "M" section, then click the **triangle** to expose the "M" index entries.

6. Drag **Miniature Pinscher** into the Referenced text box, as shown in Figure J-42.

   The words Miniature Pinscher should appear in the Referenced text box, as shown in Figure J-43.

7. Click **OK**, then scroll to the M section in the Index palette.

   A new entry for Min-Pin has been added, with the reference See Miniature Pinscher.

8. Save Toy Breeds, close the document, then click the **Save the book button** 💾 in the Book palette.

9. Verify that Index is the only open document, then click the **Generate index button** 📄 in the Index palette.

10. In the Generate Index dialog box, check the **Replace Existing Index check box** to replace the previous index, then click **OK**.

11. Click the **Save the book button** 💾 in the Book palette.

You created a new index entry that is cross-referenced to an already existing entry.

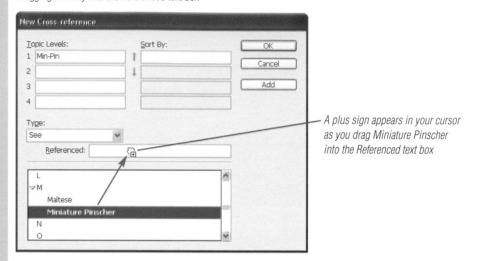

A plus sign appears in your cursor as you drag Miniature Pinscher into the Referenced text box

FIGURE J-43
Creating a cross-reference

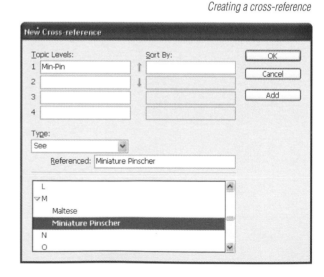

FIGURE J-44
New index entry

FIGURE J-45
Four sorted entries

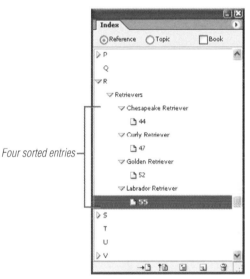

Four sorted entries —

FIGURE J-46
Updated index with four sorted entries

R

Retrievers

   Chesapeake Retriever 44

   Curly Retriever 47 ⎤

   Golden Retriever 52 ⎬— *Three sorted entries*

   Labrador Retriever 55 ⎦

Rhodesian Ridgeback 29

1. Open **Sport Breeds**.

   Sport Breeds contains four pages that profile retriever breeds of dogs.

2. Click the **Type Tool** T, double-click **page 44** in the Pages palette, then click the **headline**.

3. Click the **Index palette list arrow**, then click **New Page Reference**.

4. In the Topic Levels section, type **Retrievers** in the number 1 text box, type **Chesapeake Retriever** in the number 2 text box, click **OK**, then compare your Index palette to Figure J-44.

5. Double-click **page 47** in the Pages palette, click the **headline**, click the **Index palette list arrow**, then click **New Page Reference**.

6. Type **Retrievers** in the number 1 text box, type **Curly Retriever** in the number 2 text box, then click **OK**.

7. Using Pages 52 and 55, create new page references for the Golden Retriever and Labrador Retriever.

   Your Index palette should resemble Figure J-45.

8. Save Sport Breeds, close the document, verify that Index is the only document open, then generate a replacement index.

   As in Figure J-46, the new index has an entry for Retrievers with the four retriever breeds sorted beneath as sub-entries.

9. Save Index, close it, save the Book palette, then close it.

You created a new index entry, then sorted four other entries.

Create a book file.

1. Open ID J-8.indd, save it as **Appetizers**, then close the document.
2. Open ID J-9.indd, save it as **Soups**, then close the document.
3. Open ID J-10.indd, save it as **Entrees**, then close the document.
4. Open ID J-11.indd, save it as **Desserts**, then close the document.
5. Click File on the menu bar, point to New, then click Book.
6. Name the new file **Dinner Recipes**, then click Save.
7. Click the Book palette list arrow, then click Add Document.
8. Add Entrees.indd.
9. Click the Add documents button in the Book palette, then add Desserts.indd.
10. Add the following two documents: Soups.indd and Appetizers.indd.
11. Click the Save the book button in the Book palette.

Organize a book file.

1. Click and drag Soups to the top of the list.
2. Click and drag Appetizers to the top of the list.

3. Note that all the documents in the Book palette begin on odd page numbers. (*Hint*: For this project, you want each chapter to begin on an even left-hand page.)
4. Click the Book palette list arrow, then click Book Page Numbering Options.
5. Click the Continue on next even page option button, then click OK.
6. In the Book palette, double-click the page numbers for Appetizers.
7. Click the Start Page Numbering at option button, type **2** in the text box, then click OK.
8. Save the change, close Appetizers, then note the page range in the Book palette.
9. Click the Save the book button in the Book palette.

Create a table of contents.

1. Open ID J-12.indd, then save it as **Recipes TOC**.
2. Click the Paragraph Styles palette list arrow, then click Load Paragraph Styles.
3. Open Appetizers.indd.
4. Click File on the menu bar, then click Save.
5. With Recipes TOC.indd still open, click the Add documents button in the Book palette.

6. Add Recipes TOC.indd.
7. Drag Recipes TOC to the top of the list.
8. Click Layout on the menu bar, then click Table of Contents.
9. Delete the text in the Title text box.
10. In the Other Styles list, click Course Name, then click Add.
11. Double-click Dish Name.
12. In the Options section at the bottom of the dialog box, click the Include Book Document(Dinner Recipes.indb) check box.
13. Click OK.
14. Position your cursor over the top-left corner of the margin guides on the page, then click.
15. Click Layout on the menu bar, then click Table of Contents.
16. In the Include Paragraph Styles section, click Course Name to select it.
17. Click the Entry Style list arrow, then click TOC Course.
18. Click the Page Number list arrow, then click No Page Number.
19. In the Include Paragraph Styles section, click Dish Name to select it.

20. Click the Entry Style list arrow, then click TOC Dish Name, click the Page Number list arrow, then click After Entry.
21. Select the contents of the Between Entry and Number text box, then type .... (ten periods).
22. Click the Sort Entries in Alphabetical Order check box, then verify that the Replace Existing Table of Contents check box is checked.
23. Click OK.
24. Click the Selection Tool, select the text frame on the page, click Object on the menu bar, click Text Frame Options, change the number of columns to 2, then click OK. Your page should resemble Figure J-47.
25. Save the changes to Recipes TOC.indd, then close the document.

FIGURE J-47
Completed Skills Review, Part 1

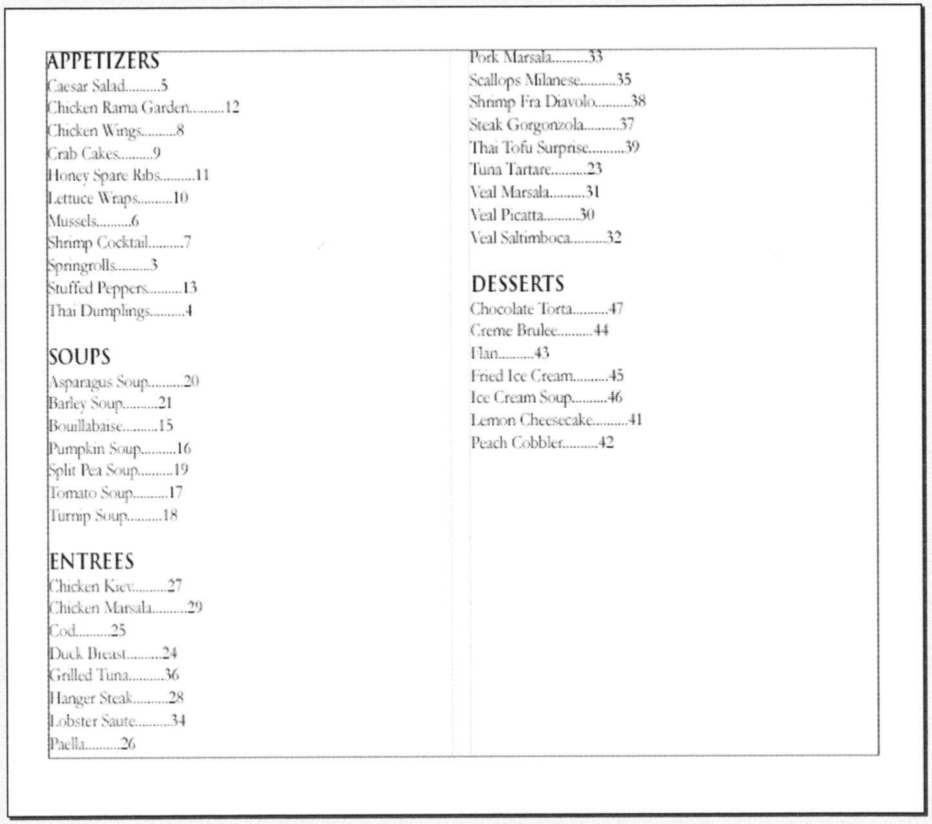

APPETIZERS
Caesar Salad..........5
Chicken Rama Garden..........12
Chicken Wings..........8
Crab Cakes..........9
Honey Spare Ribs..........11
Lettuce Wraps..........10
Mussels..........6
Shrimp Cocktail..........7
Springrolls..........3
Stuffed Peppers..........13
Thai Dumplings..........4

SOUPS
Asparagus Soup..........20
Barley Soup..........21
Bouillabaise..........15
Pumpkin Soup..........16
Split Pea Soup..........19
Tomato Soup..........17
Turnip Soup..........18

ENTREES
Chicken Kiev..........27
Chicken Marsala..........29
Cod..........25
Duck Breast..........24
Grilled Tuna..........36
Hanger Steak..........28
Lobster Saute..........34
Paella..........26

Pork Marsala..........33
Scallops Milanese..........35
Shrimp Fra Diavolo..........38
Steak Gorgonzola..........37
Thai Tofu Surprise..........39
Tuna Tartare..........23
Veal Marsala..........31
Veal Picatta..........30
Veal Saltimboca..........32

DESSERTS
Chocolate Torta..........47
Creme Brulee..........44
Flan..........43
Fried Ice Cream..........45
Ice Cream Soup..........46
Lemon Cheesecake..........41
Peach Cobbler..........42

Making Books, Tables of Contents, and Indexes

Create an index.

1. In the Book palette, double-click Entrees to open the document.
2. Click Window on the menu bar, point to Type & Tables, then click Index.
3. In the Pages palette, double-click page 23 to center it in the window, click the Type Tool, then select the Tuna Tartare headline.
4. Click the Create a new index entry button in the Index palette.
5. Click OK.
6. Click File on the menu bar, click Save, then close Entrees.
7. Open ID J-13.indd, then save it as **Recipes Index**.
8. Click the Add documents button in the Dinner Recipes Book palette, add Recipes Index.indd, then drag it to the bottom of the book palette.
9. Click the Generate index button in the Index palette.
10. Delete the text in the Title text box.
11. Remove the check mark in the Replace Existing Index check box, then click the Include Book Documents check box.

12. Click OK.
13. Position the loaded text cursor over the top-left corner of the text frame in Recipes Index.indd, then click.
14. Click File on the menu bar, then click Save.
15. Click the Save the book button in the Book palette.
16. Double-click Soups in the Book palette to open the document.
17. Click the Index palette list arrow, then click New Cross-reference.
18. In the Topic Levels section, type **Fish Stew** in the number 1 text box.
19. Click the Type list arrow, then click See.
20. In the large white box at the bottom, scroll to the "B" section, then click the triangle to expose the "B" index entries.
21. Drag Bouillabaisse into the Referenced text box, then release your mouse when the plus sign appears in your cursor.
22. Click OK.
23. Save Soups, close the document, then click the Save the book button in the Book palette.

24. Verify that Recipes Index.indd is the only open document, then click the Generate index button in the Index palette.
25. In the Generate Index dialog box, check the Replace Existing Index check box, then click OK.
26. Click the Save the book button in the Book palette.
27. Double-click Entrees in the Book palette to open the document. (*Hint*: Entrees contains three Marsala dishes—Pork, Veal, and Chicken.)
28. Click the Type Tool, double-click page 29 in the Pages palette, then click in the headline.
29. Click the Index palette list arrow, then click New Page Reference.
30. In the Topic Levels section, type **Marsala Dishes** in the number 1 text box, type **Chicken Marsala** in the number 2 text box, then click OK.
31. Double-click page 31 in the Pages palette, click in the headline, click the Index palette list arrow, then click New Page Reference.

32. Type **Marsala Dishes** in the number 1 text box, type **Veal Marsala** in the number 2 text box, then click OK.

33. Double-click page 33 in the Pages palette, click in the headline, click the Index palette list arrow, then click New Page Reference.

34. Type **Marsala Dishes** in the number 1 text box, type **Pork Marsala** in the number 2 text box, then click OK.

35. Save Entrees, close the document, verify that Recipes Index.indd is the only document open, then generate a replacement index. (*Hint*: You may need to replace the font used for the word See in the updated index.)

36. In the Paragraph Styles palette, double-click Index Section Head, click Basic Character Formats, change the font to Trajan Bold, change the size to 18 pt, click OK, then compare your index to Figure J-48.

37. Save Recipes Index.indd, close it, save the Dinner Recipes book, then close it.

FIGURE J-48
Completed Skills Review, Part 2

Index

A

Asparagus Soup 20

B

Barley Soup 21
Bouillabaisse 15

C

Caesar Salad 5
Chicken Kiev 27
Chicken Marsala 29
Chicken Rama Garden 12
Chicken Wings 8
Chocolate Torta 47
Cod 25
Crab Cakes 9
Creme Brulee 44

D

Duck Breast 24

F

Fish Stew. See Bouillabaisse
Flan 43
Fried Ice Cream 45

G

Grilled Tuna 36

H

Hanger Steak 28

Honey Spare Ribs 11

I

Ice Cream Soup 46

L

Lemon Cheesecake 41
Lettuce Wraps 10
Lobster Saute 34

M

Marsala Dishes
  Chicken Marsala 29
  Pork Marsala 33
  Veal Marsala 31
Mussels 6

P

Paella 26
Peach Cobbler 42
Pork Marsala 33
Pumpkin Soup 16

S

Scallops Milanese 35
Shrimp Cocktail 7
Shrimp Fra Diavolo 38
Split Pea Soup 19
Springrolls 3
Steak Gorgonzola 37
Stuffed Peppers 13

T

Thai Dumplings 4
Thai Tofu Surprise 39
Tomato Soup 17
Tuna Tartare 23
Turnip Soup 18

V

Veal Marsala 31
Veal Picatta 30
Veal Saltimboca 32

Making Books, Tables of Contents, and Indexes

You work for a publishing company, and you have created an index for a book on dog breeds. Your boss comes to you and tells you that the index is not complete as is; he wants you to sort three breeds under a new index entry.

1. Open ID J-14.indd, then save it as **Sort Setters**.

2. Click the Type Tool, double-click page 6 in the Pages palette, then click in the headline.

3. Click the Index palette list arrow, then click New Page Reference.

4. In the Topic Levels section, type **Setters** in the number 1 text box, type **English Setter** in the number 2 text box, then click OK.

5. Double-click page 7 in the Pages palette, click in the headline, click the Index palette list arrow, then click New Page Reference.

6. Type **Setters** in the number 1 text box, type **Gordon Setter** in the number 2 text box, then click OK.

7. Double-click page 9 in the Pages palette, click in the headline, click the Index palette list arrow, then click New Page Reference.

8. Type **Setters** in the number 1 text box, type **Irish Setter** in the number 2 text box, then click OK.

9. Scroll to the S section, then compare your index to Figure J-49.

10. Save your work, then close Sort Setters.

FIGURE J-49
Completed Project Builder 1

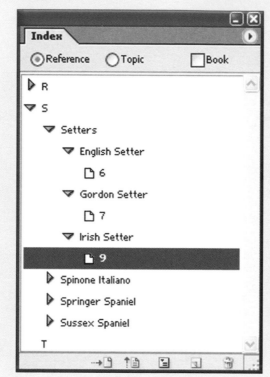

Making Books, Tables of Contents, and Indexes

You work for a publishing company, and you have created an index for a book on dog breeds. Your boss comes to you and tells you that the index is not complete as is; he wants you to create a cross-reference entry titled "Red Setter" that points to the Irish Setter page.

1. Open ID J-15.indd, then save it as **Cross-reference Setters**.
2. Click the Index palette list arrow, then click New Cross-reference.
3. In the Topic Levels section, type **Red Setter** in the number 1 text box.
4. Click the Type list arrow, then click See.
5. In the large white box at the bottom, scroll to the "I" section, then click the triangle to expose the "I" index entries.
6. Drag Irish Setter into the Referenced text box, then release your mouse when the plus sign appears in your cursor.
7. Click OK.
8. Compare your Index palette to Figure J-50.
9. Save your work, then close Cross-reference Setters.

FIGURE J-50
Completed Project Builder 2

You are a graphic designer at a publishing company. One of your clients comes to you with an InDesign file and says he needs your help. He generated a table of contents from a book file, and he was surprised that the paragraph styles used to create the TOC did not include the same formatting for the layout of the TOC. He gives you the file on disk, and you note that he didn't include the book file. This means that you can't regenerate a new TOC file. Therefore, you decide to reformat the layout directly in the InDesign document.

1. Open ID J-16.indd, then save it as **TOC Redesign**.
2. In the Paragraph Styles palette, double-click Breed Name, click Basic Character Formats, change the font size to 12, then click OK.
3. Double-click Section Name, click Basic Character Formats, change the font size to 16, click Advanced Character Formats, change the horizontal scale to 75%, then click OK.
4. Select the text frame, open the Text Frame Options dialog box, change the number of columns to 4, then click OK.
5. Triple-click the word Contents, then delete it.
6. Compare your page to Figure J-51.
7. Save your work, then close TOC Redesign.

FIGURE J-51
Completed Design Project

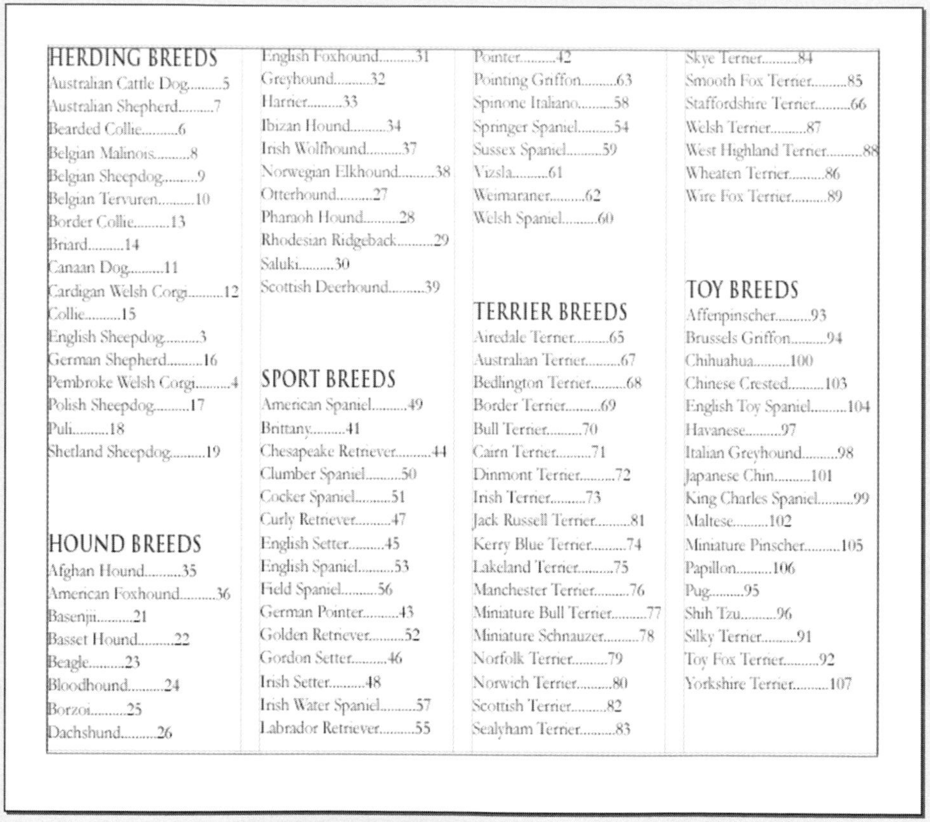

HERDING BREEDS
Australian Cattle Dog.......5
Australian Shepherd.......7
Bearded Collie.......6
Belgian Malinois.......8
Belgian Sheepdog.......9
Belgian Tervuren.......10
Border Collie.......13
Briard.......14
Canaan Dog.......11
Cardigan Welsh Corgi.......12
Collie.......15
English Sheepdog.......3
German Shepherd.......16
Pembroke Welsh Corgi.......4
Polish Sheepdog.......17
Puli.......18
Shetland Sheepdog.......19

HOUND BREEDS
Afghan Hound.......35
American Foxhound.......36
Basenji.......21
Basset Hound.......22
Beagle.......23
Bloodhound.......24
Borzoi.......25
Dachshund.......26

English Foxhound.......31
Greyhound.......32
Harrier.......33
Ibizan Hound.......34
Irish Wolfhound.......37
Norwegian Elkhound.......38
Otterhound.......27
Pharaoh Hound.......28
Rhodesian Ridgeback.......29
Saluki.......30
Scottish Deerhound.......39

SPORT BREEDS
American Spaniel.......49
Brittany.......41
Chesapeake Retriever.......44
Clumber Spaniel.......50
Cocker Spaniel.......51
Curly Retriever.......47
English Setter.......45
English Spaniel.......53
Field Spaniel.......56
German Pointer.......43
Golden Retriever.......52
Gordon Setter.......46
Irish Setter.......48
Irish Water Spaniel.......57
Labrador Retriever.......55

Pointer.......42
Pointing Griffon.......63
Spinone Italiano.......58
Springer Spaniel.......54
Sussex Spaniel.......59
Vizsla.......61
Weimaraner.......62
Welsh Spaniel.......60

TERRIER BREEDS
Airedale Terrier.......65
Australian Terrier.......67
Bedlington Terrier.......68
Border Terrier.......69
Bull Terrier.......70
Cairn Terrier.......71
Dinmont Terrier.......72
Irish Terrier.......73
Jack Russell Terrier.......81
Kerry Blue Terrier.......74
Lakeland Terrier.......75
Manchester Terrier.......76
Miniature Bull Terrier.......77
Miniature Schnauzer.......78
Norfolk Terrier.......79
Norwich Terrier.......80
Scottish Terrier.......82
Sealyham Terrier.......83

Skye Terrier.......84
Smooth Fox Terrier.......85
Staffordshire Terrier.......66
Welsh Terrier.......87
West Highland Terrier.......88
Wheaten Terrier.......86
Wire Fox Terrier.......89

TOY BREEDS
Affenpinscher.......93
Brussels Griffon.......94
Chihuahua.......100
Chinese Crested.......103
English Toy Spaniel.......104
Havanese.......97
Italian Greyhound.......98
Japanese Chin.......101
King Charles Spaniel.......99
Maltese.......102
Miniature Pinscher.......105
Papillon.......106
Pug.......95
Shih Tzu.......96
Silky Terrier.......91
Toy Fox Terrier.......92
Yorkshire Terrier.......107

This group project is designed to show the group the type of thinking that must go into creating an index. The group will open a single InDesign document that contains 17 pages, each featuring one dish. An index entry has been made for all 17 dishes. An additional index entry has been made for "Marsala Dishes," under which three Marsala dishes have been sorted.

This project is not about generating an index; it's about looking at data and deciding how an index can best refer to that data. The group should think about which dishes, if necessary, require a cross-reference. The group should also consider different ways the dishes can be sorted.

This project does not have a specific solution. Instead, the group should decide when the index has been thoroughly cross-referenced and sorted.

Discussion.

1. Open ID J-17.indd, then save it as **Group Project**.
2. Scroll through the pages and note the names of the dishes.
3. Can any of the dishes be referred to by a different name? If so, which dishes?

4. Create cross-reference index entries for dishes that can be referred to by a different name.
5. Which of the 17 dishes are similar enough that they can be sorted together?
6. Does the group think it is necessary to sort the two chicken dishes under a new entry named Chicken Dishes? Why or why not?

7. Create new index entries that are appropriate for sorting groups of dishes.
8. Save your work, compare your index to the sample shown in Figure J-52, then close Group Project.

FIGURE J-52
Sample Group Project

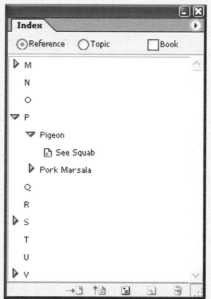

CHAPTER K

EXPLORING ADVANCED TECHNIQUES

1. Use the Pathfinder palette.

2. Create new stroke styles.

3. Create mixed ink swatches.

4. Work with nested styles.

CHAPTER K
EXPLORING ADVANCED TECHNIQUES

Welcome to the second-to-last chapter of the book! By now, having been exposed to so many of InDesign's great features, you are ready to explore some of the more advanced options that the application has to offer. In this chapter, you'll add to your drawing skills by incorporating the Pathfinder palette into your work. This palette helps you to create complex shapes by overlapping simple objects. It's fun and powerful!

You'll delve deeper into the Stroke palette and learn how to create and apply custom strokes. You'll also create mixed ink swatches, a very smart and fast way to create swatches that are mixtures of process and spot inks.

Finally, you'll be amazed by the power of nested styles, which allow you to apply multiple character styles to multiple paragraphs—simultaneously!

Tools You'll Use

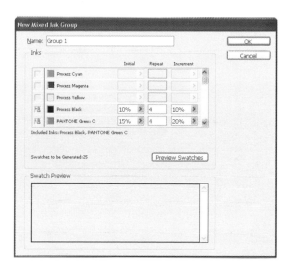

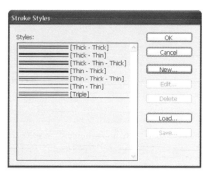

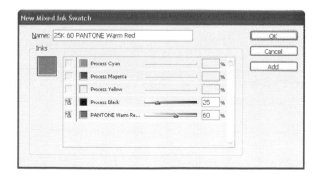

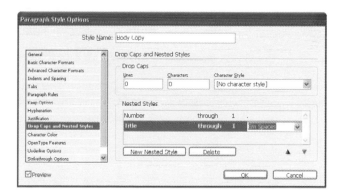

USE THE PATHFINDER PALETTE

What You'll Do

In this lesson, you will use the Pathfinder palette to create complex shapes from overlapping objects.

Using the Pathfinder Palette

The best way to think of the **Pathfinder palette**, shown in Figure K-1, is as a drawing tool. The Pathfinder palette helps you to easily create new complex shapes by overlapping simple objects. The palette does this by offering five buttons that work as follows:

Add: Combines two or more overlapping objects into one object, as shown in Figure K-2. With the Add pathfinder, the resulting object retains the color properties of the frontmost object.

Subtract: The frontmost object(s) "punch a hole" in the backmost object, as shown in Figure K-3. With the Subtract pathfinder, the resulting object retains the color properties of the backmost object.

Intersect: The resulting shape is the intersection of the overlapping object(s). With the Intersect pathfinder, the resulting object retains the color properties of the frontmost object, as shown in Figure K-4.

Exclude Overlap: A hole is created where the two objects overlap, as shown in Figure K-5. You can think of the Exclude Overlap pathfinder as the opposite of the Intersect pathfinder. Again, the resulting object retains the color properties of the frontmost object.

Minus Back: The backmost object "punches a hole" in the object(s) in front, as shown in Figure K-6. You can think of the Minus Back pathfinder as the opposite of the Subtract pathfinder.

FIGURE K-1

Pathfinder palette

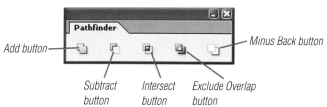

Add button

Subtract button

Intersect button

Exclude Overlap button

Minus Back button

FIGURE K-2

Add pathfinder

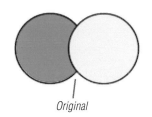

Original

Add

FIGURE K-3

Subtract pathfinder

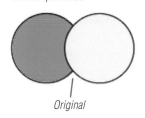

Original

Subtract

FIGURE K-4

Intersect pathfinder

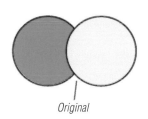

Original

Intersect

FIGURE K-5

Exclude Overlap pathfinder

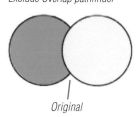 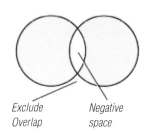

Original

Exclude Overlap

Negative space

FIGURE K-6

Minus Back pathfinder

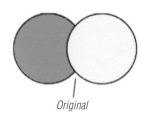 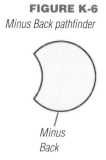

Original

Minus Back

Use the Add pathfinder

1. Open ID K-1.indd, then save it as **Add and Subtract**.

2. Click the **Selection Tool** ▶, click the **green circle**, click **Object** on the menu bar, point to **Transform**, then click **Move**.

3. Type **2** in the Horizontal text box, then click **OK**.

4. Click the **yellow circle**, click **Object** on the menu bar, point to **Transform**, then click **Move**.

5. Type **-2** in the Horizontal text box, then click **OK** so that the objects are positioned as shown in Figure K-7.

6. Select all three objects—the green and yellow circles and the red square.

7. Click **Window** on the menu bar, then click **Pathfinder**.

8. Click the **Add button** in the Pathfinder palette.

   The three objects are combined into a single object, as shown in Figure K-8.

   > **TIP** When objects are added, the resulting object assumes the color of the topmost of the original objects.

You used the Move command to align three objects, selected them, then combined them into one object using the Add pathfinder.

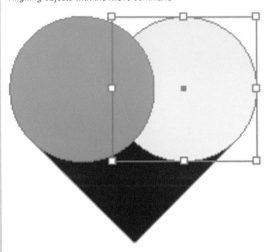

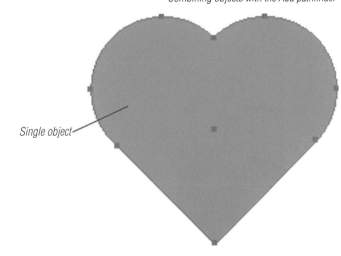

Single object

Aligning objects

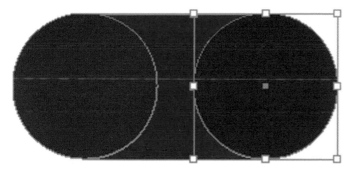

Use the Subtract pathfinder

1. Click the **red circle**, click **Object** on the menu bar, point to **Transform**, then click **Move**.

2. Type **1.5** in the Horizontal text box, then click **OK**.

3. Click the **blue circle**, click **Object** on the menu bar, point to **Transform**, then click **Move**.

4. Type **-1.5** in the Horizontal text box, then click **OK** so that the objects are positioned as shown in Figure K-9.

5. Select all three objects—the red and blue circles and the black rectangle.

6. Click the **Subtract button** 🗗 in the Pathfinder palette.

   The two front objects—the circles—"punch holes" in the backmost object, as shown in Figure K-10.

   | TIP When the Subtract pathfinder is used on multiple objects, the backmost object retains its original fill color.

7. Click the **green heart shape**, click **Object** on the menu bar, point to **Transform**, then click **Rotate**.

8. Type **180** in the Angle text box, then click **OK**.

(continued)

FIGURE K-10
Using the Subtract pathfinder to create a new shape

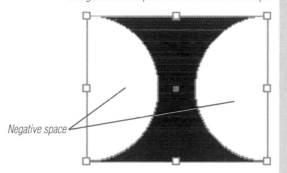

Negative space

9. Reposition the green heart shape in relation to the black shape as shown in Figure K-11.

10. Select both objects, click the **Add button** in the Pathfinder palette, deselect, then compare your work with Figure K-12.

11. Save your work, then close Add and Subtract.

You aligned three objects, selected them, then used the Subtract pathfinder to transform the backmost object into an entirely new shape. You combined that object with another using the Add pathfinder to create a spade shape.

Use the Intersect and Minus Back pathfinders

1. Open ID K-2.indd, then save it as **Intersect and Minus Back**.

2. Click the **Selection Tool** , then move the green circle so that it overlaps the red square, as shown in Figure K-13.

3. Select both objects, then click the **Intersect button** in the Pathfinder palette.

   The resulting single object is the intersection of the two overlapping objects.

   (continued)

FIGURE K-11
Repositioning an object

FIGURE K-12
Combining objects with the Add pathfinder

FIGURE K-13
Overlapping objects

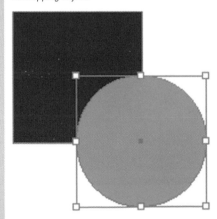

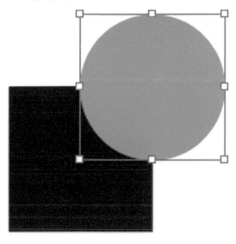

4. Move the light blue circle so that it overlaps the blue square, as shown in Figure K-14.

5. Select both objects, click the **Minus Back button** in the Pathfinder palette, deselect, then compare the shapes in your document to Figure K-15.

   Where the two objects overlap, the backmost object "punches a hole" in the frontmost object.

6. Save your work, then close Intersect and Minus Back.

You used the Intersect and Minus Back pathfinders to create new shapes from two overlapping objects.

FIGURE K-15
Viewing two shapes created from pathfinders

CREATE NEW STROKE STYLES

What You'll Do

In this lesson, you will create new stroke styles using the New Stroke Style dialog box.

Creating Stroke Styles

The Stroke palette offers a number of stroke styles that you can apply to objects. You can also create and customize your own stroke styles and make them available for use in the Stroke palette.

InDesign allows you to create and customize three types of stroke styles: Dashed, dotted, and striped. To create one of these stroke styles, you simply access the Stroke Styles dialog box by clicking the Stroke palette list arrow.

Creating a Dashed Stroke Style

To create a new dashed stroke style, open the New Stroke Style dialog box by clicking New in the Stroke Styles dialog box, then choosing Dash from the Type list, as shown in Figure K-16. First, enter a descriptive name in the Name text box. Next, enter a measurement in the Length text box to specify the length of the dash, then enter another measurement in the Pattern Length text box to specify the intervals at which the dashes will occur.

You can add additional dashes to the pattern. Simply click the white space in the ruler, as shown in Figure K-17. You can change the length of the new dash by dragging the two white triangles above the dash. As you modify the new dashed stroke style, you can see what it looks like in the preview window at the bottom of the dialog box. Using this dialog box, you can create dashed stroke styles that are complex and visually interesting.

Creating a Dotted Stroke Style

To create a new dotted stroke style, open the New Stroke Style dialog box and choose Dotted from the Type list. As with dashed strokes, you can add additional dots to the stroke pattern. Enter a value in the Center text box to specify where the additional dot will be positioned horizontally in relation to the original dot. Enter a value in the Pattern Length text box to specify the intervals at which the dot pattern will occur. See Figure K-18.

Creating a Striped Stroke Style

To create a new striped stroke style, open the New Stroke Style dialog box and choose Stripe from the Type list, as shown in Figure K-19. By default, a striped stroke style begins with two stripes, as shown in the figure. Enter a value in the Start text box to specify where the stripe will be positioned on the vertical axis. Enter a value in the Width text box to determine the width—from top to bottom—of the stripe.

Click anywhere in the white space to add additional stripes. As shown in Figure K-20, you can specify additional stripes as having different widths, thus creating a style that is unique and visually interesting.

FIGURE K-16
New Stroke Style dialog box

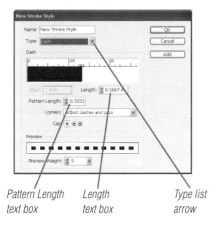

Pattern Length text box

Length text box

Type list arrow

FIGURE K-17
Adding a second dash to the stroke style

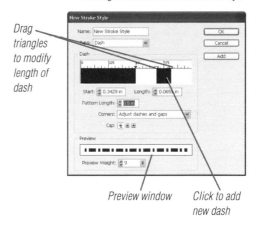

Drag triangles to modify length of dash

Preview window

Click to add new dash

FIGURE K-18
Creating a dotted stroke style

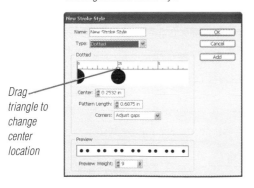

Drag triangle to change center location

FIGURE K-19
Creating a striped stroke style

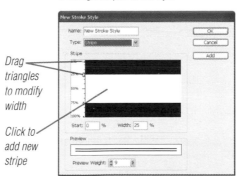

Drag triangles to modify width

Click to add new stripe

FIGURE K-20
Adding two new stripes to a stroke style

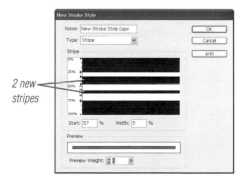

2 new stripes

Create a new dashed stroke style

1. Open ID K-3.indd, then save it as **Custom Strokes**.

2. Click **Window** on the menu bar, click **Stroke**, click the **Stroke palette list arrow**, click **Stroke Styles**, then click **New**.

3. Type **Custom Dash Style** in the Name text box, then verify that Dash is listed in the Type text box.

4. Select the value in the Length text box, type **.25**, then press **[Tab]**.

5. Select the value in the Pattern Length text box, type **.5**, press **[Tab]**, then compare your dialog box to Figure K-21.

6. Click anywhere in the **white space** in the ruler to the right of the black dash to add a new dash.

7. Type **.35** in the Start text box, press **[Tab]**, type **.1** in the Length text box, press **[Tab]**, then note the change in the preview window in the dialog box.

8. Click **OK**.

   The new stroke style is listed in the Stroke Styles dialog box, shown in Figure K-22.

You created a new dashed stroke style using the New Stroke Style dialog box.

FIGURE K-21
Defining a new dashed stroke style

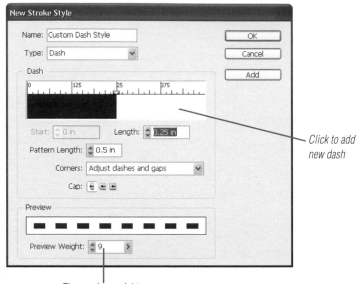

Click to add new dash

The preview weight only affects the preview size of the new stroke style, not the actual weight of the stroke

FIGURE K-22
Viewing the new stroke style in the Stroke Styles dialog box

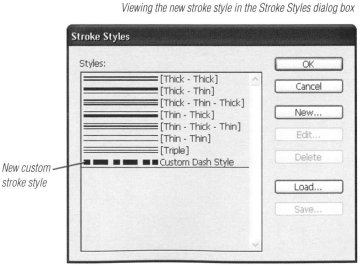

New custom stroke style

FIGURE K-23

Defining the width of the top stripe

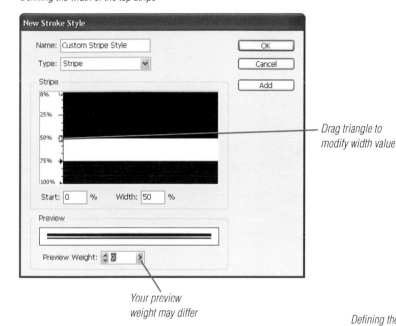

Drag triangle to
modify width value

Your preview
weight may differ

1. Click **New** in the Stroke Styles dialog box.

2. Type **Custom Stripe Style** in the Name
   text box, click the **Type list arrow**, then
   click **Stripe**.

3. Select the value in the Width text box, type
   50, then press **[Tab]**.

   As shown in Figure K-23, the top stripe dou-
   bles in width and remains selected, as noted
   by the highlighted triangles.

4. Click the **triangle** at the 50% mark and drag
   it up until the value in the Width text box
   reads 35%.

5. Click anywhere in the **white space** between
   the two stripes to add a third stripe.

6. Select the contents of the Start text box,
   type **50**, then press **[Tab]**.

7. Type **10** in the Width text box, then
   press **[Tab]**.

   Your dialog box should resemble
   Figure K-24.

8. Click **OK**, then note that the new stroke style
   has been added to the list.

*You created a new striped stroke style using the
New Stroke Style dialog box.*

FIGURE K-24

Defining the location and width of the new stripe

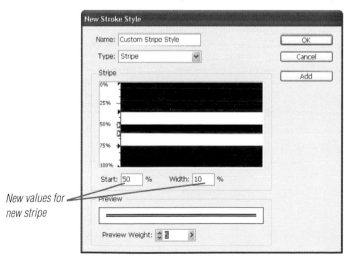

New values for
new stripe

Create a new dotted stroke style

1. Click **New** in the Stroke Styles dialog box.

2. Type **Custom Dot Style** in the Name text box, click the **Type list arrow**, then click **Dotted**.

3. In the Pattern Length text box, click the **up arrow** until the value reads 1, then note the change to the preview.

   The default dotted stroke is a pattern of dots that are evenly spaced, regardless of the pattern length.

4. Click anywhere in the **white space** (beneath the ruler) to add another dot to the pattern.

5. Click the **triangle** above the new dot and drag it until the value in the Center text box reads .25.

   Your dialog box should resemble Figure K-25.

6. Click anywhere in the **white space** to add another dot.

7. Noting the change to the preview, drag the **triangle** above the new dot until the value in the Center text box reads .5.

   Your dialog box should resemble Figure K-26.

8. Click **OK**, then note that the new stroke style has been added to the list.

You created a new dotted stroke style using the New Stroke Style dialog box.

FIGURE K-25

Positioning a new dot at the .25 mark

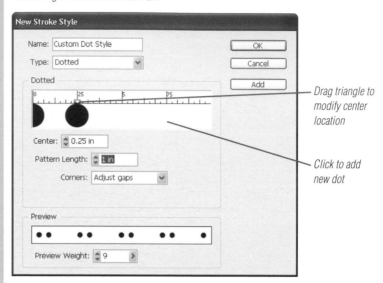

Drag triangle to modify center location

Click to add new dot

FIGURE K-26

Positioning a new dot at the .5 mark

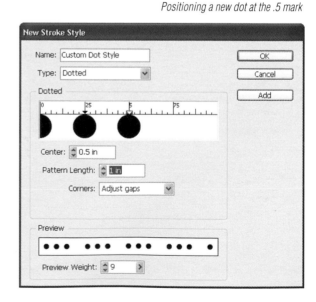

FIGURE K-27

Viewing three lines with stroke styles applied

1. Click **OK** in the Stroke Styles dialog box.
2. Click the **Selection Tool**, then click the **top line** on the page.
3. Click the **Type list arrow** in the Stroke palette, then click **Custom Dash Style**.
4. Click the **second line**, then apply the Custom Stripe Style.
5. Click the **third line**, then apply the Custom Dot Style.
6. Select all three lines on the page, then change the weight in the Stroke palette to 12 pts.
7. Deselect all, select the second line on the page, click the **Gap Color list arrow** in the Stroke palette, then click **Gold**.
8. Deselect, then compare your page to Figure K-27.
9. Save your work, then close Custom Strokes.

You applied three different stroke styles to three lines. You also applied a color to the gaps in the striped stroke style.

CREATE MIXED INK SWATCHES

What You'll Do

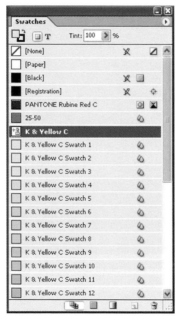

In this lesson, you will create mixed ink swatches and mixed ink groups.

Understanding the Need for Mixed Inks

Four color printing is expensive. Among other considerations, you must pay for four inks, and you must also pay for four inking stations on the press. Many designers opt to cut costs by working with two inks—usually process black ink and one spot ink.

It is important to remember that working with two inks does not mean that the document has only two colors. Just as with four color printing, you can print percentages of each of the two inks to create an array of different tints.

InDesign uses the term **mixed ink** to refer to swatches that are created by mixing a spot ink with a process ink or, occasionally, another spot ink. Mixed ink swatches must include at least one spot ink.

Creating a Mixed Ink Swatch

You create a mixed ink swatch by clicking the New Mixed Ink Swatch command on the Swatches palette menu. At least one spot ink must be present in the Swatches palette for this command to be available on the Swatches palette menu.

You define a mixed ink swatch in the New Mixed Ink Swatch dialog box, shown in Figure K-28. In this dialog box, you name the mixed ink swatch and specify which inks will be included. You also specify the percentages of each ink for the swatch.

Once created, the mixed ink swatch is available in the Swatches palette. Mixed ink swatches are identified by the **mixed ink icon**, shown in Figure K-29.

Creating a Mixed Ink Group

When you are creating a two color job—usually with a process black ink and one spot ink—you will want to work with many different ink combinations of the two colors to create a variety of tints in the document. In other words, you will want to have many mixed ink swatches available to you.

Rather than having to generate multiple mixed ink swatches one at a time, InDesign offers the option to create a mixed ink group. A **mixed ink group** is simply a group of many mixed ink swatches that are generated simultaneously. You create a mixed ink group by clicking the New Mixed Ink Group command on the Swatches palette menu. This command opens the New Mixed Ink Group dialog box.

To understand how the New Mixed Ink Group dialog box works, refer to Figure K-30.

In this figure, a mixed ink group is being generated by mixing Process Black with PANTONE Green C. The icons to the left of each ink indicate that these are the inks that will be used in the group.

The Initial setting specifies the mixture of the first swatch of the group. The Repeat setting specifies how many more tints of each will be mixed, and the Increment setting specifies how much the percentage of the ink will be increased with each subsequent mixture.

So, in the example shown in the figure, the first swatch will be 10% Process Black mixed with 15% PANTONE Green C. There will be five black percentages (the initial 10% Black plus the four more entered in the Repeat text box). Each of the five tints of black will increase by 10%, based on the value entered in the Increment text box. Thus, the first swatch will be 10% Black, the second 20%, the third 30%, the fourth 40%, and the fifth 50%.

The first PANTONE Green C swatch will be 15% and will increase by 20% in each of the subsequent four tints. Thus, the second use of PANTONE Green C will be at 35%, the third at 55%, the fourth at 75%, and the fifth at 95%.

Remember, all five percentages of Process Black must mix with all five percentages of PANTONE Green. This means that a total of 25 swatches must be generated, which is noted in the dialog box.

FIGURE K-28
New Mixed Ink Swatch dialog box

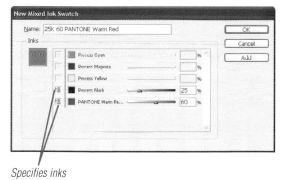
Specifies inks to be used

FIGURE K-29
Mixed ink swatch

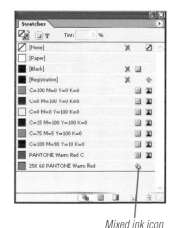
Mixed ink icon

FIGURE K-30
New Mixed Ink Group dialog box

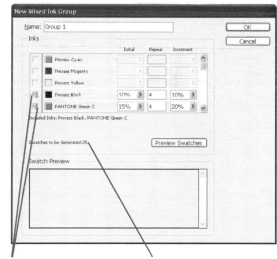
Specifies inks to be used   *Number of swatches to be generated*

Working with Mixed Ink Groups

Once generated, the swatches that compose the mixed ink group appear in the Swatches palette. If you position your cursor over a swatch, a tooltip appears showing you the ink percentages of the swatch, as shown in Figure K-31. However, you might find it easier to identify swatches by renaming them with their ink percentages.

To do so, double-click a swatch to open the Swatch Options dialog box, shown in Figure K-32. This dialog box identifies the percentages of inks used in the swatch. You can use this information to rename the swatch in the Swatch Name text box. This name will then be used in the Swatches palette as the name of the swatch.

Editing Mixed Ink Groups

When a mixed ink group is generated, a **parent swatch** is generated and appears in the Swatches palette, as shown in Figure K-33. The parent swatch has the name you entered when creating the mixed ink group.

FIGURE K-31
Identifying the percentages in a mixed ink swatch

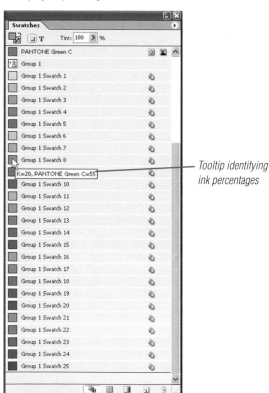

Tooltip identifying ink percentages

FIGURE K-32
Renaming a mixed ink swatch

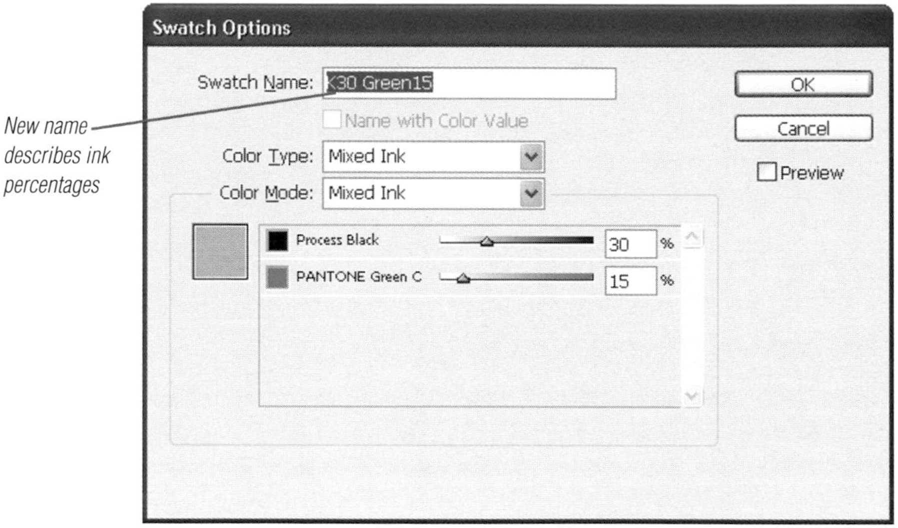

New name describes ink percentages

Exploring Advanced Techniques

It often happens that, midway through a project, a designer or a client decides to use a different spot color than the one he or she began the project with. If you've already generated a mixed ink group and applied various tints to objects in the layout, generating a new mixed ink group with the new spot color and reapplying the tints to the layout would be very time consuming. Instead, you can simply edit the parent swatch. Double-click the parent swatch to open the Mixed Ink Group Options dialog box, shown in Figure K-34. This dialog box allows you to load a different spot color (or process color) for the mixed ink group. When you click OK, all of the swatches that make up the mixed ink group will be updated with tints of the new color. The names of the swatches in the group will also be updated.

FIGURE K-33
Parent swatch

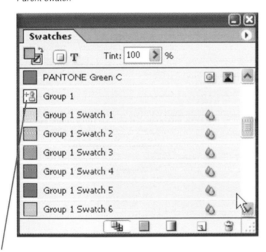

Parent swatch

FIGURE K-34
Mixed Ink Group Options dialog box

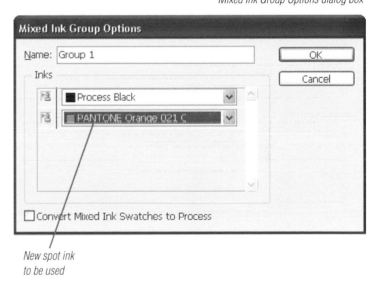

New spot ink to be used

Create a mixed ink swatch

1. Open ID K-4.indd, then save it as **Mixed Inks**.

   Note that the Swatches palette contains only one process ink—Black—and one spot ink—PANTONE Rubine Red C.

2. Click the **Swatches palette list arrow**, then click **New Mixed Ink Swatch**.

3. Type **25-50** in the Name text box.

4. Click the **empty gray squares** beside Process Black and beside PANTONE Rubine Red C so that your dialog box resembles Figure K-35.

5. Drag the **Process Black slider** to 25%, then drag the **PANTONE Rubine Red C slider** to 50%.

6. Click **OK**.

7. Position your cursor over the new swatch in the Swatches palette, so that the tooltip appears detailing the mixture of the two inks, as shown in Figure K-36.

You created a mixed ink swatch that is 25% Process Black and 50% PANTONE Rubine Red C.

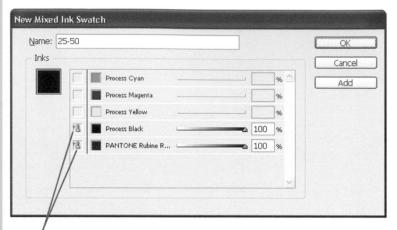

Specifies inks to be used

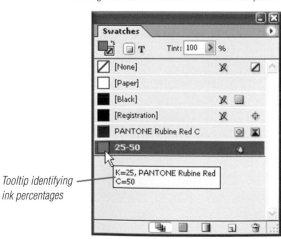

Tooltip identifying ink percentages

Exploring Advanced Techniques

FIGURE K-37
New Mixed Ink Group dialog box

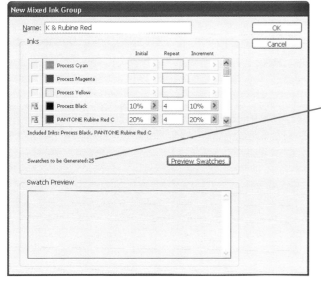

Number of
swatches to be
generated

FIGURE K-38
Identifying the percentages of Swatch 1

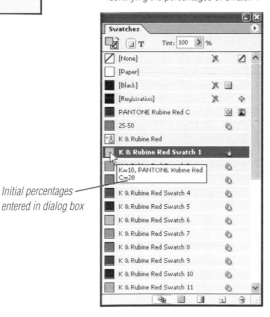

Initial percentages
entered in dialog box

1. Click the **Swatches palette list arrow**, then click **New Mixed Ink Group**.

2. Type **K & Rubine Red** in the Name text box.

3. Click the **empty gray square** beside Process Black, press **[Tab]**, type **10** in the Initial text box, then press **[Tab]** again.

4. Type **4** in the Repeat text box, press **[Tab]**, then type **10** in the Increment text box.

5. Click the **empty gray square** beside PANTONE Rubine Red C, press **[Tab]**, type **20** in the Initial text box, then press **[Tab]** again.

6. Type **4** in the Repeat text box, press **[Tab]**, type **20** in the Increment text box, then press **[Tab]** again.

   Your dialog box should resemble Figure K-37. Note that below the table is a note stating that 25 swatches will be generated.

7. Click **Preview Swatches**, then scroll to see the 25 swatches generated.

8. Click **OK**.

9. In the Swatches palette, position your cursor over a swatch until a tooltip appears detailing the mixture of the two inks.

   > TIP Swatch 1 will be composed of the values you typed in the Initial text box for each ink, as shown in Figure K-38.

You created a mixed ink group based on one process ink and one PANTONE ink.

Edit a mixed ink group

1. Click the **Swatches palette list arrow**, then click **New Color Swatch**.

2. Click the **Color Type list arrow**, click **Spot**, click the **Color Mode list arrow**, then click **PANTONE solid coated**.

3. In the list of PANTONE swatches, click **PANTONE Yellow C**, then click **OK**.

   PANTONE Yellow C is added to the Swatches palette.

4. Note the parent swatch of the K & Rubine Red mixed ink group, shown in Figure K-39.

   (continued)

FIGURE K-39

Parent swatch of the K & Rubine Red mixed ink group

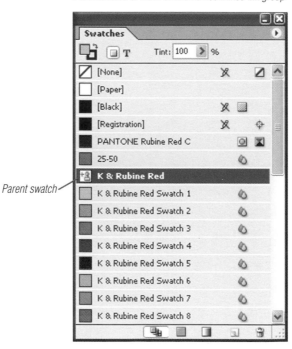

Parent swatch

FIGURE K-40

Viewing a mixed ink group modified with a different PANTONE ink

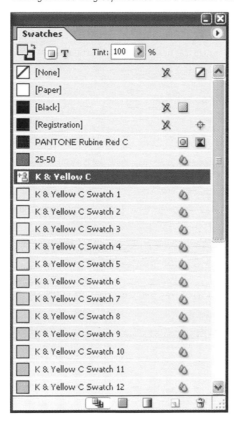

5. Double-click the **parent swatch** to open the Mixed Ink Group Options dialog box, then type **K & Yellow C** in the Name text box.

6. Click the **PANTONE Rubine Red C list arrow**, then click **PANTONE Yellow C**.

7. Click **OK**.

   As shown in Figure K-40, all of the swatches in the mixed ink group are modified as mixtures of Process Black and PANTONE Yellow C.

8. Save your work, then close Mixed Inks.

You modified all of the swatches of a mixed ink group with a different PANTONE ink.

WORK WITH NESTED STYLES

What You'll Do

 In this lesson, you will use nested styles to format a block of text.

Understanding Nested Styles

The term **nested styles** is based on real-world objects. If you like to cook, you've probably seen "nested" stainless steel mixing bowls. These are mixing bowls—usually six—of different sizes. For storage, you set the smallest one inside the next largest one, then you set those two in the next largest one, until the five small bowls are "nested" in the largest bowl. This metaphor is also used for end tables, in which one small table slides underneath a taller table and both of those slide underneath an even taller table. These are called "nested" tables.

In InDesign, nested styles are paragraph styles that contain two or more character styles. In other words, two or more character styles are "nested" within the paragraph style.

In Figure K-41, each paragraph contains elements that were formatted with character styles. The numbers were formatted with the Red Number character style, and the blue names were formatted with the Artist Name character style.

Without nested styles, you would need to apply the character styles one at a time. For example, in the first paragraph, you'd need to select the number 1 and the period that follows it, then apply the Red Number character style. Then, you'd select "Pablo Picasso:" and apply the Artist Name character style. Then you'd need to do the same for the next paragraphs. Imagine if your document profiled 100 artists!

With nested styles, you would format the entire block of text with a single paragraph style. That paragraph style would contain both the Red Number and the Artist Name character styles. They would be "nested" within the paragraph style and formatted in such a way that the first would format the number and the period and the second would format the artist's name. Then, because it's a paragraph style, the formatting would be reapplied after every paragraph break.

Applying Nested Styles

Nested styles are useful in specific situations—especially for blocks of text that contain repeating formatting at the beginning of each paragraph. Figure K-42 shows how nested styles were applied to the sample text.

In the Nested Styles section, two character styles were loaded—Red Number and Artist Name. The values entered for Red Number translate as follows: the Red Number character style will be applied to each paragraph through the first (1) period; The Artist Name character style is applied to each paragraph through the first em space.

If you regard the sample text with this in mind, you see that the Red Number character is indeed applied up to and including the first period. An em space has been inserted after each artist's name, and the Artist Name character style has indeed been applied up to that em space. If you wanted, you could also have specified that the character style be applied up to and including the colon after each artist's name. The result would have been the same.

FIGURE K-41

Viewing a document with multiple character styles

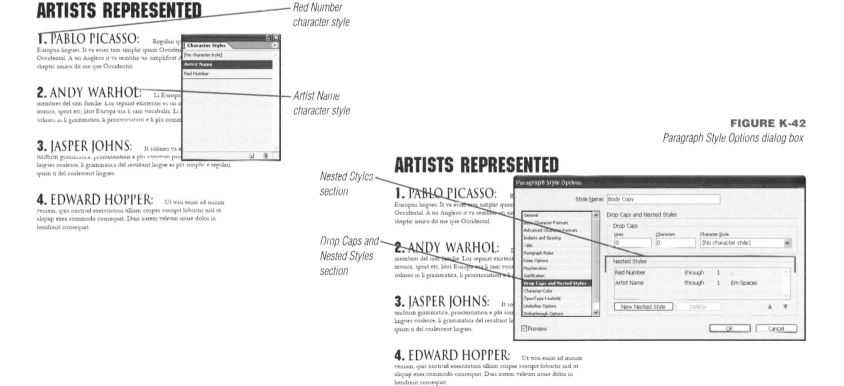

Red Number character style

Artist Name character style

Nested Styles section

Drop Caps and Nested Styles section

FIGURE K-42

Paragraph Style Options dialog box

Using the End Nested Style Here Command

Clearly, implementing nested styles requires a bit of forethought when formatting paragraphs. You must have characters that you can use to identify where a nested style ends. Periods, colons, and em or en spaces can be entered in the paragraph style to mark where a nested style should end.

But what if your layout doesn't call for periods, colons, or em spaces? No problem. Simply insert a special character using the End Nested Style Here command. This command is located within the Insert Special Character command on the Type menu—the same list that you use to insert auto page numbers on master pages or em dashes in body copy.

When you format the nested style in the paragraph style dialog box, you can specify that the nested style ends at the End Nested Style Here insertion. You do this by choosing End Nested Style Character in the Nested Styles section of the Paragraph Style Options dialog box, as shown in Figure K-43.

FIGURE K-43

Formatting a nested style using the End Nested Style Here insertion

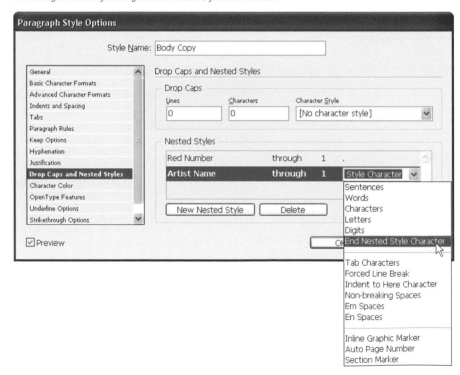

Viewing two character styles applied to text

Great American Novels

Number character style

Title character style

1. **The Grapes of Wrath:** Regulari quam li existent Europan lingues. It va esser tam simplic quam Occidental in fact, it va esser Occidental. A un Angleso it va semblar un simplificat Angles, quam un skeptic amico dit me que Occidental.

2. The Adventures of Huckleberry Finn: Li Europan lingues es membres del sam familie. Lor separat existentie es un myth. Por scientie, musica, sport etc, litot Europa usa li sam vocabular. Li lingues differe solmen in li grammatica, li pronunciation e li plu commun vocabules.

3. Tender is the Night: It solmen va esser necessi far uniform grammatica, pronunciation e plu sommun paroles. Ma quande lingues coalesce, li grammatica del resultant lingue es plu simplic e regulari quam ti del coalescent lingues.

4. To Kill a Mockingbird: Ut wisi enim ad minim veniam, quis nostrud exercitation ulliam corper suscipit lobortis nisl ut aliquip exea commodo consequat. Duis autem veleum iriure dolor in hendrerit consequat.

Apply character styles using the Character Styles palette

1. Open ID K-5.indd, then save it as **Nested Styles**.

2. Display the Paragraph Styles palette, select all the black text, then note the paragraph style highlighted in the Paragraph Styles palette.

   All of the black text has been saved with the Body Copy paragraph style.

3. Deselect all, select the number 1 and the period that follows it, then click **Number** in the Character Styles palette.

4. Select **The Grapes of Wrath** and the colon that follows it, then click **Title** in the Character Styles palette.

5. Deselect, then compare your page to Figure K-44.

   In order to format the remainder of the list, you would need to select each number and apply the Number character style, then select each title and apply the Title character style.

6. Click **File** on the menu bar, click **Revert**, then click **Yes** (Win) or **Revert** (Mac) in the dialog box that follows.

You used the Character Styles palette for applying character styles to text in a document.

Apply nested styles

1. Click the **Type Tool** T. , click to the immediate right of the colon after the word Wrath,
click **Type** on the menu bar, point to **Insert
Special Character**, then click **End Nested
Style Here**.

   | TIP Enlarge your document view if
   necessary.

   The special character is invisible, so you
   won't see any change to the text.

2. Using the same method, insert the End
Nested Style Here special character after the
colons in items 2–4.

3. Double-click **Body Copy** in the Paragraph
Styles palette, then click the **Preview check
box** in the bottom-left corner.

4. Click **Drop Caps and Nested Styles** on the
left, then click **New Nested Style**.

5. Click **[No character style]** in the Nested
Styles section to activate the list arrow, click
the **[No character style] list arrow**, then
click **Number**.

6. Click the word **Words**, then type a **period (.)**
to replace Words, so that your dialog box
resembles Figure K-45.

   The Number character style will be applied
   through the first period in each entry.

   | TIP If necessary, move the dialog box to
   the side so that you can see the format
   changes as they are applied to the text.

   (continued)

FIGURE K-45

Formatting a nested style

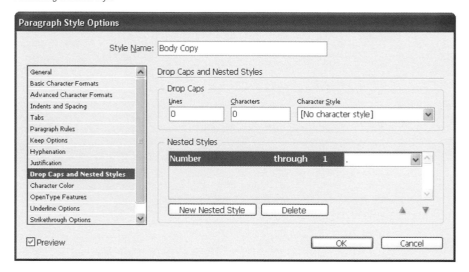

FIGURE K-46

Formatting a nested style through to the first colon

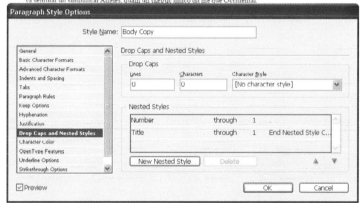

Great American Novels

1. **The Grapes of Wrath:** Regulari quam li existent Europan lingues. It va esser tam simplic quam Occidental in fact, it va esser Occidental. A un Angleso it va semblar un simplificat Angles, quam un skeptic amico dit me que Occidental.

Paragraph Style Options

Style Name: Body Copy

General
Basic Character Formats
Advanced Character Formats
Indents and Spacing
Tabs
Paragraph Rules
Keep Options
Hyphenation
Justification
Drop Caps and Nested Styles
Character Color
OpenType Features
Underline Options
Strikethrough Options

Drop Caps and Nested Styles

Drop Caps

Lines	Characters	Character Style
0	0	[No character style]

Nested Styles

Number	through	1	
Title	through	1	End Nested Style C...

New Nested Style   Delete   ▲ ▼

☑ Preview   OK   Cancel

7. Click **New Nested Style**, click the **[No character style] list arrow**, then click **Title**.

8. Click the word **Words** once, then note the format changes to the text on the page.

   TIP   The Title character style is applied to the first word only, because the nested style specifies to do so.

9. Click the **Words list arrow**, click **End Nested Style Character**, then press **[Enter]** (Win) or **[return]** (Mac) to execute the change.

   As shown in Figure K-46, the Title character style is applied to all the words up to the inserted special character End Nested Style Here.

10. Click **OK**, save your work, then close Nested Styles.

You applied two character styles to four paragraphs simultaneously by using nested styles.

Use the Pathfinder palette.

1. Open ID K-6.indd, then save it as **Chapter K Skills**.
2. Open the Layers palette, then verify that only Layer 1 is visible and targeted.
3. Select all, then click the Subtract button in the Pathfinder palette.
4. Click Edit on the menu bar, click Copy, click Edit on the menu bar, click Paste in Place, then change the fill color to PANTONE 1797 C.
5. Make Layer 2 visible, press and hold [Shift], then click the yellow star to add it to the selection.
6. Click the Exclude Overlap button in the Pathfinder palette.
7. Click PANTONE Reflex Blue C in the Swatches palette.

Create new stroke styles.

1. Deselect all.
2. Click the Stroke palette list arrow, then click Stroke Styles.
3. Click New, then type **New Dash** in the Name text box.
4. Verify that Dash is listed in the Type text box.
5. Drag the highlighted triangle left until the value in the Length text box reads .125.
6. Click the white space to the right of the dash to add a new dash.
7. Type **.19** in the Start text box, press [Tab], type **.01** in the Length text box, then press [Tab].

8. Click OK.
9. Note the New Dash stroke in the Stroke Styles dialog box, then click OK.
10. Select the circle, click the Type list arrow in the Stroke palette, then click New Dash.

Create mixed ink swatches.

1. Click the Swatches palette list arrow, then click New Mixed Ink Group.
2. Type **K & Reflex Blue** in the Name text box.
3. Click the empty gray square beside Process Black, press [Tab], type **5** in the Initial text box, then press [Tab] again.
4. Type **3** in the Repeat text box, press [Tab], then type **5** in the Increment text box.

FIGURE K-47
Completed Skills Review, Part 1

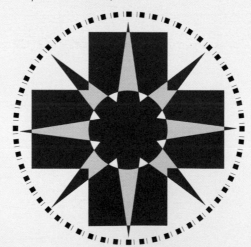

5. Scroll until you see PANTONE Reflex Blue C, then click the empty gray square beside PANTONE Reflex Blue C.
6. Type **10** in the Initial text box, press [Tab], type **3** in the Repeat text box, press [Tab], type **10** in the Increment text box, then press [Tab] again.
7. Click the Preview Swatches button, preview the 16 swatches, then click OK.
8. Click the Selection Tool, then click the green area of the star.
9. Click the K & Reflex Blue Swatch 5 swatch in the Swatches palette.
10. Switch to Preview Mode, deselect all, compare your work to Figure K-47, save your work, then close Chapter K Skills.

Work with nested styles.

1. Open ID K-7.indd, then save it as **Nested Styles Skills**.
2. Click the Type Tool, click to the immediate right of the colon after the word Picasso, click Type on the menu bar, point to Insert Special Character, then click End Nested Style Here.
3. Using the same method, insert the End Nested Style Here special character after the colons in items 2–4.
4. Double-click Body Copy in the Paragraph Styles palette, then click the Preview check box in the bottom-right corner (if necessary).
5. Click Drop Caps and Nested Styles on the left side, then click New Nested Style.
6. Click [No character style] in the Nested Styles section to activate the list arrow, click the [No character style] list arrow, click Red Number, then press [Enter] (Win) or [return] (Mac) to execute the change.
7. Click New Nested Style, click the [No character style] list arrow, then click Artist Name.
8. Click the word Words once, click the Words list arrow, click End Nested Style Character, then press [Enter] (Win) or [return] (Mac) to execute the change.
9. Click OK, compare your work to Figure K-48, save your work, then close Nested Styles Skills.

FIGURE K-48
Completed Skills Review, Part 2

ARTISTS REPRESENTED

1. **PABLO PICASSO:** Regulari quam li existent Europan lingues. It va esser tam simplic quam Occidental in fact, it va esser Occidental. A un Angleso it va semblar un simplificat Angles, quam un skeptic amico dit me que Occidental.

2. **ANDY WARHOL:** Li Europan lingues es membres del sam familie. Lor separat existentie es un myth. Por scientie, musica, sport etc, litot Europa usa li sam vocabular. Li lingues differe solmen in li grammatica, li pronunciation e li plu commun vocabules.

3. **JASPER JOHNS:** It solmen va esser necessi far uniform grammatica, pronunciation e plu sommun paroles. Ma quande lingues coalesce, li grammatica del resultant lingue es plu simplic e regulari quam ti del coalescent lingues.

4. **EDWARD HOPPER:** Ut wisi enim ad minim veniam, quis nostrud exercitation ulliam corper suscipit lobortis nisl ut aliquip exea commodo consequat. Duis autem veleum iriure dolor in hendrerit consequat.

83% |◄ ◄ 1   ▼ ► ►| ◄

Exploring Advanced Techniques

A new magazine named WEIRD is court-
ing you with the idea of hiring you in
their art department. They have asked
you to submit a sample of a cover design.
You are an avid fan of the magazine, and
you know that every month they do
something interesting with the title artwork. You decide to use a customized
stroke style to create a 70s look.

1. Open ID K-8.indd, then save it as **WEIRD**.
2. Open the Stroke Styles dialog box, click
   New, type **Vibe** in the Name text box, click
   the Type list arrow, then click Stripe.
3. Click the top stripe, then drag the top triangle down until the Start value reads 85.
4. Click the top stripe, then drag the bottom
   triangle up until the Width value reads 15.
5. Add a new stripe between the two stripes,
   change the Start value to 30, change the
   Width value to 40, then click OK twice.
6. Click the Direct Selection Tool, click the W,
   then click the Swap Fill and Stroke button in
   the Toolbox.
7. Change the stroke type to Vibe, then change
   the stroke weight to 6 pt.
8. Deselect, compare your work to
   Figure K-49, save your work, then
   close WEIRD.

FIGURE K-49
Completed Project Builder 1

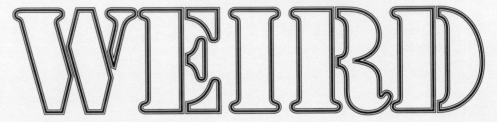

Exploring Advanced Techniques

You work for a magazine that is typically published in black and white. You have just finished designing this month's cover, when you are informed that extra money in the budget means that the cover can be printed with two colors. You realize this means that you'll need to create a mixed ink group to create a variety of colors for the cover.

1. Open ID K-9.indd, then save it as **Two Color Lab**.
2. Click the Swatches palette list arrow, then click New Mixed Ink Group.
3. Type **K & Violet** in the Name text box.
4. Click the empty gray square beside Process Black, press [Tab], type **10** in the Initial text box, then press [Tab] again.
5. Type **2** in the Repeat text box, press [Tab], then type **10** in the Increment text box.
6. Click the empty gray square beside PANTONE Violet C, type **20** in the Initial text box, press [Tab], type **2** in the Repeat text box, press [Tab], type **20** in the Increment text box, then click OK.
7. Change the fill on the black border to K & Violet Swatch 9.
8. Change the fill on the "Puppy Love" and "welcoming a new addition to your home" text to K & Violet Swatch 1.
9. Change the fill color on the inner white border to PANTONE Violet C, then change the stroke color to Paper.
10. Compare your work to Figure K-50, save your work, then close Two Color Lab.

FIGURE K-50
Completed Project Builder 2

Exploring Advanced Techniques

You design logos, and a local company has asked that you update their logo, which is a black spade shape that you would find in any deck of cards. They tell you that they want to add red to the logo, but that you can't change the shape of the logo in any way. You decide to draw a red object and position it over the spade, knowing that you will use a pathfinder to achieve the desired effect.

1. Open ID K-10.indd, then save it as **Red Lightning**.
2. Copy the black spade, paste a copy directly in front of the original, then fill it with green to help you distinguish it from the original.
3. Bring the red shape to the front of the stacking order.
4. Select the red object and the green spade.
5. Click the Intersect button in the Pathfinder palette.
6. Deselect, then compare your work to Figure K-51.
7. Save your work, then close Red Lightning.

FIGURE K-51
Completed Design Project

Exploring Advanced Techniques

This project is designed to challenge the group members' ability to recognize and distinguish pathfinders visually.

1. Open ID K-11.indd or refer to Figure K-52.
2. Each member of the group should number a piece of paper from 1 to 5.
3. Identify the pathfinder used in each of the numbered examples.

FIGURE K-52
Group Project Challenge

Original

1.

2.

3.

4.

5.

CHAPTER L

PREPARING, PACKAGING AND EXPORTING DOCUMENTS

1. Create bleeds, slugs, and printer's marks.

2. Use the Ink Manager and preview color separations.

3. Preflight and package a document.

4. Export a document.

CHAPTER 1
PREPARING, PACKAGING AND EXPORTING DOCUMENTS

When it comes time to output a document—to print it, to export it, or to send it to a printer or service bureau—you will be impressed with the many well-thought-out options that InDesign makes available for this critical phase of production.

InDesign comes complete with all the industry-standard printer's marks that you would expect from a professional layout application. Crop marks, bleed marks, color bars, and registration marks are all available in the Print dialog box. Additionally, you can create bleed and slug areas in the Document Setup dialog box, which positions a handy guide for laying out these important areas.

The Ink Manager makes it easy to specify how the document will color separate and allows you to convert spot inks to process inks with a simple click of the mouse. The Separations Preview palette is a great resource for the designer and the print professional to see at a glance how a document will color separate and to inspect each plate quickly.

If the document is going to be shipped to a printer or service bureau, the Preflight and Package commands automate these all-important steps in the production process.

Rather than print, you might want to export a document. You'll find that InDesign offers all of the file formats that you need and expect. Export a document as a PDF, which opens easily in Adobe Acrobat. You can export a selected item—or the whole layout—as a JPEG image, handy for Web viewing. And if you want to manipulate a layout in Photoshop or Illustrator, choose the EPS format in the Export dialog box.

Tools You'll Use

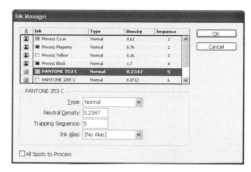

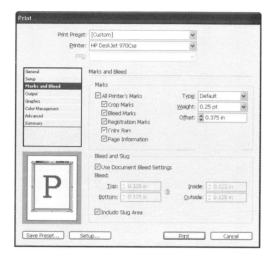

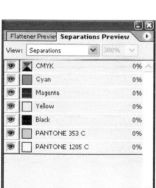

CREATE BLEEDS, SLUGS, AND PRINTER'S MARKS

What You'll Do

In this lesson, you will create bleed and slug areas, and then you will output a document with printer's marks.

Understanding Bleeds

Before discussing bleeds, it's important to define trim size. **Trim size** is the size to which a printed document will be cut—or trimmed—when it clears the printing press. For example, an 8" × 10" magazine may be printed on a page that is 12" × 14", but it will be trimmed to 8" × 10".

You might be surprised to find that documents are often printed on paper that is larger than the document's trim size, but that extra space is used to accommodate bleeds, crops, and other printer's marks. **Bleeds** are areas of the layout that extend to the trim size. In Figure L-1, the green background extends to the trim on all four sides; the yellow strip extends to the trim on the left and the right. Both are said to "bleed" off of the edge.

It's important to understand that areas of the layout that extend to the trim—areas that are meant to bleed—must actually go beyond the trim size when the document is prepared (or "prepped") for printing. Why? To accommodate for the margin of error in trimming.

Nothing and nobody is perfect—and this includes the cutting device that is used to trim printed pieces when they clear the printing press. You can target the cutting device to slice the paper exactly at the trim size, but you can never expect it to be dead-on every time. There is a margin of error, usually 1/32"–1/16".

To accommodate for this margin of error, any item that bleeds—any item that extends to the trim size—must *extend* the trim size. The standard measurement that a bleed item must extend beyond the trim size is .125".

Creating Bleeds

You define a bleed area for a document in the Bleed and Slug section of the Document Setup dialog box, shown in Figure L-2. You can do this when you create a new document or at any time after it has been created. (Many designers prefer to address the issues with items that bleed after they've designed the layout.)

Figure L-2 shows that the trim size for the document is 6" wide by 3" in height and that a .125" bleed area is to be added outside the trim size. This bleed area is reflected in the document by a red guide, shown in Figure L-3. You use this guide when you extend areas that bleed beyond the trim size.

As shown in Figure L-4, the green background has been extended to the bleed guide on all four sides, and the yellow strip has been extended on the left and the right. If the trimmer trims slightly outside of the trim size (the black line), the extra bleed material provides the room for that error.

FIGURE L-1
Identifying areas that will bleed

Green extends to the trim size on all four sides

Yellow extends to the trim size on two sides

THE ROAD TO HANA
a visual journey through Maui

FIGURE L-2
Bleed and Slug section of the Document Setup dialog box

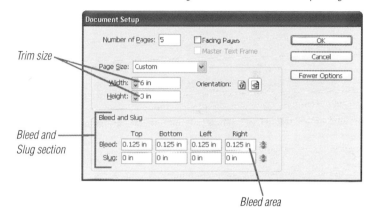

Trim size

Bleed and Slug section

Bleed area

FIGURE L-3
Identifying the bleed guide

THE ROAD TO HANA
a visual journey through Maui

Bleed guide

FIGURE L-4
Extending bleed items to the bleed guide

Bleed guide

THE ROAD TO HANA
a visual journey through Maui

Trim size

Creating Slugs

When you output a document, often you'll want to include a note on the output. Printers refer to that note as a **slug**. Slugs are often notes to the printer, phone numbers to call if there are any problems, or other information related to the file.

Obviously, slugs are not meant to be part of the final trimmed document. They must be positioned outside the trim size so that they will be discarded when the document is trimmed. InDesign allows you to create a **slug area** in the Bleed and Slug section of the Document Setup dialog box, shown in Figure L-5. In this figure, .5" has been specified for a slug area on all four sides of the document. The slug area is identified by a blue guide, shown in Figure L-6. Create a text frame, position it in the slug area, then type whatever information you want to keep with the file, as shown in Figure L-7.

When you create a slug, use the **Registration swatch** in the Swatches palette as the fill color for the text. When the document is color separated, anything filled with Registration appears on all printing plates.

FIGURE L-5
Defining the slug area

FIGURE L-6
Identifying the slug area

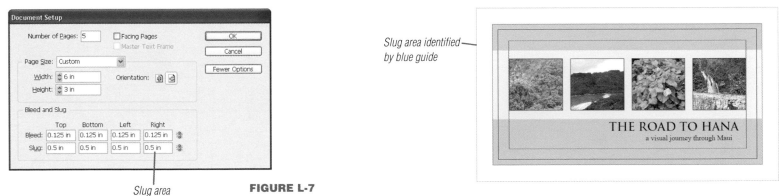

Slug area

Slug area identified by blue guide

FIGURE L-7
Adding a slug

Slug contained in the slug area

Previewing Bleeds and Slugs

When you switch to Preview Mode, the bleed and slug areas will not be visible. To preview those areas, press and hold the Preview Mode button in the Toolbox to reveal the Bleed Mode and Slug Mode buttons, shown in Figure L-8. Bleed Mode will show you a preview with the bleed area included, and Slug Mode will show you a preview with both the bleed and slug areas included.

Printing Bleeds, Slugs, and Printer's Marks

When you output a document, you can choose whether or not the bleed and slug areas will print; usually they are printed along with printer's marks. You specify these items to print in the Marks and Bleed section of the Print dialog box, shown in Figure L-9. **Printer's marks** include **crop marks**, which are guide lines that define the trim size. **Bleed marks** define the bleed size. Printers use **registration marks** to align the color-separated output. **Color bars** are used to maintain consistent color on press, and **page information** includes the title of the InDesign document.

Figure L-10 shows a printed document output with a bleed area and a slug area, and identifies all five printer's marks.

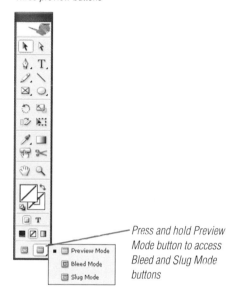

FIGURE L-8
Three preview buttons

Preview Mode
Bleed Mode
Slug Mode

Press and hold Preview Mode button to access Bleed and Slug Mode buttons

FIGURE L-9
Print dialog box

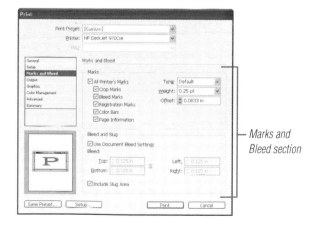

Marks and Bleed section

FIGURE L-10
Identifying bleeds, slugs, and printer's marks

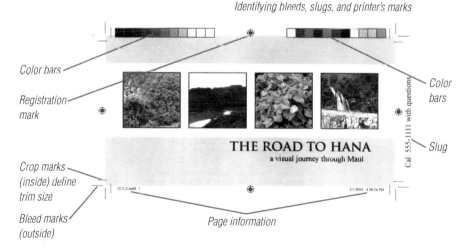

Color bars

Registration mark

Color bars

THE ROAD TO HANA
a visual journey through Maui

Slug

Crop marks (inside) define trim size

Bleed marks (outside)

Page information

Create a bleed

1. Open ID L-1.indd, then save it as **OAHU To Print**.

2. Verify that you are in Normal View Mode and that guides are visible.

3. Click **File** on the menu bar, then click **Document Setup**.

4. Click **More Options** (if necessary) to display the Bleed and Slug section, as shown in Figure L-11.

   The document's size—the trim size—is 6" × 7.5".

5. Type **.125** in the Top, Bottom, Inside, and Outside Bleed text boxes, click **OK**, then compare your page to Figure L-12.

   A bleed guide appears defining the bleed area, which is .125" outside the trim size on all four sides.

6. Click the **Selection Tool** ⯅, select the blue frame, then drag the frame corners to the bleed guide so that your document resembles Figure L-13.

You specified the bleed area in the Document Setup dialog box, and then you modified an object on the page so that it will bleed on all four sides.

FIGURE L-11
Document Setup dialog box

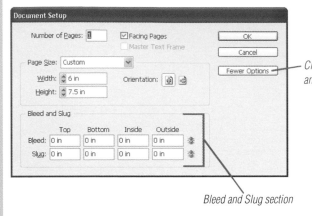

Click to hide the Bleed and Slug section

Bleed and Slug section

FIGURE L-12
Bleed area

Bleed guide

FIGURE L-13
Modifying an object's size to bleed

Preparing, Packaging, and Exporting Documents

FIGURE L-14
Slug area

Slug guide

FIGURE L-15
Typing a message in the slug area

Message to printer

Create a slug

1. Click **File** on the menu bar, then click **Document Setup**.

2. Type **.5** in the Top, Bottom, Inside, and Outside Slug text boxes, click **OK**, then compare your page to Figure L-14.

   A slug guide appears, defining the slug area, which is .5" outside the trim size on all four sides.

3. Drag the **text frame** from the pasteboard into the slug area at the right of the document, then change the stroke color of the text frame to None.

4. Click the **Type Tool T.**, then type the following in the text frame: **Printer: Any ?s call me at 800-555-1212. Kevin.**

5. Click the **Selection Tool ▸**, resize the text frame (if necessary) to see the entire message, then position the text frame in the same location shown in Figure L-15.

6. Verify that the text frame is still selected, then click the **Formatting affects text button** **T** in the Swatches palette.

7. Change the fill color of the text to **[Registration]**, then deselect the text frame.

   With a Registration fill, the slug text will appear on all printing plates if the document is color separated.

You specified a slug area in the Document Setup dialog box, you typed a message for the printer in the slug area, and then you filled the text with Registration.

Preview bleeds and slugs

1. Click the **Preview Mode button** 🔲. in the Toolbox.

   In preview mode, neither the bleed nor the slug area is visible.

2. Press and hold the **Preview Mode button** 🔲. until you see the Bleed Mode and Slug Mode buttons, then click the **Bleed Mode button** 🔲.

   The preview shows the document and the bleed area.

3. Press and hold the **Bleed Mode button** 🔲, then click the **Slug Mode button** 🔲.

   As shown in Figure L-16, in slug mode, the bleed and slug areas are previewed along with the document.

4. Click the **Normal View Mode button** 🔲.

   You viewed the layout in preview, bleed, and slug modes.

FIGURE L-16
Viewing the layout in slug mode

Slug area

Bleed area

Understanding InDesign compatibility

One of the most important features of Adobe InDesign is that it interfaces effectively with other Adobe products. An InDesign layout can be exported as a PDF, which means that the layout can be opened in both Adobe Photoshop and Adobe Acrobat. You can export the layout as an EPS, so it can be placed in both Adobe Photoshop and Adobe Illustrator. Adobe InDesign documents can also be opened by Adobe GoLive! to be used as layouts for the World Wide Web. The relationship between the Adobe products also works when importing files into an InDesign layout. If you have a Photoshop file with many layers, you don't need to save a flattened copy for use in InDesign—InDesign will place a layered Photoshop document without any problems. Similarly, InDesign will place an Illustrator file—you don't need to save it in the EPS format.

FIGURE L-17
Setup category in the Print dialog box

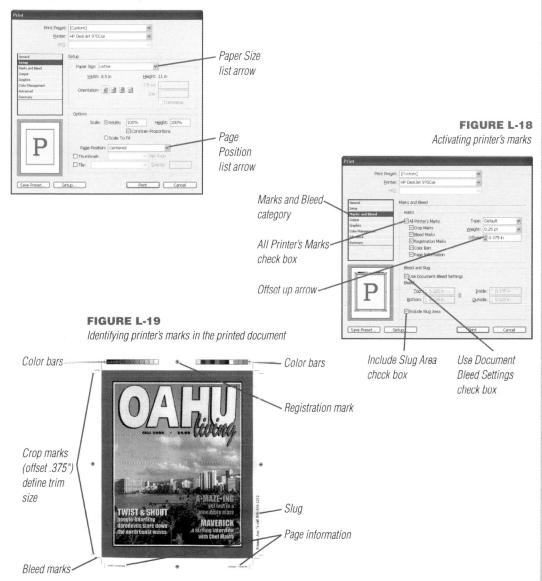

Paper Size
list arrow

Page
Position
list arrow

FIGURE L-18
Activating printer's marks

Marks and Bleed
category

All Printer's Marks
check box

Offset up arrow

FIGURE L-19
Identifying printer's marks in the printed document

Color bars

Color bars

Include Slug Area
check box

Use Document
Bleed Settings
check box

Registration mark

Crop marks
(offset .375")
define trim
size

Slug

Page information

Bleed marks

Print bleeds, slugs, and printer's marks

1. Click **File** on the menu bar, then click **Print**.

2. Verify that Copies is set to 1 and Pages is set to All, then click the **Setup category** on the left.

   TIP Don't click the Setup button at the bottom of the dialog box.

3. Click the **Paper Size list arrow**, click **Letter**, click the **Page Position list arrow**, then click **Centered**.

   Your dialog box should resemble Figure L-17.

   TIP Your letter choice may be Letter (8.5 × 11 in), depending on your printer type.

4. Click the **Marks and Bleed category** on the left.

5. In the Marks section, click the **All Printer's Marks check box**, then click the **Offset up arrow** until the value reads .375 in.

6. In the Bleed and Slug section, verify that the Use Document Bleed Settings check box is checked, then click the **Include Slug Area check box**.

   Your dialog box should resemble Figure L-18.

7. Click **Print**.

   Compare the printer's marks in Figure L-19 to your own output.

8. Save your work.

You opened the Print dialog box, set the paper size and page position, and activated all printer's marks, the document's bleed settings, and the slug area. You then printed the document.

USE THE INK MANAGER AND PREVIEW COLOR SEPARATIONS

What You'll Do

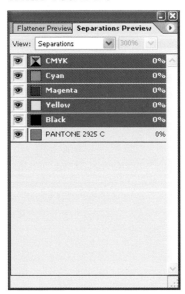

In this lesson, you will use the Ink Manager to specify swatches as process or spot colors, and then you'll preview separations in the Separations Preview palette.

Using the Ink Manager

The Ink Manager dialog box, shown in Figure L-20, gives you control over the inks that you create in the Swatches palette. One important function that the Ink Manager provides is the ability to convert spot colors easily to process inks if you should want to do so.

> **QUICKTIP**
> You can access the Ink Manager from the Swatches palette menu.

You may ask, "Why would you create a swatch as a spot color if you intend to output it as a process color?" Good question. You should know that many designers choose not to be too meticulous when creating swatches. Often, they will use the PANTONE palette to create swatches without a care as to whether they are defined as spot or process. That's why many printers are seldom surprised when they open a client's document and find that it has been saved with 22 spot inks!

The Ink Manager makes it easy to specify how the document will color separate. It is important to remember that using the Ink Manager is a function of output. The changes that you make to inks in the Ink Manager only affect the output of the document, not the inks in the document. For example, you might convert a swatch from a spot ink to a process ink in the Ink Manager, but the swatch will continue to be defined as a spot ink in the Swatches palette.

Using the Separations Preview Palette

The Separations Preview palette, shown in Figure L-21, is another palette that allows you to see at a glance the number of inks available for printing the document. The Separations Preview palette lists only the four process inks and any swatches that are defined as spot inks.

The Separations Preview palette is interactive. Click on an ink, and the areas of the document that use that ink will appear black. The areas that don't use that ink will disappear. Figure L-22 shows Black selected in the palette and only the areas of the document that contain black ink being previewed in the document.

Why is this useful? It's important to note that the Separations Preview palette comes into play in the output stages, not in the design stages. But at the output stage, it is a great resource for the print professional

to see at a glance how a document will color separate and to inspect each plate quickly.

FIGURE L-20

Ink Manager dialog box

Identifies process ink

Identifies spot ink

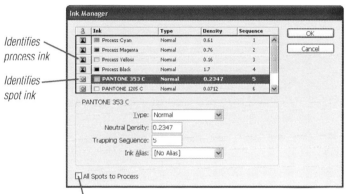

Click to convert all spot inks to process inks

FIGURE L-21

Separations Preview palette

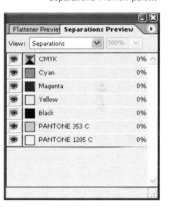

FIGURE L-22

Viewing the black inks in the document

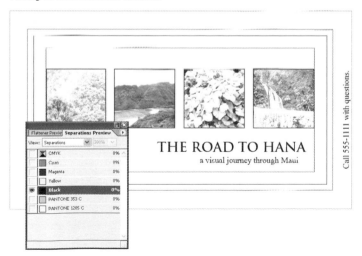

Use the Ink Manager

1. In the Swatches palette, note that there are three PANTONE spot ink swatches, as shown in Figure L-23.

2. Click the **Swatches palette list arrow**, then click **Ink Manager**.

3. Scroll in the Ink Manager and note the inks listed.

   The list of inks in the Ink Manager window is different from the list in the Swatches palette. The Ink Manager lists the four process inks (CMYK) and the three swatches specified as spot inks. Any other process swatches are not listed because they are composed of the four process inks.

4. Click **PANTONE 427 C**, then click the **spot ink icon** 🔘 to the left of PANTONE 427 C to convert it from a spot ink to a process ink, as shown in Figure L-24.

   You have converted PANTONE 427 C from a spot ink to a process ink.

5. Click **PANTONE 159 C**, click the **spot ink icon** 🔘 to the left of PANTONE 159 C, then click **OK**.

   The document will now output four process inks and 1 spot ink, for a total of five inks.

   (continued)

FIGURE L-23

Swatches palette with three spot inks

Spot inks

FIGURE L-24

Converting a spot ink to a process ink

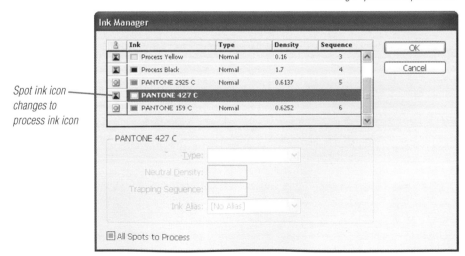

Spot ink icon changes to process ink icon

Preparing, Packaging, and Exporting Documents

FIGURE L-25

Viewing the Inks section in the Print dialog box

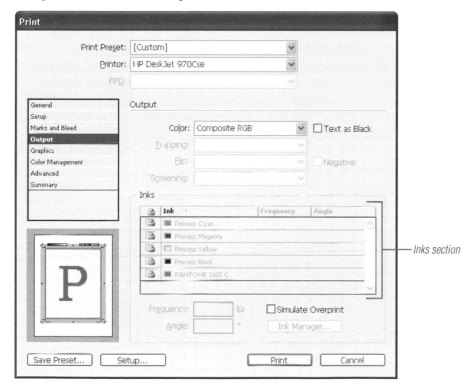

Inks section

6. Note the inks in the Swatches palette.

   Changes you make using the Ink Manager affect only the output; they do not reflect how colors are defined in the document. Though PANTONE 427 and 159 will be output as process inks, the Swatches palette continues to show a spot ink icon beside them, because that is how they were specified when created.

7. Click **File** on the menu bar, click **Print**, then click the **Output category** on the left.

   As shown in Figure L-25, the Inks section of the Print dialog box specifies that the document will separate into five inks.

8. Click **Cancel**.

You used the Ink Manager to convert two spot inks to process inks. You then switched to the Output category of the Print dialog box to verify that the document would separate into five inks, as shown in the Ink Manager dialog box.

Use the Separations Preview palette

1. Click **Window** on the menu bar, point to **Output Preview**, then click **Separations**.

2. Click the **View list arrow** in the Separations Preview palette, then click **Separations**.

   As shown in Figure L-26, the document is specified to color separate into five inks— the four process inks plus PANTONE 2925 C, which has been specified as a spot ink in the Ink Manager dialog box.

3. Move the Separations Preview palette to the side so that you can see the entire document.

4. Click **PANTONE 2925 C** in the Separations Preview palette.

   The areas of the document that have PANTONE 2925 C applied appear as black. Other areas are invisible.

   (continued)

FIGURE L-26
Viewing five inks in the Separations Preview palette

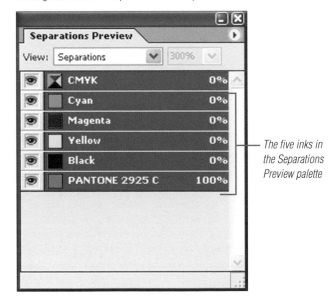

The five inks in the Separations Preview palette

FIGURE L-27

Viewing a single ink in the Separations Preview palette

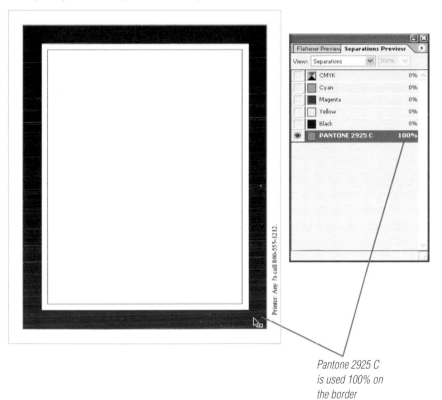

Pantone 2925 C
is used 100% on
the border

5. Position your cursor over the black border in the document.

   As shown in Figure L-27, 100% appears beside the ink listed in the palette, indicating that this area is to be printed with 100% PANTONE 2925 C.

6. Click **Cyan** in the Separations Preview palette.

   The areas of the document that have Cyan applied appear as black.

7. Move your cursor over the document and note the percentages of cyan and the other inks.

   There is 0% cyan in the title OAHU and 0% PANTONE 2925 C anywhere except in the border.

8. Click **Magenta**, then click **Yellow**, then click **Black** to preview those inks.

   Note that the slug appears on all plates because it's filled with the Registration ink, which appears on every printing plate.

9. Click **CMYK** to preview only the areas of the document that will be printed with process inks.

10. Click the **empty gray square** beside the PANTONE 2925 C ink to make the ink visible in the preview.

11. Click the **View list arrow** in the Separations Preview palette, click **Off**, then close the Separations Preview palette.

You used the Separations Preview palette to preview how the document will be color separated into five inks.

PREFLIGHT AND PACKAGE A DOCUMENT

What You'll Do

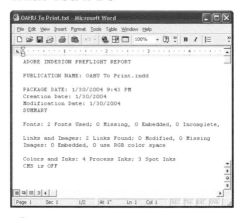

 In this lesson, you will explore options for preflighting and packaging a document.

Preflighting a Document

Before an airplane takes off, the pilots perform a preflight check. Running down a checklist, they verify that the many controls necessary to fly a plane safely are all working properly.

In the print world, designers and printers have co-opted the term "preflight" to refer to checking out a document before it's released—from the designer to the printer or service bureau—or before it's actually downloaded to an output device.

Adobe InDesign offers the very cool Preflight dialog box, shown in Figure L-28. The Preflight dialog box gives you a status report on the document. It alerts you to any problems with fonts or with placed graphics that are either modified or missing. The Preflight function of InDesign is a great resource for quickly verifying that a document is in the state it should be before releasing it to a printer or downloading it to an output device.

Packaging a Document

Once a document has been preflighted, it's ready to be packaged. Packaging a document means getting it ready to send to a printer or service bureau for outputting and printing. That sounds easy, but it's not as simple as copying the InDesign document to a disk and handing it off to a courier. Remember, a complete InDesign document is the document itself plus any and all placed graphics and any fonts that are used. The printer or service bureau requires all the components in order to output the document successfully.

Packaging has long been a tricky step in the production process—a place where many problems can and do occur. Think about how messy and disorganized some people are—not you of course—when they create and save files on their computers. Imagine trying to package a document for a fellow designer when she's called in sick and the job is due at the printer.

Any time that you're moving files on the desktop and copying them to disks, it's easy to lose track of a file or to accidentally copy over pre-existing files. And it's never fun to go into the fonts folder to find the right fonts that need to be packaged.

When you use the Package command, InDesign automatically creates a folder and packages a copy of the InDesign document, copies of all the placed graphics, and copies of all the fonts used. It also offers the Printing Instructions dialog box—shown in Figure L-29—that generates a report based on the information that you enter. By automating the process, the Package command removes much of the potential for human error.

FIGURE L-28
Preflight dialog box

FIGURE L-29
Printing Instructions dialog box

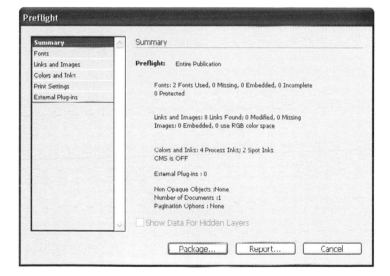

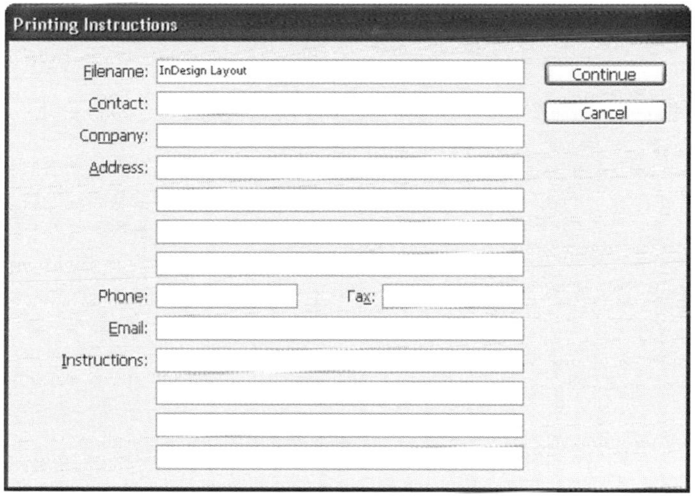

Preflight a document

1. Click **File** on the menu bar, click **Preflight**, then click the **Fonts category** on the left.

2. Note the two fonts listed, then click the **Show Problems Only check box** to add a check mark (if necessary).

   If the fonts used in the document are available on your system, the two fonts listed in the window will disappear.

3. Remove the check mark in the Show Problems Only check box.

4. Click the **Links and Images category** on the left, note the two imported graphics listed, then note the information below the window for each selected graphic.

5. Click the **Show Problems Only check box**.

   If the links to the two imported graphics have been updated, they should disappear from the window.

6. Click the **Colors and Inks category** on the left.

   Because three swatches are specified as spot inks in the Swatches palette, all three are listed here as spot inks. However, two of them have been converted to process inks using the Ink Manager dialog box, which overrides the information in this window.

7. Click **Report**, then click **Save**.

8. Open the .txt file in a word processing application (like Microsoft Word), compare your report to Figure L-30, then close the file.

9. Click **Cancel** in the Preflight dialog box.

You used the Preflight command to look for problems in the document and then you generated a preflight report.

FIGURE L-30
Viewing the Preflight report

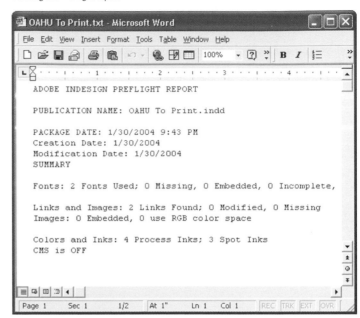

Using the Flattener Preview palette

If you prepare InDesign documents for output or prepress, you will be interested in the Flattener Preview palette. It's important to remember that InDesign is a graphic design application as well as a layout program. Designers typically create layered documents, often with blending modes between the layers to create special effects. Complex documents like these can be a challenge to print—a layered document sometimes appears differently when output than it does on the screen. The Flattener Preview palette allows you to preview how specific areas of a layout will appear when output. This palette is especially useful for previewing transparent drop shadows, objects with a feathered edge, transparent placed graphics from Illustrator or Photoshop, and the graphics that interact with the types of objects listed previously.

FIGURE L-31
Printing Instructions dialog box

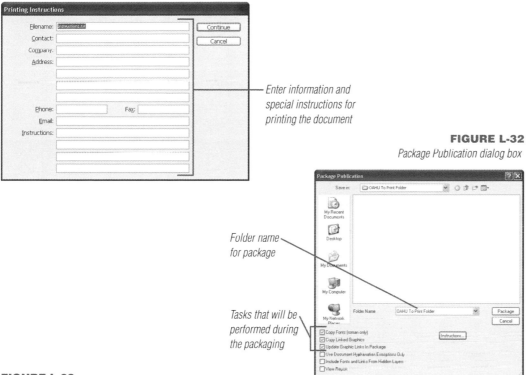

Enter information and special instructions for printing the document

FIGURE L-32
Package Publication dialog box

Folder name for package

Tasks that will be performed during the packaging

FIGURE L-33
Contents of the OAHU To Print Folder

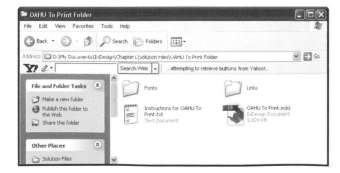

Package a document

1. Click **File** on the menu bar, then click **Save**.

   A document must be saved before it can be packaged.

2. Click **File** on the menu bar, then click **Package**.

   The Printing Instructions dialog box opens, as shown in Figure L-31. You use this dialog box to supply contact information and specific instructions for printing the document.

3. Type **Instructions for OAHU To Print.txt** (Win) or **OAHU To Print** (Mac) in the File name text box.

4. Click **Continue** to open the Package Publication dialog box (Win) or the Create Package Folder dialog box (Mac), shown in Figure L-32.

5. A folder is automatically supplied for you, and the three checked items in the lower-left corner are the tasks that will be performed during the packaging.

6. Click **Package** (Win) or **Save** (Mac), then click **OK** in the Font Alert dialog box that follows.

7. Open the OAHU To Print Folder, then compare Its contents to Figure L-33.

   The folder contains the InDesign document, the .txt instructions document, a Fonts folder, and a Links folder.

8. Close the folder, then return to the OAHU To Print document in InDesign.

You packaged a document for delivery, noting that copies of fonts and of linked graphics were stored in the delivery folder.

EXPORT A DOCUMENT

What You'll Do

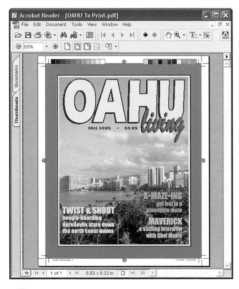

▶ In this lesson, you will explore four options for exporting a document.

Exporting a Document

Exporting a document is a different function than saving a document or printing a document. When you export a document, the document that you create is your InDesign file saved in a different file format. Figure L-34 shows the Export dialog box and the available file formats for exporting.

"Why would I do this?" you may be asking. The Export command is used most often to translate a document into another format so that it can be used in another application or uploaded to the World Wide Web.

Common exports of InDesign documents are to Adobe PDF, which allows you to open, view, and annotate an InDesign document in Adobe Acrobat. You can take an entire page of an InDesign document, export it as an EPS (encapsulated PostScript) file, then open it or place it as a bitmap graphic in Adobe Photoshop or Adobe Illustrator. You can export a page or a single selected graphic as a JPEG file, which is a common file format for bitmap images on the Internet.

FIGURE L-34

Export dialog box

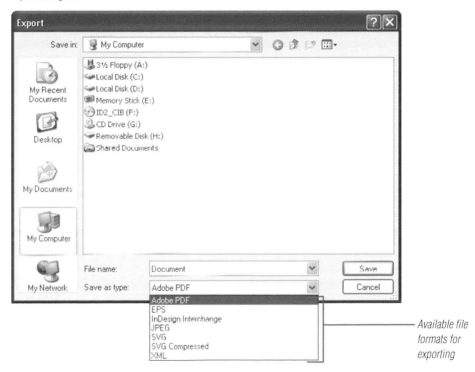

Available file formats for exporting

Export a page to EPS format

1. Click **File** on the menu bar, then click **Export**.

2. In the Export dialog box, click the **Save as type list arrow** (Win) or the **Format list arrow** (Mac), click **EPS**, as shown in Figure L-35, then click **Save**.

3. In the Export EPS dialog box, note that you can choose which pages you want to export.

   Because this document is a single page, you will accept the default in the Ranges text box.

4. Click the **Color list arrow**, click **CMYK**, then click **Export**.

5. If you have Photoshop on your computer, open Photoshop, click **File** on the menu bar, click **Open**, then open OAHU To Print.eps.

   The Rasterize Generic EPS Format dialog box opens which gives you options for converting the EPS to a bitmap image.

6. Accept the settings in the Rasterize Generic EPS Format dialog box, then click **OK**.

7. As shown in Figure L-36, the page from InDesign opens in Photoshop as a bitmap graphic.

   Like all bitmap graphics, this graphic can be edited in Photoshop.

8. Exit Photoshop without saving changes to the file, then return to the OAHU To Print document in InDesign.

Using the Export EPS option, you were able to open an InDesign page in Photoshop as a bitmap graphic.

FIGURE L-35
Exporting a page as an EPS

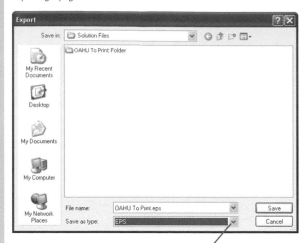

Save as type
list arrow

FIGURE L-36
Viewing the InDesign page as a bitmap graphic in Photoshop

Preparing, Packaging, and Exporting Documents

FIGURE L-37

Exporting a page as an Adobe PDF file

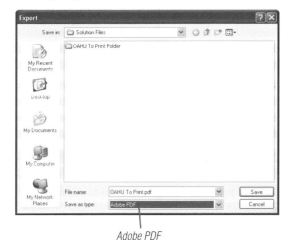

Adobe PDF

1. Click **File** on the menu bar, then click **Export**.

2. Click the **Save as type list arrow** (Win) or the **Format list arrow** (Mac), click **Adobe PDF**, as shown in Figure L-37, then click **Save**.

3. In the Export PDF dialog box, remove the check mark in the Optimize for Fast Web View check box (if necessary), then click the **Marks and Bleeds category** on the left.

4. Click the **All Printer's Marks check box**, click the **Use Document Bleed Settings check box**, then click **Export**.

   Figure L-38 shows the exported PDF file. The location of your PDF file may differ.

5. Double-click the file to open it in Adobe Acrobat Reader.

6. In Adobe Acrobat Reader, click **View** on the menu bar, click **Fit Page** (Win) or **Fit in Window** (Mac), then compare the window to Figure L-39.

7. Close the window, exit Adobe Acrobat Reader, then return to the OAHU To Print document in InDesign.

You exported the OAHU To Print document as an Adobe PDF file, then opened it in Adobe Acrobat Reader.

FIGURE L-38

Identifying the PDF file

PDF file

FIGURE L-39

Viewing the PDF file

Export a selected item to JPEG format

1. Click the **Selection Tool** ↖, then click the **photograph** on the OAHU cover.

   Your selection should resemble Figure L-40.

2. Click **File** on the menu bar, then click **Export**.

3. In the Export dialog box, click the **Save as type list arrow** (Win) or the **Format list arrow** (Mac), click **JPEG**, then click **Save**.

4. In the Export JPEG dialog box, click the **Selection option button**, click the **Image Quality list arrow**, click **High**, then click **Export**.

(continued)

FIGURE L-40

Selecting an object to export

Preparing, Packaging, and Exporting Documents

FIGURE L-41

Viewing the JPEG file

6. Open your Web browser software, click **File** on the menu bar, click **Open**, then open **OAHU To Print.jpg**.

   | TIP   Depending on your browser software, you may be prompted to browse for the JPEG file in the Open dialog box.

   The JPEG file will open in your browser window or using Windows Picture and Fax Viewer, as shown in Figure L-41.

7. Close your browser or Windows Picture and Fax Viewer, then return to the OAHU To Print document in InDesign.

8. Save your work, then close OAHU To Print.indd.

You exported only the photograph in the InDesign layout as a JPEG file, then viewed it in your Web browser or Windows Picture and Fax Viewer.

Create bleeds, slugs, and printer's marks.

1. Open ID L-2.indd, then save it as **Chapter L Skills Review**.
2. Verify that you are in Normal View Mode and that guides are showing.
3. Click File on the menu bar, then click Document Setup.
4. Click the More Options button (if necessary) to display the Bleed and Slug section of the dialog box.
5. Type **.125** in the Top, Bottom, Left and Right Bleed text boxes, then click OK.
6. Click the Selection Tool, select the green frame on Page 1, then drag the frame's corners to the bleed guide on all four sides.
7. Select the yellow frame on page 1, then drag the left and right sides of the frame to the left and right edges of the bleed guide.
8. Using the same methodology, create bleeds for the green and yellow frames on pages 2–5.
9. Click the Preview Mode button in the Toolbox.
10. Press and hold the Preview Mode button, then click the Bleed Mode button.
11. Click the Normal View Mode button.
12. Click File on the menu bar, then click Print.
13. Verify that Copies is set to 1 and Pages is set to All, then click the Setup category on the left.
14. Verify that Paper Size is set to Letter, click the leftmost Orientation icon, click the Page Position list arrow, then click Centered.
15. Click the Marks and Bleed category on the left.
16. In the Marks section, click the All Printer's Marks check box, then click the Offset up arrow until the value reads .375 in.
17. In the Bleed and Slug section, verify that the Use Document Bleed Settings check box is checked.
18. Click Print.

Use the Ink Manager and preview color separations.

1. In the Swatches palette, note that three swatches are specified as spot inks.
2. Click the Swatches palette list arrow, then click Ink Manager.
3. Scroll in the Ink Manager and note the inks listed.
4. Click Royal, then click the spot ink icon to the left of Royal to convert it to a process ink.
5. Click PANTONE 1205 C, then click the spot ink icon to the left of Pantone 1205 C to convert it to a process ink.
6. Click OK.
7. Click Window on the menu bar, point to Output Preview, then click Separations.
8. Click the View list arrow in the Separations Preview palette, then click Separations.
9. Move the Separations Preview palette to the side so that you can see the entire document.
10. Click PANTONE 353 C in the Separations Preview palette.
11. Click Cyan in the Separations Preview palette.
12. Move your cursor over the document and note the percentages of cyan and the other inks.
13. Click Magenta, then click Yellow, then click Black to preview those inks.
14. Click CMYK to preview only the areas of the document that will be printed with process inks.
15. Click the empty gray square beside the PANTONE 353 C ink to make the ink visible in the preview.
16. Click the View list arrow, click Off, then close the Separations Preview palette.

Preflight and package a document.

1. Click File on the menu bar, click Preflight, then click the Fonts category on the left.
2. Verify that the Show Problems Only check box is not checked.
3. Note the two fonts listed.
4. Click the Links and Images category on the left, note the two imported graphics listed, then note the information below the window for each selected graphic.
5. Click the Show Problems Only check box.
6. Click Report, use the filename given (Win) or name the file **Report** (Mac), then click Save.

7. Open the .txt file in a word processing application (like Microsoft Word), examine it, then close the file.
8. Click Cancel in the Preflight dialog box.
9. Click File on the menu bar, then click Save.
10. Click File on the menu bar, then click Package.
11. Type **Brochure Instructions.txt** in the File name text box.
12. Click Continue to go to the Package Publication dialog box (Win) ot the Create Package Folder dialog box (Mac).
13. Note that a folder name has been supplied for you, then note the three checked items to the left.
14. Click Package (Win) or Save (Mac).
15. Click OK in the Font Alert dialog box that follows.
16. Open the Chapter L Skills Review Folder, then note its contents.
17. Open the Links folder to view its contents.
18. Close the folders, then return to the Chapter L Skills Review document in InDesign.

Export a document.

1. Click File on the menu bar, then click Export.
2. In the Export dialog box, click the Save as type list arrow (Win) or the Format list arrow (Mac), click Adobe PDF (if necessary), then click Save.
3. In the Export PDF dialog box, click the All option button in the Pages section.
4. Remove the check mark in the Optimize for Fast Web View check box (if necessary),

then click the Marks and Bleeds category on the left.
5. Activate the All Printer's Marks check box, activate the Use Document Bleed Settings check box, then click Export.
6. Double-click the PDF file to open it in Adobe Acrobat Reader.
7. Compare your document in Adobe Acrobat Reader to Figure L-42.

FIGURE L-42
Completed Skills Review

8. Scroll through the document to verify that all five pages were exported.
9. Close the window to exit Adobe Acrobat Reader.
10. Return to InDesign, then close Chapter L Skills Review.

As part of your job at a prepress service company, you open customers' documents, preflight them, then output them to film. Starting on a new project, you open the customer's InDesign layout and note that the job ticket says that this page is to be printed at letter size. You notice immediately that the document has been built to letter size, but the customer failed to created bleeds.

1. Open ID L-3.indd, then save it as **Multiple Bleeds**. (*Hint*: After updating links, click No in the following dialog box which asks if you want to update items that have been edited.)
2. Verify that you are in Normal View Mode and that guides are showing.
3. Open the Document Setup dialog box.
4. Type **.125** in all four Bleed text boxes, then click OK.
5. Click the Selection Tool, select the large background graphic, then drag the frame's four corners to the bleed guide on all four sides.
6. Click Object on the menu bar, point to Fitting, then click Fit Content to Frame.
7. Select the Windmill Silhouette.psd graphic in the bottom-left corner, then drag the left and bottom sides of the frame to the left and bottom sides of the bleed guide.

8. Select the Windmills Color.psd graphic on the right side of the layout, then drag the right side of the frame to the right side of the bleed guide.

FIGURE L-43
Completed Project Builder 1

9. Click Object on the menu bar, point to Fitting, then click Fit Content to Frame.
10. Compare your work to Figure L-43, save your work, then close Multiple Bleeds.

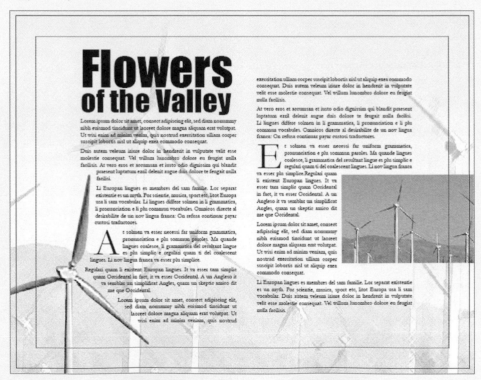

You work for a prepress service bureau, opening customers' documents, preflighting them, then outputting them to film. You've just opened the file for the cover of a monthly dog magazine. The job ticket says that it will print with five colors—CMYK + PANTONE 117 C. You decide to check that the customer specified inks properly.

1. Open ID L-4.indd, then save it as **Lab Separations**.
2. Open the Separations Preview palette, turn separations on, then note that the document is currently specified to separate into seven colors.
3. Click the Swatches palette list arrow, then click Ink Manager.
4. Convert PANTONE 183 C and PANTONE 2706 C to process inks, then click OK.
5. In the Separations Preview palette, verify that the document will now separate into five colors.
6. Click PANTONE 117 C in the Separations Preview palette to preview where the spot ink will print, then compare your screen to Figure L-44.
7. Turn separations off in the Separations Preview palette, then close the Separations Preview palette.
8. Save your work, then close Lab Separations.

FIGURE L-44
Previewing PANTONE 117 C

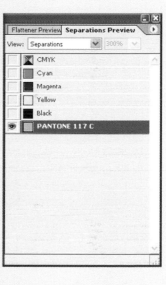

You are the Web master at LAB magazine. Every month, you update the Web site with the contents from the current issue. The art director from the print department has sent you the InDesign layout for this month's cover. You will need to resize it to 50% of its original size, then upload it to the Web site. But first, you need to export it from InDesign so that you can manipulate it in Photoshop. Note: If you do not have Photoshop, end the exercise after Step 5.

1. Open ID L-5.indd, then save it as **Lab Web Cover**.
2. Click File on the menu bar, then click Export.
3. Export the file in EPS format, then click Save.
4. In the Export EPS dialog box, click the Color list arrow, then click RGB. (*Hint*: Color bitmap graphics for the Web are saved in RGB mode.)
5. Click Export.
6. Open Photoshop, click File on the menu bar, click Open, then open Lab Web Cover.eps.
7. In the Rasterize Generic EPS Format dialog box, verify that the Mode text box reads RGB (Win) or RGB color (Mac), then click OK.
8. Compare your Photoshop file to Figure L-45.
9. Close the Photoshop file without saving changes.
10. Return to InDesign, then close Lab Web Cover.

FIGURE L-45
Completed Design Project

This group project is designed to challenge the group to figure out how to create a bleed for a tricky document. Finch Design has sent an InDesign file to be printed as a business card. Its main graphic is a large letter F, which has been specified in the Impact font. The top and bottom of the letter F must bleed. Enlarging the letter F to create the bleed is not an option; the client has noted that the relationship between the letter F and the company name (finch design) must not be altered in any way.

The challenge for the group is to figure out the best way to create the bleed at the top and bottom.

1. Open ID L-6.indd, then save it as **Finch Bleed**.
2. Verify that you are in Normal View Mode and that guides are visible.
3. Open the Document Setup dialog box.
4. Type **.125** in the Top and Bottom Bleed text boxes, then click OK.
5. Click the Selection Tool, then select the letter F text frame.
6. Create outlines.
7. Click the Direct Selection Tool, then select the top two anchor points of the letter F.
8. Move the top line of the letter F up to the bleed guide.

9. Select the bottom two anchor points of the letter F, then move the bottom line of the letter F down to the bleed guide.
10. Click the Selection Tool, select the letter F, then send it to the back.

FIGURE L-46
Completed Group Project

11. Deselect, compare your work to Figure L-46, save your work, then close Finch Bleed.

Topic Area	Objectives	Chapter
1. General Knowledge	■ List and describe key features and benefits of Adobe InDesign. (Key features include XML support, books, page layout features, text handling.)	Chapters A–L
	■ List and describe the features that allow users to manage workspaces.	Chapter A
	■ Explain how Adobe InDesign provides support for interoperability with other Adobe products. (Products include Photoshop, Illustrator, GoLive, Acrobat.)	Chapters F & L
2. Setting up Documents	■ Given a scenario, describe what is affected by selecting various settings. (Scenarios include no documents open, a document open, a specific object selected.)	Chapters A & C
	■ Given a scenario, create a new document by using the Document Setup dialog box.	Chapter A
	■ Create and apply document presets.	Chapter A
	■ Given a scenario, create the structure of a document by using guides and grids.	Chapter C
	■ Given a scenario, work with Master pages. (Scenarios include creating, applying, basing a new Master page off an existing Master page, overriding Master page items.)	Chapter C
	■ Create and use graphic and text placeholders and containers.	Chapter C
	■ Explain how objects are organized in InDesign by using layers. (Options include viewing, locking, stacking, rearranging, selecting, copying, merging, flattening.)	Chapter D
3. Working with Text	■ Given a scenario, format text by using the appropriate palette or menu item.	Chapter B
	■ Insert special characters by using the Type menu, Glyph palette, or contextual menu.	Chapters B & K
	■ Manipulate text by using text frame options. (Frame options include threading, frame properties, resizing, text wrap, selecting text.)	Chapters B, C, & D
	■ Create, apply, import, and modify styles by using the Character Style and Paragraph Style palettes.	Chapter B
	■ List and describe the advantages and disadvantages of using OpenType, TrueType, or Type 1 fonts.	Chapter L
	■ Edit text by using the Story editor.	Chapter D
	■ Create and apply a nested style.	Chapter K
4. Drawing, Arranging, and Transforming Objects	■ Describe how you can create and edit paths by using the appropriate InDesign tools.	Chapter G
	■ Create, edit, and thread text on a path.	Chapter G
	■ Modify and transform objects by using various InDesign features.	Chapters D & F
	■ Modify the contents of frames by using various InDesign features.	Chapter D
	■ Describe information that is displayed in the Info palette.	Chapter C
	■ Create a stroke style by using the Stroke palette.	Chapter K

Topic Area	Objectives	Chapter
5. Working with Color	■ Describe information that is displayed in the Info palette.	Chapter C
	■ Create, edit, and apply colors to objects by using the appropriate palettes.	Chapter E
	■ Explain when you would use the Swatches palette versus the Color palette.	Chapter E
	■ Given a scenario, create, modify and apply gradients to objects by using the appropriate palettes and tools.	Chapter E
	■ Explain the purpose of color management, and discuss color management workflows in Adobe InDesign.	Chapter L
	■ Describe how to create mixed inks.	Chapter K
6. Working with Transparency	■ Given a scenario, apply transparency to an object.	Chapter H
	■ Describe how Adobe InDesign supports transparency features in Placed files. (File formats include Photoshop, Illustrator.)	Chapter F
	■ Given a scenario, create and/or apply the proper flattening style to achieved the desired output.	Chapter L
7. Importing and Exporting Files	■ Select the appropriate method and file format for importing text and graphics.	Chapter F
	■ Given a scenario, select the appropriate options for exporting an Adobe InDesign document to PDF.	Chapter L
	■ Manage placed graphics by using the Links palette including editing the original in the source application.	Chapter F
8. Managing Long Documents	■ Create a book by using the Book palette.	Chapter J
	■ Create a Table of Contents and Index by using the appropriate palettes and commands.	Chapter J
	■ Create and manage hyperlinks by using the Hyperlinks palette.	Chapter F
	■ Synchronize styles and swatches in a book.	Chapter J
9. Preparing Documents for Crossmedia Support	■ Describe workflows that are enabled by using XML.	Online Companion Chapter F
	■ Import an XML file into an InDesign document.	Online Companion Chapter F
	■ Define and assign XML tags, and export an XML file.	Online Companion Chapter F
	■ Map styles to XML tags by using the Tags palette and the Structure view	Online Companion Chapter F
	■ Import a DTD and validate XML structure against the DTD.	Online Companion Chapter F

Topic Area	Objectives	Chapter
10. Working with Tables	■ Create and import tables.	Chapter I
	■ Modify tables.	Chapter I
	■ Format a table.	Chapter I
	■ Create headers and footers in tables.	Chapter I
11. Prepress and Outputting to Print	■ Describe which elements are checked and flagged during the preflight process.	Chapter L
	■ Describe the resulting objects when a package is prepared.	Chapter L
	■ Configure print settings in the Print dialog box for various types of output.	Chapter L
	■ Select the correct options in the Separations Preview palette in order to view separations on	Chapter L
	■ screen.	
	■ Select the correct options in the Flattener Preview palette in order to view output.	Chapter L
12. eBook Authoring	■ Create interactivitiy for an InDesign document that will be exported as an eBook.	Online Companion Chapter L
	■ Add a movie to an InDesign document that will be exported as an eBook	Online Companion Chapter L
	■ Link sounds to interactive elements in an InDesign document that will be exported as an eBook	Online Companion Chapter L

Read the following information carefully!

Find out from your instructor the location where you will store your files.

- To complete many of the chapters in this book, you need to use the Data Files provided on the CD at the back of the book.

- Your instructor will tell you whether you will be working from the CD or copying the files to a drive on your computer or on a server. Your instructor will also tell you where you will store the files you create and modify.

Copy and organize your Data Files.

- Use the Data Files List to organize your files to a zip drive, network folder, hard drive, or other storage device if you won't be working from the CD.

- Create a subfolder for each chapter in the location where you are storing your files, and name it according to the chapter title (e.g., Chapter A).

- For each chapter you are assigned, copy the files listed in the **Data File Supplied** column into that chapter's folder. If you are working from the CD, you should still store the files you modify or create in each chapter in the chapter folder.

Find and keep track of your Data Files and completed files.

- Use the **Data File Supplied** column to make sure you have the files you need before starting the chapter or exercise indicated in the **Chapter** column.

- Use the **Student Creates File** column to find out the filename you use when saving your new file for the exercise.

Adobe InDesign CS

Chapter	Data File Supplied	Student Creates File	Used In
A	ID A-1.indd		Lesson 1, 2, 3, & 4
	ID A-2.indd		Skills Review
	None	Student creates file, explores interface, no solution file	Project Builder 1
	ID A-3.indd		Project Builder 2
	None	Student uses Web site, no solution file	Design Project
	ID A-4.indd		Group Project
B	ID B-1.indd		Lesson 1 & 2
	ID B-2.indd		Lesson 3
	ID B-3.indd		Lesson 4
	ID B-4.indd		Skills Review
	ID B-5.indd		Skills Review
	ID B-6.indd		Skills Review
	ID B-7.indd		Project Builder 1
	ID B-8.indd		Project Builder 2
	ID B-9.indd		Design Project
	ID B-10.indd		Group Project
C	None	Setup	Lessons 1, 2, 3, 4, 5, & 6
	None	Skills Review	Skills Review
	ID C-1.indd		Project Builder 1
	ID C-2.indd		Project Builder 2
	ID C-3.indd		Design Project
	ID C-4.indd		Group Project
D	ID D-1.indd		Lesson 1
	ID D-2.indd		Lesson 1
	ID D-3.indd		Lesson 2
	ID D-4.indd		Lesson 2
	ID D-5.indd		Lesson 3

Chapter	Data File Supplied	Student Creates File	Used In
	ID D-6.indd		Lesson 4
	ID D-7.indd		Skills Review
	ID D-8.indd		Skills Review
	ID D-9.indd		Project Builder 1
	ID D-10.indd		Project Builder 2
	ID D-11.indd		Design Project
	ID D-12.indd		Group Project
E	ID E-1.indd		Lessons 1, 2, & 3
	ID E-2.indd		Lesson 4
	ID E-3.indd		Skills Review
	ID E-4.indd		Skills Review
	ID E-5.indd		Project Builder 1
	ID E-6.indd		Project Builder 2
	ID E-7.indd		Design Project
	ID E-8.indd		Group Project
F	ID F-1.indd		Lessons 1, 2, 3, & 4
	ID F-2.indd		Lesson 4
	ID F-3.indd		Skills Review
	ID F-4.indd		Project Builder 1
	ID F-5.indd		Project Builder 2
	ID F-6.indd		Design Project
	ID F-7.indd		Group Project
G	ID G-1.indd		Lesson 1
	ID G-2.indd		Lessons 2, 3, & 4
	ID G-3.indd		Skills Review
	ID G-4.indd		Project Builder 1
	ID G-5.indd		Project Builder 2
	ID G-6.indd		Design Project
	ID G-7.indd		Group Project
H	ID H-1.indd		Lessons 1, 2, 3, & 4
	ID H-2.indd		Skills Review
	ID H-3.indd		Project Builder 1

Chapter	Data File Supplied	Student Creates File	Used In
	ID H-4.indd		Project Builder 2
	ID H-5.indd		Design Project
	ID H-6.indd		Group Project
I	ID I-1.indd		Lesson 1
	ID I-2.indd		Lessons 2 & 3
	ID I-3.indd		Lessons 3 & 4
	ID I-4.indd		Skills Review
	ID I-5.indd		Skills Review
	ID I-6.indd		Skills Review
	ID I-7.indd		Project Builder 1
	ID I-8.indd		Project Builder 2
	ID I-9.indd		Design Project
	None	Holiday Chart	Group Project
J	ID J-1.indd		Lessons 1, 2, 3 & 4
	ID J-2.indd		Lessons 1, 2, 3 & 4
	ID J-3.indd		Lessons 1, 2, 3 & 4
	ID J-4.indd		Lessons 1, 2, 3 & 4
	ID J-5.indd		Lessons 1, 2, 3 & 4
	ID J-6.indd		Lesson 3
	ID J-7.indd		Lesson 4
	ID J-8.indd		Skills Review
	ID J-9.indd		Skills Review
	ID J-10.indd		Skills Review
	ID J-11.indd		Skills Review
	ID J-12.indd		Skills Review
	ID J-13.indd		Skills Review
	ID J-14.indd		Project Builder 1
	ID J-15.indd		Project Builder 2
	ID J-16.indd		Design Project
	ID J-17.indd		Group Project

Chapter	Data File Supplied	Student Creates File	Used In
K	ID K-1.indd		Lesson 1
	ID K-2.indd		Lesson 1
	ID K-3.indd		Lesson 2
	ID K-4.indd		Lesson 3
	ID K-5.indd		Lesson 4
	ID K-6.indd		Skills Review
	ID K-7.indd		Skills Review
	ID K-8.indd		Project Builder 1
	ID K-9.indd		Project Builder 2
	ID K-10.indd		Design Project
	ID K-11.indd		Group Project
L	ID L-1.indd		Lessons 1, 2, 3, & 4
	ID L-2.indd		Skills Review
	ID L-3.indd		Project Builder 1
	ID L-4.indd		Project Builder 2
	ID L-5.indd		Design Project
	ID L-6.indd		Group Project

Alpha channel
Selections made in Photoshop that have been saved with a descriptive name.

Apply color button
Displays the last color you've used, which makes for quick and easy access when you are using the same color repeatedly.

Apply gradient button
Displays the last gradient you've used, which makes for quick and easy access when you are using the same gradient repeatedly.

Apply None button
Button available for removing the fill or stroke from a selected object, depending on which button (Fill or Stroke) is active in the Toolbox.

Autoflowing
A powerful option for quickly adding text to your document using the Place command.

Baseline
The imaginary line on which a line of text sits.

Bitmap images
Images that consist of pixels created in a program such as Adobe Photoshop. They can also be digital photos. Anything that has been scanned is a bitmap image.

Bleed marks
Marks that define the bleed size.

Bleeds
Areas of the layout that extend to the trim size.

Blending modes
An InDesign feature that allows you to create different transparency and color effects where two or more objects overlap.

Book
A collection of two or more InDesign documents, which are paginated as a single book.

Bounding box
Always rectangular, the frame that defines the horizontal and vertical dimensions of the graphic.

Caps
Define the appearance of end points when a stroke is added to a path. The Stroke palette offers three types of caps: butt, round, and projecting.

Cell
A rectangle in a table row or column.

Clipping path
A graphic that you draw in Photoshop that outlines the areas of the image that you want to show when the file is placed in a layout program like InDesign.

Closed path
Continuous lines that do not contain end points.

Color bars
Used to maintain consistent color on press.

Column break
A typographic command that forces text to the next column.

Columns
A type of layout guide that plays an important role in flowing text.

Compound paths
One or more closed paths joined using the Compound Path command to create one complete path. You create compound paths when you want to use one object to cut a hole in another object.

Corner points
Anchor points that create a corner between the two segments.

Crop marks
Guide lines that define the trim size.

Dashed strokes
Created and formatted using the Stroke palette, strokes that consist of a series of dashes and gaps.

Default Fill and Stroke button
Reverts the Fill and Stroke buttons to their default colors—no fill and a black stroke. Clicking this button will apply a black stroke and no fill to a selected object.

Direction handle
The round blue circle at the top of the direction line.

Direction lines
Two lines attached to a smooth point. Direction lines determine the arc of the curved path, depending on their direction and length.

Drop cap
A design element in which the first letter or letters of a paragraph are increased in size to create a visual effect.

Drop shadow
A soft-edged graphic behind another graphic that appears as though it is the shadow of the graphic.

Em space
A type of white space inserted into a text box. The width of an em space is equivalent to that of the lowercase letter m in the current typeface and type size.

En space
A type of white space inserted into a text box. The width of an en space is equivalent to that of the lowercase letter n in the current typeface and type size.

Ending color
The last color in a gradient.

Facing pages
Left and right pages that face each other in a spread, such as you would find in a magazine.

Fill
A color you apply that fills an object.

Gradient
A graduated blend between two or more colors.

Graphic
In an InDesign document, refers to a bitmap or vector image.

Grayscale image
A digital image reproduced using only one color. In most cases, that color is black.

Guides
Horizontal or vertical lines that you position on a page. As their name suggests, guides are used to help guide you in aligning objects on the page.

Gutter
The space between two columns.

Hard return
See Paragraph return.

Highlights
The light areas of a graphic.

Indicates current drawing layer icon
The pen tool icon next to a layer's name in the Layers palette. This icon indicates that newly drawn objects will be added to that layer.

Indicates selected items button
A small button that appears to the right of the name of the layer and indicates that object(s) on that layer are selected.

Joins
Define the appearance of a corner point when a path has a stroke applied to it. There are three types of joins: miter, round, and bevel.

Kerning
A long-standing process of increasing or decreasing space between a pair of characters.

Layers palette
A smart solution for organizing and managing elements of a layout. When you create a new object, the object will be added to whichever layer is targeted in the Layers palette.

Libraries
Files you create that appear as a palette in your InDesign document. You can use this "library palette" to organize and store graphics that you use most often. Also called Object Libraries.

Line screen
A measurement of the number of ink dots per inch that make up the printed image.

Linear gradient
A series of straight lines that gradate from one color to another (or through multiple colors).

Margins
A type of layout guide. Margins play an important role in flowing text.

Miter limit
Determines when a miter join will be squared off to a beveled edge. The miter is the length of the point, from the inside to the outside.

Mixed ink
InDesign uses this term to refer to swatches that are created by mixing a spot ink with a process ink or another spot ink. Mixed ink swatches must include at least one spot ink. A mixed ink swatch is most often created from one process and one spot ink.

Mixed ink group
An array of mixed ink swatches that is generated simultaneously.

Multiply
A practical and useful blending mode; be sure to familiarize yourself with it. When Multiply is applied to an object, the object becomes transparent but retains its color.

Nested styles
Paragraph styles that contain two or more character styles. In other words, two or more character styles are "nested" within the paragraph style.

Opacity
Derived from the word opaque. An object that is opaque is neither transparent nor translucent—it can't be seen through.

Open path
A path whose end points are not connected.

Page information
A type of printer's marks that includes the title of the InDesign document.

Paragraph
A word, a line of text, or a block of text that is followed by a paragraph return.

Paragraph return
Inserted into the text formatting by pressing [Enter] (Win) or [return] (Mac). Also called a hard return.

Parent swatch
When a mixed ink group is generated, a parent swatch is generated and appears in the Swatches palette. The parent swatch is named with whatever name you entered when creating the mixed ink group.

Pasteboard
The area surrounding the document.

Paths
Straight or curved lines. Paths, which consist of anchor points and line segments, are created by clicking the Pen Tool on the page.

Pixels
A rectangular grid of colored squares used to create bitmap graphics.

Placeholder
The frame created for text or graphics on a master page.

Preflight
Refers to checking out a document before it's released—from the designer to the printer or service bureau—or before it's actually downloaded to an output device.

Preview
A low-resolution version of the placed graphic file. As such, its file size is substantially smaller than the average graphic file.

Printer's marks
Include crop marks, bleed marks, registration marks, color bars, and page information.

Process colors
Colors you create (and eventually print) by mixing varying percentages of cyan, magenta, yellow, and black (CMYK) inks.

Process inks
See Process colors.

Proxy
A group of nine reference points that correspond to the nine points available on a selected item's bounding box.

Pull quote
A typographical design solution in which text is used at a larger point size and positioned prominently on the page.

Radial gradient
A series of concentric circles. With a radial gradient, the starting color appears at the center of the gradient, then radiates out to the ending color.

Registration marks
Printers use registration marks to align the color-separated output.

Registration swatch
When you create a slug, use the Registration swatch in the Swatches palette as the fill color for the text. When the document is color separated, anything filled with Registration appears on all printing plates.

Resolution independent
Graphics professionals refer to vector graphics as being resolution independent because they are not made of pixels and therefore have no resolution issues.

Sections
Pages in a document where page numbering changes.

Semi-autoflowing
Semi-autoflowing text allows you to flow text from frame to frame manually instead of autoflowing.

Shadows
The dark areas of a graphic.

Silhouette
A selection you make in Photoshop using selection tools, such as the Pen Tool.

Slug
A note you include on your document for a printer. A slug usually contains special instructions for outputting your document.

Slug area
The area for a slug, positioned outside of the document's trim size, so that it will be discarded when the document is trimmed.

Smooth points
Anchor points that connect curved segments.

Spot colors
Non-process inks that are manufactured by companies. Spot colors are special pre-mixed inks that are printed separately from process inks.

Square-up
Refers to an image that has been placed in its entirety.

Stacking order
Refers to how objects are "stacked." When you create multiple objects, every object is on its own hierarchical level.

Starting color
The first color in a gradient.

Stroke
A color that you apply to the outline of an object.

Stroke weight
Refers to how heavy the outline of a stroke appears.

Swap Fill and Stroke button
When you click this button, the fill and stroke colors of the selected object are swapped.

Swatches palette
The palette that contains pre-defined color swatches.

Tables
An efficient method for communicating large amounts of information. Tables consist of squares or rectangles in horizontal rows and vertical columns.

Tabs
You use tabs to position text at specific horizontal locations within a text frame.

Threading
A term used to describe linking text from one text frame to another.

Tracking
Affects the spaces between letters, but it is applied globally to an entire word or paragraph.

Trim size
The size to which a printed document will be cut—or trimmed—when it clears the printing press.

Unnamed colors
Any colors you create that aren't saved to the Swatches palette.

Vector graphics
Usually illustrations created in and imported from drawing programs like Adobe Illustrator.

Workspace
The arrangement of windows and palettes that you see on your monitor after starting InDesign.